italian

DeMYSTiFieD

Demystified Series

Accounting Demystified
Advanced Calculus Demystified
Advanced Physics Demystified
Advanced Statistics Demystified
Algebra Demystified
Alternative Energy Demystified
Anatomy Demystified
asp.net 2.0 Demystified
Astronomy Demystified
Audio Demystified
Biology Demystified
Biotechnology Demystified
Business Calculus Demystified
Business Math Demystified
Business Statistics Demystified
C++ Demystified
Calculus Demystified
Chemistry Demystified
Circuit Analysis Demystified
College Algebra Demystified
Corporate Finance Demystified
Databases Demystified
Data Structures Demystified
Differential Equations Demystified
Digital Electronics Demystified
Earth Science Demystified
Electricity Demystified
Electronics Demystified
Engineering Statistics Demystified
Environmental Science Demystified
Everyday Math Demystified
Fertility Demystified
Financial Planning Demystified
Forensics Demystified
French Demystified
Genetics Demystified
Geometry Demystified
German Demystified
Home Networking Demystified
Investing Demystified
Java Demystified
JavaScript Demystified
Lean Six Sigma Demystified
Linear Algebra Demystified

Macroeconomics Demystified
Management Accounting Demystified
Math Proofs Demystified
Math Word Problems Demystified
MATLAB ® Demystified
Medical Billing and Coding Demystified
Medical Terminology Demystified
Meteorology Demystified
Microbiology Demystified
Microeconomics Demystified
Nanotechnology Demystified
Nurse Management Demystified
OOP Demystified
Options Demystified
Organic Chemistry Demystified
Personal Computing Demystified
Pharmacology Demystified
Physics Demystified
Physiology Demystified
Pre-Algebra Demystified
Precalculus Demystified
Probability Demystified
Project Management Demystified
Psychology Demystified
Quality Management Demystified
Quantum Mechanics Demystified
Real Estate Math Demystified
Relativity Demystified
Robotics Demystified
Sales Management Demystified
Signals and Systems Demystified
Six Sigma Demystified
Spanish Demystified
sql Demystified
Statics and Dynamics Demystified
Statistics Demystified
Technical Analysis Demystified
Technical Math Demystified
Trigonometry Demystified
uml Demystified
Visual Basic 2005 Demystified
Visual C# 2005 Demystified
xml Demystified

italian DeMYSTiFieD

Marcel Danesi

New York   Chicago   San Francisco   Lisbon   London   Madrid   Mexico City
Milan   New Delhi   San Juan   Seoul   Singapore   Sydney   Toronto

Copyright © 2007 by The McGraw-Hill Companies, Inc. All rights reserved. Printed in the
United States of America. Except as permitted under the United States Copyright Act of
1976, no part of this publication may be reproduced or distributed in any form or by any
means, or stored in a database or retrieval system, without the prior written permission of
the publisher.

3 4 5 6 7 8 9 10 11 12 13 14 15 16 17 18 19 20 21 22   DOC/DOC   0 9 8

ISBN 978-0-07-147659-1
MHID   0-07-147659-8
Library of Congress Control Number: 2006940169

Maps created by Douglas Norgord, Geographic Techniques.

McGraw-Hill books are available at special quantity discounts to use as premiums and
sales promotions or for use in corporate training programs. To contact a representative,
please visit the Contact Us pages at www.mhprofessional.com.

This book is printed on acid-free paper.

CONTENTS

Contents

INTRODUCTION

This book is for those who want to learn the basics of the Italian language without taking a formal course. It can also serve as a supplementary, complementary, or even primary text in a classroom, tutored, or homeschooled environment, given its comprehensiveness in covering the main points of Italian grammar, vocabulary, and communication. You'll find a straightforward explanation of key Italian grammar points including all of the major verb tenses. In addition to grammar points, you will learn key vocabulary through vocabulary lists and example sentences. The most common words will also appear in the glossaries in the back of this book.

There are two ways you can use this book. You can start at the beginning and go straight through, without skipping any part or omitting any exercise. Or, you can jump around, using the Table of Contents to pick and choose the grammar points you most need *demystified* for you.

This book contains an abundance of practice material. After a topic is introduced in each chapter, you will come across an Oral Practice section, which will allow you to become familiar with the topic by simple imitation and reading practice. This is usually followed by a Written Practice section, which will give you the opportunity to practice what you've learned by supplying the answers on your own. In the latter case, you can check your answers for correctness in the Answer Key at the back of the book and then move on with confidence. There is a quiz at the end of every chapter. The quizzes will help you to review the contents of each chapter and will reinforce your knowledge of the grammar points discussed. These are open-book quizzes. This means that you may, and should, refer to the relevant sections in that chapter as you work through a particular question. Write down your answers, and then check them in the Answer Key. Try to achieve a score of 80 percent on the quiz before moving on to the next chapter.

There are four major parts within this book, each organized in order of increasing complexity and focused on what you will need to know in order to use the Italian language in common situations. Grammatical accuracy and knowledge are emphasized in each chapter, and information on communication skills and Italian culture is interspersed throughout, forming the backbone of what you will be learning to do with the Italian vocabulary and grammar.

Each part contains five chapters, and each chapter contains from four to eight topics, making the overall learning easy to digest in small capsules. However, as you progress, you will have to recall what you have learned in previous chapters and use it along with the new material. The best way to do this is to review the chapter quizzes, which are designed to test you on the contents of each chapter. You may find that you need to review just a section in a chapter, or you may have to review the entire chapter.

At the end of each of the four major parts in this book, you will find a fifty-question multiple-choice test. Take the test only when you've completed the previous five chapters in that part. Each test is a closed-book test, which means that you should not look back through the text for the correct answers. The questions are not as specific in the tests as in the quizzes, but will help you gauge your knowledge to that point. A satisfactory score on each of these tests is 75 percent of the answers correct. You can check your answers in the Answer Key at the back of this book.

There is a 100-question Final Exam at the end of the book. The questions in this exam cover the main aspects of the Italian language and culture and are drawn from all four parts. Take the Final Exam only after completing all twenty chapters. A satisfactory score on the exam is at least 75 percent of the answers correct.

It is recommended that you complete one chapter per week, studying it for about one to two hours each day. Don't rush through a chapter. Give your mind time to absorb the material in it. But do not go too slowly either. Take it at a steady pace and keep it up throughout the course. Languages are not easy to learn. They require time and effort. But the way in which this book is organized allows you to absorb each concept of the Italian language in small pieces, and doing so enables you to come out of the course with a firm knowledge of basic Italian.

When you've completed this course, you can use this book as a permanent reference manual to review Italian concepts whenever you need to. There is an Index at the back to help you find the topics covered.

Learning a foreign language is exciting and fun, so above all else, enjoy yourself!

PART ONE

BASIC SKILLS

CHAPTER 1

Italian Pronunciation and Spelling

Here's what you will learn in this chapter:

Pronunciation of Italian Vowels

Come si pronuncia? *How does one pronounce it?* This chapter will address the important aspects of Italian pronunciation. There are two kinds of sounds in any language: vowels and consonants. Vowels are produced by expelling air through the mouth without blockage. The letters that represent these sounds in Italian are the same as those used in English: **a, e, i, o, u**.

Because Italian and English use many of the same alphabet characters, be careful! Some sounds represented by certain letters in Italian are different from the sounds those letters represent in English. Also, stressed vowels (vowels bearing the main accent) in Italian are not pronounced with a "glide" as in English (such as the added *w* sound in the middle of the word *going*).

Throughout this chapter there are pronunciation guides. These will help you become familiar with Italian sounds. Follow them carefully.

A

A is pronounced like the English *a* in *father*, or as in the exclamation *ah!*: **Anna** (Ahn-nah) *Anne* and *Anna*. Here are a few more Italian names that start with this vowel.

Arturo	(ahr-tOOh-roh)	*Arthur*
Arnaldo	(ahr-nAhl-doh)	*Arnold*
Andrea	(ahn-drEh-ah)	*Andrew*
Amelia	(ah-mEh-leeh-ah)	*Amelia*

E

E is pronounced like the *e* in *bet*, or as in the exclamation *eh!*: **Emma** (Ehm-mah) *Emma*. Here are a few more Italian names that start with this vowel.

Erminia	(ehr-mEEh-neeh-ah)	*Hermione*
Edoardo	(eh-doh-Ahr-doh)	*Edward*
Eleonora	(eh-leh-oh-nOh-rah)	*Eleanor*
Elena	(Eh-leh-nah)	*Helen*

I

I is pronounced like the *i* sound in *machine*, or as in the exclamation *eeh!*: **Ida** (EEh-dah) *Ida*. Here are a few more Italian names that start with this vowel.

Irma	(EEhr-mah)	*Irma*
Ignazio	(eeh-nyAh-tseeh-oh)	*Ignatius*
Ilaria	(eeh-lAh-reeh-ah)	*Hilary*
Isabella	(eeh-zah-bEhl-lah)	*Isabel*

O

O is pronounced like the *o* sound in *sorry*, or as in the exclamation *oh!* as in **Otto** (Oht-toh), *Otto*. Here are a few more Italian names that start with this vowel.

Orlando	(ohr-lAhn-doh)	*Roland*
Olivia	(oh-lEEh-vyah)	*Olivia*
Omero	(oh-mEh-roh)	*Homer*
Orfeo	(ohr-fEh-oh)	*Orpheus*

U

U is pronounced like the *oo* sound in *boot*, or as in the exclamation *ooh!*: **Ugo** (OOh-goh), *Hugh* and *Hugo*. Here are a few more Italian names that start with this vowel.

Uberto	(ooh-bEhr-toh)	*Hubert*
Umberto	(oohm-bEhr-toh)	*Humbert*
Ulisse	(ooh-lEEh-seh)	*Ulysses*

DIFFERENCES IN PRONUNCIATION

The vowels **e** and **o** are pronounced differently in various parts of Italy. In some regions they are spoken with the mouth more open; in others, more closed. In many areas, however, both pronunciations are used. This is analogous to how the English *a* in *tomato* is pronounced in North America. In some areas it is pronounced like the *a* in *father*; in others it is pronounced like the *a* in *pay*. However, whether it is pronounced one way or the other, no one will have much difficulty understanding that the word is still *tomato*. Similarly, whether **Elena** is pronounced with the first **e** open, similar to the English word *led*, or closed, similar to the English word *bet*, Italians will still know it is the same word.

DIPHTHONGS

The Italian letter **i** stands for a sound similar to the English *y* in *yes* if it comes before a stressed vowel. Similarly, the letter **u** stands for a sound similar to the English *w* in *way* if it comes before a stressed vowel. This type of syllable is called a diphthong.

Bia**g**io	(byAh-joh)	*Blaise*
Bianca	(byAhn-kah)	*Blanche, Bianca*
Pietro	(pyEh-troh)	*Peter*
Guido	(gwEEh-doh)	*Guy*
Pas**qu**ale	(pahs-kwAh-leh)	*Pascal*

Be careful! In some words **i** and **u** are pronounced as belonging to a separate syllable, even if followed by another vowel. In Italian there is no accent mark to show this feature.

Mar**i**a	(mah-rEEh-ah)	*Mary*
Vittor**i**o	(veeht-tOh-reeh-oh)	*Victor*
L**u**igi	(looh-EEh-jeeh)	*Louis*

In most words, the stress (main accent) falls on the next-to-last syllable.

Ornella	(ohr-nEhl-lah)	*Ornella*
Arturo	(ahr-tOOh-roh)	*Arthur*

But, again, be careful! This is not always the case.

Elena	(Eh-leh-nah)	*Helen*
Agata	(Ah-gah-tah)	*Agatha*
Cesare	(chEh-zah-reh)	*Caesar*

Some words are written with an accent mark on the final vowel. This means, of course, that you must put the main stress on that vowel.

Niccolò	(neehk-koh-lOh)	*Nicholas*

Introducing Yourself

To ask someone's name directly in Italian you can say:

Come ti chiami?   *What is your name?*

You answer with:

Mi chiamo…   *My name is . . .*

If you're speaking about a third party, you would say:

Lui come si chiama?   *What is his name?*
Lei come si chiama?   *What is her name?*

Or:

Come si chiama il tuo amico?   *What is your (male) friend's name?*
Come si chiama la tua amica?   *What is your (female) friend's name?*

Oral Practice

Practice saying the following sentences out loud. The focus here is on pronouncing vowels as they occur in names.

Come ti chiami?   *What is your name?*
Mi chiamo Anna.   *My name is Anna.*
Come ti chiami?   *What is your name?*
Mi chiamo Ugo.   *My name is Hugh.*
Lui come si chiama?   *What is his name?*
Lui si chiama Cesare.   *His name is Caesar.*
Lei come si chiama?   *What is her name?*
Lei si chiama Elena.   *Her name is Helen.*
Come si chiama il tuo amico?   *What is your (male) friend's name?*

Il mio amico si chiama Guglielmo.　*My friend's name is William.*

Come si chiama la tua amica?　*What is your (female) friend's name?*

La mia amica si chiama Pasqualina.　*My friend's name is Pasqualina.*

Pronunciation of Italian Consonants

E adesso come si pronuncia? *And now, how does one pronounce it?* Note two useful words within this question:

e		*and*
adesso	(ah-dEhs-soh)	*now*

Single consonant sounds are produced by a blockage (partial or complete) of the air expelled through the mouth. Most Italian consonants are pronounced in the same way they are pronounced in English.

Bruno	(brOOh-noh)	*Bruno*
Franco	(frAhn-koh)	*Frank*
Mario	(mAh-reeh-oh)	*Mario*
Nora	(nOh-rah)	*Nora*
Vittoria	(veeht-tOh-ryah)	*Victoria*

There are some differences, however. The consonant sound represented by the letter **p** is not accompanied by a small puff of air, as it is at the beginning of some English words.

Piero	(pyEh-roh)	*Pierre*
Pina	(pEEh-nah)	*Pina*

In addition, the sounds represented by the letters **t** and **d** in Italian do not correspond exactly to the English sounds represented by these letters. In Italian you must place the tongue on the upper teeth, not just above them (as in English).

Tina	(tEEh-nah)	*Tina*
Tommaso	(tohm-mAH-zoh)	*Thomas*
Dina	(dEEh-nah)	*Dina*
Daniele	(dah-nyEh-leh)	*Daniel*

The sound represented by the letter **l** is identical to the English *l* sound in *love*. However, in English, the back of the tongue is raised toward the back of the mouth when *l* occurs at the end of a syllable or word, as in *bill* or *filler*. This feature, known as the "dark *l*," is not found in Italian pronunciation.

Aldo	(Ahl-doh)	*Aldo*
Paolo	(pah-Oh-loh)	*Paul*

The sound represented by **gli** is similar to the English *lli* in *million*, but much more forceful. And the sound represented by **gn** is similar to the English *ny* in *canyon*, but, again, much more forceful.

Guglielmo	(gooh-lyEhl-moh)	*William*
Benigna	(beh-nEEh-nyah)	*Benigna (Benign)*
Ignazio	(eeh-nyAh-tsyoh)	*Ignatius*

The letter **s** can stand for both the *s* sound in the English word *sip* or the *z* sound in *zip*. The Italian **z** sound is used before **b, d, g, l, m, n, r, v**, and between vowels; otherwise, the **s** sound is used.

z sound

Cesare	(chEh-zah-reh)	*Caesar*
Osvaldo	(oh-zvAhl-doh)	*Oswald*
Giuseppe	(jooh-zEhp-peh)	*Joseph*

s sound

Cristofero	(kreeh-stOh-fehroh)	*Christopher*
Pasqualina	(pah-s-kwah-lEEh-nah)	*Pasqualina*
Sara	(sAh-rah)	*Sarah*
Sandra	(sAhn-drah)	*Sandra*

The letter **z** stands for the *ts* sound as in the English word *cats* or the *ds* sound as in *lads*.

Vincenzo	(veehn-chEhn-tsoh *or* veehn-chEhn-dsoh)	*Vincent*
Renzo	(rEhn-tsoh *or* rEhn-dsoh)	*Lawrence*

The letter **r** stands for a sound that is different from the English *r*. To pronounce the Italian sound, roll your tongue a few times on the ridge above your top front teeth.

Rachele	(rah-kEh-leh)	*Rachel*
Riccardo	(reehk-kAhr-doh)	*Richard*

The hard **k** sound is spelled as **c** before consonants and the vowels **a**, **o**, **u**. It is spelled as **ch** before the vowels **e** and **i**. The sound sequence **kw** is spelled (usually) as **qu**.

Claudia	(klAh-ooh-deeh-ah)	*Claudia*
Carlo	(kAhr-loh)	*Carlo, Charles*
Concetta	(kohn-chEht-tah)	*Concetta (Connie)*
Marco	(mAhr-koh)	*Mark*
Chiara	(kyAh-rah)	*Claire*
Achille	(ah-kEEhl-leh)	*Achilles*
Michele	(meeh-kEh-leh)	*Michael*
Pasquale	(pahs-kwAh-leh)	*Pascal*

The soft **ch** sound (as in *church*) is spelled as **c** before the vowels **e** and **i**. It is spelled as **ci** before the vowels **a**, **o**, **u**.

Cecilia	(cheh-chEEh-leeh-ah)	*Cecile*
Ciro	(chEEh-roh)	*Cyrus*
Felicia	(feh-lEEh-chah)	*Felicia*
Lucio	(lOOh-choh)	*Lucius*

The hard **g** sound is spelled as **g** before consonants and the vowels **a**, **o**, **u**. It is spelled as **gh** before the vowels **e** and **i**. The sound sequence **gw** is spelled (usually) as **gu**.

Gloria	(glOh-reeh-ah)	*Gloria*
Gabriella	(gah-breeh-Ehl-lah)	*Gabrielle*
Gustavo	(goohs-tAh-voh)	*Gustav*
il signor Gherli	(gEhr-leeh)	*Mr. Gherli*

The soft **j** sound is spelled as **g** before the vowels **e** and **i**. It is spelled as **gi** before the vowels **a**, **o**, and **u**.

Gerardo	(jeh-rAhr-doh)	*Gerard*
Gino	(jEEh-noh)	*Gino*
Giacomo	(jAh-koh-moh)	*Jack*
Giovanni	(joh-vAhn-neeh)	*John*
Giulia	(jOOh-leeh-ah)	*Julia*

The sound sequence **sk** is spelled as **sc** before consonants and the vowels **a, o, u.** It is spelled as **sch** before the vowels **e** and **i.** The soft **sh** sound (as in *shoe*) is spelled as **sc** before the vowels **e** and **i.**

Francesco   (frahn-chEhs-koh)   *Francis*
Francesca   (frahn-chEhs-kah)   *Frances*

Surnames
il signor Franceschi   (frahn-chEhs-keeh)   *Mr. Franceschi*
la signora Boschi   (bOhs-keeh)   *Mrs. Boschi*
il signor Cascina   (kah-shEEh-nah)   *Mr. Cascina*
la signora Guscini   (gooh-shEEh-neeh)   *Mrs. Guscini*

DOUBLE CONSONANTS

Each single consonant has a corresponding double pronunciation in Italian, which lasts twice as long and is slightly more forceful. The double consonant is shown, generally, with double letters.

Ri**cc**ardo   (reehk-kAhr-doh)   *Richard*
Giova**nn**i   (joh-vAhn-neeh)   *John*
To**mm**aso   (tohm-mAh-zoh)   *Thomas*
Giuse**pp**e   (jooh-zEhp-peh)   *Joseph*
A**nn**abella   (ahn-nah-bEhl-lah)   *Annabelle*
Fe**rr**uccio   (fehr-rOOh-choh)   *Ferruccio*
Santu**zz**a   (sahn-tOOh-tsah)   *Santuzza*
Vi**tt**oria   (veeht-tOh-reeh-ah)   *Victoria*
Ale**ss**andro   (ah-lehs-sAhn-droh)   *Alexander*
Ra**ff**aele   (rahf-fah-Eh-leh)   *Ralph*

The letters **gl** and **gn** between vowels are pronounced more forcefully than their English counterparts *lly* and *ny.*

Gu**gl**ielmo   (gooh-lyEhl-moh)   *William*
I**gn**azio   (eeh-nyAh-tsyoh)   *Ignatius*

The double or lengthened version of **ch, ci, gh,** and **gi** is achieved by doubling the first letter.

il signor Vecchiarelli	(vehk-kyah-rEhl-leeh)	*Mr. Vecchiarelli*
la signora Roccia	(rOh-chah)	*Mrs. Roccia*
il signor Loggia	(lOhj-jah)	*Mr. Loggia*

Introducing People

To introduce someone with a casual address in Italian, you would say:

Ti presento…   *Let me introduce you to . . .*

In a more formal situation, you would say:

Le presento il signor…   *Let me introduce you to Mr. . . .*

Le presento la signora…   *Let me introduce you to Mrs. . . .*

Oral Practice

Practice saying the following sentences out loud.

Ti presento Carlo.	*Let me introduce you to Charles.*
Ciao, Carlo.	*Hi, Charles.*
Ti presento Chiara.	*Let me introduce you to Claire.*
Ciao, Chiara.	*Hi, Claire.*
Ti presento Felicia.	*Let me introduce you to Felicia.*
Ciao, Felicia.	*Hi, Felicia.*
Ti presento Giacomo.	*Let me introduce you to Jack.*
Ciao, Giacomo.	*Hi, Jack.*
Le presento il signor Michele Franceschi.	*Let me introduce you to Mr. Michael Franceschi.*
Piacere, signor Franceschi.	*A pleasure, Mr. Franceschi.*
Le presento la signora Sara Marchi.	*Let me introduce you to Mrs. Sarah Marchi.*
Piacere, signora Marchi.	*A pleasure, Mrs. Marchi.*

Le presento il signor Pasquale Boschi.

Let me introduce you to Mr. Pasquale Boschi.

Piacere, signor Boschi.

A pleasure, Mr. Boschi.

Written Practice 1

Introduce each person with either the familiar or polite form. For example:

Raffaele (*familiar*) Ralph

Ti presento Raffaele. _____ *Let me introduce you to Ralph.*

Ciao, Raffaele. _____ *Hi, Ralph.*

1. Giuseppe (*familiar*) *Joseph*

   Ti presento Giuseppe _____ . *Let me introduce you to Joseph.*

   Ciao, Giuseppe. _____ . *Hi, Joseph.*

2. Alessandro (*familiar*) *Alexander*

   Ti presento Alessandro _____ . *Let me introduce you to Alexander.*

   Ciao, Alessandro. _____ . *Hi, Alexander.*

3. il signor Vecchiarelli (*polite*) *Mr. Vecchiarelli*

   Le presento il signor Vecchiarelli *Let me introduce you to Mr. Vecchiarelli.*

   Piacere, Signor Vecchiarelli. *A pleasure, Mr. Vecchiarelli.*

Italian Spelling and Capitalization

Come si scrive? *How does one write it?* Italian uses many of the same alphabet characters as English, except for the letters **j, k, w, x,** and **y**. The latter are found, however, in words that Italian has borrowed from other languages, primarily English.

il karatè	*karate*	il weekend	*weekend*
il jazz	*jazz*	lo yacht	*yacht*

The letter **h** exists in Italian, but it is not pronounced. It is used to achieve the hard **k** and **g** sounds, as you have seen: **mi chiamo, il signor Gherli**. It is also found in four forms of the verb **avere**: **io ho** (*I have*), **tu hai** (*you have*), **lui/lei ha** (*he/she has*), **loro hanno** (*they have*)—which will be discussed later in this book. Whenever an **h** appears in Italian, it is a silent **h**, as it is in English words such as *hour*.

The accent mark in Italian is not used to indicate differences in pronunciation. The grave accent mark (`) is used in words that are stressed on the last vowel: **-à, -è, -ì, -ò, -ù**. Here are some cognates that are written with final accent marks. Cognates are words that have the same root or origin in two languages (English and Italian in this case).

città	*city*	sì	*yes*
caffè	*coffee*	università	*university*
tassì	*taxi*		

The grave accent mark is also used to distinguish a few single-syllable words, so as to avoid confusion.

è	*it is*	dà	*he gives*
e	*and*	da	*from*

Many of the spelling conventions used in English with regard to capitalization apply to Italian as well. For example, like English, capital letters are used at the beginning of sentences and to write proper nouns (**Alessandro, Sara, Italia, Milano**, etc.).

However, there are a few differences, too. For example, the pronoun **io** (*I*) is not capitalized (unless it is the first word of a sentence), but the pronoun **Lei** (*you, polite*) is, to distinguish it from **lei** (*she*).

Titles are not capitalized, although this is optional, especially with professional titles used in direct speech.

il signor Marchi	*Mr. Marchi*
la signora Dini	*Mrs. Dini*
la signorina Bruni	*Miss/Ms. Bruni*
il professor Rossini	*Professor Rossini* (male)
la professoressa Dini	*Professor Dini* (female)

il dottor Franceschi   *Dr. Franceschi* (male)
la dottoressa Martini   *Dr. Martini* (female)

Other spelling peculiarities will be identified as they surface throughout this book.

Using the Verb *Piacere*

The verb **piacere** means *to like*, but it is a tricky one in Italian. Observe how it is used by practicing your first set of examples with it. **Piacere** will be discussed in more detail later in this book.

Oral Practice

Practice saying the following sentences out loud.

Ti piace la città?   *Do you like the city?*
Sì, mi piace.   *Yes, I like it.*
Ti piace il karatè?   *Do you like karate?*
Sì, mi piace.   *Yes, I like it.*
Ti piace il jazz?   *Do you like jazz?*
Sì, mi piace.
Ti piace il caffè?   *Do you like coffee?*
Sì, mi piace.
Ti piace l'università?   *Do you like the university?*
Sì, mi piace.

Asking People How They Are

To ask someone in Italian how they are doing you say:

Come va?   *How is it going?*

Oral Practice

Practice saying the following phrases and sentences out loud.

il signor Marchi	*Mr. Marchi*	Come va, signor Marchi?	*How is it going, Mr. Marchi?*
la signora Dini	*Mrs. Dini*	Come va, signora Dini?	*How is it going, Mrs. Dini?*
la signorina Bruni	*Miss Bruni*	Come va, signorina Bruni?	*How is it going, Miss Bruni?*
il professor Rossini	*Professor Rossini*	Come va, professor Rossini?	*How is it going, Professor Rossini?*

Written Practice 2

Using the same pattern, ask how each of the following people are doing.

1. la professoressa Dini *Professor Dini*
   <u>Come va, signora Dini</u>. *How is it going, Professor Dini?* *la professoressa*

2. il dottor Franceschi *Dr. Franceschi*
   <u>Come va, il dottor Franceschi</u>. *How is it going, Dr. Franceschi?*

3. la dottoressa Martini *Dr. Martini*
   <u>Come va, la dottoressa Martini</u>. *How is it going, Dr. Martini?*

Names and Surnames

As you probably noticed, Italian names (**nomi**) are marked for gender: that is, the ending of a name generally tells you if the person is male or female. If the name ends in **-o**, it is (usually) the name of a male; if it ends in **-a**, it is (again, usually) the name of a female. Some names end in **-e**. These can refer to either a male or a female.

Male Name	Female Name
Mario	Maria
Pino	Pina
Pasquale	Rachele

Italian surnames or family names (**cognomi**) can also end in vowels, but no gender distinction is made because these apply to both males and females.

Male Name	Female Name
Mario Franceschi	Maria Franceschi
Pino Vecchiarelli	Pina Vecchiarelli
Pasquale Di Tommaso	Rachele Di Tommaso

QUIZ

Answer the following question using the names given. For example:

Come ti chiami? *What is your name?*

Anne Mi chiamo Anna. _My name is Anne._

1. Come ti chiami?

Arnold _Mi chiamo Arnaldo._

Edward _Mi chiamo Edoardo._

Eleanor _Mi chiamo, Eleanore_

Hilary _Mi chiamo, Ilaria_

Isabel _Mi chiamo Isabella_

Indicate what each man's name is in Italian. Recall that **lui** means *he*. For example:

Mark _Lui si chiama Marco._ _His name is Mark._

2. Humbert _Lui si chiama Umberto_

Peter _Lui si chiama Pietro._

Thomas _Lui si chiama Tommaso._

John _Lui si chiama Giovanni._

Now, indicate what each woman's name is in Italian. Recall that **lei** means *she*. For example:

Helen   _Lei si chiama Elena._   *Her name is Helen.*

3. Mary   _Lei si chiama Maria_ .

    Pina   _Lei si chiama Pina_ .

    Claudia   _Lei si chiama Claudia_ .

    Blanche   _Lei si chiama Blanca_ .

Using the male names provided answer the question appropriately. For example:

Come si chiama il tuo amico?   *What is your friend's name?*

Ignazio   _Il mio amico si chiama Ignazio._   *My friend's name is Ignatius.*

4. Come si chiama il tuo amico?

    Guglielmo   _Il mio amico si chiama Guglielmo_ .

    Cesare   _Il mio amico si chiama Cesare_ .

    Osvaldo   _Il mio amico si chiama Osvaldo_ .

    Cristofero   _Il mio amico Cristofero si chiama_ .

    Giuseppe   _Il mio amico si chiama Giuseppe_ .

Using the female names provided answer the question appropriately. For example:

Come si chiama la tua amica?   *What is your friend's name?*

Claudia   _La mia amica si chiama Claudia._   *My friend's name is Claudia.*

5. Come si chiama la tua amica?

    Pasqualina   _La mia amica si chiama_ .

    Sara   _La mia amica_ .

    Rachele   _La mia amica_ .

    Maria   _La mia amica_ .

    Chiara   _La mia amica_ .

Introduce the following people using the familiar form of address. For example:

　　Marco *Ti presento Marco.* _____

6. Alessandro _____ .
　 Annabella _____ .

Introduce each person using the polite form of address this time. For example:

　　il signor Gino Marchi *Le presento il signor Gino Marchi.* _____

7. il professor Giovanni Rossini _____ .
　 la professoressa Gina Marchi _____ .
　 la signorina Maria Franceschi _____ .
　 la signora Vittoria Dini _____ .
　 il signor Marco Rossi _____ .
　 il dottor Piero Roccia _____ .
　 la dottoressa Sara Loggia _____ .

Say that you like the following things. (Do not worry at this point about the article in front of the noun. You will learn about definite articles in Chapter 5.) For example:

　　la città *Mi piace la città.* _____

8. il jazz *Mi piace il pany.* _____ .
　 il weekend _____ .
　 la città _____ .
　 il caffè _____ .
　 l'università _____ .

Personal Matters! Answer each question appropriately.

   9. Come ti chiami? (*Give your name.*)

     Mi chiamo Jessica   .

  10. Ti piace il caffè? (*If you do not like something, say* **No, non mi piace.**)

     Mi piace il caffè.   .

CHAPTER 2

Meeting and Greeting People

Here's what you will learn in this chapter:

Italian Nouns

Asking Chi è?

Asking Che cosa è?

Plural Nouns

Asking Chi sono? *and* Che cosa sono?

Italian Titles

Meeting and Greeting Expressions

Italian Nouns

Come si chiama? *What is it called?* This section will teach you how to answer this question by naming things in Italian. You will be learning about Italian nouns—the words that allow you to name persons, objects, places, concepts, and so on. In Italian a noun can be recognized easily by its vowel ending, which indicates its gender—masculine or feminine.

NOUNS REFERRING TO PEOPLE

Nouns ending in **-o** are generally masculine and nouns ending in **-a** are generally feminine. Also, the gender of the noun and the sex (male or female) of the being to which it refers, typically correspond (with some exceptions, of course). Note that, unlike English, nouns referring to nationalities are not capitalized.

Masculine		**Feminine**	
il ragazzo	*the boy*	la ragazza	*the girl*
l'amico	*the (male) friend*	l'amica	*the (female) friend*
lo zio	*the uncle*	la zia	*the aunt*
il figlio	*the son*	la figlia	*the daughter*
l'americano	*the (male) American*	l'americana	*the (female) American*
l'italiano	*the (male) Italian*	l'italiana	*the (female) Italian*
Carlo	*Charles*	Carla	*Carla*
Paolo	*Paul*	Paola	*Paula*

Some nouns end in **-e**, and when they do, they can refer to either males or females. Since the article that precedes the noun gives you a clue to the noun's gender, you should learn the nouns along with their articles (**il, lo,** and **l'** with masculine nouns and **la** and **l'** with feminine nouns). However, do not worry too much about these article forms right now. They will be discussed further in Chapter 5. For now, simply learn them along with the noun as best you can. The advantage for you is that by the time you reach Chapter 5, you will already be familiar with them.

Masculine		**Feminine**	
il padre	*the father*	la madre	*the mother*
il francese	*the French man*	la francese	*the French woman*
l'inglese	*the English man*	l'inglese	*the English woman*
il canadese	*the Canadian man*	la canadese	*the Canadian woman*

NOUNS REFERRING TO THINGS

Nouns are marked as masculine or feminine, even when they do not refer to people. Everything remains the same, grammatically speaking. If the noun ends in **-o**, it is generally masculine; if it ends in **-a**, it is generally feminine.

Masculine		Feminine	
il muro	*the wall*	la casa	*the house*
il giardino	*the garden*	la porta	*the door*
il tetto	*the roof*	la cucina	*the kitchen*
il salotto	*the living room*	la finestra	*the window*
il pavimento	*the floor*	la tavola	*the table*
il divano	*the couch*	la sedia	*the chair*

Nouns ending with the vowel **-e** are, again, either masculine or feminine. It is best to just memorize these since they follow no particular pattern or rule. To be sure about the gender of a noun of this type, consult a dictionary. In the set of nouns below, the indefinite article is shown, which will also be taken up in Chapter 5. Again, for now, just try to remember the forms for the oral exercises coming up.

Masculine		Feminine	
un giornale	*a newspaper*	una parete	*a partition* (*internal wall*)
un nome	*a name*	una chiave	*a key*
un cognome	*a surname*	una lente	*a magnifying glass*
un mobile	*a piece of furniture*	un'automobile	*an automobile*

Nouns ending in an accented **-à** or **-ù** are feminine; those ending in other accented vowels are masculine.

Masculine		Feminine	
il tè	*the tea*	la città	*the city*
il caffè	*the coffee*	l'università	*the university*
il tassì	*the taxi*	la gioventù	*youth*

There are a few exceptions to this pattern, notably: **il papà** (*dad*).

BORROWED NOUNS

Nouns that have been borrowed from other languages, primarily English, are generally masculine. These typically end in a consonant.

lo sport	*the sport*
il computer	*the computer*
il tennis	*tennis*
l'autobus	*the bus*

But the following are feminine:

la mail (l'e-mail)	*e-mail*
la chat	*chatroom*

Asking *Chi è?*

To ask *Who is it?* in Italian, say:

Chi è?

Oral Practice

Practice saying the following sentences out loud.

Chi è?	*Who is it?*
È il padre di Maria.	*He is Mary's father.*
Chi è?	*Who is it?*
È l'amica di Paolo.	*She is Paul's friend.*
Chi è?	*Who is it?*
È la madre di Alessandro.	*She is Alexander's mother.*
Chi è?	*Who is it?*
È il figlio di Sara.	*He is Sarah's son.*
Chi è?	*Who is it?*
È la figlia di Giovanni.	*She is John's daughter.*
Chi è?	*Who is it?*
È lo zio di Claudia.	*He is Claudia's uncle.*

Chi è?

Who is it?

È la zia di Pasquale.

She is Pascal's aunt.

Written Practice 1

Write the feminine equivalent of each noun following the example.

il ragazzo *the boy*

<u>la ragazza</u> *the girl*

1. l'americano *the (male) American*

   <u>l' americana</u> *the (female) American*

2. l'italiano *the (male) Italian*

   <u>l'italiana</u> *the (female) Italian*

3. il francese *the French man*

   <u>la francese</u> *the French woman*

4. l'inglese *the English man*

   <u>l'inglese</u> *the English woman*

5. il canadese *the (male) Canadian*

   <u>la canadese</u> *the (female) Canadian*

6. Carlo *Charles*

   <u>Carla</u> *Carla*

7. Paolo *Paul*

   <u>Paola</u> *Paula*

Asking *Che cosa è?*

To ask *What is it?* in Italian, you say:

Che cosa è?

What is it?

Oral Practice

Practice saying the following sentences out loud.

Che cosa è?	*What is it?*
È un muro.	*It is a wall.*
Che cosa è?	*What is it?*
È una casa.	*It is a house.*
Che cosa è?	
È un giardino.	*It is a garden.*
Che cosa è?	
È una porta.	*It is a door.*
Che cosa è?	
È un tetto.	*It is a roof.*
Che cosa è?	
È una cucina.	*It is a kitchen.*
Che cosa è?	
È un salotto.	*It is a living room.*
Che cosa è?	
È una finestra.	*It is a window.*

Written Practice 2

Fill in the blanks with the answer to each question as shown in the example. Don't worry about the article forms for now (**un, uno, una, un'**). These will be discussed in depth in later chapters. For now, try your best from memory.

Che cosa è? *What is it?*

È un giornale. _____ *It is a newspaper.*

1. Che cosa è?

   È un pavimento. *It is a floor.*

2. Che cosa è?

   È un cognome. *It is a surname.*

3. Che cosa è?

È una parete. *It is a partition.*

4. Che cosa è?

È un nome. *It is a name.*

5. Che cosa è?

È un'automobile *It is an automobile.*

6. Che cosa è?

È un divano. *It is a couch.*

7. Che cosa è?

È una chiave. *It is a key.*

8. Che cosa è?

È un mobile. *It is a piece of furniture.*

9. Che cosa è?

È una sedia. *It is a chair.*

Plural Nouns

Most common nouns can be made plural. Here's how: if the noun ends in **-o**, change the **-o** to **-i**.

Singular		Plural	
ragazzo	*boy*	ragazzi	*boys*
divano	*couch*	divani	*couches*
italiano	*Italian*	italiani	*Italians*
americano	*American*	americani	*Americans*

If the noun ends in **-a**, change the **-a** to **-e**.

Singular		Plural	
ragazza	*girl*	ragazze	*girls*
casa	*house*	case	*houses*
porta	*door*	porte	*doors*
finestra	*window*	finestre	*windows*

If the noun ends in **-e**, change the **-e** to **-i**.

Singular		Plural	
padre	*father*	padri	*fathers*
madre	*mother*	madri	*mothers*
chiave	*key*	chiavi	*keys*
automobile	*automobile*	automobili	*automobiles*

The main exception to these rules pertains to nouns ending in an accented vowel or a consonant, either of which do not make a change in the plural form.

Singular		Plural	
caffè	*coffee*	caffè	*coffees*
città	*city*	città	*cities*
computer	*computer*	computer	*computers*
e-mail	*e-mail*	e-mail	*e-mails*

Che cosa è
Che cos'è?

Asking *Chi sono?* and *Che cosa sono?*

You already know how to ask **Chi è?** (*Who is it?*) and **Che cosa è?** or **Che cos'è?** (*What is it?*) in the singular. To ask *Who are they?* and *What are they?* in Italian, use the plural form of the verb **essere**, which is **sono**.

Chi sono?	*Who are they?*
Che cosa sono?	*What are they?*

Che cosa sono?

Oral Practice

Practice saying the following sentences out loud.

Chi sono?	*Who are they?*
Sono due americani.	*They are two Americans.*
Chi sono?	*Who are they?*
Sono due italiani.	*They are two Italians.*

Chi sono?

Sono due zii.   *They are two uncles.*

Chi sono?

Sono due zie.   *They are two aunts.*

Che cosa sono?   *What are they?*

Sono due tavole.   *They are two tables.*

Che cosa sono?   *What are they?*

Sono due chiavi.   *They are two keys.*

Che cosa sono?

Sono due caffè.   *They are two coffees.*

Che cosa sono?

Sono due computer.   *They are two computers.*

Written Practice 3

Following the same pattern, change the noun provided into its plural form to match the question and response.

1. Che cosa sono? *What are they?*
   Sono due giardini . They are two gardens.

2. Che cosa sono?
   Sono due sedie . They are two chairs.

3. Che cosa sono?
   Sono due giornali . They are two newspapers.

4. Che cosa sono?
   Sono due parete . They are two partitions.

5. Che cosa sono?
   Sono due tassi . They are two taxis.

6. Che cosa sono?
   Sono due chat . They are two chatrooms.

Italian Titles

You learned some personal and professional titles in Chapter 1. These are repeated here. Notice that the final **-e** of a masculine title is dropped before a name. This rule does not apply to feminine titles. This is more a rule of style than of strict grammar. As such, it is not technically wrong to keep the **-e**, but very few Italians do so.

Masculine Title		Used Before a Name	
il signore	*the gentleman*	il signor Marchi	*Mr. Marchi*
il professore	*the professor*	il professor Binni	*Professor Binni*
il dottore	*the doctor*	il dottor Franchi	*Dr. Franchi*

Feminine Title		Used Before a Name	
la signora	*the lady*	la signora Marchi	*Mrs. Marchi*
la signorina	*the (unmarried) lady*	la signorina Bruni	*Miss/Ms. Bruni*
la professoressa	*the professor*	la professoressa Binni	*Professor Binni*
la dottoressa	*the doctor*	la dottoressa Franchi	*Dr. Franchi*

USE OF TITLES

Italians use titles much more than North Americans do. In addition to those you have already learned, here are two more commonly used titles. The same title is used for both males and females. The final **-o** in masculine titles is not dropped.

Title		Used Before a Name
l'avvocato	*the lawyer*	l'avvocato Dini
l'ingegnere	*the engineer*	l'ingegner Vecchiarelli

When addressing someone, such as saying *Good morning* to him or her, the article is dropped.

Ecco il dottor Bruni.	*Here is Dr. Bruni.*
Buongiorno, dottor Bruni.	*Good morning, Dr. Bruni.*

The title of **dottore/dottoressa** is used not only with medical doctors but also with any person who has a university degree. The title of **professore/professoressa** is used not only with university professors but also with high school and middle school teachers.

Oral Practice

Practice saying the following sentences out loud.

Ecco il dottor Marchi.	*Here is Dr. Marchi.*
Buongiorno, dottor Marchi.	*Good morning, Dr. Marchi.*
Ecco l'avvocato Bruni.	*Here is lawyer Bruni.*
Buongiorno, avvocato Bruni.	*Good morning, lawyer Bruni.*
Ecco la signora Binni.	*Here is Mrs. Binni.*
Buongiorno, signora Binni.	*Good morning, Mrs. Binni.*
Ecco la dottoressa Dini.	*Here is Dr. Dini.*
Buongiorno, dottoressa Dini.	*Good morning, Dr. Dini.*
Ecco il signor Vecchiarelli.	*Here is Mr. Vecchiarelli.*
Buongiorno, signor Vecchiarelli.	*Good morning, Mr. Vecchiarelli.*

Meeting and Greeting Expressions

Buongiorno! *Good morning!* or *Good day*! Here are the main formulas for greeting and taking leave of people.

buongiorno (*also written* buon giorno)	*good morning/good day*
buon pomeriggio	*good afternoon*
buonasera (*also written* buona sera)	*good evening*
buonanotte (*also written* buona notte)	*good night*

These expressions are used mainly in polite or formal speech—when greeting people with whom you are not on a first-name basis (strangers, superiors, etc.). However, they can also be used to greet and take leave of those with whom you are on a first-name basis.

The following expressions are used in familiar speech—those with whom you are on familiar terms.

ciao	*hi/bye*	A presto!	*See you soon!*
arrivederci	*good-bye*	Ci vediamo!	*See you later!*

arrivederla

NOTE: *The polite form of* good-bye *is **arrivederLa**.*

Here are a few common expressions used when meeting and greeting people:

Come stai?	*How are you?* (familiar)
Come sta?	*How are you?* (polite)
Come va?	*How is it going?*
Bene, grazie.	*Well, thanks.*
Prego.	*You're welcome.*
Non c'è male.	*Not bad.*
Così, così.	*So-so.*
per favore/per piacere	*please*

Oral Practice

Practice saying the following sentences out loud.

Buongiorno!	*Good morning!*
Buon pomeriggio!	*Good afternoon!*
Buonasera!	*Good evening!*
Buonanotte!	*Good night!*
Ciao!	*Hi!/Bye!*
A presto!	*See you soon!*
Ci vediamo!	*See you later!*
Bene, grazie.	*Well, thanks.*
Prego.	*You're welcome.*
Non c'è male.	*Not bad.*
Così, così.	*So-so.*

Written Practice 4

Translate the following sentences into Italian, using the familiar or polite form as necessary.

1. How are you, Mary?

   Come stai, Maria? ?

2. How are you, Mrs. Bianchi?

   Come sta, signora Bianchi ?

3. How is it going, Claudia?

   Come va, Claudia ?

4. How is it going, Mr. Marchi?

   Come va, Signor Marchi ?

5. Good-bye, Mark!

   Ciao, Marco! !

6. Good-bye, Mrs. Dini.

   Arrivederla, signora Dini .

QUIZ

Fill in each blank with the missing male or female noun.

Masculine	**Feminine**
1. il ragazzo	_la ragazza_
il padre	la madre
l'americano	_l'americana_
l'amico	l'amica
il figlio	_la figlia_
l'italiano	l'italiana
lo zio	_la zia_
la francese	la francese
l'inglese	_l'inglese_
il canadese	la canadese

Fill in each blank with the singular or plural form as required.

Singular	Plural
2. muro	*muri*
casa	case
giardino	*giardini*
sedia	sedie
tavola	*tavole*
pavimento	pavimenti
caffè	*caffè*
città	città
sport	*sport*
tassì	tassì
chat	*chat*
computer	computer

Answer each question with the phrases provided. For example:

Chi è?   *Who is it?*

È la madre di Maria. _____ *It is Mary's mother.*

3. Chi è?

Alexander's son

È il figlio di Alessandro.

Sarah's daughter

È la figlia di Sara.

Che cosa è?

Alexander's house

È la casa di Alessandro.

Sarah's key

È la chiave di Sara.

Greet the following people in the morning. For example:

Tommaso   *Thomas*

Buongiorno/Ciao, Tommaso. _____ *Good morning, Thomas./Hi, Thomas.*

il signor Torelli   *Mr. Torelli*

Buongiorno, signor Torelli. _____ *Good morning, Mr. Torelli.*

4. Maria

   Buongiorno / Ciao, Maria. _____.

   la signorina Giusti

   Buongiorno, signorina Giusti _____.

   Marco

   Ciao Marco _____

   il professor Marchi

   Buongiorno, professor Marchi _____.

Greet the following people in the evening, asking each one how he or she is. Then, give the person's response as indicated. For example:

Marco/*Well, thanks.*

Buonasera/Ciao, Marco. Come stai?   *Good evening/Hi, Mark. How are*
                                      you?

Bene, grazie.   *Well, thanks.*

Il signor Dini/*So-so.*

Buonasera, signor Dini. Come sta?   *Good evening. Mr. Dini. How are*
                                      you?

Così, così.   *So-so.*

5. Claudia/*Well thanks.*

   Buonsera, Claudia. Come stai? → Bene, grazie.

   la professoressa Giusti/*Not bad.*

   Buonsera, professoressa Giusti Come sta?
   Non c'è male.

Giovanni/*So-so.*

Ciao, Giovanni. Come sta? → Così, così.

il dottor Bruni/*Well, thanks.*

Buonasera, dottor Bruni. Come sta?
Bene, grazie.

Circle the letter of the word or phrase that best completes each sentence.

6. How would you greet Ms. Marchi in the afternoon, asking her how she is?

  (a) Ciao, signorina Marchi. Come stai?

  (b) Buon pomeriggio, signorina Marchi. Come sta?

7. How would you introduce Mr. Bruni to Mrs. Vecchiarelli?

  (a) Signora Vecchiarelli, ti presento il signor Bruni.

  (b) Signora Vecchiarelli, Le presento il signor Bruni.

8. How would you ask a stranger what his or her name is?

  (a) Come si chiama?

  (b) Come ti chiami?

Personal Matters! Fill in each blank with your name, using a complete sentence.

9. Nome

  Mi chiamo Jessica.

10. Cognome

  Mi cognome è Morena.

CHAPTER 3

Asking Questions

Here's what you will learn in this chapter:

More Plural Nouns

In Chapter 2 we began our discussion of Italian nouns. However, there's much more to learn about nouns, as you might imagine. Let's look now at masculine nouns ending in **-co** and **-go**. How are they put into the plural form? Are the hard sounds of the consonants retained or not?

Generally speaking, the hard **c** sound in **-co** is retained if the preceding sound in the word is one of the vowels **a**, **o**, or **u**, or any consonant. The plural ending in this case is spelled **-chi**, which, as you know from Chapter 1, represents a hard sound.

Singular		Plural	
gioco	*game*	giochi	*games*
buco	*hole*	buchi	*holes*
tedesco	*German*	tedeschi	*Germans*

Again, generally speaking, the soft **c** sound is required in the plural if the preceding vowel in the word is **e** or **i**. The plural ending in this case is spelled **-ci**, which, as you also know from Chapter 1, represents a soft sound.

Singular		Plural	
amico	*friend*	amici	*friends*
greco	*Greek*	greci	*Greeks*

In the case of **-go**, the tendency is to retain the hard sound. But there are a number of exceptions. Mainly that most nouns ending in **-logo** are pluralized to **-logi**.

Singular		Plural	
luogo	*place*	luoghi	*places*
lago	*lake*	laghi	*lakes*
biologo	*biologist*	biologi	*biologists*

NOTE: *You should consider these to be guidelines rather than strict grammatical rules.*

There is only one way to change the feminine noun endings **-ca** and **-ga** to the plural—that is to **-che** and **-ghe**, which represent hard sounds.

Singular		Plural	
amica	*female friend*	amiche	*female friends*
banca	*bank*	banche	*banks*
riga	*ruler*	righe	*rulers*

There is also only one way to change the masculine noun endings **-cio** and **-gio** to the plural—that is to **-ci** and **-gi**, which represent soft sounds.

Singular		**Plural**	
bacio	*kiss*	baci	*kisses*
orologio	*watch*	orologi	*watches*

There are two possibilities for changing the feminine noun endings **-cia** and **-gia** to the plural. The first is that if the **i** in the ending is stressed in the singular form of the noun, it is pronounced in the plural form and retained in spelling.

Singular		**Plural**	
farmacia	*pharmacy*	farmacie	*pharmacies*
(fahr-mah-chEEh-ah)		(fahr-mah-chEEh-eh)	
bugia	*lie*	bugie	*lies*
(booh-jEEh-ah)		(booh-jEEH-eh)	

If the **i** is not stressed, it is not pronounced and not retained in the plural spelling.

Singular		**Plural**	
valigia (vah-lEEH-jah)	*suitcase*	valige (vah-LEEH-jeh)	*suitcases*
faccia (fAh-chah)	*face*	facce (fAh-cheh)	*faces*

The main exception to these rules applies to the Italian word for *shirt*.

camicia	*shirt*	camicie	*shirts*

Oral Practice

Practice saying the following sentences out loud.

Chi sono?	*Who are they?*
Sono tedeschi.	*They are Germans.*
Chi sono?	*Who are they?*
Sono greci.	*They are Greeks.*
Che cosa sono?	*What are they?*
Sono luoghi.	*They are places.*
Che cosa sono?	*What are they?*
Sono righe.	*They are rulers.*
Sono facce.	*They are faces.*

Sono bugie.	*They are lies.*
Sono camicie.	*They are shirts.*

Written Practice 1

Write the plural form for each of the given nouns. For example:

Chi sono? *Who are they?*

Sono amici.   *They are friends.*

1. Chi sono? *Who are they?*
   Sono amiche.   *They are (female) friends.*

2. Che cosa sono? *What are they?*
   Sono giochi   *They are games.*

3. Che cosa sono?
   Sono buchi   *They are holes.*

4. Che cosa sono?
   Sono banche   *They are banks.*

5. Che cosa sono?
   Sono laghi   *They are lakes.*

6. Che cosa sono?
   Sono orologi   *They are watches.*

7. Che cosa sono?
   Sono farmacie   *They are pharmacies.*

8. Che cosa sono?
   Sono valigie   *They are suitcases.*

Days of the Week and Months of the Year

The names of days and months are not capitalized in Italian (unless they are the first word in a sentence).

I giorni della settimana (*The days of the week*)

lunedì	*Monday*
martedì	*Tuesday*
mercoledì	*Wednesday*
giovedì	*Thursday*
venerdì	*Friday*
sabato	*Saturday*
domenica	*Sunday*

lunedì
martedì
mercoledì
giovedì
venerdì
sabato
domenica

Che giorno è?

To ask what day of the week it is in Italian, you say:

Che giorno è?   *What day is it?*

I mesi dell'anno (*The months of the year*)

gennaio	*January*
febbraio	*February*
marzo	*March*
aprile	*April*
maggio	*May*
giugno	*June*
luglio	*July*
agosto	*August*
settembre	*September*
ottobre	*October*
novembre	*November*
dicembre	*December*

novembre
dicembre

Che mese è

gennaio   *agosto*
febbraio   *settembre*
marzo   *ottobre*
aprile   *novembre*
maggio   *dicembre*
giugno
luglio

To ask what month it is in Italian, you say:

Che mese è?   *What month is it?*

Oral Practice

Practice saying the following sentences out loud.

Che giorno è?	*What day is it?*
È lunedì.	*It is Monday.*
Che giorno è?	*What day is it?*

È domenica.	*It is Sunday.*
Che giorno è?	
È sabato.	*It is Saturday.*
Che mese è?	*What month is it?*
È gennaio.	*It is January.*
Che mese è?	*What month is it?*
È febbraio.	*It is February.*
Che mese è?	
È marzo.	*It is March.*
Che mese è?	
È aprile.	*It is April.*

Written Practice 2

Answer each of the following questions in Italian.

1. Che giorno è? *What day is it?*
   _____È mercoledì_____. *It is Wednesday.*

2. Che giorno è?
   _____È giovedì_____. *It is Thursday.*

3. Che giorno è?
   _____È venerdì_____. *It is Friday.*

4. Che mese è? *What month is it?*
   _____È agosto_____. *It is August.*

5. Che mese è?
   _____È settembre_____. *It is September.*

6. Che mese è?
   _____È ottobre_____. *It is October.*

7. Che mese è?
   _____È novembre_____. *It is November.*

8. Che mese è?
   _____È dicembre_____. *It is December.*

Languages and Nationalities

Quante lingue parli? *How many languages do you speak?* If you know more than one language, here is your chance to be able to say so in Italian.

The names of languages and nationalities are generally the same. Notice that they are not capitalized in Italian. The endings **-o** or **-a** are the masculine and feminine endings used when referring to males or females.

Languages		Nationalities
l'italiano	*Italian*	italiano/a
l'inglese	*English*	inglese, americano/a, canadese, australiano/a
lo spagnolo	*Spanish*	spagnolo/a
il francese	*French*	francese
il tedesco	*German*	tedesco/a
il russo	*Russian*	russo/a
il giapponese	*Japanese*	giapponese
il cinese	*Chinese*	cinese
il portoghese	*Portuguese*	portoghese

To ask someone what language he or she speaks, you would say:

Quale lingua parli?   *Which language do you speak?*

To ask someone what nationality he or she is, you would say:

Di quale nazionalità sei?   *Of what nationality are you?*

Oral Practice

Practice saying the following sentences out loud.

Quale lingua parli?	*Which language do you speak?*
Parlo portoghese.	*I speak Portuguese.*
Quale lingua parli?	*Which language do you speak?*
Parlo cinese.	*I speak Chinese.*
Di quale nazionalità sei?	*Of what nationality are you?*
Sono giapponese.	*I am Japanese.*
Di quale nazionalità sei?	*Of what nationality are you?*

Sono tedesco/a.	*I am German.*
Di quale nazionalità sei?	*Of what nationality are you?*
Sono italiano/a.	*I am Italian.*

Written Practice 3

Answer each of the following questions in Italian, using the English translations as a guide.

1. Quale lingua parli? *Which language do you speak?*
   <u>Parlo russo</u>. *I speak Russian.*

2. Quale lingua parli?
   <u>Parlo spagnolo</u>. *I speak Spanish.*

3. Di quale nazionalità sei? *Of what nationality are you?*
   <u>Sono americana</u>. *I am American.*

4. Di quale nazionalità sei?
   <u>Sono inglese</u>. *I am English.*

5. Di quale nazionalità sei?
   <u>Sono australiano</u>. *I am Australian.*

Question Words

Come ti chiami? *What is your name?* (Literally: *How do you call yourself?*)

You've already learned how to ask this question in Italian. In fact, you already know quite a bit about asking questions. To get information from someone, a question begins with a question word. The following list illustrates some of the question words in Italian.

che	*what*	perché	*why*
chi	*who*	quale	*which*
come	*how*	quando	*when*
dove	*where*	quanto	*how much*

CHE

You might also see the question word **che** replaced by **che cosa** or **cosa** when used as a pronoun.

Che giorno è?	*What day is it?*	È venerdì.	*It is Friday.*
Che mese è?	*What month is it?*	È settembre.	*It is September.*
Che cosa è?	*What is it?*	È una chiave.	*It is a key.*

CHI

Chi parla italiano?	*Who speaks Italian?*	Marco parla italiano.	*Mark speaks Italian.*
Chi è?	*Who is it?*	È l'amica di Maria.	*It is Mary's friend.*

COME

Maria, come stai?	*Mary, how are you?*	Bene, grazie.	*Well, thanks.*
Come si chiama?	*What is your name?*	Mi chiamo Pino Dini.	*My name is Pino Dini.*

DOVE

The final **-e** in **dove** (*where*) can be dropped before the verb form **è** (*is*), making an Italian contraction.

Dov'è Maria?	Where is *Mary?*	Ecco Maria.	*Here is Mary.*
Dove sei?	Where *are you?*	Sono qui.	*I am here.*

PERCHÉ

Note that **perché** (*why*) also means *because* and that the accent on the final vowel slants to the right (acute).

Perché parli?	Why *are you speaking?*	**Perché** mi piace.	Because *I like it.*
Perché ti piace?	Why *do you like it?*	**Perché** è italiano.	Because *it is Italian.*

QUALE AND *QUANTO*

In the case of both **quale** and **quanto**, the endings change according to the gender and number of the noun, when they are used as adjectives.

Quale lingua parli?	Which *language do you speak?*	Parlo italiano.	*I speak Italian.*
Quali lingue parli?	Which *languages do you speak?*	Inglese e italiano.	*English and Italian.*
Quanto caffè?	How much *coffee?*	Poco, grazie.	*A little, thanks.*
Quanti figli hai?	How many *children do you have?*	Ho due figli.	*I have two children.*

QUANDO

Quando means *when* and is invariable—that is, its **-o** ending never changes.

Quando vai in Italia?	When *are you going to Italy?*	A gennaio.	*In January.*

ABBREVIATIONS WITH QUESTION WORDS

In writing, it is normal to drop the **-e** from **come**, **dove**, and **quale** before the verb form **è**. In the case of both **come** and **dove** an apostrophe is added. But this is not the case for **quale**.

Com'è?	*How is it?*
Dov'è?	*Where is it?*
Qual è?	*Which is it?*

Oral Practice

Practice saying the following sentences out loud.

Che cosa è (Che cos'è)?	*What is it?*
È un'automobile.	*It is an automobile.*
Chi è?	*Who is it?*

È il padre di Alessandro.	*He is Alexander's father.*
Come si chiama?	*What is your name?*
Mi chiamo Marco Vecchiarelli.	*My name is Mark Vecchiarelli.*
Dove vai?	*Where are you going?*
Vado in Italia.	*I am going to Italy.*
Quando vai?	*When are you going?*
A luglio.	*In July.*
Perché?	*Why?*
Perché mi piace.	*Because I like it.*
Quali lingue parli?	*Which languages do you speak?*
Parlo italiano e francese.	*I speak Italian and French.*
Quante lingue parli?	*How many languages do you speak?*
Solo l'italiano.	*Only Italian.*

ASKING YES/NO QUESTIONS

In some cases you might have to ask a question that requires simply a yes or no answer. The most common method of forming a question designed to get such a response in Italian is to add a question mark at the end of the corresponding affirmative sentence. Notice that **non** means *not*.

Anna è italiana?	*Is Anne Italian?*
Sì, Anna è italiana.	*Yes, Anne is Italian.*
Betty è italiana?	*Is Betty Italian?*
No, Betty non è italiana.	*No, Betty is not Italian.*
Lui parla francese?	*Does he speak French?*
Sì, lui parla francese.	*Yes, he speaks French.*
Lei parla francese?	*Does she speak French?*
No, lei non parla francese.	*No, she does not speak French.*

Another way to form this type of question is to put the subject at the end.

È italiana Anna?	*Is Anne Italian?*
Parla francese lui?	*Does he speak French?*

TAG QUESTIONS

Some questions are designed to elicit consent, agreement, or verification. These are called tag questions because they end with an expression "tagged on." In Italian that expression can be one of the following:

Vero?	*Right?*
Non è vero?	*Isn't that correct?*
No?	*No?*

Lui è americano, non è vero?	*He is American, isn't he?*
Lei parla francese, vero?	*She speaks French, doesn't she?*
Oggi è lunedì, no?	*Today is Monday, isn't it?*

Oral Practice

Practice saying the following sentences out loud.

È russa Maria?	*Is Mary Russian?*
Sì, Maria è russa.	*Yes, Mary is Russian.*
Ti chiami Marco, vero?	*Your name is Mark, isn't it?*
Sì, mi chiamo Marco.	*Yes, my name is Mark.*
Lui parla cinese?	*Does he speak Chinese?*
No, lui non parla cinese.	*No, he does not speak Chinese.*
Ti piace il caffè, no?	*You like coffee, don't you?*
Sì, mi piace.	*Yes, I like it.*

Written Practice 4

Answer each of the following questions in Italian.

1. È americana Sara? *Is Sarah American?*

   Sì, Sara è americana *Yes, Sarah is American.*

2. Ti piace il caffè, non è vero? *You like coffee, don't you?*

   No, non mi piace il caffè. *No, I do not like coffee.*

3. Ti piace il tè, no? *You like tea, don't you?*

   Sì, mi piace il tè. *Yes, I like tea.*

Italian-Speaking World

There are many speakers of Italian worldwide—in Italy alone there are more than 56 million of them. You will also find them in southern Switzerland in a region called **il Ticino** and, of course, throughout North America, as well as in many other countries. The two countries that use Italian as their official language or as one of their official languages are:

l'Italia	*Italy*
la Svizzera	*Switzerland*

Other Countries Around the World

Notice that names of countries require a definite article.

gli Stati Uniti	*the United States*
il Canada	*Canada*
l'Inghilterra	*England*
l'Australia	*Australia*
la Francia	*France*
la Germania	*Germany*
la Spagna	*Spain*
la Cina	*China*
il Giappone	*Japan*
la Russia	*Russia*

l'Inghilterra

To say that you are *in* a country, however, use **in** plus the country name without the article. A major exception to this is with the United States. It presents a different situation because it is always in the plural form. In this instance use **negli Stati Uniti** (*in the United States*). Don't worry too much at this point about the form **negli**, which is a contraction of **in** + **gli**. We will discuss this later.

in Italia	*in Italy*
in Francia	*in France*
negli Stati Uniti	*in the United States*

To Italians, home is the place where one was born. So, if you ask an Italian where he or she is from, you will get an answer such as *I am from Milan.*

Di dove sei?	*Where are you from?*
Sono di Milano.	*I am from Milan.*
Di dove sei?	*Where are you from?*
Sono di Roma.	*I am from Rome.*

Oral Practice

Practice saying the following sentences out loud.

Dove vai?	*Where are you going?*
In Francia.	*To France.*
Dove vai?	*Where are you going?*
In Inghilterra.	*To England.*
Dove vai?	*Where are you going?*
In Germania.	*To Germany.*
Dove vai?	*Where are you going?*
Negli Stati Uniti.	*To the United States.*

Written Practice 5

Using the English translations as a guide, fill in the blanks with the answers to the questions. When the city name is different in Italian, it is provided for you.

1. Di dove sei? (Napoli) *Where are you from?*
   Sono di napoli . *I am from Naples.*
2. Di dove sei?
   Sono di Palermo . *I am from Palermo.*
3. Di dove sei? (Venezia)
   Sono di Venezia . *I am from Venice.*
4. Di dove sei? (Firenze)
   Sono di Firenze . *I am from Florence.*

5. Di dove sei? (Genova)

Sono di Genova. *I am from Genoa.*

6. Di dove sei?

Sono di Perugia. *I am from Perugia.*

7. Di dove sei?

Sono di Bari. *I am from Bari.*

QUIZ

Write the plural form of each of the following nouns.

1. tedesco _tedeschi_

   buco _buchi_

   gioco _giochi_

   greco _greci_

   amico _amici_

   luogo _luoghi_

   lago _laghi_

   biologo _biologi_

   amica _amiche_

Write the singular form of each of the following nouns.

2. righe _riga_

   banche _banca_

   orologi _orologio_

   baci _bacio_

   facce _faccia_

   farmacie _farmacia_

   camicie _camicia_

Answer each question, using the day after the one provided. Note that **oggi** means *today*. For example:

lunedì   *Monday*

Oggi è martedì. _____ *Today is Tuesday.*

3. Che giorno è?

Su. domenica _Oggi è domenica_ .

M. lunedì _Oggi è lunedì_ .

Tu martedì _Oggi è martedì_ .

Fri venerdì _Oggi è venerdì_ .

Wed mercoledì _Oggi è mercoledì._ .

Answer each question, using the month after the one provided. For example:

gennaio   *January*

È il mese di febbraio _____ *It is the month of February.*

4. Che mese è?

dicembre _È il mese di dicembre_ .

maggio _È il mese di maggio._ .

settembre _È il mese di settembre_ .

aprile _È il mese di aprile._ .

gennaio _È il mese di gennaio_ .

febbraio _È il mese di febbraio_ .

marzo _È il mese di marzo._ .

Write sentences saying that you speak each of the following languages, but that you are not of that nationality. Note that **ma** means *but*. For example:

French

Parlo francese, ma non sono francese. *I speak French, but I am not French.*

5. Portuguese

Parlo portoghese, ma non sono portoghese.

Italian

Parlo italiano, ma non sono italiana.

Russian

Parlo russo, ma non sono russa.

English

Parlo inglese, ma non sono inglese.

German

Parlo tedesco, ma non sono tedesca.

Personal Matters! Answer each question appropriately.

6. Qual è il tuo giorno preferito della settimana?

Domenica è il mio giorno preferito della settimana.

7. Di quale nazionalità sei?

Sono americana.

8. Quali lingue parli?

Parlo inglese e italiano.

9. Come ti chiami?

Mi chiamo Jessica.

10. Di dove sei?

Sono di New York.

CHAPTER 4

Describing People and Things

Here's what you will learn in this chapter:

Personal Pronouns

To conjugate verbs, you will first have to learn the subject personal pronouns. Personal pronouns are called this because they refer to a person or persons (*I, you, we,* etc.). They are classified according to the person(s) speaking (= first person), the person(s) spoken to (= second person), or the person(s) spoken about (= third person). The pronoun can, of course, be in the singular (= referring to one person) or in the plural (= referring to more than one person).

	Singular	**Plural**
1st person	**io** (*I*)	**noi** (*we*)
2nd person	**tu** (*you*, familiar singular)	**voi** (*you*, familiar plural)
3rd person	**Lei** (*you*, polite singular)	**Loro** (*you*, polite plural)
	lui/lei (*he/she*)	**loro** (*they*)

Notice that **io** is not capitalized (unless it is the first word in a sentence). Also, note that *you* has both familiar (**tu, voi**) and polite (**Lei, Loro**) forms in Italian. In writing, the polite forms are capitalized in order to distinguish them from **lei** meaning *she* and **loro** meaning *they*. In current Italian the **voi** forms are used commonly as the plural of both **tu** and **Lei** forms. The **Loro** form is restricted to very formal situations. For example:

Familiar Singular		**Familiar Plural**	
Chi sei tu?	*Who are you?*	Chi siete voi?	*Who are you?*
Tu sei italiano.	*You are Italian.*	Voi siete italiani.	*You are Italians.*

Polite Singular		**Polite Plural**	
Chi è Lei?	*Who are you?*	Chi siete voi?	*Who are you?*
Lei è italiano.	*You are Italian.*	Voi siete italiani.	*You are Italians.*
Chi è Lei?	*Who are you?*	Chi sono Loro?	*Who are you?* (very polite)
Lei è italiano.	*You are Italian.*	Loro sono italiani.	*You are Italians.* (very polite)

USE OF PERSONAL PRONOUNS

The personal pronouns are optional in simple affirmative sentences, because it is easy to tell from the verb form itself which person is the subject.

Io sono americano.	I am *American.*
Sono americano.	I am *American.*

Noi siamo in Italia.	We are *in Italy.*
Siamo in Italia.	We are *in Italy.*

However, the pronouns must be used for emphasis, to avoid ambiguity, or if more than one subject pronoun is required.

Marco, sei tu?	*Mark, is it you?*
Lui e io siamo in Italia.	*He and I are in Italy.*

They must also be used after the following words. Try to memorize these words for future use.

anche	*also, too*
neanche	*neither, not even, not . . . either*
proprio	*really*

Anche tu sei italiano, vero?	*You, too, are Italian, aren't you?*
Non è italiano neanche lui.	*He is not Italian either.*
Signor Rossini, è proprio Lei?	*Mr. Rossini, is it really you?*

In English sentences the subject pronoun *it* must be stated, however, in Italian it can be omitted.

È vero.	*It is true.*

Using the Verb *Essere*

Chi sei tu? *Who are you?* It's time to learn your first verb, **essere** (*to be*). This unconjugated form of the verb **essere** is called the infinitive. The infinitive is the form of the verb given to you in a dictionary. In this chapter you will learn how to conjugate **essere** in the present indicative tense. The indicative mood is used to express or indicate facts. It is the most commonly used mood in everyday conversation. The present indicative, as its name implies, is used to form statements and questions in the present tense.

Singular

io sono	*I am*
tu sei	*you are* (familiar)
Lei è	*you are* (polite)
lui è	*he is*
lei è	*she is*

Plural

noi siamo	*we are*
voi siete	*you are* (familiar)
Loro sono	*you are* (polite)
loro sono	*they are*

To make the verb negative in a sentence, simply put the word **non** before it.

Affirmative

Lui è spagnolo.	*He is Spanish.*
Sono italiano.	*I am Italian.*

Negative

Lui **non** è spagnolo.	*He is not Spanish.*
Non sono italiano.	*I am not Italian.*

Oral Practice

Practice reading the following sentences out loud.

Di che nazionalità sei tu?	*Of what nationality are you?*
Io sono canadese.	*I am Canadian.*
Di che nazionalità è lui?	*Of what nationality is he?*
Lui è americano.	*He is American.*
Di che nazionalità è lei?	*Of what nationality is she?*
Lei è americana.	*She is American.*
Di che nazionalità è Lei, signor Marchi?	*Of what nationality are you, Mr. Marchi?*
Io sono italiano.	*I am Italian.*
Di che nazionalità siete voi?	*Of what nationality are you?*
Noi siamo francesi.	*We are French.*
Di che nazionalità sono loro?	*Of what nationality are they?*
Loro sono inglesi.	*They are English.*

Sono
sei
è

siamo
siete
sono

Written Practice 1

Fill in the blanks with the appropriate form of the verb **essere**.

1. Marco, di che nazionalità sei? *Mark, of what nationality are you?*
   Io _sono_ italiano. *I am Italian.*

2. Di che nazionalità è Claudia? *Of what nationality is Claudia?*
   Claudia _è_ tedesca. *Claudia is German.*

3. Di che nazionalità è Alessandro? *Of what nationality is Alexander?*
   Alessandro _è_ canadese. *Alexander is Canadian.*

4. Di che nazionalità è Sara? *Of what nationality is Sarah?*
   Sara _è_ americana. *Sarah is American.*

5. Di che nazionalità siete voi, Paolo e Elena? *Of what nationality are you, Paul and Helen?*
   Noi _siamo_ francesi. *We are French.*

6. Di che nazionalità sono Franco e Maria? *Of what nationality are Frank and Mary?*
   Loro _sono_ spagnoli. *They are Spanish.*

Adjectives

Com'è? *How is it?* Answering this question requires knowing how to use descriptive adjectives (*new, nice, expensive, tall,* etc.). Descriptive adjectives are words that modify or describe nouns. They are usually placed after the noun they modify in a sentence.

È una casa nuova.	*It is a new house.*
Sono automobili italiane.	*They are Italian automobiles.*

In Italian, as in English, descriptive adjectives can be separated by the verb **essere** in sentences.

La casa è nuova.	*The house is new.*
Le automobili sono italiane.	*The automobiles are Italian.*

Italian adjectives agree in gender (masculine or feminine) and number (singular or plural) with the nouns they modify. This means that the final vowel is changed according to the gender and number of the noun being modified. There are two types of adjectives in Italian: (1) adjectives that end in **-o**, such as **alto** (*tall*), and (2) those that end in **-e**, such as **intelligente** (*intelligent*). These are the default forms—that is, the forms that are given to you in a dictionary.

When modifying masculine nouns, adjectives such as **alto** end in **-o** if the noun is singular and **-i** if it is plural; adjectives such as **intelligente** end in **-e** if the noun is singular and **-i** if it is plural.

Singular		**Plural**	
il ragazzo alto	*the tall boy*	i ragazzi alti	*the tall boys*
il ragazzo intelligente	*the intelligent boy*	i ragazzi intelligenti	*the intelligent boys*
il padre alto	*the tall father*	i padri alti	*the tall fathers*
il padre intelligente	*the intelligent father*	i padri intelligenti	*the intelligent fathers*

With feminine nouns, adjectives such as **alto** end in **-a** if the noun being modified is singular and **-e** if it is plural; adjectives such as **intelligente** end in **-e** if the noun is singular and **-i** if it is plural.

Singular		**Plural**	
la ragazza alta	*the tall girl*	le ragazze alte	*the tall girls*
la ragazza intelligente	*the intelligent girl*	le ragazze intelligenti	*the intelligent girls*
la madre alta	*the tall mother*	le madri alte	*the tall mothers*
la madre intelligente	*the intelligent mother*	le madri intelligenti	*the intelligent mothers*

The following are some common Italian color adjectives:

azzurro	*blue*	nero	*black*
bianco	*white*	rosso	*red*
giallo	*yellow*	verde	*green*

Oral Practice

Practice saying the following sentences out loud.

Com'è il ragazzo?	*How is the boy?*
Il ragazzo è alto.	*The boy is tall.*
Com'è la ragazza?	*How is the girl?*
La ragazza è alta.	*The girl is tall.*
Come sono i ragazzi?	*How are the boys?*
I ragazzi sono alti.	*The boys are tall.*
Come sono le ragazze?	*How are the girls?*
Le ragazze sono alte.	*The girls are tall.*
Com'è il padre?	*How is the father?*
Il padre è intelligente.	*The father is intelligent.*
Com'è la madre?	*How is the mother?*
La madre è intelligente.	*The mother is intelligent.*
Come sono gli zii di Maria?	*How are Mary's uncles?*
Gli zii di Maria sono intelligenti.	*Mary's uncles are intelligent.*
Come sono le zie di Maria?	*How are Mary's aunts?*
Le zie di Maria sono intelligenti.	*Mary's aunts are intelligent.*

Written Practice 2

Fill in the blanks using the correct forms of the adjectives provided in the English translations.

1. Com'è l'automobile di Pina? *How is Pina's car?*

   L'automobile di Pina è *nuovo* . *Pina's car is new.*

2. Com'è il divano di Maria? *How is Mary's sofa?*

   Il divano di Maria è *bianco* . *Mary's sofa is white.*

3. Come sono le automobili? *How are the cars?*

   Le automobili sono *neri* . *The cars are black.*

4. Come sono i pantaloni di Pina? *How are Pina's pants?*

   I pantaloni di Pina sono _azzurri_ . *Pina's pants are blue.*

5. Com'è la valigia di Marco? *How is Mark's suitcase?*

   La valigia di Marco è ___Verde___ . *Mark's suitcase is green.*

6. Com'è la camicia di Marco? *How is Mark's shirt?*

   La camicia di Marco è ___giallo___ . *Mark's shirt is yellow.*

7. Come sono gli amici di Marco? *How are Mark's friends?*

   Gli amici di Marco sono _intelligenti_ . *Mark's friends are intelligent.*

8. Come sono le amiche di Marco? *How are Marks (female) friends?*

   Le amiche di Marco sono _intelligenti_ . *Mark's friends are intelligent.*

INVARIABLE ADJECTIVES

A few adjectives are invariable—that is, their endings never change, no matter what gender or number the noun is. The color adjectives **marrone** (*brown*), **arancione** (*orange*), **viola** (*violet, purple*), **rosa** (*pink*), and **blu** (*dark blue*) are invariable. These, and other color adjectives are often used to describe clothes and accessories (as you might imagine). Following is a list of commonly used words for clothing and accessories.

marrone
arancione
viola
rosa
blu

la giacca	*the jacket*	il vestito	*the dress*
il cappello	*the hat*	la sciarpa	*the scarf*
lo zaino	*the backpack*		

Singular		**Plural**	
la giacca marrone	*the brown jacket*	le giacche marrone	*the brown jackets*
il cappello arancione	*the orange hat*	i cappelli arancione	*the orange hats*
lo zaino viola	*the purple backpack*	gli zaini viola	*the purple backpacks*
il vestito rosa	*the pink dress*	i vestiti rosa	*the pink dresses*
la sciarpa blu	*the dark blue scarf*	le sciarpe blu	*the dark blue scarves*

Adjectives ending in **-co**, **-go**, **-cio**, and **-gio** undergo the same spelling changes when pluralized as do nouns ending in these sounds, which you can review in Chapter 3 if necessary.

Singular

l'uomo simpati**co**	*the nice man*
la donna simpati**ca**	*the nice woman*
il vestito lun**go**	*the long dress*
la strada lun**ga**	*the long street*
il vestito gri**gio**	*the gray dress*
la camicia gri**gia**	*the gray shirt*

Plural

gli uomini simpati**ci**	*the nice men*
le donne simpati**che**	*the nice women*
i vestiti lun**ghi**	*the long dresses*
le strade lun**ghe**	*the long streets*
i vestiti gri**gi**	*the gray dresses*
le camicie gri**ge**	*the gray shirts*

When two nouns are modified by one adjective, the adjective must be in the plural. If the two nouns are feminine, then the appropriate feminine plural form is used; if the two nouns are both masculine, or of mixed gender, then the appropriate masculine plural form is used.

Both Feminine

La camicia e la sciarpa sono rosse.   *The shirt and the scarf are red.*

Both Masculine

Il vestito e lo zaino sono rossi.   *The dress and the backpack are red.*

Mixed Gender

La sciarpa e il cappello sono rossi.   *The scarf and the hat are red.*

Oral Practice

Practice saying the following sentences out loud.

Di che colore è la giacca?	*Of what color is the jacket?*
La giacca è marrone.	*The jacket is brown.*
Di che colore sono le giacche?	*Of what color are the jackets?*
Le giacche sono blu.	*The jackets are dark blue.*
Di che colore è il cappello?	*Of what color is the hat?*
Il cappello è arancione.	*The hat is orange.*
Di che colore sono i cappelli?	*Of what color are the hats?*
I cappelli sono viola.	*The hats are purple.*
Di che colore è la sciarpa?	*Of what color is the scarf?*

La sciarpa è grigia.   The scarf is gray.   *La sciarpe è grigie.*

Di che colore sono le sciarpe?   Of what color are the scarves?   *Di che colore sono le sciarpe?*

Le sciarpe sono rosa.   The scarves are pink.   *Le sciarpe sono rose.*

Com'è l'uomo?   How is the man?   *Com'è l'uomo?*

L'uomo è simpatico.   The man is nice.   *L'uomo è simpatico.*

Come sono gli uomini?   How are the men?   *Come sono gli uomini?*

Gli uomini sono simpatici.   The men are nice.   *L'uomo è*
                                                                     Gli uomini sono simpatici.

Written Practice 3

Fill in the blanks with the correct forms of the adjectives provided in the English translations.

1. Com'è la donna? *How is the woman?*
   La donna è _simpatica_. *The woman is nice.*

2. Come sono le donne? *How are the women?*
   Le donne sono _simpatiche_. *The women are nice.*

3. Com'è l'amico di Paolo? *How is Paul's friend?*
   L'amico di Paolo è _simpatico_. *Paul's friend is nice.*

4. Come sono gli amici di Paolo? *How are Paul's friends?*
   Gli amici di Paolo sono _simpatici_. *Paul's friends are nice.*

5. Com'è il vestito? *How is the dress?*
   Il vestito è _lungo_. *The dress is long.*

6. Come sono i vestiti? *How are the dresses?*
   I vestiti sono _lunghi_. *The dresses are long.*

7. Com'è la sciarpa? *How is the scarf?*
   La sciarpa è _lunga_. *The scarf is long.*

8. Come sono le sciarpe? *How are the scarves?*
   Le sciarpe sono _lunghe_. *The scarves are long.*

Numbers from 0 to 20

Quanto costa? *How much does it cost?* To answer this question in Italian, you will have to know how to count. Let's start here with the numbers from 0 to 20. You will learn more about numbers in upcoming chapters.

0	zero	11	undici
1	uno	12	dodici
2	due	13	tredici
3	tre	14	quattordici
4	quattro	15	quindici
5	cinque	16	sedici
6	sei	17	diciassette
7	sette	18	diciotto
8	otto	19	diciannove
9	nove	20	venti
10	dieci		

zero, uno, due, tre, quattro, cinque, sei, ~~sette~~ otto, nove, dieci
undici, dodici, tredici, quattordici, quindici, sedici, diciasette,
diciotto, diannove, venti

Italian Currency

As you may know, the euro is used in Italy as the basic unit of currency, as it is in many other European countries. It replaced the **lira** on January 1, 1999, which was the previous Italian unit of currency. One euro is designed to provide the same buying power as one dollar, **un dollaro** (dOh-llah-roh), although the exchange rates always seem to vary. Do you know what the rate is right now?

The spelling of the noun **euro** in Italian is invariable.

un euro	*one euro*
cinque euro	*five euros*

Oral Practice

Practice saying the following sentences out loud.

Quanto costa?	*How much does it cost?*
Forse costa uno o due euro.	*Maybe it costs one or two euros.*

Quanto costa?

Forse costa uno o due euro.

Quanto costa?

Forse costa tre o quattro euro.	*Maybe it costs three or four euros.*
Forse costa cinque o sei dollari.	*Maybe it costs five or six dollars.*
Forse costa sette o otto dollari.	*Maybe it costs seven or eight dollars.*
Forse costa nove o dieci euro.	*Maybe it costs nine or ten euros.*
Forse costa undici o dodici euro.	*Maybe it costs eleven or twelve euros.*

Written Practice 4

Answer the questions using the English translations as a guide.

1. Quanto costa? *How much does it cost?*

Forse costa <u>tredici o quattordici dollari</u>. *Maybe it costs thirteen or fourteen dollars.*

2. Quanto costa?

<u>quindici o sedici</u>. *Maybe it costs fifteen or sixteen dollars.*

3. Quanto costa?

<u>diciassette diciotto</u>. *Maybe it costs seventeen or eighteen euros.*

4. Quanto costa?

<u>diciannove venti</u>. *Maybe it costs nineteen or twenty euros.*

Numbers from 21 to 100

The number words between 20 and 100 are shown in the following list, however, keep these points in mind:

- In front of **uno** and **otto** (the two number words that start with a vowel), drop the final vowel of the higher value word to which these are added on. For example:

  21 venti + uno = ventuno

  38 trenta + otto = trentotto

- When **tre** is added on, it must be written with an accent (to show that the stress is on the final vowel).

  23 venti + tre = ventitré

  33 trenta + tre = trentatré

Here are the number words representing the tens values. Only the twenties are given to you in full, since you can easily complete the others on your own.

21	ventuno	50	cinquanta
22	ventidue	51	cinquantuno
23	ventitré	52	cinquantadue
24	ventiquattro	53	cinquantatré
25	venticinque	60	sessanta
26	ventisei	61	sessantuno
27	ventisette	62	sessantadue
28	ventotto	63	sessantatré
29	ventinove	70	settanta
30	trenta	71	settantuno
31	trentuno	72	settantadue
32	trentadue	73	settantatré
33	trentatré	80	ottanta
40	quaranta	81	ottantuno
41	quarantuno	82	ottantadue
42	quarantadue	83	ottantatré
43	quarantatré	90	novanta
		91	novantuno
		92	novantadue
		93	novantatré
		100	cento

Handwritten notes in margin: Ventuno / trentotto / Ventitré / trentatré

Handwritten notes in margin: Vent / trent / quar / cinc / sess / sett / ott / nov / cent

Oral Practice

Practice saying the following sentences out loud.

Quanto costa?	*How much does it cost?*
Forse costa ventuno o trentadue euro.	*Maybe it costs 21 or 32 euros.*

Quanto costa?

Forse costa quarantatré o
    cinquantacinque euro.   *Maybe it costs 43 or 55 euros.*

Forse costa sessantotto o
    settantasei dollari.   *Maybe it costs 68 or 76 dollars.*

Forse costa ottantasette o
    novantaquattro dollari.   *Maybe it costs 87 or 94 dollars.*

Forse costa trentotto o ventiquattro   *Maybe it costs 38 or 24 euros.*
    euro.

Written Practice 5

Answer the questions using the digits in the English translations as a guide.

1. Quanto costa?
   Settantatré   novantotto _____. *Maybe it costs 73 or 98 euros.*

2. Quanto costa?
   quarantanove cinquantasette _____. *Maybe it costs 49 or 57 dollars.*

3. Quanto costa?
   Zero o cento _____. *Maybe it costs 0 or 100 dollars.*

Asking Questions with Prepositions

Di chi è? *Whose is it?* (literally: *Of whom is it?*). Many questions begin with a
preposition. The following are some of the most commonly used prepositions:

a	*to*	con	*with*
di	*of*	in	*in*
da	*from*	di chi	*whose*

Here are a few examples of questions beginning with these prepositions:

Di chi è la camicia?   Whose *shirt is it?*

A chi parli?   To whom *are you speaking?*

Di dove sei?   Where *are you from?*

Con chi parli?   With whom *are you speaking?*

Using *Quanto* and *Quale*

Recall **quanto** (*how much*) from Chapter 3. Note that when used as an adjective its endings change according to the required gender and number.

Quanto caffè prendi?   *How much coffee are you having?*

Quanta pizza mangi?   *How much pizza are you eating?*

Quanti caffè prendi?   *How many coffees are you having?*

Quante pizze mangi?   *How many pizzas are you eating?*

However, when used as a pronoun, the only form possible is **quanto**.

Quanto costa?   *How much does it cost?*

Similarly, when **quale** (*which*) is used as an adjective its endings also change in the usual manner.

Quale caffè prendi?   *Which coffee are you having?*

Quale pizza mangi?   *Which pizza are you eating?*

Quali caffè prendi?   *Which coffees are you having?*

Quali pizze mangi?   *Which pizzas are you eating?*

Oral Practice

Practice saying the following sentences out loud.

Di chi è l'automobile?   *Whose car is it?*

È di Mario.   *It is Mario's.*

A chi parli?   *To whom are you speaking?*

Parlo a Maria.   *I am speaking to Mary.*

Da dove vieni?   *Where are you coming from?*

Vengo da Milano.	*I am coming from Milan.*
Con chi parli?	*With whom are you speaking?*
Parlo con Giovanni.	*I am speaking with John.*
Dove sono Marco e Maria?	*Where are Mark and Mary?*
Forse sono in Italia.	*Maybe they are in Italy.*
Quanto caffè ti piace?	*How much coffee do you like?*
Non mi piace il caffè.	*I do not like coffee.*
Quale caffè ti piace?	*Which coffee do you like?*
Non mi piace il caffè.	*I do not like coffee.*
Quanti caffè prendi?	*How many coffees are you having?*
Due, grazie.	*Two, thanks.*

(Handwritten answers in the right margin:)
Vengo da Milano.
Con chi parli?
Parlo con Giovanni.
Dove sono Marco e Maria?
Forse sono in Italia.
Quanto caffè prendi? / ti piace?
Non mi piace il caffè.
Quale caffè ti piace?
Non mi piace il caffè.
Quanti caffè prendi?
Due, grazie.

QUIZ

Using the pronouns in parentheses, write sentences giving that person's nationality. Be sure to make all appropriate changes to the adjective. For example:

Marco è italiano. (Maria)   *Mark is Italian. (Mary)*

Anche Maria è italiana.   *Mary is also Italian.*

1. Io sono americano. (tu)

Anche tu sei americano.

Tu sei australiano. (lei)

Anche lei è australiano.

Lui è inglese. (noi)

Anche noi siamo inglesi.

Lei è francese. (voi)

Anche voi siete francesi

Noi siamo canadesi. (loro)

Anche sono canadesi

Voi siete russi. (io)

Sono russo.

Loro sono cinesi. (lui)

Anche so lui è cinese.

Maria è italiana. (Paolo)

Anche Paolo è italiano.

Marco e Claudia sono italiani. (il signor Giusti)

Anche il signor Giusti è italiano.

La signora Marchi è americana. (la signorina Dini)

Anche la signorina Dini è americana.

Circle the letter of the word or phrase that best completes each sentence.

2. Di che nazionalità è Lei, signora Marchi?

   (a) Sono italiana.

   (b) È italiana.

3. Di che colore è la giacca?

   (a) È rossa.

   (b) Sono rosse.

4. Come sono le donne?

   (a) Sono simpatici.

   (b) Sono simpatiche.

Write each phrase in its corresponding masculine or feminine form.

Masculine	Feminine
5. ragazzo intelligente	_ragazza intelligente_
amico alto	amica alta
zio alto	_zia alta_
uomo intelligente	donna intelligente
padre simpatico	_madre simpatica_
amico italiano	amica italiana
ragazzo francese	_ragazza francese_
uomo simpatico	donna simpatica

Write each phrase in its corresponding singular or plural form. Note: The plural of **uomo** (*man*) is **uomini** (*men*).

Singular	Plural
6. vestito rosa	*vestiti rosa*
sciarpa rossa	sciarpe rosse
uomo alto	*uomini alti*
zaino marrone	zaini marrone
uomo simpatico	*uomini simpatici*
scarpe grigie	sciarpe grige

Answer each question, writing out the numbers in words. For example:

Quanto costa?

2 or 3 dollars   *Forse costa due o tre dollari.*

7. Quanto costa?
   78 or 79 euros   *settantotto o settantanove*
   87 or 88 dollars   *ottantasette o ottantotto*
   16 or 17 dollars   *sedici o diciassette*
   23 or 24 euros   *ventitré o ventiquattro*
   61 or 62 euros   *sessantuno o sessantadue*

Personal Matters! Write full sentences in Italian indicating the following:

8. Your favorite color
   Mi colore favorito è rosa.
9. Your nationality
   La mia nazionalità è americana.
10. The name of your friend
    La mia amica è Kristine.

CHAPTER 5

Expressing Likes and Dislikes

Here's what you will learn in this chapter:

Forms of the Indefinite Article

Chi è? Che cos'è? *Who is it?* or *What is it?* There are two basic ways to answer these questions, according to who or what someone or something is. For example, if you answer that it is *a book*, then you mean to say that it is *a book* in general, distinct from, say, *a magazine* or *a record*. However, if you answer that it is *the book*, then you mean to say that it is a specific book, such as *the book* that you read yesterday. The words *a* and *the* allow you to make this distinction. They are called articles. The former is called the indefinite article and the latter the definite article.

In Italian the indefinite article varies according to the gender and initial sound of the noun it precedes. The indefinite article can only be used with singular nouns, of course, because when using it you can only refer to one person or thing: *a student, an uncle*, and so on. Here are some rules for using the indefinite article in Italian:

- The indefinite article **uno** is used before a masculine noun beginning with **z, s** + consonant, **gn**, or **ps**. For example:

uno zio	*an uncle*	uno gnocco	*a dumpling*
uno studente	*a student*	uno psicologo	*a psychologist*

- **Un** is used before a masculine noun beginning with any other sound (consonant or vowel).

un ragazzo	*a boy*	un gatto	*a cat*
un cane	*a dog*	un amico	*a friend*

- **Una** is used before a feminine noun beginning with any consonant (including **z, s** + consonant, **gn**, or **ps**).

una zia	*an aunt*	una ragazza	*a girl*
una studentessa	*a female student*	una psicologa	*a (female) psychologist*

- **Un'** is used before a feminine noun beginning with any vowel.

un'amica	*a friend*	un'americana	*an American*
un'ora	*an hour*	un'isola	*an island*
		(EEh-zoh-lah)	

When an adjective precedes the noun, it is necessary to adjust the indefinite article according to the beginning sound of the adjective.

uno zio	*an uncle*	but:	un caro zio	*a dear uncle*
un'amica	*a friend*	but:	una cara amica	*a dear friend*

In **uno zio** the indefinite article is before **z** so **uno** must be used, while in **un caro zio** it is before the **c** so **un** is used. It may help to remember that a similar pattern applies in English (albeit for different reasons).

a boy	but:	*an intelligent boy*
an apple	but:	*a good apple*

The indefinite article in Italian has basically the same uses as it does in English. However, there are a few differences. It is omitted in some Italian exclamations. For example:

Che ragazzo simpatico!	*What a nice boy!*
Che camicia bella!	*What a beautiful shirt!*

On the other hand, it must be repeated before every noun.

un ragazzo e una ragazza	*a boy and girl*
un amico e uno zio	*a friend and uncle*

Oral Practice

Practice saying the following sentences out loud.

Chi è?	*Who is he?*
È uno zio.	*He is an uncle.*
Chi è?	*Who is he?*
È uno studente.	*He is a student.*
Chi è?	
È un ragazzo.	*He is a boy.*
Chi è?	*Who is she?*
È una zia.	*She is an aunt.*
È una studentessa.	*She is a student.*
È una psicologa.	*She is a psychologist.*
Chi è?	*Who is she?*
È un'americana.	*She is an American.*
Chi è?	*Who is he?*

È un caro zio.	*He is a dear uncle.*
Chi è?	*Who is she?*
È una cara amica.	*She is a dear friend.*
Chi sono?	*Who are they?*
Sono uno zio e una zia.	*They are an uncle and aunt.*

Written Practice 1

Fill in the blanks with the appropriate form of the indefinite article.

1. Chi è? *Who is it?*

   È _____ psicologo. *It is a (male) psychologist.*

2. Chi è?

   È _____ amico. *It is a (male) friend.*

3. Chi è?

   È _____ ragazza. *It is a girl.*

4. Chi è?

   È _____ amica. *It is a (female) friend.*

5. Chi è? *Who is it?*

   È _____ caro studente. *It is a dear student.*

6. Chi sono? *Who are they?*

   Sono _____ studente e _____ donna. *They are a student and a woman.*

7. Che cos'è? *What is it?*

   È _____ gatto. *It is a cat.*

8. Che cos'è?

   È _____ isola. *It is an island.*

9. Che cos'è?

   È _____ bella isola. *It is a beautiful island.*

10. Che cosa sono? *What are they?*

    Sono _____ cane e _____ gatto. *They are a dog and cat.*

Forms of the Definite Article

Chi è? Che cos'è? *Who is it?* and *What is it?* If you answer these questions with the definite article *the*, then you mean to say that it is something specific, such as *the book* that belongs to Mary, rather than *any book*.

Like the indefinite article, the definite article varies according to the gender and initial sound of the noun it precedes. Unlike it, the definite article also varies according to the number, singular or plural, of the noun.

SINGULAR FORMS

Let's start with the singular forms of the definite article:

- The definite article **lo** is used before a masculine singular noun beginning with **z**, **s** + consonant, **gn**, or **ps**.

lo zio	*the uncle*	lo gnocco	*the dumpling*
lo studente	*the student*	lo psicologo	*the psychologist*

- **Il** is used before a masculine singular noun beginning with any other consonant.

il ragazzo	*the boy*
il cane	*the dog*
il gatto	*the cat*

- **La** is used before a feminine singular noun beginning with any consonant (including **z**, **s** + consonant, **gn**, or **ps**).

la zia	*the aunt*	la ragazza	*the girl*
la studentessa	*the student*	la psicologa	*the psychologist*

- And **l'** is used before a masculine or feminine singular noun beginning with any vowel.

  masculine

l'amico	*the (male) friend*	l'orologio	*the watch*

  feminine

l'amica	*the (female) friend*	l'ora	*the hour*

PLURAL FORMS

The corresponding plural forms of the definite article are as follows:

- The plural form **gli** is used before a masculine plural noun beginning with **z, s** + consonant, **gn, ps**, or any vowel; it is the plural of both **lo** and **l'**.

gli zii	*the uncles*	gli psicologi	*the psychologists*
gli studenti	*the students*	gli amici	*the friends*
gli gnocchi	*the dumplings*	gli orologi	*the watches*

- The plural form **i** is used before a masculine plural noun beginning with any other consonant (but not a vowel); it is the plural of **il**.

i ragazzi	*the boys*	i fratelli	*the brothers*
i cani	*the dogs*	i cugini	*the cousins*
i gatti	*the cats*		

- And **le** is used before a feminine plural noun beginning with any sound (consonant or vowel); it is the plural of both **la** and **l'**.

le zie	*the aunts*	le isole	*the islands*
le ragazze	*the girls*	le sorelle	*the sisters*
le ore	*the hours*	le cugine	*the (female) cousins*

Oral Practice

Practice saying the following sentences out loud.

Chi è?	*Who is he?*
È lo zio di Maria.	*He is Mary's uncle. (He is the uncle of Mary.)*
È lo studente americano.	*He is the American student.*
È il fratello di Pina.	*He is Pina's brother.*
È il cugino di Giovanni.	*He is John's cousin.*
Chi è?	*Who is she?*
È la zia di Marco.	*She is Mark's aunt.*
È la studentessa italiana.	*She is the Italian student.*
È la sorella di Giovanni.	*She is John's sister.*
È la psicologa francese.	*She is the French psychologist.*

Written Practice 2

Fill in the blanks with the appropriate forms of the definite article.

1. Chi è? *Who is he?*

   È _____ psicologo italiano. *He is the Italian psychologist.*

2. Chi è?

   È _____ fratello di Pasqualina. *He is Pasqualina's brother.*

3. Chi è?

   È _____ amico di Maria. *He is Mary's friend.*

4. Chi è? *Who is she?*

   È _____ amica di Marco. *She is Mark's friend.*

5. Chi è?

   È _____ sorella di Andrea. *She is Andrew's sister.*

6. Che cos'è? *What is it?*

   È _____ gatto di Paola. *It is Paula's cat.*

7. Che cos'è?

   È _____ orologio di Claudia. *It is Claudia's watch.*

Oral Practice

Practice saying the following sentences out loud.

Chi sono?	*Who are they?*
Sono gli zii di Carlo.	*They are Charles's uncles.*
Sono gli studenti americani.	*They are the American students.*
Sono gli amici di Maria.	*They are Mary's friends.*
Sono i cugini di Pina.	*They are Pina's cousins.*
Sono le studentesse americane.	*They are the American students.*
Sono le amiche di Carlo.	*They are Charles's friends.*

Written Practice 3

Fill in the blanks with the appropriate forms of the definite article.

1. Chi sono? *Who are they?*

   Sono _____ fratelli di Carlo. *They are Charles's brothers.*

2. Chi sono?

   Sono _____ zii di Maria. *They are Mary's uncles.*

3. Chi sono?

   Sono _____ amici di Giuseppe. *They are Joseph's friends.*

4. Chi sono?

   Sono _____ sorelle di Pina. *They are Pina's sisters.*

5. Chi sono?

   Sono _____ amiche di Gina. *They are Gina's friends.*

USING DEFINITE ARTICLES

Just as with the indefinite article, when an adjective precedes the noun remember to adjust the definite article according to the beginning sound of the adjective.

lo zio	*the uncle*	but:	il caro zio	*the dear uncle*
l'amica	*the friend*	but:	la cara amica	*the dear friend*

And the definite article, too, must be repeated before every noun.

il ragazzo e la ragazza	*the boy and girl*
l'amico e lo zio	*the friend and uncle*

Also, as you have seen, definite articles are used to indicate possession.

lo zio di Maria	*Mary's uncle = the uncle of Mary*
gli amici di Stefano	*Stephen's friends = the friends of Stephen*

Definite articles are also used with titles, unless the person is being directly spoken to.

Il dottor Rossi è italiano.	*Dr. Rossi is Italian.*
La professoressa Bianchi è italiana.	*Professor Bianchi is Italian.*

But:

Dottor Rossi, come va?	*Dr. Rossi, how is it going?*
Professoressa Bianchi, come sta?	*Professor Bianchi, how are you?*

Oral Practice

Practice saying the following sentences out loud.

Chi è?	*Who is it?*
È l'amico di Maria.	*He is Mary's friend.*
È il caro amico di Maria.	*He is Mary's dear friend.*
Chi sono?	*Who are they?*
Sono gli zii di Paolo.	*They are Paul's uncles.*
Chi è?	*Who is it?*
È il dottor Rossi.	*It is Dr. Rossi.*
Buongiorno, dottor Rossi.	*Good morning, Dr. Rossi.*
Come sta?	*How are you?*
Chi sono?	*Who are they?*
Sono il signor Martini e la dottoressa Marchi.	*They are Mr. Martini and Dr. Rossi.*
Buonasera, signor Martini e dottoressa Marchi.	*Good evening, Mr. Martini and Dr. Rossi.*

Written Practice 4

Fill in the blanks with the appropriate forms of the definite article, if required.

1. Chi è? *Who is it?*

   È _____ amica di Giovanni. *It is John's friend.*

2. Chi sono? *Who are they?*

   Sono _____ zie di Maria. *They are Mary's aunts.*

3. Chi è? *Who is it?*

   È _____ professoressa Binni. *It is Professor Binni.*

   Buongiorno, _____ professoressa. *Good morning, professor.*

Expressing Here and There with *Essere*

C'è Marco? *Is Marco here/there?* This question is formed with the verb **essere** (*to be*) + **ci** (*here* or *there*), which produces the expression **esserci** meaning *to be here/ there*. This verbal phrase is used to indicate or ask if people or things are here or there. Use the regular conjugation of **essere** (Chapter 4) with **ci** placed before the conjugated verb. Note, however, that it can only be used in the third person. Here are some example sentences:

C'è Marco?	*Is Marco here/there?*
Sì, c'è.	*Yes, he is here.*
Quanti studenti ci sono?	*How many students are there?*
Ci sono molti studenti.	*There are many students.*

To make the expression negative, just put **non** in front of it.

C'è il professor Giusti?	*Is Professor Giusti here?*
No, **non** c'è.	*No, he is not here.*
Ci sono molti studenti in classe?	*Are there many students in the class?*
Non, **non** ci sono molti studenti.	*No, there are not many students.*

The word **ecco** in Italian means *here is* or *there are*. It is used to indicate or point out something or someone directly.

Dov'è Maria?	*Where is Mary?*
Ecco Maria.	*Here is Mary.*
Dove sono gli studenti?	*Where are the students?*
Ecco gli studenti.	*There are the students.*

When to use **essere**, **esserci**, or **ecco** may seem confusing. Just keep in mind the differences between them, as the following table illustrates.

Singular   **Plural**

Essere (*to be*)

Che cosa è?	*What is it?*	Che cosa **sono**?	*What are they?*
È un libro.	It is *a book.*	**Sono** due libri.	They are *two books.*

Esserci (*to be here/there*)

C'è Marco?	Is *Marco* there?	**Ci sono** Marco e Maria?	Are *Marco and Maria* there?
Sì, c'è.	*Yes,* he is there/here.	Sì, **ci sono**.	*Yes,* they are there/here.

Ecco (pointing out: *here is/are*; *there is/are*)

Dov'è Marco?	*Where is Marco?*	Dove sono Marco e Maria?	*Where are Marco and Maria?*
Ecco Marco.	Here/There is *Marco.*	**Ecco** Marco e Maria.	Here/There *they* are.

Oral Practice

Practice saying the following sentences out loud. Note the new vocabulary words.

Che cos'è?	*What is it?*
È il libro d'italiano.	*It is the Italian book.*
Chi è?	*Who is it?*
È un amico.	*He is a friend.*
Che cosa sono?	*What are they?*

Sono una penna e una matita.	*They are a pen and pencil.*
È il computer di Marco?	*Is it Mark's computer?*
No, è il computer di Maria.	*No, it is Mary's computer.*
C'è una matita qui?	*Is there a pencil here?*
Sì, c'è.	*Yes, there is.*
Ci sono studenti là?	*Are there students there?*
Sì, ci sono molti studenti là.	*Yes, there are lots of students there.*
C'è un portatile qui?	*Is there a laptop here?*
No, non c'è.	*No, there is not.*
Dov'è Maria?	*Where is Mary?*
Ecco Maria.	*There is Mary.*
Dove sono i libri?	*Where are the books?*
Ecco i libri.	*Here are the books.*

Written Practice 5

Supply the appropriate forms of **essere**, **esserci**, or **ecco**.

1. Che cos'è? *What is it?*

   _____ il portatile di Maria. *It is Mary's laptop.*

2. Che cosa sono? *What are they?*

   _____ le penne di Marco. *They are Mark's pens.*

3. C'è Marco là? *Is Mark there?*

   No, Marco non _____. *No, Mark is not there.*

4. Ci sono molti studenti oggi in classe? *Are there many students in class?*

   Sì, _____ molti studenti oggi. *Yes, there are many students today.*

5. Dove sono le matite? *Where are the pencils?*

   _____ le matite. *Here are the pencils.*

Using the Verb *Avere*

Quanti anni hai? *How old are you?* (Or literally, *How many years do you have?*) To be able to use this expression, and many others like it, you will have to learn how to conjugate the verb **avere**, which means *to have*. In Chapter 4 you learned how to conjugate the verb **essere**. All verbs are conjugated according to the same pattern (first person singular, second person singular, and so on). Here are the forms of **avere** in the present indicative:

Singular		**Plural**	
(io) ho	*I have*	(noi) abbiamo	*we have*
(tu) hai	*you have* (familiar)	(voi) avete	*you have* (familiar)
(Lei) ha	*you have* (polite)	(Loro) hanno	*you have* (polite)
(lui/lei) ha	*he/she has*	(loro) hanno	*they have*

As you might recall, the **h** is not pronounced in Italian. It is silent. So the pronunciation of the verb conjugation **io ho** would look like this: (EE-oh oh) and **lui ha** would be: (LOO-ee ah), and so forth. Also, recall that you must distinguish between familiar and polite forms with verb conjugations.

Familiar Singular	**Familiar Plural**
Marco, quanti anni hai?	Ragazzi, quanti anni avete?
Marco, how old are you?	*Kids, how old are you?*

Polite Singular	**Polite Plural**
Signora Marchi, quanti anni ha?	Signori, quanti anni avete (*or* hanno)?
Mrs. Marchi, how old are you?	*Gentlemen, how old are you?*

As you know, to make any verb negative, simply put **non** before it in the sentence.

Non ho ventidue anni.	*I am not twenty-two years old.*
Non ho trent'anni ancora.	*I am not thirty years old yet.*

The verb **avere** is used in many common idiomatic expressions. This can be a bit tricky because these same expressions are translated with the verb *to be* (not *to have*) in English.

avere fame	*to be hungry* (literally: *to have hunger*)
avere sete	*to be thirsty* (literally: *to have thirst*)
avere sonno	*to be sleepy* (literally: *to have sleep*)
avere ragione	*to be right* (literally: *to have reason*)
avere torto	*to be wrong* (literally: *to have crookedness*)

Oral Practice

Practice saying the following sentences out loud.

Marco, hai fame?	*Mark, are you hungry?*
Sì, ho fame.	*Yes, I am hungry.*
Signora Marchi, ha sete?	*Mrs. Marchi, are you thirsty?*
No, non ho sete.	*No, I am not thirsty.*
Maria ha sonno?	*Is Mary sleepy?*
Sì, Maria ha sonno.	*Yes, Mary is sleepy.*
Giovanni ha sonno?	*Is John sleepy?*
Sì, anche Giovanni ha sonno.	*Yes, John is also sleepy.*
Marco e Maria, avete fame?	*Mark and Mary, are you hungry?*
No, non abbiamo fame.	*No, we are not hungry.*
Loro hanno ragione?	*Are they right?*
Sì, (loro) hanno ragione.	*Yes, they are right.*
(Io) ho ragione, vero?	*I am right, aren't I?*
Sì, (tu) hai ragione.	*Yes, you are right.*
(Noi) abbiamo torto?	*Are we wrong?*
Sì, (voi) avete torto.	*Yes, you are wrong.*
Quanti anni hai, Marco?	*Mark, how old are you?*
Ho venticinque anni.	*I am twenty-five years old.*
Quanti anni ha, signora Marchi?	*How old are you, Mrs. Marchi?*
Ho trenta anni.	*I am thirty years old.*

Written Practice 6

Fill in the blanks with the appropriate forms of **avere**.

1. (Tu) hai sete, vero? *You are thirsty, aren't you?*

   Sì, (io) _____ sete. *Yes, I am thirsty.*

2. Anch'io ho ragione, vero? *I, too, am right, aren't I?*

   Sì, anche tu _____ ragione. *Yes, you, too, are right.*

3. Pierina ha sonno, vero? *Pierina is sleepy, isn't she?*

   Sì, Pierina _____ sonno. *Yes, Pierina is sleepy.*

4. Voi avete ragione, vero? *You are right, aren't you?*

   Sì, (noi) _____ ragione. *Yes, we are right.*

5. Noi abbiamo torto, vero? *We are wrong, aren't we?*

   No, voi non _____ torto. *No, you are not wrong.*

6. Gli studenti hanno sonno, vero? *The students are sleepy, aren't they?*

   Sì, gli studenti _____ sonno. *Yes, the students are sleepy.*

Using the Verb *Stare*

The commonly used verb **stare** means *to stay*, but quite often it takes on the meaning of being. Here are its present indicative forms:

Singular		Plural	
(io) sto	*I stay (I am)*	(noi) stiamo	*we stay (we are)*
(tu) stai	*you stay (you are)* (familiar)	(voi) state	*you stay (you are)* (familiar)
(Lei) sta	*you stay (you are)* (polite)	(Loro) stanno	*you stay (you are)* (polite)
(lui/lei) sta	*he/she stays (he/she is)*	(loro) stanno	*they stay (they are)*

Stare (like **avere**) is used in many idiomatic expressions. Here are some of the commonly used expressions with **stare**.

stare bene	*to be (feel) well*
stare assai bene	*to be rather well*

stare molto bene	*to be very well*
stare male	*to be (feel) bad*
stare così, così	*to be so-so*

Oral Practice

Practice saying the following sentences out loud.

Come stai, Marco?	*How are you, Mark?*
Sto molto bene, grazie.	*I am very well, thank you.*
Come sta, professor Bruni?	*How are you, Professor Bruni?*
Non sto bene.	*I am not well.*
Come sta Maria?	*How is Mary?*
Maria sta assai male.	*Mary feels rather bad.*
Come state voi?	*How are you?*
Noi stiamo così, così.	*We are so-so.*
Loro come stanno?	*How are they?*
Loro stanno bene.	*They are well.*

Written Practice 7

Fill in the blanks with the appropriate forms of the verb **stare**.

1. Come sta, Dottoressa Dini? *How are you, Dr. Dini?*

   _____ assai bene, grazie. *I am quite well, thank you.*

2. Come _____, Giovanni? *How are you, John?*

   Sto così, così. *I am so-so.*

3. Come state, ragazzi? *How are you, boys?*

   _____ molto bene. *We are very well.*

4. Professore, come _____? *Professor, how are you?*

   Sto assai bene, grazie. *I am rather well, thank you.*

5. Come stanno Marco e Maria? *How are Mark and Mary?*

Loro _____ assai bene. *They are quite well.*

6. E voi come _____? *And how are you?*

Anche noi stiamo bene. *We, too, are well.*

More About Using the Verb *Piacere*

Ti Piace? *Do you like it?* You already know that **Mi piace** means *I like it.* The verb **piacere** (*to like, to be pleasing to*) can be very confusing for English speakers. The following points will help you make some sense of it.

Think of the pronouns **mi** and **ti** as subjects when used with this verb, even though this is not correct (it's just a rule of thumb). Then make the verb agree with the noun or noun phrase that follows it in normal speech. For example:

- If the noun is singular use **piace**: **mi piace** (*I like it*); **ti piace** (*you like it*).
- If the noun is plural, use **piacciono** (pyAh-choh-noh): **mi piacciono** (*I like them*); **ti piacciono** (*you like them*).

Singular	**Plural**
Mi piace la pizza.	Mi piacciono le pizze.
I like pizza. (= The pizza is pleasing to me.)	*I like the pizzas. (= The pizzas are pleasing to me.)*

Note that **ti** is the familiar form of the pronoun for *you*. If speaking formally or politely, you must use the pronoun **Le**.

(familiar *you* form)

Ti piace il gelato, Marco?	Ti piacciono gli spaghetti, Marco?
Do you like ice cream, Mark?	*Do you like spaghetti, Mark?*

(polite *you* form)

Le piace la minestra, signora Marchi?	Le piacciono i ravioli, signora Marchi?
Do you like the soup, Mrs. Marchi?	*Do you like the ravioli, Mrs. Marchi?*

To say that you do not like something, simply put **non** before the pronoun in the normal fashion: **Non mi piace la minestra.** (*I do not like soup.*)

Oral Practice

Practice saying the following sentences out loud.

Marco, ti piace la pizza?	*Mark, do you like the pizza?*
Sì, mi piace molto.	*Yes, I like it a lot.*
Dottor Marchi, Le piace la pizza?	*Dr. Marchi, do you like the pizza?*
No, non mi piace.	*No, I do not like it.*
Maria, ti piacciono gli spaghetti?	*Mary, do you like the spaghetti?*
Sì, mi piacciono assai.	*Yes, I like it quite a bit.*
Signora Dini, Le piacciono le lasagne?	*Mrs. Dini, do you like the lasagna?*
No, non mi piacciono affatto.	*No, I do not like it at all.*

Written Practice 8

Fill in the blanks with the correct form of **piacere**. Don't forget the pronoun!

1. Maria, _____ il gelato? *Mary, do you like the ice cream?*

    Sì, mi piace molto. *Yes, I like it a lot.*

2. Signora, _____ la minestra? *Madam, do you like the soup?*

    No, non mi piace affatto. *No, I do not like it at all.*

3. Marco, _____ i ravioli? *Mark, do you like the ravioli?*

    Sì, mi piacciono assai. *Yes, I like them a lot.*

4. Dottor Marchi, _____ gli gnocchi? *Dr. Marchi, do you like the gnocchi?*

    Sì, mi piacciono assai. *Yes, I like them, a lot.*

QUIZ

Change the indefinite article form to its corresponding definite article form. For example:

un giornale *il giornale* _____ *a newspaper/the newspaper*

1. un ragazzo _____

   una ragazza _____

   un americano _____

   un'italiana _____

   uno studente _____

   un'amico _____

Fill in each blank with the corresponding plural form of each noun phrase. For example:

la chiave *le chiavi* _____ *the key/the keys*

2. il ragazzo _____

   la madre _____

   l'americano _____

   la studentessa _____

   lo studente _____

   l'italiano _____

   il cane _____

   l'orologio _____

   lo gnocco _____

   l'ora _____

Match the questions in the left column with the answers in the right column.

3.

_____ a. Chi sono?

_____ b. Che cos'è?

_____ c. Dove sono i libri?

_____ d. Sono qui i libri?

_____ e. C'è Marco qui?

_____ f. Quante matite ci sono?

_____ g. Dov'è il computer?

h. È il portatile di Franco.

i. No, i libri sono là.

j. Sì, c'è.

k. Ci sono tante matite.

l. Ecco il computer.

m. Sono gli studenti d'italiano.

n. Ecco i libri.

Say that the person or persons in parentheses is/are also hungry, fine, and so on, as indicated. For example:

Marco ha fame. (noi)   *Marco is hungry. (we)*

Anche noi abbiamo fame. _____ *We, too, are hungry.*

4. Giovanni ha sete. (io)

_____.

Loro hanno sonno. (il fratello di Maria)

_____.

Pasquale ha ragione. (tu)

_____.

Marco sta bene. (io)

_____.

Loro stanno assai bene. (noi)

_____.

Choose the correct form of the verb **piacere**.

5. Marco, _____ gli spaghetti?

(a) ti piace

(b) ti piacciono

6. Signora Marchi, _____ la minestra?

    (a) Le piace

    (b) Le piacciono

Personal Matters! Answer each question appropriately.

7. Quanti anni hai?

    _____.

8. Come stai?

    _____.

9. Ti piace la lingua italiana?

    _____.

10. Ti piacciono gli spaghetti?

    _____.

Circle the letter of the word or phrase that best completes each sentence.

1. Come ti chiami?

   (a) Mi chiamo Maria.

   (b) Si chiama Maria.

2. Come si chiama?

   (a) Mi chiamo Maria.

   (b) Si chiama Maria.

3. Signora, come si chiama?

   (a) Mi chiamo Maria Signorelli.

   (b) Si chiama Maria Signorelli.

4. Il mio amico si chiama _____.

   (a) Marco

   (b) Maria

5. La mia amica si chiama _____.

   (a) Marco

   (b) Maria

6. Ti presento _____.

   (a) il professor Marco Tucci

   (b) Marco

7. Le presento _____.

   (a) il professor Marco Tucci

   (b) Marco

8. Ecco la _____ di Paolo.

   (a) madre

   (b) padre

9. Carla è la _____ di Giovanni.

   (a) sorella

   (b) fratello

10. Abbiamo una _____ in casa.

   (a) sedie

   (b) sedia

11. Ci sono due _____ nella casa.

   (a) pareti

   (b) parete

12. Chi è?

   (a) È l'orologio di Carlo.

   (b) È lo zio di Carlo.

13. Chi sono?

   (a) Sono le camicie di Marco.

   (b) Sono gli amici di Maria.

14. Che cos'è?

   (a) È la cugina di Bruno.

   (b) È la giacca di Bruno.

15. Buongiorno, _____.

   (a) signor Torelli

   (b) il signor Torelli

16. Buonasera, dottoressa _____.

   (a) Come sta?

   (b) Come stai?

17. Ciao, Pasquale _____.

   (a) Come sta?

   (b) Come stai?

18. Grazie.

   (a) Prego.

   (b) Per favore.

19. Ciao.

   (a) Arrivederci.

   (b) ArrivederLa.

20. Ci vediamo!

   (a) A presto!

   (b) Buon pomeriggio!

21. Quali lingue parli?

   (a) Parlo italiano e inglese.

   (b) Sono italiano.

22. I due ragazzi sono _____ .

   (a) greci

   (b) greche

23. Le mie amiche sono _____ .

   (a) tedeschi

   (b) tedesche

24. Che giorno è?

   (a) È mercoledì.

   (b) È gennaio.

25. Che mese è?

   (a) È sabato.

   (b) È settembre.

26. Di quale nazionalità sei?

   (a) Sono studente.

   (b) Sono americano.

27. Di dove sei?

   (a) Sono di Roma.

   (b) Sono italiano.

28. Il mio amico è _____ .

   (a) italiano

   (b) italiana

29. Le amiche di Paolo sono _____ .

   (a) russi

   (b) russe

30. Tu _____ inglese, vero?

    (a) sei

    (b) è

31. Di che nazionalità è Lei, signora Vecchiarelli?

    (a) Sono italiana.

    (b) È italiana.

32. Com'è la donna?

    (a) È simpatico.

    (b) È simpatica.

33. Come sono le donne?

    (a) Sono simpatici.

    (b) Sono simpatiche.

34. Lui è un uomo _____.

    (a) alto

    (b) simpatici

35. Quanto costa?

    (a) Novanta euro.

    (b) Non è vero?

36. Sono _____ amici di Paolo.

    (a) gli

    (b) i

37. È _____ zaino.

    (a) uno

    (b) un

38. È _____ orologio di Marco.

    (a) l'

    (b) il

39. Sono _____ amiche di Pasqualina.

    (a) gli

    (b) le

40. Ecco _____ ragazzi italiani.

   (a) i

   (b) gli

41. Dove sono i libri?

   (a) Ecco i libri.

   (b) Ci sono i libri.

42. Ci sono studenti in classe oggi?

   (a) Sì, ecco.

   (b) Sì, ci sono.

43. Avete fame?

   (a) No, non abbiamo fame.

   (b) No, non hanno fame.

44. Quanti anni _____, Maria?

   (a) hai

   (b) ha

45. Quanti anni _____, signora Marchi?

   (a) hai

   (b) ha

46. Come _____, Giovanni?

   (a) stai

   (b) sta

47. Come _____, signor Vecchiarelli?

   (a) stai

   (b) sta

48. Rosa, _____ il gelato?

   (a) ti piace

   (b) ti piacciono

49. Signora Marchi, _____ i ravioli?

   (a) Le piace

   (b) Le piacciono

50. Non _____ la pizza.

    (a) mi piace

    (b) mi piacciono

PART TWO

EXPANDING ON THE BASICS

CHAPTER 6

Learning the Present Indicative with *-are* Verbs

Here's what you will learn in this chapter:

Present Indicative of -*are* Verbs

Parli italiano? *Do you speak Italian?* The verb used in this question is **parlare**, which means *to speak*. **Parlare** is the infinitive form of the verb. **Parli** is its second-person singular (*you*) form.

Infinitives ending in **-are**, such as **parlare**, are called first-conjugation verbs. Such verbs, when classified as *regular*, are conjugated by adding the endings **-o**, **-i**, **-a**, **-iamo**, **-ate**, **-ano** to the stem of the verb (in this case, it would be **parl-**). Any **-are** verb that is not conjugated like this is called, logically enough, *irregular*, which means it does not follow the normal rules of conjugation.

The indicative is used in all languages to express or indicate facts. It is the most commonly used mood in everyday conversation. The present, as its name implies, is the particular tense that allows us to express facts in the present time or related to it in some way.

As mentioned, to conjugate regular first-conjugation verbs in the present indicative, drop the infinitive ending **-are** (**parl-**), and add on the endings according to the person (first, second, third) and number (singular and plural).

Singular

(io) parlo	*I speak, am speaking, do speak*
(tu) parli	*you* (familiar) *speak, are speaking, do speak*
(Lei) parla	*you* (polite) *speak, are speaking, do speak*
(lui/lei) parla	*he/she speaks, is speaking, does speak*

Plural

(noi) parliamo	*we speak, are speaking, do speak*
(voi) parlate	*you* (familiar plural) *speak, are speaking, do speak*
(Loro) parlano	*you* (polite plural) *speak, are speaking, do speak*
(loro) parlano (pAhr-lah-noh)	*they speak, are speaking, do speak*

NOTE: *The Italian present indicative is a versatile tense that translates three different ways in English (I speak, I am speaking, I do speak).*

Let's quickly review some of what you have previously learned in Part I of this book. It's important to understand this now before moving on to subsequent chapters.

1. To make a verb negative, simply add **non** before it.

Affirmative	**Negative**
Giovanni parla francese.	Giovanni non parla francese.
John speaks French.	*John does not speak French.*

2. The subject pronouns are optional in simple sentences. The reason for this is that the verb endings make it clear which person is being referred to.

Io parlo italiano.	= Parlo italiano.	*I speak Italian.*
Tu parli inglese.	= Parli inglese.	*You speak English.*

3. However, the pronouns must be used after words such as **anche**.

Anche noi parliamo italiano.   *We also speak Italian.*

4. Pronouns must also be used when more than one person is indicated.

Lui parla italiano e lei parla inglese.   *He speaks Italian and she speaks English.*

5. Second person (**tu**) forms are used for familiar (informal) singular address; third person (**Lei**) forms are used for polite (formal) singular address. Recall that **voi** forms are used in colloquial Italian as the plural of both **tu** (familiar) and **Lei** (polite) forms. **Loro** forms are used in plural formal polite speech.

Familiar

Maria, parli francese?	*Mary, do you speak French?*
Marco e Maria, parlate inglese?	*Mark and Mary, do you speak English?*

Polite

Professore, parla francese?	*Professor, do you speak French?*
Professori, parlate russo?	*Professors, do you speak Russian?*

Or:

Professori, parlano russo?	*Professors, do you speak Russian?*

6. The English subject pronoun *it* (plural *they*) is not normally expressed in Italian.

È vero.	*It is true.*
Non è vero.	*It is not true.*

7. Some common *-are* verbs in Italian are:

arrivare	*to arrive*	guardare	*to watch, look at*
chiamare	*to call*	imparare	*to learn*
entrare	*to enter*	tornare	*to return, come back*

Expressions of Time

Here are some adverbs of time commonly used in present indicative sentences.

spesso	*often*	mai	*ever*
adesso	*now*	non... mai	*never*
domani	*tomorrow*	ogni	*every, each*
sempre	*always*		

Oral Practice

Practice saying the following sentences out loud.

(Tu) parli italiano?	*Do you speak Italian?*
Sì, (io) parlo italiano molto bene.	*Yes, I speak Italian very well.*
(Voi) chiamate spesso, vero?	*You call often, don't you?*
No, noi non chiamiamo mai.	*No, we never call.*
Quando entrano in classe gli studenti?	*When do students enter the class?*
Entrano in classe adesso.	*They are entering the class now.*
Chi guarda la televisione ogni sera?	*Who watches television every night?*
Noi guardiamo la televisione spesso.	*We watch television often.*
Giovanni, che cosa impari?	*John, what are you learning?*

Imparo la lingua russa.	*I am learning the Russian language.*
Dottoressa, quando torna in Italia?	*Doctor, when are you going back to Italy?*
Non torno in Italia.	*I am not going back to Italy.*
Anche loro parlano sempre francese, vero?	*They also always speak French, don't they?*
No, loro non parlano mai francese.	*No, they never speak French.*

Written Practice 1

Fill in the blanks with the appropriate present indicative forms of the given verbs.

1. Signorina, Lei _____ italiano, vero? *Miss, you speak Italian, don't you?*

   Sì, io _____ italiano molto bene. *Yes, I speak Italian very well.*

2. Quando _____ gli amici di Carla? *When are Carla's friends arriving?*

   Loro _____ domani. *They are arriving tomorrow.*

3. Chi _____ in classe? *Who is entering the class?*

   Il professore _____ in classe. *The professor is entering the class.*

4. Anche voi _____ spesso la televisione? *Do you also watch television often?*

   Sì, noi _____ la televisione ogni sera. *Yes, we watch television every night.*

5. Marco, anche tu _____ l'italiano, vero? *Mark, you are learning Italian, too, right?*

   Sì, anch'io _____ l'italiano. *Yes, I am learning Italian, too.*

6. Signori, _____ spesso in Italia, Loro? *Gentlemen, do you go back to Italy often?*

   Sì, noi _____ ogni anno in Italia. *Yes, we go back to Italy every year.*

Verbs Ending in *-care*, *-gare*, *-ciare*, and *-giare*

Che cosa cerchi, Maria? *What are you looking for, Mary?* The verb used in this question is **cercare** (*to look for, to search*). Notice the unusual spelling of the **tu** verb form (**cerchi**). Certain verbs will have spelling variations in order to keep the hard or soft sound of the consonant.

- If the verb ends in **-care** or **-gare**, the hard sound of the **c** and the **g** is preserved by inserting an **h** before the **tu** and **noi** endings **-i** and **-iamo**.

cercare	*to look for, search for*
(io) cerco	*I search, am searching, do search*
(tu) cerchi	*you (familiar) search, are searching, do search*
(Lei) cerca	*you (polite) search, are searching, do search*
(lui/lei) cerca	*he/she searches, is searching, does search*
(noi) cerchiamo	*we search, are searching, do search*
(voi) cercate	*you (familiar plural) search, are searching, do search*
(Loro) cercano	*you (polite plural) search, are searching, do search*
(loro) cercano	*they search, are searching, do search*

pagare	*to pay*
(io) pago	*I pay, am paying, do pay*
(tu) paghi	*you (familiar) pay, are paying, do pay*
(Lei) paga	*you (polite) pay, are paying, do pay*
(lui/lei) paga	*he/she pays, is paying, does pay*
(noi) paghiamo	*we pay, are paying, do pay*
(voi) pagate	*you (familiar plural) pay, are paying, do pay*
(Loro) pagano	*you (polite plural) pay, are paying, do pay*
(loro) pagano	*they pay, are paying, do pay*

- If the verb ends in **-ciare** or **-giare**, the **-i-** is dropped before adding the **-i** and **-iamo** endings. As you may recall, the **-i-** in such cases simply tells us that the soft sound of **c** and **g** is to be preserved.

cominciare	*to start, begin*
(io) comincio	*I start, am starting, do start*
(tu) cominci	*you (familiar) start, are starting, do start*
(Lei) comincia	*you (polite) start, are starting, do start*
(lui/lei) comincia	*he/she starts, is starting, does start*
(noi) cominciamo	*we start, are starting, do start*
(voi) cominciate	*you (familiar plural) start, are starting, do start*
(Loro) cominciano	*you (polite plural) start, are starting, do start*
(loro) cominciano	*they start, are starting, do start*

mangiare	*to eat*
(io) mangio	*I eat, am eating, do eat*
(tu) mangi	*you* (familiar) *eat, are eating, do eat*
(Lei) mangia	*you* (polite) *eat, are eating, do eat*
(noi) mangiamo	*we eat, are eating, do eat*
(voi) mangiate	*you* (familiar plural) *eat, are eating, do eat*
(Loro) mangiano	*you* (polite plural) *eat, are eating, do eat*
(loro) mangiano	*they eat, are eating, do eat*

Italian Food and Drink

Before a meal, Italians say **Buon appetito!** which means *Have a good appetite!* This is an important expression, culturally. Also, before taking your first sip, it is polite to say: **Salute!** *To your health!*

Here are some food and drink vocabulary words to memorize. Some of these you may have encountered already.

la carne	*meat*	la colazione	*breakfast*
la pasta	*pasta*	il pranzo	*lunch*
la patata	*potato*	la cena	*dinner*
il pomodoro	*tomato*	l'antipasto	*starter, hors d'oeuvres*
la frutta	*fruit*	il primo piatto	*first dish, serving, course*
il conto	*the bill, check*	il secondo piatto	*second dish, serving,*
il caffè	*coffee*		*course*
l'espresso	*espresso*	il dolce	*dessert, sweet*
il cappuccino	*cappuccino*	il formaggio	*cheese*
il tè	*tea*	il panino	*sandwich, bun*
la bibita	*soft drink*	il bar	*coffee bar*
la bevanda	*drink, beverage* (in general)	il ristorante	*(formal) restaurant*
il succo	*juice*	la trattoria	*(family) restaurant*
il vino	*wine*		

Oral Practice

Practice saying the following sentences out loud.

Con che cosa cominci, Marco?	*With what are you starting, Mark?*
(Io) comincio con gli spaghetti.	*I am starting with the spaghetti.*

Chi paga il conto?	*Who is paying the bill?*
(Io) pago il conto.	*I will pay the bill.*
Che cosa mangi, Maria?	*What are you eating, Mary?*
(Io) mangio solo la carne.	*I am eating only the meat.*
Che cosa cerca, signorina Marchi?	*What are you looking for, Ms. Marchi?*
(Io) cerco il gelato italiano.	*I am looking for Italian ice cream.*
Anche tu mangi la frutta, vero?	*You are also eating fruit, aren't you?*
Sì, anch'io mangio la frutta.	*Yes, I am also eating fruit.*
Anche loro cominciano con le patate?	*Are they also starting with the potatoes?*
No, loro cominciano con la pasta.	*No, they are starting with pasta.*
Voi pagate sempre il conto, vero?	*You always pay the bill, don't you?*
Sì, noi paghiamo sempre il conto.	*Yes, we always pay the bill.*

Written Practice 2

Fill in the blanks with the appropriate forms of the verbs provided.

1. (Io) _____ con i ravioli. *I am starting with the ravioli.*

2. Tu invece _____ con la carne e le patate. *You instead are starting with meat and potatoes.*

3. Maria invece _____ con gli gnocchi e la carne. *Maria instead is starting with gnocchi and meat.*

4. Noi _____ con la frutta. *We are starting with the fruit.*

5. Noi _____ il gelato italiano. *We are looking for Italian ice cream.*

6. Loro invece _____ il gelato americano. *They instead are looking for American ice cream.*

7. Anche voi _____ il gelato, no? *You, too, are looking for ice cream, right?*

8. Marco, che cosa _____? *Mark, what are you looking for?*

9. Maria, _____ tu il conto? *Mary, are you paying the bill?*

10. Sì, io _____ sempre il conto. *Yes, I always pay the bill.*

11. Voi non _____ mai! *You never pay!*

12. No, noi _____ sempre! *No, we always pay!*

13. Che cosa _____ Giovanni? *What are you eating John?*

14. (Io) _____ i ravioli. *I am eating the ravioli.*

15. Signora Marchi, cosa _____? *Mrs. Marchi, what are you eating?*

16. Loro non _____ mai la carne. *They never eat meat.*

Using the Verbs *Bere* and *Dare*

Che cosa bevi? A chi dai la pasta? *What are you drinking?* and *To whom are you giving the pasta?* These questions are constructed with the verbs **bere** (*to drink*) and **dare** (*to give*). Like **essere**, **avere**, and **stare** of previous chapters, **bere** and **dare** are irregular verbs and do not use the regular verb endings. This means that you must memorize their forms. Here are their conjugations in the present indicative:

bere	*to drink*
(io) bevo	*I drink, am drinking, do drink*
(tu) bevi	*you drink* (familiar), *are drinking, do drink*
(Lei) beve	*you drink* (polite), *are drinking, do drink*
(lui/lei) beve	*he/she drinks, is drinking, does drink*
(noi) beviamo	*we drink, are drinking, do drink*
(voi) bevete	*you drink* (familiar plural), *are drinking, do drink*
(Loro) bevono	*you drink* (polite plural), *are drinking, do drink*
(loro) bevono	*they drink, are drinking, do drink*

dare	*to give*
(io) do	*I give, am giving, do give*
(tu) dai	*you give* (familiar), *are giving, do give*
(Lei) dà	*you give* (polite), *are giving, do give*
(lui/lei) dà	*he/she gives, is giving, does give*
(noi) diamo	*we give, are giving, do give*
(voi) date	*you give* (familiar plural), *are giving, do give*

(Loro) danno	*you give* (polite plural), *are giving, do give*
(loro) danno	*they give, are giving, do give*

NOTE: *Notice the accent on the form* **dà**—*easy to miss!*

Oral Practice

Practice saying the following sentences out loud. Notice the new vocabulary words.

A chi dai la bevanda?	*To whom are you giving the drink?*
Do la bevanda a Carlo.	*I am giving the drink to Charles.*
A chi dà il caffè, signora?	*To whom are you giving the coffee, madam?*
Do il caffè a mio marito.	*I am giving the coffee to my husband.*
A chi dà il succo, il signore?	*To whom is the man giving the juice?*
Lui dà il succo al bambino.	*He is giving the juice to the child.*
A chi date il vino?	*To whom are you giving the wine?*
Noi diamo il vino a loro.	*We are giving the wine to them.*
A chi danno le bibite?	*To whom are they giving the soft drinks?*
Loro danno le bibite ai bambini.	*They are giving the soft drinks to the children.*
Che cosa bevi, Maria?	*What are you drinking, Mary?*
Bevo il cappuccino.	*I am drinking cappuccino.*
Che cosa beve, signora?	*What are you drinking, madam?*
Bevo l'espresso.	*I am drinking espresso.*
Che cosa beve il tuo amico?	*What is your friend drinking?*
Il mio amico beve solo il caffè.	*My friend only drinks coffee.*
Che cosa bevete voi?	*What are you drinking?*
Noi beviamo solo il caffè.	*We drink only coffee.*
Che cosa bevono i bambini?	*What are the children drinking?*
I bambini bevono le bibite.	*The children are drinking the soft drinks.*

Written Practice 3

Fill in the blanks with the appropriate forms of the present indicative for either **dare** or **bere**.

1. Carla, a chi _____ la bevanda? *Carla, to whom are you giving the drink?*

2. (Io) _____ la bevanda a Gina. *I am giving the drink to Gina.*

3. Che cosa _____, Franca? *What are you drinking, Franca?*

4. (Io) _____ il tè. *I am drinking tea.*

5. A chi _____ il caffè, signor Dini? *To whom are you giving the coffee, Mr. Dini?*

6. (Io) _____ il caffè a mia moglie. *I am giving the coffee to my wife.*

7. Che cosa _____, signorina? *What are you drinking, miss?*

8. (Io) _____ una bibita. *I am drinking a soft drink.*

9. A chi _____ il succo, l'uomo? *To whom is the man giving the juice?*

10. Lui _____ il succo al bambino. *He is giving it to the child.*

11. Che cosa _____ la tua amica? *What is your friend drinking?*

12. La mia amica _____ l'espresso. *My friend is drinking espresso.*

13. A chi _____ il vino, voi? *To whom are you giving the wine?*

14. Noi _____ il vino a loro. *We are giving them the wine.*

15. Che cosa _____ voi? *What are you drinking?*

16. Noi _____ solo il tè. *We are drinking only the tea.*

17. A chi _____ le bibite, i genitori? *To whom are the parents giving the soft drinks?*

18. Loro _____ le bibite ai bambini. *They are giving the soft drinks to the children.*

19. Che cosa _____ i bambini? *What are the children drinking?*

20. I bambini _____ le bibite. *They are drinking the soft drinks.*

Oral Practice

Practice saying the following sentences out loud.

Che cosa bevi a colazione?	*What do you drink for breakfast?*
Di solito bevo il caffè.	*Usually I drink coffee.*
Che cosa mangi a pranzo?	*What do you eat for lunch?*
Di solito mangio un panino.	*Usually I eat a sandwich.*
Che cosa mangiate a cena.	*What do you eat for dinner?*
Di solito mangiamo la pasta.	*Usually we eat pasta.*
Ti piace l'antipasto?	*Do you like the appetizer?*
Sì, mi piace.	*Yes, I like it.*
Che cosa mangiano per il primo piatto?	*What are they eating for the first course?*
Loro mangiano gli spaghetti.	*They are eating spaghetti.*
Che cosa mangia lui per il secondo piatto?	*What is he eating for the second course?*
Lui mangia la carne.	*He is eating meat.*
Buon appetito!	*Eat up! / Enjoy your meal!*

Written Practice 4

Fill in the blanks with the appropriate verb forms.

1. Che cosa _____ tu, dopo il secondo piatto? *What are you eating after the second course?*

2. _____ solo il dolce. *I am eating only dessert.*

3. E voi, che cosa _____? *And you, what do you eat?*

4. Noi di solito _____ il formaggio. *We usually eat cheese.*

5. Dove _____ il caffè, di solito, Marco? *Where do you drink coffee, usually, Mark?*

6. Di solito _____ il caffè a un bar qui vicino. *Usually I drink coffee at a coffee bar nearby.*

7. Che cosa _____ voi per cena al ristorante? *What do you eat for dinner at a restaurant?*

8. _____ solo alla trattoria per pranzo. *We eat only at a family restaurant for lunch.*

More About Nouns and Gender

In Chapters 2 and 3 you learned about Italian nouns. It might be good to review them now if you need to. Recall that a noun ending in **-o** referring to a male being usually has a corresponding noun ending in **-a**, which refers to a female being.

Masculine		Feminine	
il ragazzo	*the boy*	la ragazza	*the girl*
l'amico	*the friend*	l'amica	*the friend*

Here are a few more noun patterns:

- Sometimes, a masculine noun ending in **-e** corresponds to a feminine noun ending in **-a**.

Masculine		Feminine	
l'infermiere	*the male nurse*	l'infermiera	*the female nurse*
il cameriere	*the waiter*	la cameriera	*the waitress*

- A few nouns ending in **-a** refer to both males and females.

la spia	*spy* (male or female)
la persona	*person* (male or female)

- Nouns ending in **-ista** refer to both male and female persons. Many of these nouns indicate a person's occupation. Notice in the following table that it is the definite article that shows whether one is referring to a male or a female.

Masculine		Feminine	
il dentista	*the (male) dentist*	la dentista	*the (female) dentist*
il pianista	*the (male) pianist*	la pianista	*the (female) pianist*
il farmacista	*the (male) pharmacist*	la farmacista	*the (female) pharmacist*
lo specialista	*the (male) specialist*	la specialista	*the (female) specialist*

To make these plural, change the masculine nouns to **-isti** and the feminine to **-iste**.

Masculine		**Feminine**	
i dentisti	*the (male) dentists*	le dentiste	*the (female) dentists*
i pianisti	*the (male) pianists*	le pianiste	*the (female) pianists*
i farmacisti	*the (male) pharmacists*	le farmaciste	*the (female) pharmacists*
gli specialisti	*the (male) specialists*	le specialiste	*the (female) specialists*

Oral Practice

Practice saying the following sentences out loud.

Chi è?	*Who is it?*
È un infermiere.	*He is a nurse.*
Chi è?	*Who is it?*
È un'infermiera.	*She is a nurse.*
Chi è?	*Who is it?*
È una spia.	*He/She is a spy.*
Chi sono?	*Who are they?*
Sono due persone simpatiche.	*They are two nice people.*
Chi è?	*Who is it?*
È il mio dentista.	*He is my dentist.*
Chi sono?	*Who are they?*
Sono due pianisti.	*They are two pianists.*
Chi è?	*Who is it?*
È la mia farmacista.	*She is my pharmacist.*
Chi sono?	*Who are they?*
Sono due specialiste.	*They are two (female) specialists.*

Written Practice 5

Fill in the blanks with the required forms of the nouns in the singular or plural, as necessary.

1. Chi è? *Who is it?*

   È un _____. *He is a nurse.*

2. Chi sono? *Who are they?*

   Sono due _____. *They are two (female) nurses.*

3. Chi sono?

   Sono due _____. *They are two spies.*

4. Chi è?

   È una _____ simpatica. *He is a nice person.*

5. Chi sono?

   Sono due _____. *They are two (male) dentists.*

6. Chi sono?

   Sono due _____. *They are two (female) pianists.*

7. Chi è?

   È il mio _____. *He is my pharmacist.*

8. Chi è?

   È una _____. *She is a specialist.*

Numbers from 101 to 1000

Remember learning the numbers from 0 (**zero**) to 100 (**cento**) in Chapter 4? If not, review them now. This chapter will discuss the numbers from 101 to 1000. Learning these numbers is easy. Simply add on each consecutive number to the word for one hundred, two hundred, and so on—up to one thousand.

101	centuno
102	centodue
103	centotré
104	centoquattro
199	centonovantanove (*or* cento novantanove)

To form the numbers 200, 300, and so on, simply add the word **cento**, as shown here:

200	duecento
300	trecento
400	quattrocento
500	cinquecento
600	seicento
700	settecento
800	ottocento
900	novecento

To continue counting, make number words as before. Simply add on each consecutive number to the word for one hundred, two hundred, and so on—up to one thousand.

201	duecentuno (*or* duecento uno)
302	trecentodue (*or* trecento due)
403	quattrocentotré (*or* quattrocento tre)
504	cinquecentoquattro (*or* cinquecento quattro)
1000	mille

Here are a few words used in mathematical phrases:

più	*plus*
meno	*minus*
per	*times, multiplied by*
diviso per	*divided by*
fa	*equals, is, makes*

Oral Practice

Practice saying the following sentences out loud.

Quanto fa cento più cento?	*How much is 100 plus 100?*
Duecento.	*Two hundred.*
Quanto fa quattrocento meno cento?	*How much is 400 minus 100?*
Trecento.	*Three hundred.*

Quanto fa due per trecento quattro?	*How much is 2 times 304?*
Seicentotto.	*Six hundred eight.*
Quanto fa mille diviso per due?	*How much is 1000 divided by 2?*
Cinquecento.	*Five hundred.*
Quanto fa seicento novanta più due?	*How much is 690 plus 2?*
Seicento novantadue.	*Six hundred ninety-two.*
Quanto fa novecento trenta meno tre?	*How much is 930 minus 3?*
Novecento ventisette.	*Nine hundred twenty-seven.*
Quanto fa due per duecento dieci?	*How much is 2 times 210?*
Quattrocento venti.	*Four hundred twenty.*
Quanto fa settecento due diviso per due?	*How much is 702 divided by 2?*
Trecento cinquantuno.	*Three hundred fifty-one.*

Written Practice 6

On each blank write out the answer to the mathematical question.

1. Quanto fa centonovanta due più trecento quattro? *How much is 192 plus 304?*

   _____.

2. Quanto fa mille meno cento? *How much is 1000 minus 100?*

   _____.

3. Quanto fa tre per trecento cinque? *How much is 3 times 305?*

   _____.

4. Quanto fa ottocento quattro diviso per due? *How much is 804 divided by 2?*

   _____.

5. Quanto fa settecento più centotré? *How much is 700 plus 103?*

   _____.

6. Quanto fa quattrocento meno trentanove? *How much is 400 minus 39?*

   _____.

7. Quanto fa tre per duecento dieci? *How much is 3 times 210?*

   _____ .

8. Quanto fa quattrocento quattro diviso per due? *How much is 404 divided by 2?*

   _____ .

QUIZ

Fill in the blanks with the appropriate ending for each verb.

1. Quando arriv_____ i genitori di Maria?

   Quando guard_____ la televisione di solito, Alessandro?

   Che cosa impar_____ la tua amica a scuola?

   Quando chiam_____ voi di solito la sera?

   Noi torn_____ in Italia spesso.

   Quali lingue parl_____ gli amici di Carlo?

   Chi chiam_____ Lei di solito, signora Marchi?

Circle the letter of the word or phrase that best completes each sentence.

2. Marco, chi _____ adesso?

   (a) cerchi

   (b) cerca

3. Professore, perché _____ sempre Lei?

   (a) paghi

   (b) paga

4. Noi _____ a mangiare.

   (a) cominciamo

   (b) cominciate

5. E voi, che cosa _____?

    (a) mangiano

    (b) mangiate

Write the feminine forms corresponding to each of the masculine forms provided. Be sure to pay attention to whether the nouns are in the singular form or the plural.

Masculine	Feminine
6. l'infermiere	_____
i camerieri	_____
il dentista	_____
i pianisti	_____
il farmacista	_____
gli specialisti	_____

Circle the letter of the word or phrase that best answers the question.

    7. Quanto fa trecento più cento meno cinquanta per due?

        (a) Settecento.

        (b) Seicento cinquanta.

    8. Quanto fa ottocento più duecento meno cento diviso per due?

        (a) Quattrocento.

        (b) Quattrocento cinquanta.

Personal Matters! Answer each question appropriately.

    9. Che cosa mangi e bevi di solito per colazione?

    _____.

    10. Che cosa mangi e bevi di solito per pranzo?

    _____.

CHAPTER 7

Prepositions and the Present Indicative of *-ere* Verbs

Here's what you will learn in this chapter:

Present Indicative of -ere *Verbs*
Using the Verbs Fare *and* Dire
Prepositional Contractions
Numbers Over 1000
Telling Time

Present Indicative of -*ere* Verbs

Che cosa scrivi? *What are you writing?* The verb used in this question is **scrivere** (skrEEh-veh-reh), which means *to write*. Notice that it ends in **-ere** (instead of **-are**). It is called a second-conjugation verb.

To conjugate regular second-conjugation verbs in the present indicative, drop the infinitive ending **-ere** from the verb root (in this case, **scriv-**), and add on the endings **-o, -i, -e, -iamo, -ete, -ono**, according to the person (first, second, third) and number (singular and plural).

(io) scrivo	*I write, am writing, do write*
(tu) scrivi	*you* (familiar) *write, are writing, do write*
(Lei) scrive	*you* (polite) *write, are writing, do write*
(lui/lei) scrive	*he/she writes, is writing, does write*
(noi) scriviamo	*we write, are writing, do write*
(voi) scrivete	*you* (familiar plural) *write, are writing, do write*
(Loro) scrivono	*you* (polite plural) *write, are writing, do write*
(loro) scrivono	*they write, are writing, do write*

Here are some common **-ere** verbs:

vedere (veh-dEh-reh)	*to see*
vivere (vEEh-veh-reh)	*to live*
ripetere (reeh-pEh-teh-reh)	*to repeat*
vendere (vEhn-deh-reh)	*to sell*
leggere (lEh-jjeh-reh)	*to read*
prendere (prEhn-deh-reh)	*to take, have* (something to eat/drink)
mettere (mEh-tteh-reh)	*to put*

Oral Practice

Practice saying the following sentences out loud. As you practice, you will come across a few new useful words.

(Tu) scrivi in italiano?	*Do you write in Italian?*
Sì, (io) scrivo in italiano molto bene.	*Yes, I write in Italian very well.*
(Voi) ripetete spesso in classe, vero?	*You often repeat in class, don't you?*
No, noi non ripetiamo mai.	*No, we never repeat.*
Quando vendono l'automobile?	*When are they selling the car?*

Vendono l'automobile domani.	*They are selling it tomorrow.*
Chi legge il giornale ogni giorno?	*Who reads the newspaper every day?*
Noi leggiamo il giornale ogni giorno.	*We read the newspaper every day.*
Giovanni, che cosa prendi?	*John, what are you having?*
Prendo un succo di frutta.	*I am having a fruit juice.*
Dottoressa, dove mette la borsa, di solito?	*Doctor, where do you put your purse, usually?*
Metto la borsa di solito sul tavolo.	*Usually I put my purse on the table.*
Marco, chi vedi?	*Mark, who do you see?*
Vedo Maria.	*I see Mary.*
Giovanni, dove vivono i tuoi genitori?	*John, where do your parents live?*
Loro vivono in Italia.	*They live in Italy.*

Written Practice 1

Fill in the blanks with the appropriate present indicative forms of the verbs provided.

1. Signorina, chi _____, Lei? *Miss, who do you see?*

   _____ la mia amica. *I see my friend.*

2. Quando _____ i tuoi amici in classe? *When do your friends repeat in class?*

   Loro _____ sempre. *They always repeat.*

3. Chi _____ l'automobile? *Who is selling the car?*

   Il professore _____ l'automobile. *The professor is selling the car.*

4. Anche voi _____ il giornale? *You, too, are reading the newspaper?*

   Sì, noi _____ il giornale ogni giorno. *Yes, we read the newspaper every day.*

5. Marco, anche tu _____ il caffè? *Mark, are you also having coffee?*

   Sì, anch'io _____ il caffè. *Yes, I am also having coffee.*

6. Signori, dove _____ l'automobile, Loro? *Gentlemen, where do you put the car?*

Noi _____ l'automobile nel garage *We put the car in the garage.*

7. Maria, dove _____? *Mary, where do you live?*

_____ in America. *I live in America.*

Using the Verbs *Fare* and *Dire*

Che cosa fai? Che cosa dici? *What are you doing?* and *What are you saying?* These questions are constructed with the verbs **fare** (*to do, make*) and **dire** (*to say, tell*). Like **essere**, **avere**, **stare**, **bere**, and **dare** of previous chapters, they are irregular verbs and memorization of them is the key to using them correctly.

fare	*to do, to make*
(io) faccio	*I do/make, am doing/making, do/make*
(tu) fai	*you do/make* (familiar), *are doing/making, do do/make*
(Lei) fa	*you do/make* (polite), *are doing/making, do do/make*
(lui/lei) fa	*he/she does/makes, is doing/making, does do/make*
(noi) facciamo	*we do/make, are doing/making, do do/make*
(voi) fate	*you do/make* (familiar plural), *are doing/making, do do/make*
(Loro) fanno	*you do/make* (polite plural), *are doing/making, do do/make*
(loro) fanno	*they do/make, are doing/making, do do/make*

dire	*to say, to tell*
(io) dico	*I say/tell, am saying/telling, do say/tell*
(tu) dici	*you say/tell* (familiar), *are saying/telling, do say/tell*
(Lei) dice	*you say/tell* (polite), *are saying/telling, do say/tell*
(lui/lei) dice	*he/she says/tells, is saying/telling, does say/tell*
(noi) diciamo	*we say/tell, are saying/telling, do say/tell*
(voi) dite	*you say/tell* (familiar plural), *are saying/telling, do say/tell*
(Loro) dicono	*you say/tell* (polite plural), *are saying/telling, do say/tell*
(loro) dicono	*they say/tell, are saying/telling, do say/tell*

Oral Practice

Practice saying the following sentences out loud. Note the new vocabulary words.

Marco, che fai domani?	*Mark, what are you doing tomorrow?*
Non faccio niente.	*I am not doing anything.*
E Lei, che fa, signora?	*And what are you doing, madam?*
Faccio delle spese.	*I am doing some shopping.*
Che fa il signore?	*What is the gentleman doing?*
Lui fa la spesa con la moglie.	*He is shopping for food with his wife.*
Che fate domani, Bruno e Dina?	*What are you doing tomorrow, Bruno and Dina?*
Non facciamo niente.	*We are not doing anything.*
Che cosa fanno gli studenti?	*What are the students doing?*
Gli studenti studiano.	*The students are studying.*
Che cosa dici, Maria?	*What are you saying, Mary?*
Non dico niente.	*I am not saying anything.*
Che cosa dice, signora?	*What are you saying, madam?*
Dico la verità.	*I am telling the truth.*
Che cosa dice il tuo amico?	*What is your friend saying?*
Il mio amico dice solo la verità.	*My friend is telling only the truth.*
Che cosa dite voi?	*What are you saying?*
Noi non diciamo niente.	*We are not saying anything.*
Che cosa dicono i bambini?	*What are the children saying?*
I bambini dicono la verità.	*The children are telling the truth.*

Written Practice 2

Fill in the blanks with the appropriate present indicative forms of **fare** or **dire**.

1. Carla, che cosa _____? *Carla, what are saying?*
2. (Io) _____ la verità. *I am telling the truth.*

3. Che cosa _____ domani, Franca? *What are you doing tomorrow, Franca?*

4. (Io) _____ delle spese. *I am doing some shopping.*

5. Che cosa _____ domani, Marco e Maria? *What are you doing tomorrow, Mark and Mary?*

6. Domani _____ delle spese insieme. *Tomorrow we are doing some shopping together.*

7. Che cosa _____, signorina? *What are you saying, miss?*

8. (Io) non _____ niente. *I am not saying anything.*

9. Che cosa _____ gli amici? *What are the friends doing?*

10. Loro _____ delle spese insieme. *They are doing some shopping together.*

11. Che _____ insieme, Dina e Pina? *What do you do together, Dina and Pina?*

12. Ogni giorno _____ la spesa insieme. *Every day we do the shopping together.*

13. Che _____ gli studenti? *What are the students saying?*

14. Loro non _____ niente. *They are not saying anything.*

SHOPPING FOR FOOD

From the previous practice sessions, note the difference between going shopping in general (**fare delle spese**) and shopping for food (**fare la spesa**), which indicates that Italians see the two things as separate. Also, note that **il tavolo** refers to a table in general, whereas **la tavola** refers to an eating table (with some exceptions). Again, this indicates a cultural difference.

Prepositional Contractions

Facciamo delle spese domani. *We are doing some shopping tomorrow.* Take note of the form **delle** in this sentence. It is actually a contraction of the preposition **di** (*of*) plus the definite article form **le**. This is called a prepositional contraction.

When the following prepositions immediately precede a definite article form, they contract to form one word.

a	*to, at*	in	*in*
di	*of*	su	*on*
da	*from*		

Questo è il libro del fratello di Francesca.   *This is the book of Francesca's brother.*

del = di + il (fratello)

Ci sono due euro nella scatola (skAh-toh-lah).   *There are two euros in the box.*

nella = in + la (scatola)

Loro arrivano dall'Italia domani.   *They are arriving from Italy tomorrow.*

dall' = da + l' (Italia)

The following chart summarizes the contracted forms:

+	il	i	lo	l'	gli	la	le
a	al	ai	allo	all'	agli	alla	alle
da	dal	dai	dallo	dall'	dagli	dalla	dalle
di	del	dei	dello	dell'	degli	della	delle
in	nel	nei	nello	nell'	negli	nella	nelle
su	sul	sui	sullo	sull'	sugli	sulla	sulle

Forming a contraction with the preposition **con** (*with*) is optional. In fact, only the forms **col** (= **con** + **il**) and **coll'** (= **con** + **l'**) are found today in Italian, with any degree of frequency.

Lui parla col professore domani.   *He will speak with the professor tomorrow.*

Loro arrivano coll'Alitalia.   *They will arrive with Alitalia.*

The other prepositions in Italian do not contract.

tra, fra	*between, among*	sopra	*above, on top*
per	*for, through, on account of*	sotto	*under, below*

Metto la scatola tra la tavola e la sedia.	*I am putting the box between the table and the chair.*
Metto il libro sotto la tavola.	*I am putting the book under the table.*

The definite article is dropped in expressions that have a high degree of usage or that have become idiomatic.

Sono a casa.	*I am at home.*
Arrivo in automobile.	*I am arriving by car.*

However, if the noun in such expressions is modified in any way, the article must be used and prepositional contractions are formed.

Siamo alla casa nuova di Michele.	*We are at Michael's new home.*
Arriviamo nell'automobile di Marco.	*We are arriving in Marco's car.*

Oral Practice

Practice saying the following sentences out loud.

Dov'è il libro?	*Where is the book?*
È sul tavolo.	*It is on the table.*
Dov'è Maria?	*Where is Mary?*
È alla partita di calcio.	*She is at the soccer game.*
Di chi è il giornale?	*Whose newspaper is it?*
È il giornale degli studenti.	*It is the students' newspaper.*
Dove vivono?	*Where do they live?*
Vivono negli Stati Uniti.	*They live in the United States.*
Da dove arrivate?	*From where are you arriving?*
Arriviamo dall'Italia.	*We are arriving from Italy.*
Dov'è la scatola?	*Where is the box?*
La scatola è tra il tavolo e la sedia.	*The box is between the table and chair.*
Per chi è il libro?	*For whom is the book?*
È per mio fratello.	*It is for my brother.*
Dov'è la penna?	*Where is the pen?*

La penna è sul pavimento.   *The pen is on the floor.*

Dove sono le matite?   *Where are the pencils?*

Le matite sono sotto la sedia.   *The pencils are under the chair.*

Dove siete?   *Where are you?*

Noi siamo a casa.   *We are at home.*

Written Practice 3

Fill in the blanks with the appropriate preposition or prepositional contraction.

1. A chi dai le bibite? *To whom are you giving the soft drinks?*

   Do le bibite _____ bambini. *I am giving the drinks to the children.*

2. Chi è? *Who is it?*

   È il fratello _____ zio. *He is the uncle's brother (= the brother of the uncle).*

3. Dov'è il computer? *Where is the computer?*

   Il computer è _____ tavolo. *The computer is on the table.*

4. Che fai domani? *What are you doing tomorrow?*

   Domani faccio _____ spese. *I am doing some shopping tomorrow.*

5. Dove vivi? *Where do you live?*

   Vivo _____ Stati Uniti. *I live in the United States.*

6. Con chi parli? *With whom are you speaking?*

   Parlo _____ professoressa. *I am speaking with the professor.*

7. Dov'è la scatola? *Where is the box?*

   È _____ sedia. *It is under the chair.*

SPECIAL USES OF PREPOSITIONS

Prepositions have many uses and are important to everyday communication. Keep in mind the following special uses for **a**, **in**, **di**, and **da** within sentences.

- The preposition **a** is used in front of a city name to render the idea of being "in a city."

Vivo a Roma.	*I live in Rome.*

- Otherwise, the preposition **in** is used.

Vivo in Italia.	*I live in Italy.*
Vivo nell'Italia centrale.	*I live in central Italy.*

NOTE: *Remember that the definite article is used with a modified noun. (In the previous example sentence the definite article is contracted with the preposition.)*

- Use the preposition **di** to indicate possession or relationship.

È l'automobile nuova di Alessandro.	*It is Alexander's new car.*
Come si chiama la figlia del professore?	*What is the name of the professor's daughter?*

- The preposition **da** translates to *from* or *at* in expressions such as the following:

Arrivo dalla farmacia.	*I am arriving from the pharmacy.*
Sono dal medico.	*I am at the doctor's.*

- But **da** translates to both *since* and *from* in time constructions.

Vivo qui dal 2004.	*I have been living here since 2004.*
Vivo qui da undici anni.	*I have been living here for eleven years.*

Oral Practice

Practice saying the following sentences out loud.

Dove vivete?	*Where do you live?*
Viviamo a Pisa.	*We live in Pisa.*
Dove sono i tuoi amici?	*Where are your friends?*
Sono in Italia.	*They are in Italy.*
Dove vivono?	*Where do they live?*
Vivono nell'Italia centrale.	*They live in central Italy.*
Chi sono?	*Who are they?*

Sono i figli della signora Marchi.	*They are Mrs. Marchi's children.*
Dove sono le tue amiche?	*Where are your friends?*
Sono dal medico.	*They are at the doctor's.*
Da quando vivi qui?	*Since when have you been living here?*
Vivo qui dal 2005.	*I have been living here since 2005.*

Written Practice 4

Fill in the blanks with the appropriate preposition or prepositional contraction.

1. Dove sono i tuoi amici? *Where are your friends?*

   Sono _____ Chicago. *They are in Chicago.*

2. Dove sono i tuoi genitori? *Where are your parents?*

   Sono _____ America centrale. *They are in Central America.*

3. Chi sono? *Who are they?*

   Sono gli studenti _____ professore. *They are the professor's students.*

4. Dove sono Maria e Dina? *Where are Mary and Dina?*

   Sono _____ genitori. *They are at their parents' house.*

5. Da quando vivi qui? *Since when have you been living here?*

   Vivo qui _____ venti anni. *I have been living here for twenty years.*

Numbers Over 1000

Previously you learned the numbers from 0 to 1000, and how to form them. The same pattern of construction applies to the numbers over 1000.

1001	milleuno
1002	milledue
2000	duemila
3000	tremila
100.000	centomila
200.000	duecentomila

1.000.000	un milione
2.000.000	due milioni
3.000.000	tre milioni

Notice that the plural of **mille** is **mila**, whereas **milione** is pluralized in the normal way.

duemila	*two thousand*
due milioni	*two million*

Milione is always followed by the preposition **di** before a noun.

due milioni di euro	*two million euros*
un milione di dollari	*one million dollars*

As you know, the cardinal numbers may be written as one word. But for large numbers, it is better to separate them, so that they can be read easily.

30.256	trentamila duecento cinquantasei

NOTE: *Italians use periods where Americans use commas in numbers.*

Italian	**American**
30.256,50	30,256.50

When the number **uno** (or any number constructed with it, such as **ventuno**, **trentuno**, etc.) is used with a noun, it follows the same rules as the indefinite article.

uno zio	*one uncle*
ventun anni	*twenty-one years*
trentuna ragazze	*thirty-one girls*

The word **nessuno** means *no* in the sense of *none*. It is made up of **ness** + **uno**, and thus it is treated, again, like the indefinite article when used with a noun. In this case, however, the noun is always in the singular, even if its meaning is plural.

nessuno zio	*no uncles*
nessun amico	*no friends*
nessuna zia	*no aunts*

The definite and indefinite articles also vary when used with the word **altro** (*other*).

Masculine

un altro zio   *another uncle*

l'altro zio   *the other uncle*

Feminine

un'altra ragazza   *another girl*

l'altra ragazza   *the other girl*

Oral Practice

Practice saying the following sentences out loud.

Quante persone vivono nella città?   *How many people live in the city?*

Quasi ventidue mila.   *Almost twenty-two thousand.*

Qual è la popolazione d'Italia?   *What is the population of Italy?*

La popolazione è di circa sessanta milioni.   *The population is around 60 million.*

Quanti anni hai?   *How old are you?*

Ho trentun anni.   *I am thirty-one years old.*

Quanti anni ha la tua amica?   *How old is your friend?*

Lei ha quasi quarantun anni.   *She is almost forty-one years old.*

Quanto costa l'automobile?   *How much does the car cost?*

Costa quasi ventimila euro.   *It costs almost 20,000 euros.*

Quanto costa l'altra casa?   *How much does the other house cost?*

Costa circa cinquecento mila dollari.   *It costs almost 500,000 dollars.*

Quanti amici italiani hai?   *How many Italian friends do you have?*

Non ho nessun amico italiano.   *I have no Italian friends.*

Quante amiche americane hai?   *How many (female) American friends do you have?*

Non ho nessun'amica americana.   *I have no American friends.*

Written Practice 5

Fill in the blanks with the appropriate number word(s).

1. Quante persone ci sono nella città? *How many people are there in the city?*
   Circa _____. *Almost nine million.*

2. Qual è la popolazione degli Stati Uniti? *What is the population of the United States?*
   Circa _____. *Almost 300 million.*

3. Quanti anni hai? *How old are you?*
   Ho _____ anni. *I am fifty-one years old.*

4. Quanti anni ha il tuo amico? *How old is your friend?*
   Lui ha quasi _____ anni. *He is almost thirty-one years old.*

5. Quanto costa l'automobile? *How much does the car cost?*
   Costa quasi _____ dollari. *It costs almost 22,000 dollars.*

6. Quanto costa l'altra automobile? *How much does the other car cost?*
   Costa circa _____ euro. *It costs almost 18,000 euros.*

7. Quanti cugini italiani hai? *How many Italian cousins do you have?*
   Non ho _____ cugino italiano. *I have no Italian cousins.*

8. Quante zie americane hai? *How many American aunts do you have?*
   Non ho _____ zia americana. *I have no American aunts.*

Telling Time

In this section you will learn to tell time in Italian. To inquire about the time, you would say **Che ora è?** *What time is it?* (literally: *What hour is it?*) The plural form **Che ore sono?** (literally: *What hours are they?*) can also be used.

The hours are feminine in gender. Therefore, the feminine forms of the definite article are used.

l'una	*one o'clock* (= the only singular form)
le due	*two o'clock*
le tre	*three o'clock*
le quattro	*four o'clock*

In ordinary conversation, morning, afternoon, and evening hours are distinguished by the following expressions:

di mattina (della mattina)   *in the morning*
di pomeriggio   *in the afternoon*
di sera (della sera)   *in the evening*
di notte (della notte)   *in the night/at night*

Here are some example sentences:

Sono le otto di mattina.   *It is eight o'clock in the morning.*

Sono le nove di sera.   *It is nine o'clock in the evening.*

Officially, however, telling time in Italian is carried out using the twenty-four-hour clock. Thus, after the noon hour, continue with the numbers as follows:

le tredici   *1:00 p.m. (thirteen hundred hours)*

le quattordici   *2:00 p.m. (fourteen hundred hours)*

le quindici   *3:00 p.m. (fifteen hundred hours)*

le sedici   *4:00 p.m. (sixteen hundred hours)*

Sono le quindici.   *It is 3:00 p.m.*

Sono le venti.   *It is 8:00 p.m.*

Sono le ventiquattro.   *It is (twelve) midnight.*

Minutes are simply added to the hour with the conjunction **e** (*and*).

Sono le tre e venti.   *It is three-twenty.*

È l'una e quaranta.   *It is one-forty.*

Sono le sedici e cinquanta.   *It is 4:50 p.m.*

Sono le ventidue e cinque.   *It is 10:05 p.m.*

As the next hour approaches, an alternative way of expressing the minutes is by saying the next hour minus (**meno**) the number of minutes left to go. For example:

8:58   =   le otto e cinquantotto *or* le nove meno due

10:50   =   le dieci e cinquanta *or* le undici meno dieci

The expressions **un quarto** (*a quarter*) and **mezzo** or **mezza** (*half*) can be used for the quarter and half hour.

3:15	=	le tre e quindici *or*
		le tre e un quarto
4:30	=	le quattro e trenta *or*
		le quattro e mezzo/mezza
5:45	=	le cinque e quaranta cinque *or*
		le sei meno un quarto *or*
		le cinque e tre quarti (*three quarters*)

Noon and *midnight* can also be expressed by using the words **mezzogiorno** and **mezzanotte**, respectively.

Sono le dodici.	=	È mezzogiorno.	*It is noon.*
Sono le ventiquattro.	=	È mezzanotte.	*It is midnight.*

Finally, note the following useful expressions:

preciso	*exactly*
È l'una precisa.	*It is exactly one o'clock.*
Sono le otto precise.	*It is exactly eight o'clock.*

in punto	*on the dot*
È l'una in punto.	*It is one o'clock on the dot.*
Sono le otto in punto.	*It is eight o'clock on the dot.*

Oral Practice

Practice saying the following sentences out loud.

Che ora è?	*What time is it?*
Sono le due e venti del pomeriggio.	*It is 2:20 in the afternoon.*
Che ore sono?	*What time is it?*
È l'una precisa.	*It is exactly one o'clock.*
A che ora arriva Maria?	*At what time is Mary arriving?*

Maria arriva alle quattro e mezzo.	*Maria is arriving at 4:30.*
A che ora arriva Paolo?	*At what time is Paul arriving?*
Arriva alle nove e un quarto di sera.	*He is arriving at 9:15 in the evening.*
A che ora c'è il film?	*At what time is the movie?*
Il film c'è alle sette meno dieci.	*The movie is at ten to seven.*
Quando arrivano i tuoi genitori?	*When are your parents arriving?*
Arrivano a mezzogiorno.	*They are arriving at noon.*
Che ora è?	*What time is it?*
Sono le otto e mezzo di mattina.	*It is 8:30 in the morning.*
Che ore sono?	*What time is it?*
Sono le ventidue in punto.	*It is 10:00 on the dot.*
Che ora è?	*What time is it?*
Sono le diciannove e quarantadue.	*It is 7:42.*
Che ore sono?	*What time is it?*
Sono le venti meno cinque.	*It is five minutes to eight.*

Written Practice 6

Fill in the blanks with the times provided.

1. Che ora è? *What time is it?*

   Sono _____. *It is two thirty.*

2. Che ore sono? *What time is it?*

   È _____. *It is 1:35 in the afternoon.*

3. A che ora arriva il professore? *At what time is the professor arriving?*

   Arriva _____. *He is arriving at 7:45 in the evening.*

4. A che ora arrivano? *At what time are they arriving?*

   Arrivano _____. *They are arriving at midnight.*

5. A che ora c'è il film? *At what time is the movie?*

   Il film c'è _____. *The movie is at 5:00 in the afternoon on the dot.*

6. Quando arrivano i tuoi amici? *When are your friends arriving?*

   Arrivano _____. *They are arriving at 4:15.*

7. Che ora è? *What time is it?*

Sono _____ . *It is 6:01.*

8. Che ore sono? *What time is it?*

Sono _____ . *It is twenty to four.*

QUIZ

Fill in the blanks with the missing ending from each verb.

1. Maria, chi ved_____ stasera?

Dove viv_____ i tuoi genitori?

Anch'io ripet_____ sempre tutto (*everything*) in classe.

Perché anche voi vend_____ la casa?

Noi legg_____ sempre il giornale.

Signora, Lei che cosa prend_____?

Giovanni che cosa mett_____ nel caffè?

Give the appropriate prepositional contraction for each phrase.

2. a + lo zio _____

di + gli amici _____

da + il medico _____

in + i ristoranti _____

su + la sedia _____

con + l'amico _____

a + l'amica _____

di + le amiche _____

Fill in each blank with the appropriate preposition and article (simple or contracted) as required.

3. Le penne sono _____ scatola.

   Ecco i libri _____ amici.

   Le matite sono _____ tavola.

   Mio cugino è _____ medico.

   Arrivano _____ nove stasera.

   Maria sta _____ casa domani tutto il giorno.

   Siamo _____ casa nuova di mio fratello.

Circle the letter of the word or phrase that best answers the question.

4. 32.345

   (a) trentadue mila trecento quarantacinque

   (b) trentadue milioni trecento quarantacinque

5. A che ora arrivano gli amici?

   (a) Alle nove e mezzo.

   (b) Sono le nove e mezzo.

6. Che ore sono?

   (a) A mezzogiorno.

   (b) È l'una e un quarto.

7. Quando arrivano?

   (a) Le due meno venti.

   (b) Alle due meno venti.

Personal Matters! Answer each question appropriately.

8. Quanti anni hai?

    _____ .

9. Che ora è adesso?

    _____ .

10. A che ora studi di solito?

    _____ .

CHAPTER 8

Demonstratives and the Present Indicative of *-ire* Verbs

Here's what you will learn in this chapter:

Present Indicative of *-ire* Verbs

Quando parti per l'Italia? *When are you leaving for Italy?* The verb used in this question is **partire** which means *to leave*. Notice that it ends in **-ire** (instead of **-are** or **-ere**). Verbs ending in **-ire** are called, logically, third-conjugation verbs.

To conjugate regular third-conjugation verbs in the present indicative, drop the infinitive ending **-ire** from the verb root (in this case, **part-**), and add on the endings **-o, -i, -e, -iamo, -ite, -ono** according to the person (first, second, third) and number (singular and plural).

(io) parto	*I leave, am leaving, do leave*
(tu) parti	*you (familiar) leave, are leaving, do leave*
(Lei) parte	*you (polite) leave, are leaving, do leave*
(lui/lei) parte	*he/she leaves, is leaving, does leave*
(noi) partiamo	*we leave, are leaving, do leave*
(voi) partite	*you (familiar plural) leave, are leaving, do leave*
(Loro) partono	*you (polite plural) leave, are leaving, do leave*
(loro) partono	*they leave, are leaving, do leave*

COMMON *-IRE* VERBS

Here are some common useful **-ire** verbs.

dormire	*to sleep*
sentire	*to hear, feel*
aprire	*to open*

Oral Practice

Practice saying the following sentences out loud.

Quando parti, Maria?	*When are you leaving, Mary?*
Parto domani.	*I am leaving tomorrow.*
Chi dorme adesso?	*Who is sleeping now?*
Mia sorella dorme adesso.	*My sister is sleeping now.*
Quando aprono tutti i negozi?	*When do all the stores open?*
Aprono alle sette.	*They open at seven.*

Che cosa sentite? *What do you hear?*

Sentiamo una voce strana. *We hear a strange voice.*

Written Practice 1

Fill in the blanks with the appropriate present indicative forms of the verbs provided.

1. Quando _____, signorina? *When are you leaving, miss?*

   _____ domani. *I am leaving tomorrow.*

2. Marco, tu _____ in classe? *Mark, do you sleep in class?*

   No, non _____ mai in classe. *No, I never sleep in class.*

3. Quando _____ il negozio? *When does the store open?*

   Tutti i negozi _____ alle sette. *All the stores open at seven.*

4. Che cosa _____, Dino e Dina? *What do you hear, Dino and Dina?*

   _____ una voce strana. *We hear a strange voice.*

Using the Verb *Capire*

Capisci l'italiano? Sì, capisco l'italiano. *Do you understand Italian? Yes, I understand Italian.* The verb used in this case is **capire** (*to understand*), which is also, as you can see, a third-conjugation verb. However, it is conjugated differently than the **-ire** verbs previously discussed. With **capire** and a few other **-ire** verbs, **-isc** is added to the verb stem before the endings are added except **-iamo** and **-ite**. Pay special attention to this conjugation.

(io) cap*isc*o	*I understand, am understanding, do understand*
(tu) cap*isc*i	*you (familiar) understand, are understanding, do understand*
(Lei) cap*isc*e	*you (polite) understand, are understanding, do understand*
(lui/lei) cap*isc*e	*he/she understands, is understanding, does understand*
(noi) cap*iamo*	*we understand, are understanding, do understand*
(voi) cap*ite*	*you (familiar plural) understand, are understanding, do understand*
(Loro) cap*isc*ono	*you (polite plural) understand, are understanding, do understand*
(loro) cap*isc*ono	*they understand, are understanding, do understand*

So, **-ire** verbs have two sets of endings and learning to which category an **-ire** verb belongs must be memorized, as there are no rules governing this. If you are unsure, consult an Italian verb dictionary.

Here are a few other common third-conjugation verbs conjugated with **-isc**:

finire	*to finish*
preferire	*to prefer*
pulire	*to clean*

CHE

Before the Oral Practice, you should learn the relative pronoun **che**, meaning *that, which,* or *who.* Do not confuse **che** with **che (cosa)**, which, as you know, means *what.* Note how **che** and **che cosa** are used in the following sentences:

Oral Practice

Practice saying the following sentences out loud.

Capisci che non è vero?	*Do you understand that it is not true?*
Sì, capisco.	*Yes, I understand.*
Che cosa preferite, voi due?	*What do the two of you prefer?*
Preferiamo un cappuccino.	*We prefer a cappuccino.*
Chi pulisce la casa oggi?	*Who is cleaning the house today?*
Loro puliscono la casa oggi.	*They are cleaning the house today.*
Quando finisce di lavorare Marco?	*When does Mark finish working?*
Lui finisce di lavorare alle sei.	*He finishes working at six.*
Che fate domani?	*What are you doing tomorrow?*
Finiamo di fare le spese.	*We are finishing the shopping.*
Anche voi pulite la casa oggi?	*You, too, are cleaning the house today?*
Sì, anche noi puliamo la casa.	*Yes, we, too, are cleaning the house.*
Signora, Lei capisce il francese?	*Madam, do you understand French?*
No, capisco solo l'italiano.	*No, I understand only Italian.*

Written Practice 2

Fill in the blanks with the appropriate present indicative forms of the verbs provided.

1. Signora, _____ che non è vero? *Madam, do you understand that it is not true?*

   No, non _____. *No, I do not understand.*

2. Che cosa _____, loro? *What do they prefer?*

   _____ un cappuccino. *They prefer a cappuccino.*

3. Tu _____ la casa oggi, Mario? *Are you cleaning the house today, Mario?*

   Sì, _____ la casa oggi. *Yes, I am cleaning the house today.*

4. Quando _____ di lavorare voi? *When are you finishing work?*

   _____ alle sei. *We are finishing at six.*

5. Che cosa _____ domani? *What are they finishing tomorrow?*

   _____ di fare le spese. *They are finishing the shopping.*

6. Anche voi _____ la casa domani? *You, too, are cleaning the house tomorrow?*

   Sì, anche noi _____ la casa. *Yes, we, too, are cleaning the house.*

7. Il ragazzo _____ il francese? *Does the boy understand French?*

   Sì, il ragazzo _____ il francese. *Yes, the boy understands French.*

Using the Verbs *Andare, Uscire,* and *Venire*

Dove vai? A che ora esci? Quando vieni? *Where are you going? At what time are you going out?* and *When are you coming?* These questions are constructed with the verbs **andare** (*to go*), **uscire** (*to go out*), and **venire** (*to come*). Like some of the other verbs you have learned in previous chapters, these are irregular verbs. This means, once again, that you will have to memorize their conjugations.

andare	*to go*
(io) vado	*I go, am going, do go*
(tu) vai	*you go* (familiar), *are going, do go*
(Lei) va	*you go* (polite), *are going, do go*
(lui/lei) va	*he/she goes, is going, does go*
(noi) andiamo	*we go, are going, do go*
(voi) andate	*you go* (familiar plural), *are going, do go*
(Loro) vanno	*you go* (polite plural), *are going, do go*
(loro) vanno	*they go, are going, do go*

uscire	*to go out*
(io) esco	*I go out, am going out, do go out*
(tu) esci	*you go out* (familiar), *are going out, do go out*
(Lei) esce	*you go out* (polite), *are going out, do go out*
(lui/lei) esce	*he/she goes out, is going out, does go out*
(noi) usciamo	*we go out, are going out, do go out*
(voi) uscite	*you go out* (familiar plural), *are going out, do go out*
(Loro) escono	*you go out* (polite plural), *are going out, do go out*
(loro) escono	*they go out, are going out, do go out*

venire	*to come*
(io) vengo	*I come, am coming, do come*
(tu) vieni	*you come* (familiar), *are coming, do come*
(Lei) viene	*you come* (polite), *are coming, do come*
(lui/lei) viene	*he/she comes, is coming, does come*
(noi) veniamo	*we come, are coming, do come*
(voi) venite	*you come* (familiar plural), *are coming, do come*
(Loro) vengono	*you come* (polite plural), *are coming, do come*
(loro) vengono	*they come, are coming, do come*

Oral Practice

Practice saying the following sentences out loud.

Dove vai oggi, Giovanni?	*Where are you going today, John?*
Vado in centro.	*I am going downtown.*
E Maria dove va?	*And where is Mary going?*
Maria va a scuola.	*Mary is going to school.*
Dove andate voi stasera?	*Where are you going tonight?*
Andiamo a una festa.	*We are going to a party.*
Dove vanno i tuoi amici stasera?	*Where are your friends going tonight?*
Vanno al cinema.	*They are going to the movies.*
A che ora esci, Maria?	*At what time are you going out, Mary?*
Esco verso le otto stasera.	*I am going out around eight o'clock tonight.*
E quando esce la tua amica?	*And when is your friend going out?*
Lei esce nel pomeriggio.	*She is going out in the afternoon.*
E voi due quando uscite?	*And when are the two of you going out?*
Noi usciamo domani.	*We are going out tomorrow.*
A che ora escono stasera, loro?	*When are they going out tonight?*
Loro escono alle otto e mezzo.	*They are going out at eight thirty.*
Maria, vieni anche tu alla festa?	*Mary, are you also coming to the party?*
No, non vengo.	*No, I am not coming.*
Chi viene al cinema con noi?	*Who is coming to the movies with us?*
Viene solo mio fratello.	*Only my brother is coming.*
Venite anche voi due alla discoteca?	*Are the two of you also coming to the disco?*
Sì, veniamo anche noi.	*Yes, we are also coming.*
Vengono anche Alessandro e Sara?	*Are Alexander and Sarah also coming?*
Sì, vengono anche loro.	*Yes, they are coming, too.*

Written Practice 3

Fill in the blanks with the appropriate present indicative forms of the verbs provided.

1. Dove _____ oggi, Pina? *Where are you going today, Pina?*

   _____ a scuola. *I am going to school.*

2. E la professoressa dove _____? *And where is the professor going?*

   Lei _____ in centro. *She is going downtown.*

3. Dove _____ voi due domani? *Where are the two of you going tomorrow?*

   _____ in centro. *We are going downtown.*

4. Dove _____ loro stasera? *Where are they going tonight?*

   _____ a una discoteca. *They are going to a disco.*

5. A che ora _____, Marco? *At what time are you going out, Mark?*

   _____ verso le nove stasera. *I am going out around nine o'clock tonight.*

6. Quando _____ di solito la tua amica? *When does your friend usually go out?*

   Lei _____ di solito la sera. *She usually goes out in the evenings.*

7. E voi due quando _____? *And when are the two of you going out?*

   Noi _____ nel pomeriggio. *We are going out in the afternoon.*

8. A che ora _____ stasera loro? *When are they going out tonight?*

   _____ alle ventuno. *They are going out at 9:00 p.m.*

9. Sara, _____ anche tu al cinema? *Sarah, are you also coming to the movies?*

   Sì, _____ anch'io. *Yes, I am coming, too.*

10. Chi _____ alla festa con noi? *Who is coming to the party with us?*

    _____ solo lui. *Only he is coming.*

11. _____ anche voi due al cinema? *Are the two of you also coming to the movies?*

    No, non _____. *No, we are not coming.*

12. _____ anche loro? *Are they also coming?*

    Sì, _____ anche loro. *Yes, they are coming, too.*

Ordinal Numbers

Lunedì è il primo giorno della settimana. *Monday is the first day of the week.* This sentence uses the ordinal number word **primo** (*first*). Ordinal numbers indicate the order of something (first, second, third, etc.). Here are the first ten ordinal numbers in Italian:

1st primo (1°)	6th sesto (6°)
2nd secondo (2°)	7th settimo (7°)
3rd terzo (3°)	8th ottavo (8°)
4th quarto (4°)	9th nono (9°)
5th quinto (5°)	10th decimo (10°)

The remaining ordinal numbers are easily constructed in the following manner:

- Take the corresponding cardinal number, drop its vowel ending, and add **-esimo**.

11th	undici + -esimo = undicesimo
40th	quaranta + -esimo = quarantesimo

- But, in the case of numbers ending in **-tré**, remove the accent mark, but keep the **-e**.

23rd	ventitré + -esimo = ventitreesimo
33rd	trentatré + -esimo = trentatreesimo

- And if the number ends in **-sei**, do not drop the vowel.

26th	ventisei + -esimo = ventiseiesimo

Unlike the cardinal numbers, ordinal numbers are adjectives. Therefore, they agree with the noun being modified in both gender and number. It may be necessary to review the information on adjectives in Chapter 4 if you need to now. Also, notice that the ordinals are put before (not after) the nouns they modify.

il primo (1°) giorno	*the first day*
la ventesima (20ª) settimana	*the twentieth week*
tutti gli ottavi mesi (8ⁱ)	*all the eighth months*

Oral Practice

Practice saying the following sentences out loud.

Vai in centro oggi?	*Are you going downtown today?*
Sì, è già la seconda volta.	*Yes, it is already the second time.*
A quale piano stai?	*On which floor do you live (stay)?*
Al quinto piano.	*On the fifth floor.*
Che giorno è?	*What day is it?*
È il primo giorno della settimana.	*It is the first day of the week.*
In quali mesi vai in vacanza?	*In which months do you go on vacation?*
Nel terzo, quarto e sesto mese.	*In the third, fourth, and sixth month.*
Chi è?	*Who is it?*
È la settima persona che vedo oggi.	*It is the seventh person that I have seen today.*
In quale mese è il tuo compleanno?	*In which month is your birthday?*
Nell'ottavo mese.	*In the eighth month.*
In che mese prendi le vacanze?	*In which month do you take a vacation?*
Nel nono o decimo mese.	*In the ninth or tenth month.*
Quante volte vai in centro?	*How many times do you go downtown?*
Molte. Questa è la sedicesima volta.	*Many. This is the sixteenth time.*

Written Practice 4

Provide the appropriate ordinal number in its correct form. For example:

> 13ª volta
>
> *la tredicesima volta* _____ *the thirteenth time*

1. 26° piano

   _____ *the twenty-sixth floor*

2. 12ª volta

   _____ *the twelfth time*

3. 43° giorno

   _____ *the forty-third day*

4. 58ª volta

   _____ *the fifty-eighth time*

5. 6ª settimana

   _____ *the sixth week*

6. 8° mese

   _____ *the eighth month*

Demonstratives

Che cosa è questa cosa? *What is this thing?* Note the word **questa** in this question, which means *this*. **Questa** is called a demonstrative because it allows you to demonstrate or point out where things are.

DEMONSTRATIVES INDICATING OBJECTS THAT ARE NEAR

Some demonstratives indicate the relative nearness of an object, while other demonstratives indicate objects that are farther away. The one used above (**questa**) is referring to something that is near. In this case, it is used as an adjective, so its forms vary the same as other adjectives.

- Use **questo** (plural: **questi** [*these*]) before a masculine noun or adjective.

Singular		**Plural**	
questo zio	*this uncle*	questi zii	*these uncles*
questo studente	*this student*	questi studenti	*these students*
questo ragazzo	*this boy*	questi ragazzi	*these boys*
questo cane	*this dog*	questi cani	*these dogs*
questo amico	*this friend*	questi amici	*these friends*

- Use **questa** (plural: **queste** [*these*]) before a feminine noun or adjective.

Singular		**Plural**	
questa zia	*this aunt*	queste zie	*these aunts*
questa studentessa	*this student*	queste studentesse	*these students*
questa ragazza	*this girl*	queste ragazze	*these girls*
questa camicia	*this shirt*	queste camicie	*these shirts*
questa amica	*this friend*	queste amiche	*these friends*

- The word **quest'** can be used (optionally) before a singular noun or adjective beginning with a vowel.

  questo amico *or* quest'amico

  questa amica *or* quest'amica

Oral Practice

Practice saying the following sentences out loud.

Ti piace questo vestito?	*Do you like this dress?*
Sì, mi piace molto questo vestito.	*Yes, I like this dress a lot.*
Ti piacciono anche questi vestiti?	*Do you like these dresses, too?*
No, non mi piacciono questi vestiti.	*No, I do not like these dresses.*
Ti piace questo zaino?	*Do you like this backpack?*
Sì, mi piace molto questo zaino.	*Yes, I like this backpack a lot.*
Ti piacciono anche questi zaini?	*Do you also like these backpacks?*
No, non mi piacciono questi zaini.	*No, I do not like these backpacks.*
Ti piace quest'espresso?	*Do you like this espresso?*
Sì, mi piace molto quest'espresso.	*Yes, I like this espresso a lot.*
Ti piacciono anche questi orologi?	*Do you also like these watches?*

No, non mi piacciono questi orologi.   *No, I do not like these watches.*

Ti piace questa borsa?   *Do you like this purse?*

Sì, mi piace molto questa borsa.   *Yes, I like this purse a lot.*

Ti piacciono anche queste borse?   *Do you also like these purses?*

No, non mi piacciono queste borse.   *No, I do not like these purses.*

Ti piace quest'amica?   *Do you like this friend?*

Sì, mi piace molto quest'amica.   *Yes, I like this friend a lot.*

Ti piacciono anche queste amiche?   *Do you also like these friends?*

No, non mi piacciono queste amiche.   *No, I do not like these friends.*

Written Practice 5

Supply the appropriate form of the demonstrative **questo** in front of the given noun or expression. For example:

    <u>questo ragazzo</u> ragazzo   *this boy*

1. _____ amico   *this friend*
2. _____ amici   *these friends*
3. _____ bambino   *this child*
4. _____ altro bambino   *this other child*
5. _____ bambini   *these children*
6. _____ zio   *this uncle*
7. _____ zii   *these uncles*
8. _____ ragazza   *this girl*
9. _____ ragazze   *these girls*
10. _____ altra amica   *this other friend*
11. _____ amiche   *these friends*

DEMONSTRATIVES INDICATING OBJECTS THAT ARE FAR AWAY

The second type of demonstrative, **quello/a** (*that*), indicates objects that are relatively far away. Its forms vary in the same way as those of the definite article. If you need to now, review the definite article information in Chapter 5.

- Use **quello** (plural: **quegli** [*those*]) before a masculine noun or adjective beginning with **z**, **s + consonant**, **gn**, or **ps**.

Singular		Plural	
quello zio	*that uncle*	quegli zii	*those uncles*
quello studente	*that student*	quegli studenti	*those students*
quello gnocco	*that dumpling*	quegli gnocchi	*those dumplings*
quello psicologo	*that psychologist*	quegli psicologi	*those psychologists*

- Use **quel** (plural: **quei** [*those*]) before a masculine noun or adjective beginning with any other consonant.

Singular		Plural	
quel ragazzo	*that boy*	quei ragazzi	*those boys*
quel cane	*that dog*	quei cani	*those dogs*

- Use **quell'** (plural: **quegli** [*those*]) before a masculine noun or adjective beginning with a vowel.

Singular		Plural	
quell'amico	*that friend*	quegli amici	*those friends*
quell'orologio	*that watch*	quegli orologi	*those watches*

- Use **quella** (plural: **quelle** [*those*]) before a feminine noun or adjective beginning with any consonant.

Singular		Plural	
quella zia	*that aunt*	quelle zie	*those aunts*
quella studentessa	*that student*	quelle studentesse	*those students*
quella ragazza	*that girl*	quelle ragazze	*those girls*

- And use **quell'** (plural: **quelle** [*those*]) before a feminine noun or adjective beginning with any vowel.

Singular		Plural	
quell'amica	*that friend*	quelle amiche	*those friends*
quell'ora	*that hour*	quelle ore	*those hours*

Note however, that, as with the articles, when an adjective precedes a noun, you must change the demonstrative according to the adjective's initial sound.

quello zio	*that uncle*
quegli amici	*those friends*

quel simpatico zio	*that nice uncle*
quei simpatici amici	*those nice friends*

And also as with the articles, remember to repeat the demonstratives before every noun.

questo ragazzo e questa ragazza	*this boy and girl*
quel ragazzo e quella ragazza	*that boy and girl*

Oral Practice

Practice saying the following sentences out loud.

Ti piace quel cane?	*Do you like that dog?*
Ti piacciono quei cani?	*Do you like those dogs?*
Ti piace quello zaino?	*Do you like that backpack?*
Ti piacciono quegli zaini?	*Do you like those backpacks?*
Ti piace quell'espresso?	*Do you like that espresso?*
Ti piacciono quegli espressi?	*Do you like those espressos?*
Ti piace quella camicia?	*Do you like that shirt?*
Ti piacciono quelle camicie?	*Do you like those shirts?*
Ti piace quell'amica?	*Do you like that friend?*
Ti piacciono quelle amiche?	*Do you like those friends?*

Written Practice 6

Supply the appropriate form of the demonstrative before the given noun or expression. For example:

*quel ragazzo*____ ragazzo   *that boy*

1. _____ amico   *that friend*
2. _____ amici   *those friends*
3. _____ bambino   *that child*

4. _____ altro bambino	*that other child*
5. _____ bambini	*those children*
6. _____ zio	*that uncle*
7. _____ zii	*those uncles*
8. _____ ragazza	*that girl*
9. _____ ragazze	*those girls*
10. _____ altra ragazza	*that other girl*
11. _____ amiche	*those friends*

Expressing Dates

Dates are expressed by the following formula:

il quindici settembre	*September 15* (literally: *the fifteen September*)
il ventun settembre	*September 21* (literally: *the twenty-one September*)

The exception to this formula is the first day of every month, in which case you use the ordinal number **primo**.

È il primo ottobre.	*It is October 1.*
È il primo giugno.	*It is June 1.*

Years are always preceded by the definite article.

È il 2007.	*It is 2007.*
Sono nato/a nel 1994.	*I was born in 1994.*

(nel 1994 = in + il 1994)

However, when stating complete dates, the article is omitted before the year.

Oggi è il 5 febbraio, 2012.	*Today is February 5, 2012.*

Oral Practice

Practice saying the following sentences out loud.

Che giorno è?	*What day is it?*
È il trenta agosto.	*It is August 30.*
Che data è?	*What is the date?*
È il 5 novembre, 2009 (duemila nove).	*It is November 5, 2009.*
Quando sei nato, Giovanni?	*When were you born, John?*
Sono nato il 12 febbraio.	*I was born on February 12.*
E tu, Maria, quando sei nata?	*And when were you born, Mary?*
Io sono nata il primo gennaio.	*I was born on January 1.*

Written Practice 7

Fill in the blanks with the answer to each question.

1. Che giorno è? *What day is it?*

   È _____. *It is August 16.*

2. Che data è? *What is the date?*

   È _____. *It is July 9, 2009.*

3. Quando sei nato, Marco? *When were you born, Mark?*

   Io _____. *I was born on March 25.*

4. E tu, Claudia, quando sei nata? *And when were you born, Claudia?*

   Io _____. *I was born on April 1.*

Italian Holidays

Italy, like all countries, has national holidays. The main Italian holidays are as follows:

il Natale (il venticinque dicembre)	*Christmas*
il Capo d'Anno (il primo gennaio)	*New Year's Day*

L'Epifania (eh-peeh-fah-nEEh-ah) (il sei gennaio)   *the Epiphany*
la Pasqua (primavera)   *Easter*
il Ferragosto (il quindici agosto)   *the Assumption*

In Italy most homes and churches have a **presepio** (*Nativity scene*) for Christmas. A bread called **il panettone**, which is made with raisins and candied fruit, is also popular at Christmas. Italian children receive gifts from **la Befana**, a kindly old lady, on the eve of the Epiphany, January 6.

Easter is preceded by **il Carnevale** (*Carnival*) throughout Italy. Most carnivals today are small and are held in towns and small cities, setting up their attractions in streets and parking lots. The Mardi Gras in New Orleans is a similar famous American carnival.

QUIZ

Supply the missing ending from each verb.

1. Maria, che cosa sent_____?

   I negozi apr_____ alle sette e mezzo?

   Anch'io part_____ per l'Italia domani.

   Marco cap_____ molte lingue.

   Noi prefer_____ la lingua italiana.

   Anche voi pul_____ la casa oggi, non è vero?

   Loro fin_____ di lavorare alle sei.

Circle the letter of the word or phrase that best answers each question or completes each sentence.

2. Dove vai oggi pomeriggio, Maria?

   (a) Vado in centro.

   (b) Va in centro.

3. A che ora uscite?

   (a) Usciamo alle sei.

   (b) Escono alle sei.

4. Quando viene la professoressa?

   (a) Vengo domani.

   (b) Viene domani.

5. Lui vive _____ piano.

   (a) al ventesimo

   (b) alla ventesima

6. Che giorno è oggi?

   (a) È il cinque gennaio.

   (b) È gennaio.

7. Quando sei nata, Maria?

   (a) Sono nato il sei gennaio.

   (b) Sono nata il sei gennaio.

Give the corresponding demonstrative showing nearness or farness, as necessary. For example, if you are given **questo ragazzo** (*this boy*), you would give **quel ragazzo** (*that boy*).

8. quei bambini _____

   questa ragazza _____

   quegli amici _____

   quest'amica _____

   queste ragazze _____

   quelle bambine _____

   questo studente _____

   questi zii _____

   quest'uomo _____

Vero o falso? Indicate whether each statement is true (**vero**) or false (**falso**).

9. _____ Il Natale si festeggia (*is celebrated*) il venticinque dicembre.

   _____ La Befana si festeggia il sei gennaio.

_____ Il Carnevale c'è prima di Pasqua.

_____ Il Ferragosto si festeggia il quindici agosto.

Personal Matters! Answer the question appropriately.

10. Quante lingue capisci?

_____ .

CHAPTER 9

Present Progressives and Possessives

Here's what you will learn in this chapter:

Present Progressive Tense
Using the Verbs Potere, Volere, *and* Dovere
Possessives
Talking About the Weather
Italian Cities

Present Progressive Tense

Maria, che cosa stai leggendo? Anche lui sta dormendo, vero? *Mary, what are you reading?* and *He is also sleeping, isn't he?* The verbs in these two sentences are in the present progressive tense. This is an alternative tense to the present indicative when speaking of an ongoing action.

The present progressive tense uses the verb **stare**, which you already know from Chapter 5, plus the gerund form of the verb showing the action. To form a gerund in Italian, simply drop the infinitive ending and add **-ando** to the stem of first-conjugation verbs and **-endo** to the stems of the other two conjugations.

-are Verbs		**-ere Verbs**		**-ire Verbs**	
parlare	*to speak*	mettere	*to put*	dormire	*to sleep*
parl**ando**	*speaking*	mett**endo**	*putting*	dorm**endo**	*sleeping*

Here is an example of each verb type conjugated in the present progressive tense:

guardare   *to watch*
(io) sto guardando   *I am watching*
(tu) stai guardando   *you (familiar) are watching*
(Lei) sta guardando   *you (polite) are watching*
(lui/lei) sta guardando   *he/she is watching*
(noi) stiamo guardando   *we are watching*
(voi) state guardando   *you (familiar plural) are watching*
(Loro) stanno guardando   *you (polite plural) are watching*
(loro) stanno guardando   *they are watching*

leggere   *to read*
(io) sto leggendo   *I am reading*
(tu) stai leggendo   *you (familiar) are reading*
(Lei) sta leggendo   *you (polite) are reading*
(lui/lei) sta leggendo   *he/she is reading*
(noi) stiamo leggendo   *we are reading*
(voi) state leggendo   *you (familiar plural) are reading*
(Loro) stanno leggendo   *you (polite plural) are reading*
(loro) stanno leggendo   *they are reading*

finire   *to finish*
(io) sto finendo   *I am finishing*
(tu) stai finendo   *you (familiar) are finishing*
(Lei) sta finendo   *you (polite) are finishing*

(lui/lei) sta finendo	*he/she is finishing*
(noi) stiamo finendo	*we are finishing*
(voi) state finendo	*you* (familiar plural) *are finishing*
(Loro) stanno finendo	*you* (polite plural) *are finishing*
(loro) stanno finendo	*they are finishing*

There are a few verbs that have irregular gerund forms. Of the verbs you have encountered in this book so far, only the following four have irregular forms. As always, there is no other way to learn these irregularities but to memorize them.

dire	*to say, tell*	dicendo	*saying, telling*
dare	*to give*	dando	*giving*
bere	*to drink*	bevendo	*drinking*
fare	*to do*	facendo	*doing*

Oral Practice

Practice saying the following sentences out loud.

Che cosa stai guardando in questo momento?	*What are you watching at this moment?*
Sto guardando la televisione.	*I am watching television.*
Che cosa sta leggendo lui?	*What is he reading?*
Sta leggendo un romanzo.	*He is reading a novel.*
Che cosa state finendo, Maria e Marco?	*What are you finishing, Mary and Mark?*
Stiamo finendo di mangiare.	*We are finishing eating.*
Che cosa stanno parlando loro due?	*What are the two of them speaking?*
Stanno parlando italiano.	*They are speaking Italian.*
Che cosa stai facendo, Marco?	*What are you doing, Mark?*
Sto studiando.	*I am studying.*
Che cosa stanno dicendo quei due?	*What are those two saying?*
Non stanno dicendo niente.	*They aren't saying anything.*
Che cosa sta bevendo, dottoressa Rossi?	*What are you drinking, Dr. Rossi?*
Sto bevendo un caffè.	*I am drinking a coffee.*

Written Practice 1

Fill in the blanks with the missing part of the progressive verb forms.

1. Che cosa stai _____ in questo momento? *What are you doing at this moment?*

   Sto _____. *I am eating.*

2. Che cosa _____ scrivendo lui? *What is he writing?*

   Lui _____ scrivendo una e-mail. *He is writing an e-mail.*

3. Che cosa state _____, Maria e Marco? *What are you doing, Mary and Mark?*

   Stiamo _____ la casa insieme. *We are cleaning the house together.*

4. Che cosa _____ facendo loro due? *What are the two of them doing?*

   _____ uscendo. *They are going out.*

5. Che cosa stai _____, Marco? *What are you doing, Mark?*

   _____ cominciando un romanzo. *I am beginning a novel.*

6. Che cosa stanno _____ quei due? *What are those two saying?*

   Non stanno _____ niente. *They aren't saying anything.*

7. Che cosa _____ bevendo il bambino? *What is the boy drinking?*

   _____ bevendo una bibita. *He is drinking a soft drink.*

Using the Verbs *Potere*, *Volere*, and *Dovere*

Puoi venire alla festa, Maria? Voglio venire, ma non posso. Devo studiare. *Can you come to the party, Mary? I want to come, but I cannot. I have to study.* These sentences are constructed with the verbs **potere** (*to be able to*), **volere** (*to want, to want to*), and **dovere** (*to have to*). Like other verbs you have learned in previous chapters, these verbs are irregular verbs. This means, of course, that you will have to memorize their conjugations. The following shows the present indicative conjugation of each of these verbs:

potere	*to be able to*
(io) posso	*I am able to (I can)*
(tu) puoi	*you are able to (you can)* (familiar)
(Lei) può	*you are able to (you can)* (polite)
(lui/lei) può	*he/she is able to (he/she can)*
(noi) possiamo	*we are able to (we can)*
(voi) potete	*you are able to (you can)* (familiar plural)
(Loro) possono	*you are able to (you can)* (polite plural)
(loro) possono	*they are able to (they can)*

volere	*to want to*
(io) voglio	*I want to*
(tu) vuoi	*you want to* (familiar)
(Lei) vuole	*you want to* (polite)
(lui/lei) vuole	*he/she wants to*
(noi) vogliamo	*we want to*
(voi) volete	*you want to* (familiar plural)
(Loro) vogliono	*you want to* (polite plural)
(loro) vogliono	*they want to*

dovere	*to have to*
(io) devo	*I have to*
(tu) devi	*you have to* (familiar)
(Lei) deve	*you have to* (polite)
(lui/lei) deve	*he/she has to*
(noi) dobbiamo	*we have to*
(voi) dovete	*you have to* (familiar plural)
(Loro) devono	*you have to* (polite plural)
(loro) devono	*they have to*

Oral Practice

Practice saying the following sentences out loud.

Marco, tu puoi venire alla festa?	*Mark, can you come to the party?*
No, non posso venire.	*No, I cannot come.*
Marco e Maria, potete uscire stasera?	*Mark and Mary, can you go out tonight?*

Sì, possiamo uscire.	*Yes, we can go out.*
Anche loro possono venire, vero?	*They can also come, right?*
Maria, che cosa vuoi?	*Mary, what do you want?*
Voglio un altro panino.	*I want another sandwich.*
Che cosa vuole fare la tua amica?	*What does your friend want to do?*
E voi due, che cosa volete?	*And what do the two of you want?*
Noi vogliamo mangiare gli spaghetti.	*We want to eat spaghetti.*
E loro che cosa vogliono?	*And what do they want?*
Maria, che cosa devi fare oggi?	*Mary, what do you have to do today?*
Oggi devo studiare.	*Today I have to study.*
E la tua amica che cosa deve fare?	*And what does your friend have to do?*
Marco e Maria, che cosa dovete fare?	*Mark and Mary, what do you have to do?*
Non dobbiamo fare niente.	*We do not have to do anything.*

Written Practice 2

Fill in the blanks with the appropriate forms of the suggested verbs.

1. Maria, tu _____ venire in centro? *Mary, can you come downtown?*

   Sì, oggi _____ venire. *Yes, today I can come.*

2. Tuo fratello non _____ uscire, vero? *Your brother cannot go out, right?*

   Non è vero, lui _____ uscire oggi. *It is not true, he can go out today.*

3. Franco e Bruno, _____ uscire oggi? *Frank and Bruno, can you go out today?*

   Sì, _____ uscire. *Yes, we can go out.*

4. E anche loro _____ uscire, vero? *They can also go out, right?*

   Sì, loro _____ uscire. *Yes, they can go out.*

5. Giovanni, che cosa _____? *John, what do you want?*

   _____ un piatto di ravioli. *I want a plate of ravioli.*

6. Che cosa _____ il professore? *What does the professor want?*

   Lui _____ un panino. *He wants a sandwich.*

7. E voi due che cosa _____? *And what do the two of you want?*

   Noi non _____ niente. *We do not want anything.*

8. E loro che cosa _____? *And what do they want?*

   Loro _____ gli gnocchi. *They want dumplings.*

9. Dove _____ andare oggi? *Where do you have to go today?*

   Oggi _____ andare in centro. *Today I have to go downtown.*

10. E la tua amica dove _____ andare? *And where does your friend have to go?*

    Anche lei _____ andare in centro. *She also has to go downtown.*

11. Marco e Maria, dove _____ andare? *Mark and Mary, where do you have to go?*

    _____ andare alla festa. *We have to go to the party.*

12. E loro dove _____ andare? *And where do they have to go?*

    _____ andare in centro. *They have to go downtown.*

Possessives

Dov'è il mio libro? *Where is my book?* You have been using **il mio** and **il tuo** from the moment you started using this book. So, you are already somewhat familiar with possessive adjectives.

Possessive adjectives, like descriptive adjectives, are variable and agree in number and gender with the noun or nouns they modify. The only invariable possessive adjective is **loro**. Unlike many descriptive adjectives, however, the possessive adjectives are always placed before the noun. In addition, the definite article always appears with the possessive adjective. Here are the forms of the possessives:

mio	*my*	
	Singular	**Plural**
masculine	il mio amico	i miei amici
	my (male) friend	*my (male) friends*
feminine	la mia amica	le mie amiche
	my (female) friend	*my (female) friends*

tuo	*your* (familiar singular)	
	Singular	**Plural**
masculine	il tuo orologio	i tuoi orologi
	your watch	*your watches*
feminine	la tua camicia	le tue camicie
	your shirt	*your shirts*

suo **Suo**	*his/her/its* *your* (polite singular)	
	Singular	**Plural**
masculine	il suo orologio	i suoi orologi
	his/her watch	*his/her watches*
feminine	la sua camicia	le sue camicie
	his/her shirt	*his/her shirts*
masculine	il Suo orologio	i Suoi orologi
	your watch	*your watches*
feminine	la Sua camicia	le Sue camicie
	your shirt	*your shirts*

nostro	*our*	
	Singular	**Plural**
masculine	il nostro amico	i nostri amici
	our friend	*our friends*
feminine	la nostra amica	le nostre amiche
	our friend	*our friends*

vostro	*your* (familiar plural)	
	Singular	**Plural**
masculine	il vostro orologio	i vostri orologi
	your watch	*your watches*
feminine	la vostra camicia	le vostre camicie
	your shirt	*your shirts*

loro **Loro**	*their* (invariable) *your* (polite plural) (invariable)	
	Singular	**Plural**
masculine	il loro amico	i loro amici
	their friend	*their friends*

feminine	la loro amica	le loro amiche
	their friend	*their friends*
masculine	il Loro amico	i Loro amici
	your friend	*your friends*
feminine	la Loro amica	le Loro amiche
	your friend	*your friends*

Oral Practice

Practice saying the following sentences out loud.

È il tuo orologio, Maria?	*Is it your watch, Mary?*
Sì, è il mio orologio.	*Yes, it is my watch.*
È la tua bibita, Sandra?	*Is it your drink, Sandra?*
No, non è la mia bibita.	*No, it is not my drink.*
Esci con i tuoi amici stasera, Dino?	*Are you going out with your friends tonight, Dino?*
Sì, esco con i miei amici.	*Yes, I am going out with my friends.*
Posso avere le tue chiavi?	*Can I have your keys?*
Va bene, ecco le mie chiavi.	*Okay, here are my keys.*
Signora Marchi, dov'è la Sua borsa?	*Mrs. Marchi, where is your purse?*
Signor Marchi, dove sono i Suoi figli?	*Mr. Marchi, where are your children?*
Maria sta cercando il suo portatile.	*Mary is looking for her laptop.*
Anche Marco sta cercando il suo portatile.	*Mark is also looking for his laptop.*
Maria sta cercando la sua giacca.	*Mary is looking for her jacket.*
Anche Mario sta cercando la sua giacca.	*Mario is also looking for his jacket.*
Maria cerca i suoi stivali.	*Mary is looking for her boots.*
Anche Mario cerca i suoi stivali.	*Mario is also looking for his boots.*
Maria cerca le sue scarpe.	*Mary is looking for her shoes.*
Anche Mario cerca le sue scarpe.	*Mario is also looking for his shoes.*
Lui è il vostro amico?	*Is he your friend?*

Sì, lui è il nostro amico.	*Yes, he is our friend.*
E lei è pure la vostra amica?	*And is she your friend as well?*
Sì, lei è pure la nostra amica.	*Yes, she is our friend as well.*
Loro sono i vostri genitori?	*Are they your parents?*
Sì, loro sono i nostri genitori.	*Yes, they are our parents.*
Quelle sono le vostre scarpe?	*Are those your shoes?*
Sì, sono le nostre scarpe.	*Yes, they are our shoes.*
Marco è il loro amico?	*Is Marco their friend?*
Chi sono i loro genitori?	*Who are their parents?*
Dove sono le loro scarpe?	*Where are their shoes?*
Ecco le loro scarpe.	*Here are their shoes.*

Written Practice 3

Fill in the blanks with the missing possessive adjectives.

1. È _____ computer, Maria? *Is it your computer, Mary?*

   Sì, è _____ computer. *Yes, it is my computer.*

2. È _____ borsa, Sandra? *Is it your purse, Sandra?*

   No, non è _____ borsa. *No, it is not my purse.*

3. Esci con _____ genitori stasera, Dino? *Are you going out with your parents tonight, Dino?*

   Sì, esco con _____ genitori. *Yes, I am going out with my parents.*

4. Posso avere _____ scarpe? *Can I have your* (familiar) *shoes?*

   Va bene, ecco _____ scarpe. *Okay, here are my shoes.*

5. Signora Marchi, dov'è _____ penna? *Mrs. Marchi, where is your pen?*

   Ecco _____ penna. *Here is my pen.*

6. Signor Marchi, dove sono _____ stivali? *Mr. Marchi, where are your boots?*

   _____ stivali sono qui. *My boots are here.*

7. Maria sta cercando _____ cane. *Mary is looking for her dog.*

   Anche Marco sta cercando _____ cane. *Mark is also looking for his dog.*

8. Maria sta cercando _____ chiave. *Mary is looking for her key.*

   Anche Mario sta cercando _____ chiave. *Mario is also looking for his key.*

9. Maria cerca _____ libri. *Mary is looking for her books.*

   Anche Mario cerca _____ libri. *Mario is also looking for his books.*

10. Maria cerca _____ matite. *Mary is looking for her pencils.*

    Anche Mario cerca _____ matite. *Mario is also looking for his pencils.*

11. Lui è _____ professore? *Is he your (familiar plural) professor?*

    Sì, lui è _____ professore. *Yes, he is our professor.*

12. E lei è pure _____ professoressa? *And is she your (familiar plural) professor as well?*

    Sì, lei è pure _____ professoressa. *Yes, she is our professor as well.*

13. Loro sono _____ genitori? *Are they your (familiar plural) parents?*

    Sì, loro sono _____ genitori. *Yes, they are our parents.*

14. Quelle sono _____ scarpe? *Are those your (familiar plural) shoes?*

    Sì, sono _____ scarpe. *Yes, they are our shoes.*

15. Lui è _____ amico? *Is he their friend?*

    No, lei è _____ amica. *No, she is their friend.*

16. Chi sono _____ genitori? *Who are their parents?*

    Il signor e la signora Dini sono _____ genitori. *Mr. and Mrs. Dini are their parents.*

17. Dove sono _____ amiche? *Where are their friends?*

    Ecco _____ amiche. *Here are their friends.*

USING ARTICLES WITH KINSHIP NOUNS

The definite article is dropped from all forms except **loro** when the noun is a singular, unmodified kinship noun (**padre**, **madre**, etc.).

Singular Kinship Noun		**Plural Kinship Noun**	
tuo cugino	*your (male) cousin*	i tuoi cugini	*your cousins*
mia sorella	*my sister*	le mie sorelle	*my sisters*
nostro fratello	*our brother*	i nostri fratelli	*our brothers*

Singular Kinship Noun		**Modified Kinship Noun**	
tuo cugino	*your (male) cousin*	il tuo cugino americano	*your (male) American cousin*
nostra cugina	*our (female) cousin*	la nostra cugina italiana	*our (female) Italian cousin*

The preceding rule is optional with the following kinship nouns (when singular and unmodified):

nonno	*grandfather*	mamma	*mom*
nonna	*grandmother*	papà	*dad*
mia mamma	*my mom*	*or*	la mia mamma	*my mom*
tuo papà	*your dad*	*or*	il tuo papà	*your dad*
mio nonno	*my grandfather*	*or*	il mio nonno	*my grandfather*
mia nonna	*my grandmother*	*or*	la mia nonna	*my grandmother*

Remember, that the article is always retained with **loro**.

il loro figlio	*their son*
la loro figlia	*their daughter*
il loro fratello	*their brother*

Oral Practice

Practice saying the following sentences out loud.

Chi è quella donna?	*Who is that woman?*
È mia zia.	*She is my aunt.*
Chi è quella donna?	*Who is that woman?*
È la mia zia italiana.	*She is my Italian aunt.*

Chi è quell'uomo?	*Who is that man?*
È nostro cugino.	*He is our cousin.*
Chi sono quegli uomini?	*Who are those men?*
Sono i nostri cugini.	*They are our cousins.*
Chi è quella ragazza?	*Who is that girl?*
È sua cugina.	*She is his/her cousin.*
Chi è quella ragazza?	*Who is that girl?*
È la sua cugina americana.	*She is his/her American cousin.*
Chi è quel ragazzo?	*Who is that boy?*
È il loro figlio.	*He is their son.*
Chi è quell'uomo?	*Who is that man?*
È mio nonno./È il mio nonno.	*He is my grandfather.*

Written Practice 4

Fill in the blanks with the missing possessives, with or without the articles as necessary.

1. Chi è quella donna? *Who is that woman?*

   È _____ nonna. *She is my grandmother.*

2. Chi è quella donna? *Who is that woman?*

   È _____ mamma. *She is my mom.*

3. Chi è quell'uomo? *Who is that man?*

   È _____ papà. *He is our dad.*

4. Chi sono quegli uomini? *Who are those men?*

   Sono _____ zii. *They are our uncles.*

5. Chi è quella ragazza? *Who is that girl?*

   È _____ cugina. *She is his/her cousin.*

6. Chi è quella ragazza? *Who is that girl?*

   È _____ cugina americana. *She is our American cousin.*

7. Chi è quel ragazzo? *Who is that boy?*

   È _____ fratello. *He is their brother.*

USE OF THE POSSESSIVE ADJECTIVE *SUO*

Both *his* and *her* are expressed, as you've seen, by the same possessive adjective **suo**. **Suo** agrees in number and gender with the noun being modified—not with whether its meaning in a sentence is *his* or *hers*. This can be confusing so take careful note of the following examples:

His		**Her**	
il suo libro	*his book*	il suo libro	*her book*
i suoi libri	*his books*	i suoi libri	*her books*
la sua penna	*his pen*	la sua penna	*her pen*
le sue penne	*his pens*	le sue penne	*her pens*

Again, it's important to remember that **suo** agrees with the noun being modified.

Oral Practice

Practice saying the following sentences out loud.

È il cellulare di Marco?	*Is it Mark's cell phone?*
Sì, è il suo cellulare.	*Yes, it is his cell phone.*
È il cellulare di Maria?	*Is it Mary's cell phone?*
Sì, è il suo cellulare.	*Yes, it is her cell phone.*
Sono gli stivali di tuo fratello?	*Are they your brother's boots?*
Sì, sono i suoi stivali.	*Yes, they are his boots.*
Sono gli stivali di tua sorella?	*Are they your sister's boots?*
Sì, sono i suoi stivali.	*Yes, they are her boots.*
Sono le scarpe di tua madre?	*Are they your mother's shoes?*
Sì, sono le sue scarpe.	*Yes, they are her shoes.*
Sono le scarpe di tuo padre?	*Are they your father's shoes?*
Sì, sono le sue scarpe.	*Yes, they are his shoes.*

Written Practice 5

Fill in the blanks with the correct form of the possessive adjective **suo**.

1. È il cellulare di tuo cugino? *Is it your cousin's cell phone?*

   Sì, è _____ cellulare. *Yes, it is his cell phone.*

2. È il cellulare di tua nonna? *Is it your grandmother's cell phone?*

   Sì, è _____ cellulare. *Yes, it is her cell phone.*

3. Sono gli stivali del professore? *Are they the professor's boots?*

   Sì, sono _____ stivali. *Yes, they are his boots.*

4. Sono gli stivali della signora Verdi? *Are they Mrs. Verdi's boots?*

   Sì, sono _____ stivali. *Yes, they are her boots.*

5. Sono le scarpe di tua zia? *Are they your aunt's shoes?*

   Sì, sono _____ scarpe. *Yes, they are her shoes.*

6. Sono le scarpe di tuo zio? *Are they your uncle's shoes?*

   Sì, sono _____ scarpe. *Yes, they are his shoes.*

Talking About the Weather

Che tempo fa oggi? *How is the weather today?* Notice that this expression uses the word **tempo**, which means both *time* and *weather*, and the verb **fare**, which you have encountered already.

When talking about the weather in Italian, the following words and expressions are often used.

le stagioni	*the seasons*	l'inverno	*winter*
la primavera	*spring*	il tempo	*the weather*
l'estate	*summer*	nevicare	*to snow*
l'autunno	*fall*	piovere	*to rain*

Here are some example sentences:

Che tempo fa?	*How is the weather?*
Fa bel tempo!	*It is nice/beautiful weather!*

Fa brutto tempo!	*The weather is awful!*
Fa freddo!	*It is cold!*
Fa caldo!	*It is hot/warm!*
Tira vento!	*It is windy!*

Oral Practice

Practice saying the following sentences out loud.

Che tempo fa oggi?	*How is the weather today?*
Fa bel tempo!	*It is beautiful!*
Che tempo fa domani?	*How is the weather going to be tomorrow?*
Domani fa brutto tempo!	*Tomorrow, it is going to be awful!*
Che tempo fa di solito in inverno?	*What is the weather usually like in the winter?*
Fa freddo e nevica molto!	*It is cold and it snows a lot!*
Che tempo fa di solito in estate?	*What is the weather usually like in the summer?*
Fa caldo!	*It is hot!*
Che tempo fa di solito in primavera?	*What is the weather usually like in the spring?*
Fa caldo, ma tira vento!	*It is warm, but it is windy!*
Che tempo fa di solito in autunno?	*What is the weather usually like in the fall?*
Fa bel tempo!	*It is nice!*

Written Practice 6

Answer each question using the English translations as a guide.

1. Che tempo fa oggi? *How is the weather today?*

_____ ! *It is awful!*

2. Che tempo fa domani? *How is the weather going to be tomorrow?*

_____! *Tomorrow, it is going to be beautiful!*

3. Che tempo fa di solito in inverno? *What is the weather usually like in the winter?*

_____! *It snows a lot!*

4. Che tempo fa di solito in estate? *What is the weather usually like in the summer?*

_____! *It is hot!*

5. Che tempo fa di solito in primavera? *What is the weather usually like in the spring?*

_____! *It is windy and it rains!*

6. Che tempo fa di solito in autunno? *What is the weather usually like in the fall?*

_____! *It is cold and often it snows!*

Italian Cities

Italy has a rich history. Italian cities (**le città italiane**) were originally run as city-states—little nations, each with its own government (**il governo**) and often ruled by a king (**un re**), a nobleman, or a small group of powerful citizens. In some cases political life was controlled by city dwellers, and in other cases by people of both the countryside and the city.

Some well-known Italian cities are:

Ancona	*Ancona*	Napoli	*Naples*
Bari	*Bari*	Perugia	*Perugia*
Bologna	*Bologna*	Potenza	*Potenza*
Cagliari	*Cagliari*	Roma	*Rome*
Catanzaro	*Catanzaro*	Siena	*Siena*
Firenze	*Florence*	Siracusa	*Syracuse*
Genova	*Genoa*	Torino	*Turin*
L'Aquila	*Aquila*	Trieste	*Trieste*
Milano	*Milan*	Venezia	*Venice*

QUIZ

Provide the missing form of each verb in either the present indicative or the present progressive.

1. **Present Indicative**   **Present Progressive**

   _____   io sto cominciando

   tu metti   _____

   _____   lui sta dormendo

   noi facciamo   _____

   _____   lei sta dando

   voi bevete   _____

   _____   loro stanno dicendo

Supply the corresponding present indicative forms of the indicated verbs.

2. potere   3. volere   4. dovere

   _____   _____   io devo

   tu puoi   _____   _____

   _____   lui vuole   _____

   _____   _____   lei deve

   noi possiamo   _____   _____

   _____   voi volete   _____

   _____   _____   loro devono

Fill in each blank with the corresponding singular or plural form of the possessive, as necessary.

5. Singular   6. Plural

   il mio orologio   _____

   _____   le nostre amiche

   la mia camicia   _____

   _____   i nostri libri

il tuo cane

_____

_____

le vostre amiche

la tua automobile

_____

_____

i vostri amici

il suo gatto

_____

_____

le sue amiche

il loro amico

_____

_____

le loro case

Fill in each blank with the appropriate form of the definite article, when necessary.

7. Lui è _____ mio fratello.

Lei è _____ nostra sorella.

Quel ragazzo è _____ loro figlio.

Lei è _____ sua figlia.

Signora Marchi, come si chiama _____ Sua figlia?

Signora e signor Marchi, come si chiama _____ Loro figlio?

Lui è _____ mio amico.

Anche lei è _____ mia amica.

Fill in each blank with the appropriate form of **suo**, **Suo**, **loro**, or **Loro**.

8. Questo è il libro di mia sorella. È _____ libro. *This is her book.*

Questo è il libro di mio fratello. È _____ libro. *This is his book.*

Queste sono le riviste di mia madre. Sono _____ riviste. *These are her magazines.*

Queste sono le riviste di mio padre. Sono _____ riviste. *These are his magazines.*

Signora Verdi, come si chiama _____ figlia? *Mrs. Verdi, what is your daughter's name?*

Signor Verdi, come si chiama _____ figlia? *Mr. Verdi, what is your daughter's name?*

Signora e signor Verdi, come si chiama _____ figlia? *Mrs. and Mr. Verdi, what is your daughter's name?*

Personal Matters! Answer each question appropriately.

9. Dove vuoi andare in Italia?

    _____.

10. Che tempo fa oggi?

    _____.

CHAPTER 10

Giving Commands

Here's what you will learn in this chapter:

Imperative Tense
Negative Imperative
Using the Verbs Sapere *and* Conoscere
Partitives
Talking About Addresses

Imperative Tense

Marco, mangia la pesca! Signor Verdi, legga il giornale! *Mark, eat the peach!* and *Mr. Verdi, read the newspaper!* The verb in both of these sentences is in the imperative—a tense that allows you to give commands, advice, orders, instructions, and so on. The imperative in Italian is formed by dropping the infinitive ending of the verb, and then adding the imperative endings according to the verb type.

IMPERATIVE WITH FIRST-CONJUGATION VERBS (-ARE)

For **-are** verbs, the imperative endings are as follows. Notice that there is no first-person singular form used in the imperative tense.

aspettare	*to wait* (**for**)
(tu) aspet**ta**	*wait* (familiar)
(Lei) aspet**ti**	*wait* (polite)
(noi) aspett**iamo**	*let's wait*
(voi) aspett**ate**	*wait* (familiar plural)
(Loro) aspett**ino**	*wait* (polite plural)

In order to maintain the hard **c** and **g** sounds of verbs ending in **-care** and **-gare**, an **h** must be added to the **-i**, -**iamo**, and **-ino** endings.

cercare	*to search for*
(tu) cerca	*search* (familiar)
(Lei) cer**chi**	*search* (polite)
(noi) cer**chiamo**	*let's search*
(voi) cercate	*search* (familiar plural)
(Loro) cer**chino**	*search* (polite plural)

pagare	*to pay*
(tu) paga	*pay* (familiar)
(Lei) pa**ghi**	*pay* (polite)
(noi) pa**ghiamo**	*let's pay*
(voi) pagate	*pay* (familiar plural)
(Loro) pa**ghino**	*pay* (polite plural)

And for verbs ending in **-ciare** and **-giare**, the **-i-** is dropped so it is not repeated before the **-i**, **-iamo**, and **-ino** endings.

cominciare	*to begin*
(tu) comincia	*begin* (familiar)
(Lei) comin**ci**	*begin* (polite)
(noi) comin**ciamo**	*let's begin*
(voi) cominciate	*begin* (familiar plural)
(Loro) comin**cino**	*begin* (polite plural)

mangiare	*to eat*
(tu) mangia	*eat* (familiar)
(Lei) man**gi**	*eat* (polite)
(noi) man**giamo**	*let's eat*
(voi) mangiate	*eat* (familiar plural)
(Loro) man**gino**	*eat* (polite plural)

Oral Practice

Practice saying the following sentences out loud.

Marco, aspetta qui!	*Mark, wait here.*
Signora Verdi, aspetti qui, per favore!	*Mrs. Verdi, wait here, please.*
Aspettiamo qui, va bene?	*Let's wait here, okay?*
Marco e Maria, aspettate qui!	*Mark and Mary, wait here.*
Signori, aspettino qui, per favore!	*Gentlemen, wait here, please.*
Claudia, mangia questa pesca!	*Claudia, eat this peach.*
Signora Dini, mangi questa mela!	*Mrs. Dini, eat this apple.*
Mangiamo quelle pesche!	*Let's eat those peaches.*
Pina e Bruno, cominciate a lavorare!	*Pina and Bruno, start working.*
Signori, comincino, per favore!	*Gentlemen, begin, please.*
Maria, cerca la mia penna!	*Mary, look for my pen.*
Signora Dini, cerchi la Sua borsa!	*Mrs. Dini, look for your purse.*
Paghiamo il conto!	*Let's pay the bill.*
Bruna e Paolo, pagate il conto!	*Bruna and Paul, pay the bill.*
Signori, paghino il conto, per favore!	*Gentlemen, pay the bill, please.*

NOTE: *To indicate that the verb is in the imperative, it is better to end the sentence with an exclamation point.*

Written Practice 1

Fill in the blanks with the missing imperative form of the indicated verb.

1. Marco, _____ italiano! *Mark, speak Italian.*

   Signora Verdi, _____ italiano, per favore! *Mrs. Verdi, speak Italian, please.*

   _____ italiano, va bene? *Let's speak Italian, okay?*

2. Marco e Maria, _____ Paolo! *Mark and Mary, call Paul.*

   Signore, _____ stasera, per favore! *Ladies, call tonight, please.*

3. Gino, _____ questa mela! *Gino, eat this apple.*

   Signora Dini, _____ queste pesche! *Mrs. Dini, eat these peaches.*

   _____ quelle mele! *Let's eat those apples.*

4. Ragazzi, _____ il conto! *Guys, pay the bill.*

   Signori, _____ il conto, per favore! *Gentlemen, pay the bill, please.*

IMPERATIVE WITH SECOND-CONJUGATION VERBS (-*ERE*)

Verbs that end in **-ere** take the following endings in the imperative:

chiudere	*to close*
(tu) chiud**i**	*close* (familiar)
(Lei) chiud**a**	*close* (polite)
(noi) chiud**iamo**	*let's close*
(voi) chiud**ete**	*close* (familiar plural)
(Loro) chiud**ano**	*close* (polite plural)

IMPERATIVE WITH THIRD-CONJUGATION VERBS (-*IRE*)

The **-ire** verbs take the following endings in the imperative:

aprire   *to open*
(tu) apr**i**   *open* (familiar)
(Lei) apr**a**   *open* (polite)
(noi) apr**iamo**   *let's open*
(voi) apr**ite**   *open* (familiar plural)
(Loro) apr**ano**   *open* (polite plural)

   Remember, however, that some third-conjugation verbs require an **-isc** in their present tense conjugations. Those verbs will also require **-isc** when in the imperative, except before **-iamo** and **-ite**.

finire   *to finish*
(tu) fin**isci**   *finish* (familiar)
(Lei) fin**isca**   *finish* (polite)
(noi) finiamo   *let's finish*
(voi) finite   *finish* (familiar plural)
(Loro) fin**iscano**   *finish* (polite plural)

Oral Practice

Practice saying the following sentences out loud.

Giovanni, chiudi la porta, va bene?	*Mark, close the door, okay?*
Signor Dini, chiuda la porta, per favore!	*Mr. Dini, close the door, please.*
Chiudiamo la finestra, va bene?	*Let's close the window, okay?*
Marco e Maria, chiudete la finestra!	*Mark and Mary, close the window.*
Signori, chiudano la porta, per favore!	*Gentlemen, close the door, please.*
Marco, apri la porta, va bene?	*Mark, open the door, okay?*
Signor Dini, apra la porta, per favore!	*Mr. Dini, open the door, please.*
Apriamo la finestra, va bene?	*Let's open the window, okay?*
Marco e Maria, aprite la finestra!	*Mark and Mary, open the window.*
Signori, aprano la porta, per favore!	*Gentlemen, open the door, please.*

Written Practice 2

Fill in the blanks with the missing imperative form of the indicated verb.

1. Giovanni, _____ quel romanzo! *John, read that novel.*

   Signor Dini, _____ il giornale! *Mr. Dini, read the newspaper.*

   _____ il giornale! *Let's read the newspaper.*

2. Marco e Maria, _____ la scatola qui! *Mark and Mary, put the box here.*

   Signori, _____ la scatola qui! *Gentlemen, put the box here.*

3. Maria, _____ la porta, va bene? *Mary, open the door, okay?*

   Signor Dini, _____ la finestra, per favore! *Mr. Dini, open the window, please.*

   _____ la finestra, va bene? *Let's open the window, okay?*

4. Marco e Maria, _____ pure! *Mark and Mary, go ahead and sleep.*

   Signori, _____ pure! *Gentlemen, go ahead and sleep.*

5. Giovanni, _____ la pasta, va bene? *John, finish the pastry, okay?*

   Signora Verdi, _____ il caffè, per favore! *Mrs. Dini, finish the coffee, please.*

   _____ gli spaghetti, va bene? *Let's finish the spaghetti, okay?*

6. Marco e Maria, _____ la casa! *Mark and Mary, clean the house.*

   Signori, _____ la casa, per favore! *Gentlemen, clean the house, please.*

IMPERATIVE WITH IRREGULAR VERBS

Remember that some Italian verbs have irregular forms in the present indicative. These verbs will also be irregular in the imperative and, therefore, their imperative conjugations must be memorized. Of the verbs you have encountered so far, the following have irregular imperative forms:

andare   *to go*
(tu) va', (Lei) vada, (noi) andiamo, (voi) andate, (Loro) vadano

avere   *to have*
(tu) abbi, (Lei) abbia, (noi) abbiamo, (voi) abbiate, (Loro) abbiano

bere   *to drink*
(tu) bevi, (Lei) beva, (noi) beviamo, (voi) bevete, (Loro) bevano

dare   *to give*
(tu) da', (Lei) dia, (noi) diamo, (voi) date, (Loro) diano

dire   *to say, tell*
(tu) di', (Lei) dica, (noi) diciamo, (voi) dite, (Loro) dicano

essere   *to be*
(tu) sii, (Lei) sia, (noi) siamo, (voi) siate, (Loro) siano

fare   *to do, make*
(tu) fa', (Lei) faccia, (noi) facciamo, (voi) fate, (Loro) facciano

stare   *to stay*
(tu) sta', (Lei) stia, (noi) stiamo, (voi) state, (Loro) stiano

uscire   *to go out*
(tu) esci, (Lei) esca, (noi) usciamo, (voi) uscite, (Loro) escano

venire   *to come*
(tu) vieni, (Lei) venga, (noi) veniamo, (voi) venite, (Loro) vengano

Oral Practice

Practice saying the following sentences out loud.

Marco, va' con loro!	*Mark, go with them.*
Signora Dini, abbia pazienza!	*Mrs. Dini, have patience.*

Beviamo il caffè!	*Let's drink the coffee.*
Ragazzi, date la mela al professore!	*Guys, give the apple to the professor.*
Signori, dicano la verità!	*Gentlemen, tell the truth.*
Maria, sii brava!	*Mary, be good.*
Signor Dini, faccia questo!	*Mr. Dini, do this.*
Stiamo zitti!	*Let's be quiet.*
Marco e Maria, uscite con noi!	*Mark and Mary, go out with us.*
Signori, vengano alla festa!	*Gentlemen, come to the party.*

Written Practice 3

Fill in the blanks with the missing imperative form of the indicated verb. Don't forget to make the distinctions between familiar and polite forms!

1. Signora Verdi, _____ con loro. *Mrs. Verdi, go with them.*

   Signori, _____ con loro. *Gentlemen, go with them.*

2. Maria, _____ pazienza! *Mary, have patience.*

   Ragazzi, _____ pazienza! *Boys, have patience.*

3. Signor Verdi, _____ il caffè! *Mr. Verdi, drink the coffee.*

   Anche voi, _____ il caffè! *You, too, drink the coffee.*

4. Maria, _____ la mela al professore! *Mary, give the apple to the professor.*

   Signora, _____ la mela a noi! *Madam, give us the apple.*

5. Marco e Maria, _____ la verità! *Mark and Mary, tell the truth.*

   Signori, _____ la verità! *Gentlemen, tell the truth.*

6. Dino, _____ bravo! *Dino, be good.*

   Studenti, _____ bravi! *Students, be good.*

7. Signora, _____ questo! *Madam, do this.*

   Maria, _____ questo! *Mary, do this.*

8. Marco, _____ zitto! *Mark, be quiet.*

   Studenti, _____ zitti! *Students, be quiet.*

9. Maria, _____ con noi! *Mary, go out with us.*

   Professore, _____ con noi! *Professor, go out with us.*

10. Maria, _____ alla festa! *Mary, come to the party.*

    Dottoressa, _____ alla festa! *Doctor, come to the party.*

Negative Imperative

To form the negative imperative, add **non** before the verb in the sentence. However, you must also change the second-person singular verb forms to infinitives in the negative imperative. For example:

Affirmative		**Negative**	
(tu) Aspetta!	*Wait!*	Non aspettare!	*Do not wait!*
(tu) Scrivi!	*Write!*	Non scrivere!	*Do not write!*
(tu) Finisci!	*Finish!*	Non finire!	*Do not finish!*
(tu) Va'	*Go!*	Non andare!	*Do not go!*
(tu) Vieni!	*Come!*	Non venire!	*Do not come!*

But:

(Lei) Aspetti!	*Wait!* (polite singular)	Non aspetti!	*Do not wait!*
(noi) Scriviamo!	*Let's write!*	Non scriviamo!	*Let's not write!*
(voi) Finite!	*Finish!* (familiar plural)	Non finite!	*Do not finish!*
(Loro) Aspettino!	*Wait!* (polite plural)	Non aspettino!	*Do not wait!*

Oral Practice

Practice saying the following sentences out loud.

Marco, mangia la mela!	*Mark, eat the apple.*
No, Marco, non mangiare la mela!	*No, Mark, do not eat the apple.*
Signora, mangi la pesca!	*Madam, eat the peach.*
No, signora, non mangi la pesca!	*No, madam, do not eat the peach.*
Maria, leggi il giornale!	*Mary, read the newspaper.*

No, Maria, non leggere il giornale!   *No, Mary, do not read the newspaper.*

Andiamo in Italia!   *Let's go to Italy.*

No, non andiamo in Italia!   *No, let's not go to Italy.*

Written Practice 4

Fill in the blanks with the appropriate imperative forms of the indicated verbs.

1. Maria, non _____ quelle pesche! *Mary, do not eat those peaches.*

   Signora, non _____ quelle pesche! *Madam, do not eat those peaches.*

2. Marco, non _____ con loro! *Mark, do not go out with them.*

   Professore, non _____ con loro! *Professor, do not go out with them.*

3. Dina, non _____ delle spese! *Dina, do not do any shopping.*

   Signora, non _____ delle spese! *Madam, do not do any shopping.*

4. Ragazzi, non _____ la casa! *Guys, do not clean the house.*

   Signori, non _____ la casa! *Gentlemen, do not clean the house.*

Using the Verbs *Sapere* and *Conoscere*

Marco, sai parlare francese? Maria, conosci Franca? *Mark, do you know how to speak French?* and *Mary, do you know Franca?* The verbs **sapere** and **conoscere**, as you can see, both mean *to know*, but they are used in different ways. Before learning about these differences, note that **conoscere** is a regular second-conjugation verb, but **sapere** is irregular. The following shows **sapere** in its present indicative conjugation:

sapere	*to know*
(io) so	*I know*
(tu) sai	*you know* (familiar)
(Lei) sa	*you know* (polite)
(lui/lei) sa	*he/she knows*
(noi) sappiamo	*we know*
(voi) sapete	*you know* (familiar plural)
(Loro) sanno	*you know* (polite plural)
(loro) sanno	*they know*

Here are the different uses for **conoscere** and **sapere**:

- To express the idea of *knowing someone*, the verb **conoscere** must be used.

  Maria non conosce quell'avvocato.   *Mary does not know that lawyer.*

  Chi conosce la dottoressa Verdi?   *Who knows Dr. Verdi?*

- To express the idea of *being familiar with something*, again, use the verb **conoscere**.

  Conosci Roma?   *Are you familiar with Rome?*

  Conosco un bel ristorante qui vicino.   *I know a good restaurant nearby.*

- However, *to know how to do something* is expressed by using the verb **sapere**.

  Mia sorella sa parlare italiano.   *My sister knows how to speak Italian.*

  Sai cantare?   *Do you know how to sing?*

- *To know something/know a fact* is also expressed by using **sapere**.

  Marco non sa la verità.   *Mark does not know the truth.*

  Chi sa come si chiama quella donna?   *Who knows what that woman's name is?*

Oral Practice

Practice saying the following sentences out loud.

Chi conosce quell'avvocato?	*Who knows that lawyer?*
Maria conosce quell'avvocato.	*Mary knows that lawyer.*
Chi conosce la dottoressa Verdi?	*Who knows Dr. Verdi?*

Tutti conoscono la dottoressa Verdi.	*Everyone knows Dr. Verdi.*
Marco, tu conosci Roma?	*Mark, are you familiar with Rome?*
No, non conosco Roma.	*No, I do not know Rome.*
Ragazzi, conoscete un bel ristorante?	*Guys, do you know a nice restaurant?*
Sì, conosciamo un bel ristorante qui vicino.	*Yes, we know a good restaurant nearby.*
Chi sa parlare italiano bene?	*Who knows how to speak Italian well?*
Mia sorella sa parlare italiano bene.	*My sister knows how to speak Italian well.*
Dina, sai cantare?	*Dina, do you know how to sing?*
No, non so cantare.	*No, I do not know how to sing.*
Ragazzi, sapete la verità?	*Guys, do you know the truth?*
Sì, sappiamo la verità!	*Yes, we know the truth!*
Loro sanno come mi chiamo?	*Do they know my name?*
Sì, loro sanno come ti chiami.	*Yes, they know your name.*

Written Practice 5

Fill in the blanks with either **conoscere** or **sapere** in their appropriate forms, as necessary.

1. Voi _____ come mi chiamo? *Do you know my name?*

   Sì, noi _____ come ti chiami. *Yes, we know your name.*

2. Signora Dini, Lei _____ Roma? *Mrs. Dini, are you familiar with Rome?*

   No, non _____ Roma. *No, I do not know Rome.*

3. Chi _____ parlare francese bene? *Who knows how to speak French well?*

   Mio fratello _____ parlare francese bene. *My brother knows how to speak French well.*

4. Alessandro, _____ cantare? *Alexander, do you know how to sing?*

   No, non _____ cantare. *No, I do not know how to sing.*

5. Ragazzi, _____ la verità? *Guys, do you know the truth?*

Sì, _____ la verità! *Yes, we know the truth!*

6. Chi _____ quell'uomo? *Who knows that man?*

Maria _____ quell'uomo. *Mary knows that man.*

7. Chi _____ il professore d'italiano? *Who knows the Italian professor?*

Tutti _____ il professore d'italiano. *Everyone knows the Italian professor.*

8. Marco, tu _____ Venezia? *Mark, are you familiar with Venice?*

No, non _____ Venezia. *No, I do not know Venice.*

Partitives

Voglio dell'acqua e degli spaghetti. *I want some water and some spaghetti.* Did you notice the contraction of **di** + the article in this sentence, which translates as *some*? Using di + the definite article is called the partitive. Partitives are structures used to indicate a part of something as distinct from its whole.

dell'acqua	*some water*
degli spaghetti	*some spaghetti*

Before count nouns (nouns that have a plural form and use the indefinite article in their singular forms), the partitive can be considered to function as the plural of the indefinite article.

Singular		**Plural**	
uno sbaglio	*a mistake*	degli sbagli	*some mistakes*
un albero	*a tree*	degli alberi	*some trees*
un bicchiere	*a (drinking) glass*	dei bicchieri	*some glasses*
un coltello	*a knife*	dei coltelli	*some knives*
una forchetta	*a fork*	delle forchette	*some forks*
una sedia	*a chair*	delle sedie	*some chairs*
un'automobile	*an automobile*	delle automobili	*some automobiles*

With mass nouns (nouns that do not, normally, have a plural form), the partitive is rendered by using either **di** + the singular forms of the definite article, or by the expression **un po' di** (*a bit of*).

del vino	*some wine*	un po' di vino	*some wine, a little wine*
dello zucchero	*some sugar*	un po' di zucchero	*some sugar, a little sugar*
dell'orzo	*some barley*	un po' d'orzo	*some barley, a little barley*
della pasta	*some pasta*	un po' di pasta	*some pasta, a little pasta*
dell'acqua	*some water*	un po' d'acqua	*some water, a little water*

Oral Practice

Practice saying the following sentences out loud.

Che cosa vuoi, Maria, un po' d'orzo?	*What do you want Mary, a little barley?*
Sì, voglio dell'orzo.	*Yes, I want some barley.*
Che cosa fanno spesso gli studenti?	*What do the students often do?*
Fanno degli sbagli.	*They make some mistakes.*
Che cosa c'è davanti alla tua casa?	*What is there in front of your house?*
Ci sono degli alberi.	*There are some trees.*
Signora, vuole dello zucchero?	*Madam, would you like some sugar?*
Sì, voglio un po' di zucchero.	*Yes, I want a bit of sugar.*
Di che cosa hai bisogno?	*What do you need?*
Ho bisogno dei bicchieri.	*I need some glasses.*
Che cosa sono?	*What are they?*
Sono delle automobili nuove.	*They are some new automobiles.*
Vuoi un po' di vino?	*Would you like a little wine?*
Sì, voglio del vino.	*Yes, I would like some wine.*
Di che cosa altro hai bisogno?	*What else do you need?*
Ho bisogno dei coltelli e delle forchette.	*I need some knives and forks.*
Che cosa vuoi mangiare, Maria?	*What do you want to eat, Mary?*
Voglio mangiare della pasta.	*I would like to eat some pasta.*

Vuoi dell'acqua?   *Would you like some water?*

Sì, voglio un po' d'acqua.   *Yes, I would like a bit of water.*

Written Practice 6

Fill in the blanks with the missing partitives.

1. Che cosa vuoi, _____ zucchero? *What do you want, a little sugar?*

   Sì, voglio _____ zucchero. *Yes, I want some sugar.*

2. Che cosa fate spesso voi? *What do you often do?*

   Facciamo _____ sbagli. *We make some mistakes.*

3. Che cosa c'è davanti alla loro casa? *What is there in front of their house?*

   Ci sono _____ alberi. *There are some trees.*

4. Signora, vuole _____ carne? *Madam, would you like some meat?*

   Sì, voglio _____ carne. *Yes, I want a bit of meat.*

5. Di che cosa hai bisogno? *What do you need?*

   Ho bisogno _____ bicchieri, _____ forchette e _____ coltelli. *I need some glasses, some forks, and some knives.*

6. Vuoi _____ vino? *Would you like some wine?*

   Sì, voglio _____ vino. *Yes, I would like a little wine.*

7. Che cosa vuoi mangiare, Maria? *What do you want to eat, Mary?*

   Voglio mangiare _____ pasta. *I would like to eat some pasta.*

8. Vuoi _____ acqua? *Would you like some water?*

   Sì, voglio _____ acqua. *Yes, I would like a bit of water.*

USING PRONOUNS AS SUBSTITUTES FOR PARTITIVES

In place of these forms, the pronouns **alcuni** (masculine plural) and **alcune** (feminine plural) can be used to express more precisely the idea of *several*.

degli zii	*some uncles*	alcuni zii	*several (a few) uncles*
dei bicchieri	*some glasses*	alcuni bicchieri	*several (a few) glasses*
delle forchette	*some forks*	alcune forchette	*several (a few) forks*
delle amiche	some friends	alcune amiche	*several (a few) friends*

The invariable pronoun **qualche** can also be used to express the partitive with count nouns. But be careful with this one! It must be followed by a singular noun, even though the meaning is plural.

degli zii	*some uncles*	qualche zio	*some uncles*
dei bicchieri	*some glasses*	qualche bicchiere	*some glasses*
delle forchette	*some forks*	qualche forchetta	*some forks*
delle amiche	*some friends*	qualche amica	*some friends*

An easy way to remember this is by thinking of **qualche** as really meaning *whichever*, and then it will be easy to see why the noun is in the singular.

| qualche libro | = | *whichever book* |
| qualche amico | = | *whichever friend* |

Finally, you should know that in negative sentences, the partitive is omitted.

Affirmative Sentence		**Negative Sentence**	
Ho dei biglietti.	*I have some tickets.*	Non ho biglietti.	*I do not have any tickets.*
Ho alcune riviste.	*I have a few magazines.*	Non ho riviste.	*I do not have any magazines.*
Prendo dello zucchero.	*I will take some sugar.*	Non voglio zucchero.	*I do not want any sugar.*

Oral Practice

Practice saying the following sentences out loud.

Fanno degli sbagli, gli studenti?	*Do the students make some mistakes?*
Sì, fanno alcuni sbagli.	*Yes, they make a number of mistakes.*
Sì, fanno qualche sbaglio.	*Yes, they make some mistakes.*
Ci sono degli alberi davanti alla mia casa.	*There are some trees in front of my house.*

Ci sono alcuni alberi davanti alla mia casa.	*There are several trees in front of my house.*
C'è qualche albero davanti alla mia casa.	*There are some trees in front of my house.*
Signora, vuole dei ravioli?	*Madam, would you like some ravioli?*
Sì, voglio alcuni ravioli.	*Yes, I would like a few ravioli.*
Sì, voglio qualche raviolo.	*Yes, I would like some ravioli.*
Signore, vuole delle paste?	*Sir, would you like some pastries?*
Sì, voglio alcune paste.	*Yes, I would like a few pastries.*
Sì, voglio qualche pasta.	*Yes, I would like some pastries.*
Hai dei biglietti?	*Do you have some tickets?*
No, non ho biglietti.	*No, I do not have any tickets.*
Hai qualche rivista?	*Do you have any magazines?*
No, non ho riviste.	*I do not have any magazines.*

Written Practice 7

Fill in the blanks with the missing forms of the partitive.

1. Hai degli zii? *Do you have any uncles?*

   Sì, ho _____ zii. *Yes, I have several uncles.*

   Sì, ho _____ zio. *Yes, I have some uncles.*

2. Hai delle amiche a scuola? *Do you have any friends at school?*

   Sì, ho _____ amiche. *Yes, I have several friends.*

   Sì, ho _____ amica. *Yes, I have some friends.*

3. Signora, vuole dei libri? *Madam, would you like some books?*

   Sì, voglio _____ libri. *Yes, I would like a few books.*

   Sì, voglio _____ libro. *Yes, I would like some books.*

4. Signore, vuole delle forchette? *Sir, would you like some forks?*

   Sì, voglio _____ forchette. *Yes, I would like a few forks.*

   Sì, voglio _____ forchetta. *Yes, I would like some forks.*

5. Prendi _____ zucchero? *Do you take any sugar?*

No, non prendo zucchero. *No, I do not take any sugar.*

Talking About Addresses

Dove vivi? *Where do you live?* To give your address, or to ask someone their address, here are some vocabulary words you should know:

la città	*city*
la campagna	*countryside*
la periferia	*suburbs*
l'indirizzo	*address*
la via	*street*
la piazza	*square, plaza*

Qual è il tuo indirizzo?	*What is your address?*
Vivo in via Rossini, numero 12.	*I live at number 12 Rossini Street.*

Oral Practice

Practice saying the following sentences out loud.

Dove vivi, Maria?	*Where do you live Mary?*
Vivo in città.	*I live in the city.*
E Lei signora, dove vive?	*And you, madam, where do you live?*
Io vivo in campagna.	*I live in the countryside.*
E loro, dove vivono?	*And where do they live?*
Loro vivono in periferia.	*They live in the suburbs.*
Qual è il tuo indirizzo, Marco?	*What is your address, Mark?*
Vivo in via Dante, numero 16.	*I live at number 16 Dante Street.*
E Lei, dove vive, signore?	*And where do you live, sir?*
Vivo in piazza Donizetti, numero 18.	*I live at number 18 Donizetti Square.*

QUIZ

Supply the corresponding familiar or polite form of the imperative in the singular or plural, as necessary.

1. Familiar

   Mangia la mela!

   _____!

   Aspetta qui!

   _____!

   Finisci la mela!

   _____!

   Paga il conto!

   _____!

   Chiudi la porta!

   _____!

   Aprite le porte!

   _____!

   Finite di studiare!

   _____!

   Va' a dormire!

2. Polite

   _____!

   Cominci a mangiare!

   _____!

   Apra la porta!

   _____!

   Non cerchi la chiave!

   _____!

   Non scriva l'e-mail!

   _____!

   Dorma!

   _____!

   Non chiudano le porte!

   _____!

   Abbia pazienza!

   _____!

Tell Maria to . . .

3. *eat the apple*

   _____!

   not drink the water

   _____!

   close the door

   _____!

   open the window

   _____!

Now, tell both Mary and Mark to . . .

4. *eat the apple*

_____!

not drink the water

_____!

close the door

_____!

open the window

_____!

This time tell Mrs. Verdi to . . .

5. *eat the apple*

_____!

not drink the water

_____!

close the door

_____!

open the window

_____!

Finally, tell both Mrs. Verdi and Mr. Rossi to . . .

6. *eat the apple*

_____!

not drink the water

_____!

close the door

_____!

open the window

_____!

Fill in each blank with the equivalent partitive noun phrase. For example:

dei ragazzi	alcuni ragazzi	*qualche ragazzo*

7. delle penne   _____   _____

    _____   _____   qualche zio

    _____   alcune mele   _____

degli amici   _____   _____

    _____   _____   qualche ragazza

Personal Matters! Answer each question appropriately.

8. Qual è il tuo indirizzo?

    _____.

9. Dove vivi, in America o in Italia?

    _____.

10. Dove vuoi vivere in futuro?

    _____

PART TWO TEST

Circle the letter of the word or phrase that best answers each question or completes each sentence.

1. Quali lingue parli, Marco?

   (a) Parlo inglese e italiano.

   (b) Parlano inglese e italiano.

2. Signor Marchi, che cosa fa?

   (a) Pago il conto.

   (b) Paga il conto.

3. Che cosa bevete di solito?

   (a) Beviamo solo il caffè.

   (b) Bevono solo il caffè.

4. Gli studenti _____ l'italiano.

   (a) imparano

   (b) impariamo

5. Non mangio la carne _____ .

   (a) di solito

   (b) sempre

6. Stasera andiamo a _____ qui vicino.

   (a) un pranzo

   (b) un ristorante

7. Chi è la tua dentista?

   (a) Il dottor Previtale.

   (b) La dottoressa Previtale.

8. Che cosa fa il tuo amico?

   (a) L'infermiera.

   (b) L'infermiere.

9. Chi sono quelle _____ simpatiche?

   (a) persona

   (b) persone

10. Quanto fa duecento più cento per due?

    (a) Trecento.

    (b) Seicento.

11. Dove vivi, Marco?

    (a) In città.

    (b) Dal medico.

12. Che cosa leggi, Maria, di solito?

    (a) Leggo il giornale.

    (b) Legge il giornale.

13. Che cosa fanno i tuoi amici domani?

    (a) Fanno delle spese in città.

    (b) Facciamo delle spese in città.

14. Che cosa dice la tua amica?

    (a) Non dice niente.

    (b) Non dico niente.

15. Quanto costa la tua automobile?

    (a) Costa ventimila euro.

    (b) Costa domani.

16. Dov'è Maria?

    (a) Del medico.

    (b) Dal medico.

17. A che ora arriva?

    (a) Sono le cinque e mezzo.

    (b) Alle cinque e mezzo.

18. Che ore sono?

    (a) All'una precisa.

    (b) L'una precisa.

19. Marco, che cosa prendi?

    (a) Faccio la spesa.

    (b) Solo il caffè.

20. Dov'è la matita?

    (a) Col professore.

    (b) Sul tavolo.

21. Quando partono i tuoi genitori?

    (a) Partono domani.

    (b) Partiamo domani.

22. Quante lingue capisci?

    (a) Capisce molte lingue.

    (b) Capisco molte lingue.

23. Dove va, signora?

    (a) Vado in centro.

    (b) Vanno in centro.

24. A che ora uscite?

    (a) Usciamo alle sei.

    (b) Escono alle sei.

25. Chi viene alla festa?

    (a) Venite alla feste.

    (b) Non viene nessuno.

26. Martedì è _____ giorno della settimana.

    (a) il secondo

    (b) la seconda

27. Oggi è _____ dicembre.

    (a) il sedici

    (b) sedici

28. Di chi sono _____ libri?

    (a) quegli

    (b) questi

29. Chi sono _____ uomini?

    (a) quei

    (b) quegli

30. Quando si festeggia il Ferragosto?

    (a) Il quindici agosto.

    (b) Il primo agosto.

31. Che cosa stai dicendo?

    (a) Non sta dicendo niente.

    (b) Sto dicendo la verità.

32. Dove state andando?

    (a) Stiamo andando al cinema.

    (b) Stanno andando al cinema.

33. Dove stanno andando loro?

    (a) Stanno uscendo per andare alla discoteca.

    (b) Stiamo uscendo per andare alla discoteca.

34. Cosa sta mangiando, signora, in questo momento?

    (a) Sto mangiando un panino.

    (b) Sta mangiando un panino.

35. Cosa stai facendo, Maria?

    (a) Sto leggendo.

    (b) Stai leggendo.

36. Come si chiama _____ amica?

    (a) il loro

    (b) la loro

37. Domani arriva _____ zio dall'Italia.

    (a) il mio

    (b) mio

38. Arrivano anche _____ cugini.

    (a) i miei

    (b) miei

39. Oggi fa _____ tempo.

    (a) bel

    (b) bello

40. Qual è la capitale d'Italia?

    (a) Firenze

    (b) Roma

41. Marco, _____ tutti gli spaghetti!

    (a) mangia

    (b) mangi

42. Signora Dini, _____ alla festa anche Lei!

    (a) vieni

    (b) venga

43. Maria, non _____ stasera!

    (a) uscire

    (b) esci

44. Signori, _____ la verità!

    (a) di'

    (b) dicano

45. Maria, _____ pazienza!

    (a) abbi

    (b) abbia

46. Maria, anche tu _____ parlare francese?

    (a) sai

    (b) conosci

47. Marco, anche tu vuoi _____ carne?

    (a) qualche

    (b) un po' di

48. Anche noi vogliamo mangiare _____ .

    (a) di spaghetti

    (b) degli spaghetti

49. Preferisco _____ .

    (a) qualche minestra

    (b) della minestra

50. Vivo _____.

    (a) in via Dante, numero 12

    (b) 12 via Dante

PART THREE

BUILDING COMPETENCE

CHAPTER 11

Using Reflexive Verbs

Here's what you will learn in this chapter:

Reflexive Verbs
Imperative Forms of Reflexive Verbs
Reciprocal Forms of Verbs
Fractions and Other Numerical Expressions
Clothing

Reflexive Verbs

Come ti chiami? *What is your name?* Actually, this translates literally as *How do you call yourself?* The verb in this question is called a reflexive verb.

For the most part, you can consider a reflexive verb to be a verb that requires reflexive pronouns. More technically, it is a verb having an identical subject and direct object, as in *She dressed **herself***.

A reflexive verb infinitive in Italian is identifiable by the ending **-si** (*oneself*) that is attached to the infinitive itself minus the final **-e**. For example:

lavare + si = lavarsi *to wash oneself*

Below is a list of common reflexive verbs.

alzarsi	*to get up*
chiamarsi	*to call oneself*
divertirsi	*to enjoy oneself, have fun*
lavarsi	*to wash oneself*
mettersi	*to put on, wear*
sentirsi	*to feel*
svegliarsi	*to wake up*
vestirsi	*to get dressed*

Reflexive verbs are conjugated in exactly the same manner as nonreflexive verbs with, of course, the addition of the reflexive pronouns. These are: **mi**, **ti**, **si**, **ci**, **vi**, **si**. To conjugate a reflexive verb, drop the endings **-arsi**, **-ersi**, and **-irsi** and add on the usual verb endings according to the person (first, second, third). The reflexive pronoun is placed before the reflexive verb.

The following examples show the full present indicative conjugations of a first-conjugation reflexive verb (**alzarsi**), a second-conjugation verb (**mettersi**), and a third-conjugation verb (**divertirsi**).

alzarsi	*to get up*
(io) **mi** alzo	*I get up, am getting up, do get up*
(tu) **ti** alzi	*you (familiar) get up, are getting up, do get up*
(Lei) **si** alza	*you (polite) get up, are getting up, do get up*
(lui/lei) **si** alza	*he/she gets up, is getting up, does get up*
(noi) **ci** alz**iamo**	*we get up, are getting up, do get up*
(voi) **vi** alz**ate**	*you (familiar plural) get up, are getting up, do get up*
(Loro) **si** alz**ano**	*you (polite plural) get up, are getting up, do get up*
(loro) **si** alz**ano**	*they get up, are getting up, do get up*

mettersi	*to put on*
(io) **mi** mett**o**	*I put on, am putting on, do put on*
(tu) **ti** metti	*you (familiar) put on, are putting on, do put on*
(Lei) **si** mette	*you (polite) put on, are putting on, do put on*

(lui/lei) **si** mett**e**	*he/she puts on, is putting on, does put on*
(noi) **ci** mett**iamo**	*we put on, are putting on, do put on*
(voi) **vi** mett**ete**	*you (familiar plural) put on, are putting on, do put on*
(Loro) **si** mett**ono**	*you (polite plural) put on, are putting on, do put on*
(loro) **si** mett**ono**	*they put on, are putting on, do put on*

divertirsi	***to enjoy oneself, have fun***
(io) **mi** divert**o**	*I enjoy, am enjoying, do enjoy*
(tu) **ti** divert**i**	*you (familiar) enjoy, are enjoying, do enjoy*
(Lei) **si** divert**e**	*you (polite) enjoy, are enjoying, do enjoy*
(lui/lei) **si** divert**e**	*he/she enjoys, is enjoying, does enjoy*
(noi) **ci** divert**iamo**	*we enjoy, are enjoying, do enjoy*
(voi) **vi** divert**ite**	*you (familiar plural) enjoy, are enjoying, do enjoy*
(Loro) **si** divert**ono**	*you (polite plural) enjoy, are enjoying, do enjoy*
(loro) **si** divert**ono**	*they enjoy, are enjoying, do enjoy*

Oral Practice

Practice saying the following sentences out loud. Note the new vocabulary.

Marco, a che ora ti alzi di solito?	*Mark, at what time do you usually get up?*
Di solito mi alzo alle sei e mezzo.	*I usually get up at six-thirty.*
Signora, a che ora si sveglia di solito?	*Madam, at what time do you usually wake up?*
Di solito mi sveglio alle sette.	*Usually I wake up at seven.*
Gino e Marta, perché vi vestite così?	*Gino and Martha, why do you dress in that way?*
Ci vestiamo così perché siamo giovani.	*We dress like this because we are young.*
Come si sentono i tuoi genitori?	*How do your parents feel?*
Oggi si sentono assai bene, grazie.	*Today they feel rather well, thanks.*
Maria, che cosa ti metti per la festa?	*Mary, what are you wearing (putting on) for the party?*
Mi metto una giacca rossa.	*I am putting on a red jacket.*
Come si chiama, signore?	*What is your name, sir?*

Mi chiamo Giovanni Pierini.	*My name is John Pierini.*
Marco, è vero che ti diverti in centro?	*Mark, is it true that you have fun downtown?*
Sì, è vero, mi diverto molto in centro.	*Yes, it is true, I enjoy myself a lot downtown.*
Perché non si lavano mai quei bambini?	*Why do those children never wash?*
Non è vero. Si lavano sempre.	*It is not true. They always wash.*
Marco e Maria, come vi vestite?	*Mark and Mary, how are you dressing?*
Ci vestiamo semplicemente.	*We are dressing simply.*

Written Practice 1

Fill in the blanks with the missing reflexive verbs in their appropriate forms.

1. Ragazzi, a che ora _____ di solito? *Guys, at what time do you usually get up?*

   Di solito _____ alle sei e mezzo. *We usually get up at six-thirty.*

2. E loro, a che ora _____ di solito? *And at what time do they usually wake up?*

   Di solito loro _____ alle sette. *Usually they wake up at seven.*

3. Marta perché _____ così? *Martha, why do you dress in that way?*

   _____ così perché sono giovane. *I dress like this because I am young.*

4. Come _____, signora? *How do you feel, madam?*

   Oggi _____ assai bene, grazie. *Today I feel rather well, thanks.*

5. Che cosa _____ i tuoi amici per la festa? *What are your friends wearing for the party?*

   _____ un costume. *They are wearing a costume.*

6. Come _____, bambino? *What is your name, little boy?*

   _____ Piero. *My name is Piero.*

7. È vero che lei _____ in centro? *Is it true that she has fun downtown?*

   Sì, è vero, lei _____ molto in centro. *Yes, it is true, she enjoys herself a lot downtown.*

8. Signora e signore, come _____? *Madam and sir, how are you dressing?*

   _____ semplicemente. *We are dressing simply.*

Imperative Forms of Reflexive Verbs

In the imperative tense, reflexive verbs are conjugated the same way as nonreflexive verbs except with the addition of the reflexive pronouns. If you feel you need to, go back to Chapter 10 for a review of the imperative.

The reflexive pronouns are attached to the end of verbs when using the familiar (**tu, voi**) and first-person plural (**noi**) forms of the affirmative imperative. The pronouns are placed before the verbs when using the polite forms.

Familiar		**Polite**	
Tu Forms		**Lei Forms**	
Marco, vest**iti**!	*Marco, get dressed!*	Signor Verdi, **si** vesta!	*Mr. Verdi, get dressed!*
Maria, alz**ati**!	*Mary, get up!*	Signora Rossi, **si** alzi!	*Mrs. Rossi, get up!*
Noi Forms		**Noi Forms**	
Divertiam**oci**!	*Let's have fun!*	Laviam**oci**!	*Let's wash!*
Vestiam**oci**!	*Let's get dressed!*	Alziam**oci**!	*Let's get up!*
Voi Forms		**Loro Forms**	
Divertite**vi**!	*Enjoy yourselves!*	**Si** divertano!	*Enjoy yourselves!*
Alzate**vi**!	*Get up!*	**Si** alzino!	*Get up!*

Reflexive pronouns are also attached to the verbs in the negative imperative in the same way. Remember, though, that in the case of the second-person singular form of the negative imperative, the infinitive is required. With reflexive verbs, however, the pronoun may either be attached or may be put before the infinitive in the negative imperative. If attached, the final **-e** of the infinitive is dropped.

Affirmative		**Negative**	
Tu Forms			
Marco, alzati!	*Marco, get up!*	Marco, non ti alzare!	*Marco, do not get up!*
Maria, alzati!	*Mary, get up!*	Maria, non alzarti!	*Mary, do not get up!*

Oral Practice

Practice saying the following sentences out loud.

Maria, alzati! È tardi!	*Mary, get up! It is late!*
Signor Verdi, si alzi! Sono già le otto!	*Mr. Verdi, get up! It is already eight!*
Marco, non metterti quel vestito!	*Mark, do not put on that suit!*
Signor Rossi, non si metta quel vestito!	*Mr. Rossi, do not put on that suit!*
Marco e Maria, divertitevi al cinema!	*Mark and Mary, have fun at the movies!*
Signori, si divertano in Italia!	*Gentlemen, have fun in Italy!*
Pina, svegliati! Sono già le sette!	*Pina, wake up! It is already seven!*
Signora, si svegli! È tardi!	*Madam, wake up! It is late!*
Alziamoci presto domani!	*Let's get up early tomorrow.*
No, non alziamoci presto!	*No, let's not get up early.*
Gina, mettiti quel vestito!	*Gina, put on that dress.*
Signorina, si metta quel vestito!	*Miss, put on that dress.*
Gina, non svegliarti presto domani!	*Gina, do not wake up early tomorrow.*
Signorina, non si svegli presto domani!	*Miss, do not wake up early tomorrow.*
Dina e Pino, vestitevi subito! È tardi!	*Dina and Pino, get dressed right away! It is late!*
Signori, si vestano! È molto tardi!	*Gentlemen, get dressed! It is very late!*

Written Practice 2

Fill in the blanks with the missing reflexive verbs in their appropriate imperative forms.

1. Giovanni, _____! È tardi! *John, wake up! It is late!*

2. Signor Marchi, _____! Sono già le otto!   *Mr. Marchi, wake up! It is already eight!*

3. Claudia, non _____ quella giacca! *Claudia, do not put on that jacket.*

4. Signora, non _____ quella giacca! *Madam, do not put on that jacket.*

5. Marco e Maria, _____ in Italia! *Mark and Mary, have fun in Italy!*

6. Signori, _____ in Italia! *Gentlemen, have fun in Italy!*

7. Maria, _____! Sono già le sette! *Mary, get up! It is already seven!*

8. Signora, _____! È tardi! *Madam, get up! It is late!*

9. _____ presto domani! *Let's wake up early tomorrow.*

10. No, non _____ presto! *No, let's not wake up early.*

11. Pina, _____ subito! È tardi! *Pina, wash yourself right away. It is late!*

12. Signorina, _____, per favore! È tardi! *Miss, please get dressed. It is late!*

13. Maria, non _____ presto domani! *Mary, do not get up early tomorrow.*

14. Signorina, non _____ presto domani! *Miss, do not get up early tomorrow.*

Reciprocal Forms of Verbs

Some verbs can be turned into a reflexive form. This is called the reciprocal form of the verb.

Verb		Reciprocal	
parlare	*to speak*	parlarsi	*to speak to one another*
telefonare	*to phone*	telefonarsi	*to phone one another*
vedere	*to see*	vedersi	*to see one another*
capire	*to understand*	capirsi	*to understand one another*

Conjugate each reciprocal verb as you would any reflexive verb. Notice, however, that conjugating such verbs makes sense only in certain persons (Can you *phone yourself*?). Basically, reciprocal verbs are only used in the plural.

Noi Forms

Noi ci vediamo spesso.	*We see each other often.*
Noi ci capiamo molto bene.	*We understand each other quite well.*

Voi Forms

Voi vi vedete spesso, no?	*You see each other often, isn't that right?*
Voi vi telefonate ogni sera.	*You phone each other every evening.*

Loro Forms

Loro si parlano ogni giorno.	*They speak to each other every day.*
Loro si vedono spesso.	*They see each other often.*

Oral Practice

Practice saying the following sentences out loud.

Marco e Giulia si parlano ancora?	*Do Mark and Julia still speak to each other?*
No, non si parlano più.	*No, they do not speak to each other anymore.*
Voi vi telefonate ancora?	*Do you still phone each other?*
Sì, ci telefoniamo spesso.	*Yes, we phone each other often.*
Quanti anni sono che non vi vedete?	*How many years is it that you have not seen each other?*
Noi non ci vediamo da molti anni.	*We have not seen each other for many years.*

Gino e Pina si capiscono, vero?   *Gino and Pina understand each other,*
                                            right?

No, loro non si capiscono mai.   *No, they never understand each other.*

Written Practice 3

Fill in the blanks with the missing reciprocal verbs in their appropriate forms.

1. Quei due signori _____ spesso? *Do those two gentlemen*
   phone each other often?

   No, non _____ mai. *No, they never phone each other.*

2. Voi _____ ancora? *Do you still speak to each other?*

   Sì, _____ sempre. *Yes, we speak to each other all the*
   time.

3. Loro _____ spesso? *Do they see each other often?*

   Sì, loro _____ ogni giorno. *Yes, they see each other*
   every day.

4. Voi _____, vero? *You understand each other, right?*

   Sì, noi _____ perfettamente. *Yes, we understand each*
   other perfectly.

Fractions and Other Numerical Expressions

Remember the cardinal numbers (**uno, due, tre, quattro,**...) and the ordinal numbers (**primo, secondo, terzo, quarto,**...)? These numbers are also used to make
fractions in Italian.

  As in English, cardinal numbers are used to express the numerator and ordinal
numbers express the denominator of fractions. Note that if the numerator is greater
than one, the denominator, being an ordinal adjective, must be in the plural.

1/17 un diciassettesimo
3/4 tre quarti
5/9 cinque noni

Be careful! The fraction 1/2 is different, however. There are two ways to express *one-half* or *half*. When used as an adjective, the word **mezzo** is used. But when it is used as a noun, **metà** is used. For example:

mezzo litro	*a half liter*
la metà di tutto	*half of everything*

Here are a few useful numerical expressions:

il doppio	*double*
a due a due, a tre a tre,…	*two by two, three by three, . . .*
una dozzina	*a dozen*
una ventina, una trentina,…	*about twenty, about thirty, . . .*
un centinaio, due centinaia, tre centinaia,…	*about a hundred, about two hundred, . . .*
un migliaio, due migliaia, tre migliaia,…	*about a thousand, about two thousand . . .*

Oral Practice

Practice saying the following sentences out loud.

Quanto costa quella camicia?	*How much does that shirt cost?*
Costa un quarto di quella.	*It costs a quarter of that one.*
Quanta pasta vuoi?	*How much pasta do you want?*
Tre quarti della tua.	*Three-fourths of yours.*
Quanto fa due terzi e sette noni?	*What is two-thirds plus seven-ninths?*
Fa tredici noni.	*It equals thirteen-ninths.*
Quanta pasta vuoi?	*How much pasta do you want?*
La metà.	*Half.*
Quanto costa quella giacca?	*How much does that jacket cost?*
Costa il doppio di questa.	*It costs double this one.*
Di quanti bicchieri hai bisogno?	*How many glasses do you need?*
Una quarantina.	*About forty.*
Quante persone ci sono in quella città?	*How many people are in that city?*
Ci sono migliaia di persone.	*There are thousands of people.*

Quanti ravioli vuoi?　　　　　*How many ravioli do you want?*

Una dozzina, grazie.　　　　　*A dozen, thanks.*

Quanti studenti ci sono in quella　　*How many students are there in that*
　scuola?　　　　　　　　　　*school?*

Ci sono centinaia di studenti.　　　*There are hundreds of students.*

Written Practice 4

Fill in each blank with the correct word or expression, using what you have just learned in the Oral Practice.

1. Quanto _____ quella camicia? *How much does that shirt cost?*

   Costa _____ di quella. *It costs half that one.*

2. _____ pasta vuoi? *How much pasta do you want?*

   _____ della tua. *Three-fifths of yours.*

3. Quanto fa _____ e _____? *What is one-fourth plus seven-eighths?*

   Fa _____. *It equals nine-eighths.*

4. Quanti ravioli _____? *How much pasta do you want?*

   _____. *Double.*

5. Quanto _____ quelle scarpe? *How much do those shoes cost?*

   Costano _____ di queste. *They cost a third of these.*

6. Di quanti coltelli _____? *How many knives do you need?*

   Una _____. *About sixty.*

7. _____ studentesse ci sono in quella classe? *How many (female) students are in that class?*

   Ci sono _____ di studentesse. *There are hundreds of students.*

8. _____ gnocchi vuoi? *How many dumplings do you want?*

   _____, grazie. *Two dozen, thanks.*

9. _____ personne ci sono in quella città? *How many persons are there in that city?*

Ci sono _____ di persone. *There are thousands of persons.*

Clothing

Ti piace fare delle spese? *Do you like shopping?* If you like to shop and would like to do some shopping for clothes in Italy, here are a few useful words and expressions to learn:

- When you enter a shop, a salesclerk (**un commesso/una commessa**) will ask you:

  Desidera?   *Can I help you?*

- The following list shows some words for clothing items, some of which you already know:

la camicetta	*blouse*
la camicia	*shirt*
la cravatta	*tie*
la giacca	*jacket*
la gonna	*skirt*
il vestito	*dress, suit*
il cappello	*hat*
la scarpa	*shoe*
lo stivale	*boot*
l'impermeabile (*m.*)	*overcoat*
il cappotto	*coat*
i pantaloni	*pants*
il calzino	*sock*
la calza	*stocking*

- And here are some other shopping words that will come in handy:

comprare	*to buy*	il cliente/la cliente	*customer (m./f.)*
provarsi	*to try on*	il colore	*color*
portare	*to wear*	il saldo	*sale*
la taglia	*measurement, size*	vorrei	*I would like*
il paio (le paia, *pl.*)	*pair*	infine	*finally*

Oral Practice

Practice saying the following sentences out loud.

Desidera, signora?	*May I help you, madam?*
Vorrei comprare una camicetta.	*I would like to buy a blouse.*
Qual è la Sua taglia?	*What is your size?*
Di solito porto il quarantadue.	*Usually, I wear a size 42.*
Va bene, si provi questa!	*Okay, try this one on.*
Mi piace molto. Quanto costa?	*I like it a lot. How much does it cost?*
Solo cento euro. È in saldo.	*Only 100 euros. It is on sale.*
Quel commesso è simpatico.	*That (male) salesclerk is nice.*
Ma i clienti non sono simpatici.	*But the customers are not nice.*
Vorrei una camicia e una cravatta.	*I would like a shirt and tie.*
E anche una giacca e i pantaloni.	*And also a jacket and pants.*
Si provi questi!	*Try these on.*
Ho bisogno di un nuovo vestito.	*I need a new suit.*
Voglio un paio di scarpe e di stivali.	*I want a pair of shoes and boots.*
Forse anche dei calzini e delle calze.	*Maybe also some socks and stockings.*
Infine, un impermeabile.	*Finally, an overcoat.*

Written Practice 5

Fill in the blanks with the missing words or expressions.

1. _____, signora? *May I help you, madam?*

2. Vorrei _____ una camicetta. *I would like to buy a blouse.*

3. Qual è la Sua _____? *What is your size?*

4. Di solito _____ il quaranta. *Usually, I wear a size 40.*

5. Va bene, _____ questa! *Okay, try this one on.*

6. Mi piace molto. Quanto _____? *I like it a lot. How much does it cost?*

7. Solo novanta euro. È in _____. *Only 90 euros. It is on sale.*

8. Quel _____ è simpatico. *That (male) salesclerk is nice.*

9. Anche quella _____ è simpatica. *That (female) salesclerk is also nice.*

10. Ma _____ non sono simpatici. *But the customers are not nice.*

11. _____ signore? *Can I help you, sir?*

12. Vorrei una camicia e _____. *I would like a shirt and tie.*

13. Sì, una giacca e _____. *Yes, a jacket and pants.*

14. _____ questi! *Try these on.*

15. _____ un nuovo vestito. *I need a new suit.*

16. E _____ di scarpe e di stivali. *And a pair of shoes and boots.*

17. Forse anche _____ e _____. *Maybe also some socks and stockings.*

18. Infine, _____. *Finally, an overcoat.*

QUIZ

1. Tell Mary to . . .

   enjoy herself at the party!

   _____!

   not put on red pants!

   _____!

2. Tell Mark to . . .

   try on that coat!

   _____!

get up early tomorrow!

_____!

3. Tell Mary and Mark to . . .

enjoy themselves at the party!

_____!

not put on a costume (un costume)*!*

_____!

4. Tell Mary and Claudia to . . .

try on some new clothes!

_____!

phone each other more often!

_____!

5. Tell Mrs. Dini to . . .

enjoy herself at the party!

_____!

not put on red pants!

_____!

6. Tell Mr. Nitti to . . .

try on that coat!

_____!

get up early tomorrow!

_____!

Circle the correct word or response for the following.

7. C'è _____ di studenti in quella classe.

   (a) una trentina   (c) mezzo

   (b) centinaia   (d) niente

8. Qual è la Sua taglia?

   (a) Porto il quaranta.   (c) Ho bisogno di un paio di scarpe.

   (b) È in saldo.   (d) Desidera?

Personal Matters! Answer each question appropriately.

9. A che ora ti alzi di solito?

_____.

10. Che taglia porti?

_____.

CHAPTER 12

Using the Present Perfect Tense

Here's what you will learn in this chapter:

Present Perfect Tense with Avere
Present Perfect Tense with Essere
Irregular Past Participles
More About the Definite Article

Present Perfect Tense with *Avere*

Ieri ho mangiato tutto e Marco è andato al cinema. *Yesterday I ate everything, and Marco went to the movies.* The two verbs in this sentence are in the present perfect tense. The present perfect tense is used to express simple actions that have been completed at the time of speaking. It is a compound tense, which means that it is composed of two parts. It is formed with the present indicative form of an auxiliary verb plus the past participle of the verb showing the action, in that order.

It's not really as complicated as it sounds. You already know the auxiliary verbs. They are **avere** and **essere**. All you really need to learn now is how to form the past participle:

- Change the **-are** ending of first-conjugation verbs to **-ato**.

Verb	Past Participle
parlare	parlato
guardare	guardato

- Change the **-ere** ending of second-conjugation verbs to **-uto**.

Verb	Past Participle
vendere	venduto
ripetere	ripetuto

- Change the **-ire** ending of third-conjugation verbs to **-ito**.

Verb	Past Participle
dormire	dormito
capire	capito

Here are the complete conjugations of three verbs using **avere** as the auxiliary in the present perfect tense. Notice that this tense translates to three types of English past tenses.

parlare	*to speak*
(io) ho parlato	*I have spoken, I spoke, I did speak*
(tu) hai parlato	*you* (familiar) *have spoken, you spoke, you did speak*
(Lei) ha parlato	*you* (polite) *have spoken, you spoke, you did speak*
(lui/lei) ha parlato	*he/she has spoken, he/she spoke, he/she did speak*
(noi) abbiamo parlato	*we have spoken, we spoke, we did speak*
(voi) avete parlato	*you* (familiar plural) *have spoken, you spoke, you did speak*
(Loro) hanno parlato	*you* (polite plural) *have spoken, you spoke, you did speak*
(loro) hanno parlato	*they have spoken, they spoke, they did speak*

vendere	*to sell*
(io) ho venduto	*I have sold, I sold, I did sell*
(tu) hai venduto	*you* (familiar) *have sold, you sold, you did sell*
(Lei) ha venduto	*you* (polite) *have sold, you sold, you did sell*
(lui/lei) ha venduto	*he/she has sold, he/she sold, he/she did sell*
(noi) abbiamo venduto	*we have sold, we sold, we did sell*

(voi) avete venduto	*you* (familiar plural) *have sold, you sold, you did sell*
(Loro) hanno venduto	*you* (polite plural) *have sold, you sold, you did sell*
(loro) hanno venduto	*they have sold, they sold, they did sell*

finire	***to finish***
(io) ho finito	*I have finished, I finished, I did finish*
(tu) hai finito	*you* (familiar) *have finished, you finished, you did finish*
(Lei) ha finito	*you* (polite) *have finished, you finished, you did finish*
(lui/lei) ha finito	*he/she has finished, he/she finished, he/she did finish*
(noi) abbiamo finito	*we have finished, we finished, we did finish*
(voi) avete finito	*you* (familiar plural) *have finished, you finished, you did finish*
(Loro) hanno finito	*you* (polite plural) *have finished, you finished, you did finish*
(loro) hanno finito	*they have finished, they finished, they did finish*

The following list shows many of the most commonly used adverbs in Italian, some of which you may already have come across. Pay attention to how they are used with the present perfect verbs in some of the sentences in the Oral Practice that follows. Note that the word **già** is situated between the auxiliary verb and the past participle; the same pattern applies to **ancora** and **mai**. This is not a strict rule of grammar. It is a stylistic preference on the part of Italian speakers.

già	*already*	ieri	*yesterday*
ancora	*still, yet*	fa	*ago*
mai	*ever, never*	scorso	*last* (*last week, last month*)

Oral Practice

Practice saying the following sentences out loud.

mangiare *to eat*

Marco, hai già mangiato la pizza? *Mark, did you already eat the pizza?*

Sì, ho già mangiato tutta la pizza. *Yes, I already ate all the pizza.*

pagare *to pay*

La tua amica ha pagato il conto ieri? *Did your friend pay the bill yesterday?*

No, non ha pagato il conto. *No, she did not pay the bill.*

comprare   *to buy*

Avete comprato un televisore due giorni fa?   *Did you buy a television set two days ago?*

No, abbiamo comprato una radio.   *No, we bought a radio.*

imparare   *to learn*

Quando hanno imparato l'italiano loro?   *When did they learn Italian?*

Hanno imparato l'italiano tre anni fa.   *They learned Italian three years ago.*

vendere   *to sell*

Quando hai venduto la tua macchina, Dino?   *When did you sell your car, Dino?*

Ho venduto la macchina l'anno scorso.   *I sold the car last year.*

Anche loro hanno venduto la macchina?   *Did they also sell their car?*

Sì, hanno venduto la macchina il mese scorso.   *Yes, they sold their car last month.*

conoscere   *to know, meet*

Dove avete conosciuto il professore?   *Where did you meet the professor?*

Abbiamo conosciuto il professore in Italia.   *We met the professor in Italy.*

finire   *to finish*

Marco, hai finito di lavorare?   *Mark, did you finish working?*

Sì, ho già finito di lavorare.   *Yes, I have already finished working.*

dormire   *to sleep*

Quanto tempo ha dormito ieri, signora?   *Madam, how much time did you sleep yesterday?*

Ho dormito tutta la giornata.   *I slept all day long.*

preferire   *to prefer*

E voi, che cosa avete preferito fare? *And you, what did you prefer doing?*

Abbiamo preferito studiare.   *We preferred studying.*

capire   *to understand*

I tuoi amici hanno capito la lezione? *Did your friends understand the lesson?*

No, non hanno capito la lezione.   *No, they did not understand the lesson.*

Written Practice 1

Fill in the blanks with the present perfect forms of the indicated verbs.

cominciare   *to begin*

1. Marco e Maria, a che ora _____ a
   studiare? *Mark and Mary, at what time did you start studying?*

   _____ presto. *We began early.*

2. E tu, Paolo, quando _____? *And you, Paul,*
   when did you begin?

   Io _____ tardi. *I began late.*

3. E loro, quando _____? *And when did they*
   begin?

   Anche loro _____ tardi. *They also started*
   late.

ripetere   *to repeat*

4. Dina, che cosa _____? *Dina, what did you*
   repeat?

   Non _____ niente. *I did not repeat*
   anything.

5. E voi, che cosa _____? *And what did you*
   repeat?

   Anche noi non _____ niente. *We also did*
   not repeat anything.

6. E loro, che cosa _____? *And what did they repeat?*

Loro _____ tutto. *They repeated everything.*

pulire   *to clean*

7. Giovanni, _____ già _____ la casa? *John, did you already clean the house?*

No, non _____ ancora _____ la casa. *No, I have not yet cleaned the house.*

8. E voi, _____ la macchina ieri? *And did you clean the car yesterday?*

Sì, _____ la macchina ieri sera. *Yes, we cleaned the car last night.*

9. Anche i tuoi amici _____ la casa? *Did your friends also clean the house?*

Sì, i miei amici _____ la casa. *Yes, my friends cleaned the house.*

Present Perfect Tense with *Essere*

Most verbs are conjugated with **avere** in the compound tenses. However, there are a number of verbs that are conjugated with the auxiliary verb **essere**.

You already know how to conjugate the verb **essere** and now you know how to form the past participle of all three verb types. The only difference in this case is that when using **essere** in a compound tense, the past participle agrees in number and gender with the subject of the sentence. For example, here is how it works with the verb **arrivare** (*to arrive*):

- The ending **-o** is used when the subject is masculine singular (**arrivato**).
- The ending **-a** is used when the subject is feminine singular (**arrivata**).
- The ending **-i** is used when the subject is masculine plural (**arrivati**).
- The ending **-e** is used when the subject is feminine plural (**arrivate**).

Here is the complete conjugation of the verb **arrivare**, using **essere** as the auxiliary in the present perfect tense:

arrivare	***to arrive***
(io) sono arrivato/a	*I have arrived, I arrived, I did arrive*
(tu) sei arrivato/a	*you* (familiar) *have arrived, you arrived, you did arrive*
(Lei) è arrivato/a	*you* (polite) *have arrived, you arrived, you did arrive*
(lui) è arrivato	*he has arrived, he arrived, he did arrive*
(lei) è arrivata	*she has arrived, she arrived, she did arrive*
(noi) siamo arrivati/e	*we have arrived, we arrived, we did arrive*
(voi) siete arrivati/e	*you* (familiar plural) *have arrived, you arrived, you did arrive*
(Loro) sono arrivati/e	*you* (polite plural) *have arrived, you arrived, you did arrive*
(loro) sono arrivati/e	*they have arrived, they arrived, they did arrive*

So how do you know when to use **avere** or when to use **essere**? The best learning strategy is to assume that most verbs are conjugated with **avere** (which is true), and then memorize the verbs that are conjugated with **essere**. Also, the verbs that use **essere** are intransitive (that is, they do not take a direct object) and many of them generally refer to some type of motion (*going, arriving, staying, entering,* etc.).

Below is a list of common verbs that are conjugated using **essere** in compound tenses—these all have regular past participles. You have encountered most of them, but take some time to memorize those you don't know.

andare	*to go*	partire	*to leave*
arrivare	*to arrive*	sembrare	*to seem*
cadere	*to fall*	tornare	*to return*
diventare	*to become*	uscire	*to go out*
entrare	*to enter*		

Impersonal verbs are also all conjugated with **essere**. Impersonal verbs are those that have only third person forms.

durare	***to last***

Il film è durato tre ore.   *The movie lasted three hours.*

costare	***to cost***

Quanto sono costate le mele?   *How much did the apples cost?*

In addition, all reflexive and reciprocal verbs are conjugated with **essere**.

Io mi sono alzato tardi ieri.   *I got up late yesterday.*

Loro si sono divertiti molto in Italia.   *They had a lot of fun in Italy.*

Mia sorella si è svegliata presto ieri.   *My sister got up early yesterday.*

Le mie amiche non si sono chiamate.	*My friends did not call each other.*

Remember that third person verb forms are used in polite address. In this case, the verb ending of the past participle must agree with the sex of the person you are addressing or talking about.

Signor Verdi, è uscito ieri?	*Mr. Verdi, did you go out yesterday?*
Signora Verdi, è uscita ieri?	*Mrs. Verdi, did you go out yesterday?*

Oral Practice

Practice saying the following sentences out loud.

andare   *to go*

Dove sei andato ieri, Marco?	*Where did you go yesterday, Mark?*
Sono andato in centro.	*I went downtown.*
E tu, Maria, dove sei andata?	*And where did you go, Mary?*
Io sono andata al cinema.	*I went to the movies.*

arrivare   *to arrive*

Quando è arrivato tuo cugino ieri?	*When did your cousin arrive yesterday?*
È arrivato nel pomeriggio.	*He arrived in the afternoon.*
E i tuoi amici, quando sono arrivati?	*And when did your friends arrive?*
Loro sono arrivati tardi.	*They arrived late.*

uscire   *to go out*

Marco e Maria, quando siete usciti?	*Mark and Mary, when did you go out?*
Siamo usciti dopo cena.	*We went out after dinner.*

tornare   *to return, go back*

Le tue zie sono tornate in Italia?	*Did your aunts return to Italy?*
Sì, sono tornate l'anno scorso.	*Yes, they went back last year.*

alzarsi *to get up*

A che ora ti sei alzato, Marco?   *At what time did you get up, Mark?*

Mi sono alzato tardi.   *I got up late.*

divertirsi *to enjoy oneself, have fun*

Si sono divertiti i tuoi cugini ieri?   *Did your cousins have fun yesterday?*

Sì, i miei cugini si sono divertiti ieri.   *Yes, my cousins had fun yesterday.*

Written Practice 2

Fill in the blanks with the present perfect forms of the indicated verbs.

cadere *to fall*

1. Maria, è vero che _____ ieri? *Mary, is it true that you fell yesterday?*

   Sì, _____ . *Yes, I fell.*

durare *to last*

2. Quanto tempo _____ i due film? *How long did the two movies last?*

   I due film _____ qualche ora. *The two movies lasted a few hours.*

entrare *to enter*

3. Quando _____ tuo fratello? *When did your brother come in?*

   Mio fratello _____ un momento fa. *My brother entered a moment ago.*

sembrare *to seem*

4. Come _____ quel film? *What did the movie seem like?*

   Non _____ niente. *It did not seem like anything.*

diventare   *to become*

5. I tuoi amici _____ dolci, no? *Your friends have become sweet, haven't they?*

   Sì, _____ assai dolci. *Yes, they have become quite sweet.*

costare   *to cost*

6. Quanto _____ quella macchina? *How much did that car cost?*

   _____ molto. *It cost a lot.*

svegliarsi   *to wake up*

7. Ragazzi, a che ora _____? *Guys, at what time did you wake up?*

   _____ presto. *We got up early.*

sentirsi   *to feel*

8. Signora, come _____ ieri? *Madam, how did you feel yesterday?*

   _____ molto bene. *I felt very well.*

Irregular Past Participles

There are always irregularities when it comes to verbs. And, in fact, there are a number of verbs with irregular past participles. Here are the ones you have encountered so far. Verbs conjugated with **essere** are shown with an asterisk.

Verb		**Past Participle**	
aprire	*to open*	aperto	*opened*
bere	*to drink*	bevuto	*drunk*
chiudere	*to close*	chiuso	*closed*
dare	*to give*	dato	*given*
dire	*to say, tell*	detto	*said, told*
essere*	*to be*	stato	*been (was)*
fare	*to do, make*	fatto	*done, made*
leggere	*to read*	letto	*read*

mettere	*to put*	messo	*put*
mettersi*	*to put on*	messo	*put on*
prendere	*to take*	preso	*taken*
scrivere	*to write*	scritto	*written*
stare*	*to stay*	stato	*stayed*
vedere	*to see*	visto	*seen*
venire*	*to come*	venuto	*come*

Oral Practice

Practice saying the following sentences out loud, using the present perfect with the participles just learned.

Marco, perché hai aperto la finestra?	*Mark, why have you opened the window?*
Signora, che cosa ha bevuto?	*Madam, what have you drunk?*
Ragazzi, perché avete chiuso la porta?	*Guys, why have you closed the door?*
A chi hanno dato quella scatola?	*To whom have they given that box?*
Ha detto la verità Maria?	*Has Mary told the truth?*
Com'è stata la lezione di ieri?	*How was yesterday's class?*
Che tempo ha fatto la settimana scorsa?	*How was the weather last week?*
Marco, hai mai letto quel romanzo?	*Mark, have you ever read that novel?*
Pina, dove hai messo la mia penna?	*Pina, where have you put my pen?*
Gina, che cosa hai preso al bar?	*Gina, what did you have (take) at the coffee shop?*
Ragazzi, avete scritto l'e-mail?	*Boys, have you written the e-mail?*
Quanto tempo sono stati in centro loro?	*How long were they downtown?*
Chi ha visto il professore?	*Who has seen the professor?*
Sono venute le tue amiche alla festa?	*Have your friends come to the party?*

Written Practice 3

Fill in the blanks with the missing verbs in the present perfect tense.

1. Marco, perché _____ la finestra? *Mark, why have you closed the window?*

   _____ la finestra perché fa freddo. *I closed the window because it is cold.*

2. Signora, che cosa _____? *Madam, what did you have?*

   _____ un espresso. *I had an espresso.*

3. Ragazzi, perché _____ la porta? *Guys, why have you opened the door?*

   Non _____ la porta. *We have not opened the door.*

4. A chi _____ quella bibita? *To whom have they given that drink?*

   _____ quella bibita a Marco. *They have given that drink to Mark.*

5. _____ la verità tuo fratello? *Did your brother tell the truth?*

   Sì, mio fratello _____ la verità. *Yes, my brother told the truth.*

6. Come _____ la lezione di ieri? *How was yesterday's class?*

   La lezione _____ lunga. *The class was long.*

7. Che tempo _____ ieri? *How was the weather last week?*

   _____ brutto tempo. *The weather was bad.*

8. Sara, _____ quel romanzo? *Sarah, have you ever read that novel?*

   Sì, _____ quel romanzo. *Yes, I read that novel already.*

9. Pina, dove _____ la mia borsa? *Pina, where have you put my purse?*

_____ la tua borsa sulla sedia. *I put your purse on the chair.*

10. Gina, che cosa _____ al bar? *Gina, what did you drink at the coffee shop?*

   Non _____ niente. *I did not drink anything.*

11. Signori, _____ l'e-mail? *Gentlemen, have you written the e-mail?*

   Sì _____ l'e-mail. *Yes, we have already written the e-mail.*

12. Quanto tempo _____ in centro lei? *How long was she downtown?*

   _____ tutta la giornata. *She stayed the entire day.*

13. Chi _____ Marco? *Who has seen Mark?*

   Nessuno _____ Marco. *No one has seen Mark.*

14. _____ i tuoi amici alla festa? *Have your friends come to the party?*

   No, non _____. *No, they have not come.*

More About the Definite Article

If you feel you need to now, review Chapter 5 on the forms of the definite article. Here are a few more rules for using definite articles:

- The definite article is used before mass nouns (normally used as subjects), and with all nouns in the plural that express generalizations.

- As a guideline, remember that you cannot start an Italian sentence with a noun without its article.

Il caffè italiano è perfetto.	*Italian coffee is perfect.*
La pazienza è una virtù.	*Patience is a virtue.*
Gli italiani sono simpatici.	*Italians are nice.*
Le macchine sono care oggi.	*Cars are expensive these days.*

- The definite article must be used before geographical names (continents, countries, states, rivers, islands, mountains, etc.), except for cities.

l'Italia	*Italy*
la Sicilia	*Sicily*
gli Stati Uniti	*the United States*
la California	*California*

But:

Roma	*Rome*
Firenze	*Florence*
Venezia	*Venice*

- The definite article is dropped before an unmodified geographical noun.

Vado in Italia.	*I am going to Italy.*
Vivo in Francia.	*I live in France.*

- But when the noun is modified, the definite article must be used.

Vado nell'Italia centrale.	*I am going to central Italy.*
Vivo nella Francia meridionale.	*I live in southern France.*

- The definite article is commonly used in place of possessive adjectives when referring to family members in the singular, parts of the body, and clothing.

Oggi vado in centro con la zia.	*Today I am going downtown with my aunt.*
Mi fa male la testa.	*My head hurts.*
Franco non si mette mai la giacca.	*Franco never puts his jacket on.*

- The definite article is used with the days of the week when indicating a habitual action.

Il lunedì vado sempre in centro.	*On Mondays I always go downtown.*
La domenica guardo sempre la televisione.	*On Sundays I always watch television.*

- The definite article is used with titles, except when directly addressing someone.

Il dottor Rossi è italiano.	*Dr. Rossi is Italian.*
La professoressa Bianchi è molto brava.	*Professor Bianchi is very good.*

But:

Dottor Rossi, come va?	*Dr. Rossi, how is it going?*
Professoressa Bianchi, come sta?	*Professor Bianchi, how are you?*

- The definite article is used before the names of languages and before nouns referring to school subjects.

Studio lo spagnolo quest'anno.	*I am studying Spanish this year.*
Sto studiando la matematica.	*I am studying mathematics.*

- The definite article is dropped after the prepositions **di** and **in** in some expressions.

Ecco il mio libro di spagnolo.	*Here is my Spanish book.*
Lui è molto bravo in matematica.	*He is very good in math.*

- The definite article is used with the words **scorso** (*last*) and **prossimo** (*next*) in time expressions.

la settimana scorsa	*last week*
il mese prossimo	*next month*

Oral Practice

Practice saying the following sentences out loud.

Com'è l'espresso in Italia?	*How is espresso in Italy?*
L'espresso in Italia è perfetto!	*Espresso in Italy is perfect!*
Che cosa è la pazienza?	*What is patience?*
La pazienza è una virtù.	*Patience is a virtue.*
Come sono gli americani?	*How are Americans?*
Gli americani sono simpatici.	*Americans are nice.*
Dov'è l'Italia?	*Where is Italy?*
L'Italia è in Europa.	*Italy is in Europe.*
Dov'è Firenze?	*Where is Florence?*
Firenze è nell'Italia centrale.	*Florence is in central Italy.*
Con chi vai di solito al cinema?	*With whom do you usually go to the movies?*
Di solito vado con la zia.	*Usually, I go with my aunt.*

Dove vai di solito il venerdì?	*Where do you usually go on Fridays?*
Il venerdì vado sempre in centro.	*On Fridays I always go downtown.*
Ecco il dottor Rossi.	*Here is Dr. Rossi.*
Buongiorno, dottor Rossi.	*Good day, Dr. Rossi.*
Che cosa studi?	*What are you studying?*
Sto studiando la matematica.	*I am studying mathematics.*
Dove sei andato la settimana scorsa?	*Where did you go last week?*
Sono andato a New York.	*I went to New York.*
Dove vanno il mese prossimo?	*Where are they going next month?*
Il mese prossimo vanno in Francia.	*Next month they are going to France.*

Written Practice 4

Fill in the blanks with the appropriate forms of the missing articles or prepositions, if required.

1. Com'è _____ pizza in Italia? *How is the pizza in Italy?*

   _____ pizza in Italia è perfetta! *Pizza in Italy is perfect!*

2. Che cosa è _____ pazienza? *What is patience?*

   _____ pazienza è una virtù. *Patience is a virtue.*

3. Come sono _____ italiani? *How are Italians?*

   _____ italiani sono simpatici. *Italians are nice.*

4. Dov'è _____ Sicilia? *Where is Sicily?*

   _____ Sicilia è _____ Italia meridionale. *Sicily is in southern Italy.*

5. Dov'è Pisa? *Where is Pisa?*

   Pisa è _____ Italia centrale. *Pisa is in central Italy.*

6. Con chi vai di solito al cinema? *With whom do you usually go to the movies?*

   Di solito vado con _____ amici. *Usually, I go with my friends.*

7. Dove vai di solito _____ sabato? *Where do you usually go on Saturdays?*

   _____ sabato vado sempre in centro. *On Saturdays I always go downtown.*

8. Ecco _____dottoressa Rossi. *Here is Dr. Rossi.*

   Buongiorno, _____ dottoressa Rossi. *Good day, Dr. Rossi.*

9. Che cosa studi? *What are you studying?*

   Sto studiando _____ italiano. *I am studying Italian.*

10. Dove sei andato _____ mese scorso? *Where did you go last month?*

    Sono andato _____ Italia. *I went to Italy.*

11. Dove vai _____ settimana prossima? *Where are you going next week?*

    _____ settimana prossima vado a Pisa. *Next week I am going to Pisa.*

QUIZ

Put the verbs in parentheses in the correct forms of the present perfect tense. Don't forget the auxiliary verb! And remember that when using the auxiliary **essere**, the past participle must agree with the subject.

1. Ieri io (*comprare*) _____ una nuova macchina.

   Mio fratello (*vendere*) _____ la sua macchina la settimana scorsa.

   E tu Maria, quanto tempo (*dormire*) _____ ieri?

   Noi non (*divertirsi*) _____ in Italia.

   Anche voi (*venire*) _____ alla festa?

   I miei amici (*arrivare*) _____ tardi.

   Le tue amiche (*alzarsi*) _____ presto.

Fill in the blanks with the missing parts to each verb formation.

2. Ieri sera mia sorella _____ vist_____ un documentario alla televisione.

3. I miei amici _____ _____ divertit_____ molto in Italia.

4. Quanto _____ costat _____ quella macchina?

5. Quante ore _____ durat _____ quel film?

6. Marco e Maria, dove _____ andat _____ ieri?

Choose the appropriate response to each question.

7. Dove sono andati i tuoi amici?

    (a) In Italia.

    (b) Nell'Italia.

8. E le tue amiche, dove sono andate?

    (a) Nella Francia meridionale.

    (b) In Francia meridionale.

Personal Matters! Answer each question appropriately.

9. Che cosa fai di solito il sabato o la domenica?

    _____ .

10. Che tempo ha fatto ieri nella tua città?

    _____ .

CHAPTER 13

Using the Imperfect Tense

Here's what you will learn in this chapter:

Imperfect Tense
Irregular Verbs in the Imperfect Tense
Progressive Form of the Imperfect Tense
More About Demonstratives and Possessives

Imperfect Tense

Ieri, mentre io dormivo, lui guardava la televisione. *Yesterday, while I was sleeping, he was watching television.* The two verbs in this sentence are in the imperfect tense (**dormivo** and **guardava**). The imperfect tense differs from the present perfect in that it allows you to express a past action that continued for an indefinite period of time. The sentence does not tell us when the actions of *sleeping* and *watching television* came to an end, does it?

Remember that the present perfect tense, discussed in Chapter 12, allows you, in essence, to refer to a finished past action—an action that can be visualized as having started and ended. For example, look at the following sentence. How long did the *sleeping* activity last? Two hours.

Ieri ho dormito due ore.	*Yesterday I slept two hours.*

The imperfect is also used to refer to habitual or repeated actions in the past, and to describe the characteristics of people and things as they used to be.

Da giovane, suonavo il pianoforte.	*As a youth, I used to play the piano.*
Da bambina, lei aveva i capelli biondi.	*As a child, she had (used to have) blonde hair.*

The imperfect tense is formed by dropping the **-re** ending from all three conjugations and adding the following endings:

Endings

(io)	**-vo**	(noi)	**-vamo**
(tu)	**-vi**	(voi)	**-vate**
(Lei)	**-va**	(Loro)	**-vano**
(lui/lei)	**-va**	(loro)	**-vano**

IMPERFECT OF FIRST-CONJUGATION VERBS

suonare *to play (an instrument)*

Drop the **-re** (**suona-**) and add the imperfect tense endings:

(io) suonavo	*I was playing, used to play*
(tu) suonavi	*you (familiar) were playing, used to play*
(Lei) suonava	*you (polite) were playing, used to play*
(lui/lei) suonava	*he/she was playing, used to play*
(noi) suonavamo	*we were playing, used to play*
(voi) suonavate	*you (familiar plural) were playing, used to play*
(Loro) suonavano	*you (polite plural) were playing, used to play*
(loro) suonavano	*they were playing, used to play*

IMPERFECT OF SECOND-CONJUGATION VERBS

scrivere *to write*

Drop the **-re** (**scrive-**) and add the imperfect tense endings:

(io) scrivevo	*I was writing, used to write*
(tu) scrivevi	*you* (familiar) *were writing, used to write*
(Lei) scriveva	*you* (polite) *were writing, used to write*
(lui/lei) scriveva	*he/she was writing, used to write*
(noi) scrivevamo	*we were writing, used to write*
(voi) scrivevate	*you* (familiar plural) *were writing, used to write*
(Loro) scrivevano	*you* (polite plural) *were writing, used to write*
(loro) scrivevano	*they were writing, used to write*

IMPERFECT OF THIRD-CONJUGATION VERBS

finire *to finish*

Drop the **-re** (**fini-**) and add the imperfect tense endings:

(io) finivo	*I was finishing, used to finish*
(tu) finivi	*you* (familiar) *were finishing, used to finish*
(Lei) finiva	*you* (polite) *were finishing, used to finish*
(lui/lei) finiva	*he/she was finishing, used to finish*
(noi) finivamo	*we were finishing, used to finish*
(voi) finivate	*you* (familiar plural) *were finishing, used to finish*
(Loro) finivano	*you* (polite plural) *were finishing, used to finish*
(loro) finivano	*they were finishing, used to finish*

NOTE: *As you memorize the previous conjugations, note the various English translations that the imperfect tense allows you to cover.*

IMPERFECT OF REFLEXIVE VERBS

If the verb is reflexive, the reflexive infinitive ending is dropped in a similar way.

lavarsi   *to wash oneself*

Drop the **-rsi** (**lava-**) and add the same imperative endings. But be careful, don't forget the reflexive pronouns.

(io) mi lavavo	*I was washing myself, used to wash myself*
(tu) ti lavavi	*you (familiar) were washing yourself, used to wash yourself*
(Lei) si lavava	*you (polite) were washing yourself, used to wash yourself*
(lui/lei) si lavava	*he/she was washing himself/herself, used to wash himself/herself*
(noi) ci lavavamo	*we were washing ourselves, used to wash ourselves*
(voi) vi lavavate	*you (familiar plural) were washing yourselves, used to wash yourselves*
(Loro) si lavavano	*you (polite plural) were washing yourselves, used to wash yourselves*
(loro) si lavavano	*they were washing themselves, used to wash themselves*

Oral Practice

Practice saying the following sentences out loud.

Marco, perché andavi spesso in Italia da giovane?	*Mark, why did you used to go often to Italy as a young man?*
Andavo spesso in Italia, perché studiavo l'italiano.	*I used to go often, because I was studying Italian.*
Che cosa guardava tuo fratello ieri, mentre tua sorella studiava?	*What was your brother watching yesterday, while your sister was studying?*
Lui guardava un programma di sport, mentre lei studiava.	*He was watching a sports program, while she was studying.*
Pina e Dino, che cosa mangiavate ieri, mentre io studiavo?	*Pina and Dino, what were you eating yesterday, while I was studying?*
Mangiavamo un panino, mentre tu studiavi.	*We were eating a sandwich, while you were studying.*
A che ora si alzavano i tuoi genitori di solito?	*At what time did your parents used to get up regularly?*
Loro si alzavano sempre presto.	*They always used to get up early.*
Quanti amici avevi, Maria, da bambina?	*How many friends did you have, Mary, as a child?*
Da bambina, avevo tanti amici.	*As a child, I used to have a lot of friends.*
Quanta gente conosceva tua sorella, da giovane?	*How many people did your sister know as a youth?*

Lei conosceva tanta gente.	*She used to know a lot of people.*
Gina e Paolo, che cosa dovevate fare spesso da bambini?	*Gina and Paul, what did you have to do often as children?*
Noi dovevamo studiare molto.	*We had to study a lot.*
Che cosa si mettevano i tuoi amici da giovani per uscire?	*What did your friends used to wear to go out as youth?*
Loro si mettevano sempre vestiti alla moda.	*They always put on fashionable clothes.*
Bruno, a che ora finivi di lavorare di solito da giovane?	*Bruno, at what time did you usually finish working as a youth?*
Finivo sempre verso le sei.	*I always used to finish around six.*
Che cosa faceva tuo padre, mentre tuo fratello dormiva?	*What was your father doing, while your brother was sleeping?*
Mentre mio fratello dormiva, mio padre puliva la macchina.	*While my brother was sleeping, my father was cleaning the car.*
Che cosa faceva Gino, mentre voi uscivate?	*What was Gino doing as you were going out?*
Mentre noi uscivamo, Gino veniva alla nostra casa.	*As we were going out, Gino was coming to our house.*
È vero che i tuoi amici si divertivano sempre in Italia da bambini?	*Is it true that your friends always used to enjoy themselves in Italy as children?*
Sì, loro si divertivano sempre.	*Yes, they always used to enjoy themselves.*

Written Practice 1

Fill in the blanks with the correct forms of the imperfect tense, using the English translations as a guide.

1. Perché la signora Smith _____ spesso in Italia da giovane? *Why did Mrs. Smith used to go often to Italy as a young woman?*

   _____ spesso in Italia, perché _____ l'italiano. *She used to go often to Italy, because she was studying Italian.*

2. Che cosa _____ voi ieri, mentre noi _____
_____? *What were you watching yesterday, while we were studying?*

Noi _____ un programma di sport, mentre
voi _____. *We were watching a sports program, while you were studying.*

3. Ragazzi, che cosa _____ ieri, mentre io
_____? *Guys, what were you eating yesterday, while I was studying?*

_____ un panino, mentre tu
_____. *We were eating a sandwich, while you were studying.*

4. A che ora _____, Marco, di solito? *At what time did you used to get up usually, Mark?*

Io _____ sempre presto. *I always used to get up early.*

5. Quanti amici _____ tua sorella da bambina? *How many friends did your sister have, as a child?*

Da bambina, _____ tanti amici. *As a child, she used to have a lot of friends.*

6. Quanta gente _____ voi, da giovani? *How many people did you know as youths?*

Noi _____ tanta gente. *We used to know a lot of people.*

7. Che cosa _____ fare spesso da bambini loro? *What did they have to do often as children?*

Loro _____ studiare molto. *They had to study a lot.*

8. Che cosa _____, Maria, da giovane per uscire? *Mary, what did you used to wear to go out as a youth?*

Io _____ sempre vestiti alla moda. *I always put on fashionable clothes.*

9. A che ora _____ di lavorare di solito tuo fratello da giovane? *At what time did your brother usually finish working as a youth?*

_____ sempre verso le sei. *He always used to finish around six.*

10. Che cosa faceva il papà, mentre voi _____?
What was Dad doing, while you were sleeping?

   Mentre noi _____ , il papà _____
   la macchina. *While we were sleeping, Dad was cleaning the car.*

11. Che cosa faceva Gino, mentre tua sorella _____?
What was Gino doing as your sister was going out?

   Mentre lei _____ , Gino _____
   alla nostra casa. *As she was going out, Gino was coming to our house.*

12. È vero che tu _____ sempre in Italia da
bambino? *Is it true that you always used to enjoy yourself in Italy as a child?*

   Sì, io _____ sempre. *Yes, I always used to enjoy myself.*

Irregular Verbs in the Imperfect Tense

As you've seen, the imperfect tense allows you to refer to past actions that were continuous, to states and conditions that were habitual or recurring, and to the characteristics of people and things as they used to be or once were.

As with the other tenses, some verbs have irregular forms in the imperfect tense, too. Of the ones you have encountered so far, the following have irregular imperfect forms:

bere   *to drink*
(io) bevevo, (tu) bevevi, (lui/lei/Lei) beveva, (noi) bevevamo, (voi) bevevate, (loro/Loro) bevevano

dare   *to give*
(io) davo, (tu) davi, (lui/lei/Lei) dava, (noi) davamo, (voi) davate, (loro/Loro) davano

dire   *to say, tell*
(io) dicevo, (tu) dicevi, (lui/lei/Lei) diceva, (noi) dicevamo, (voi) dicevate, (loro/Loro) dicevano

essere   *to be*
(io) ero, (tu) eri, (lui/lei/Lei) era, (noi) eravamo, (voi) eravate, (loro/Loro) erano

fare   *to do, make*
(io) facevo, (tu) facevi, (lui/lei/Lei) faceva, (noi) facevamo, (voi) facevate, (loro/Loro) facevano

stare   *to stay*
(io) stavo, (tu) stavi, (lui/lei/Lei) stava, (noi) stavamo, (voi) stavate, (loro/Loro) stavano

Oral Practice

Practice saying the following sentences out loud.

Marco, che cosa bevevi ieri al bar?	*Mark, what were you drinking yesterday at the coffee shop?*
Bevevo un cappuccino.	*I was drinking a cappuccino.*
Che cosa dava tuo fratello ai genitori per Natale?	*What did your brother used to give to your parents for Christmas?*
Lui non dava niente ai genitori.	*He never gave anything to our parents.*
Che cosa dicevate ieri, mentre io leggevo il giornale?	*What were you saying yesterday, while I was reading the newspaper?*
Non dicevamo niente.	*We were not saying anything.*
Chi erano quegli uomini che parlavano al professore ieri?	*Who were those men talking to the professor yesterday?*
Erano i suoi cugini.	*They were his cousins.*
Che cosa faceva tua sorella ieri, mentre tu eri in centro?	*What was your sister doing yesterday, while you were downtown?*
Non faceva niente.	*She was not doing anything.*
Come stava, signora, ieri?	*How were you feeling yesterday, madam?*
Non stavo molto bene.	*I was not feeling too well.*

Written Practice 2

Fill in the blanks with the appropriate imperfect forms of the indicated verbs.

1. Che cosa _____ ieri al bar tua sorella? *What was your sister drinking yesterday at the coffee shop?*

   Lei _____ un cappuccino. *She was drinking a cappuccino.*

2. Che cosa _____ a tuo fratello per Natale, Laura? *What did you used to give to your brother for Christmas, Laura?*

   Io non _____ niente a mio fratello. *I never gave anything to my brother.*

3. Che cosa _____ ieri, mentre io _____ il giornale? *What were they saying yesterday, while I was reading the newspaper?*

   Non _____ niente. *They were not saying anything.*

4. Chi _____ quell'uomo che _____ al professore ieri? *Who was that man talking to the professor yesterday?*

   Lui _____ suo cugino. *He was his cousin.*

5. Che cosa _____ voi ieri, mentre io _____ in centro? *What were you doing yesterday, while I was downtown?*

   Non _____ niente, mentre tu _____ in centro. *We were not doing anything, while you were downtown.*

6. Come _____, Maria, ieri? *How were you feeling yesterday, Mary?*

   Non _____ molto bene. *I was not feeling too well.*

Progressive Form of the Imperfect Tense

The imperfect tense has a corresponding progressive form. If you feel you need to now, review the present progressive tense in Chapter 9. The imperfect progressive is conjugated with the imperfect indicative of **stare** and the gerund of the verb showing the action. Here is the verb **guardare** conjugated fully in the imperfect progressive:

guardare	*to watch*
(io) stavo guardando	*I was watching*
(tu) stavi guardando	*you (familiar) were watching*
(Lei) stava guardando	*you (polite) were watching*
(lui/lei) stava guardando	*he/she was watching*
(noi) stavamo guardando	*we were watching*
(voi) stavate guardando	*you (familiar plural) were watching*
(Loro) stavano guardando	*you (polite plural) were watching*
(loro) stavano guardando	*they were watching*

Recall from Chapter 9 that progressive forms allow you to zero in on an ongoing action in the past.

Mentre lei stava mangiando, io guardavo la televisione.	*While she was eating, I was watching television.*
Ieri mia sorella stava studiando, quando sei arrivata.	*Yesterday my sister was studying, when you arrived.*

Oral Practice

Practice saying the following sentences out loud.

Marco, che cosa stavi bevendo ieri al bar?	*Mark, what were you drinking yesterday at the coffee shop?*
Stavo bevendo un cappuccino.	*I was drinking a cappuccino.*
Che cosa stava leggendo tuo fratello ieri?	*What was your brother reading yesterday?*
Lui non stava leggendo niente.	*He was not reading anything.*
Che cosa stavate dicendo ieri, mentre io leggevo il giornale?	*What were you saying yesterday, while I was reading the newspaper?*
Non stavamo dicendo niente.	*We were not saying anything.*
Che cosa stavate facendo ieri, Maria, tu e tuo fratello?	*What were you and your brother doing yesterday, Mary?*
Mentre io stavo pulendo la mia macchina, lui leggeva.	*While I was cleaning my car, he was reading.*

Che cosa stava facendo tua sorella
ieri, mentre tu eri in centro?

*What was your sister doing yesterday,
while you were downtown?*

Non stava facendo niente.

She was not doing anything.

Written Practice 3

Fill in the blanks with the appropriate imperfect progressive forms of the indicated verbs.

1. Signor Marchi, che cosa _____ ieri al
   bar? *Mr. Marchi, what were you drinking yesterday at the coffee shop?*

   _____ un espresso. *I was drinking an
   espresso.*

2. Che cosa _____ tu e tuo fratello ieri? *What
   were you and your brother reading yesterday?*

   Noi non _____ niente. *We were not reading
   anything.*

3. Che cosa _____ ieri, mentre io leggevo
   il giornale? *What were they saying yesterday, while I was reading the
   newspaper?*

   Loro non _____ niente. *They were not
   saying anything.*

4. Che cosa _____ tuo fratello e tua sorella
   ieri? *What were your brother and sister doing yesterday?*

   Mentre lui _____ la sua macchina, lei ____
   _____. *While he was cleaning his car, she was
   reading.*

5. Che cosa _____ tu ieri, mentre io ero in
   centro? *What were you doing yesterday, while I was downtown?*

   Non _____ niente. *I was not doing
   anything.*

6. Marco, che cosa _____ tu, mentre tua sorella
   _____? *Mark, what were you doing, while
   your sister was getting dressed?*

   Anch'io _____. *I was also getting dressed.*

More About Demonstratives and Possessives

In Chapter 8 demonstratives were discussed when used as adjectives (if you need to, review the demonstratives in that chapter now). However, demonstratives can also be used as pronouns.

Demonstrative pronouns replace noun phrases that are constructed with demonstratives. For example:

Quel ragazzo è italiano.	*That boy is Italian.*
Quello è italiano.	*That one is Italian.*
Questa ragazza è americana.	*This girl is American.*
Questa è americana.	*This one is American.*

The demonstrative pronouns retain the gender and number of the demonstratives they replace. However, there are a few changes to be made to their forms. Here are all the possibilities:

Masculine Demonstratives

Singular Form

		Corresponding Pronoun Form	
questo ragazzo	*this boy*	questo	*this one (referring to* ragazzo*)*
quest'amico	*this friend*	questo	*this one (referring to* amico*)*
quel ragazzo	*that boy*	quello	*that one (referring to* ragazzo*)*
quello zio	*that uncle*	quello	*that one (referring to* zio*)*
quell'amico	*that friend*	quello	*that one (referring to* amico*)*

Plural Form

		Corresponding Pronoun Form	
questi ragazzi	*these boys*	questi	*these ones (referring to* ragazzi*)*
questi amici	*these friends*	questi	*these ones (referring to* amici*)*
quei ragazzi	*those boys*	quelli	*those ones (referring to* ragazzi*)*
quegli zii	*those uncles*	quelli	*those ones (referring to* zii*)*
quegli amici	*those friends*	quelli	*those ones (referring to* amici*)*

Feminine Demonstratives

Singular Form

		Corresponding Pronoun Form	
questa ragazza	*this girl*	questa	*this one (referring to* ragazza*)*
quest'amica	*this friend*	questa	*this one (referring to* amica*)*
quella ragazza	*that girl*	quella	*that one (referring to* ragazza*)*
quell'amica	*that friend*	quella	*that one (referring to* amica*)*

Plural Form

		Corresponding Pronoun Form	
queste ragazze	*these girls*	queste	*these ones* (*referring to* ragazze)
queste amiche	*these friends*	queste	*these ones* (*referring to* amiche)
quelle ragazze	*these girls*	quelle	*those ones* (*referring to* ragazze)
quelle amiche	*these friends*	quelle	*those ones* (*referring to* amiche)

Similarly, a possessive pronoun replaces a noun phrase containing a possessive adjective. The Italian possessive pronouns correspond to the English pronouns *mine, yours, his, hers, ours, theirs.*

La mia amica è simpatica, e la tua?	*My friend is nice, and yours?*
Ecco la nostra macchina. Dov'è la vostra?	*Here is our car. Where is yours?*

The definite article is always used with possessive pronoun forms, even when the noun phrase replacements contain singular, unmodified, kinship nouns.

Sua sorella è simpatica.	*His/her sister is pleasant.*
La sua non è simpatica.	*His/hers is not pleasant.*
Vostro zio è italiano.	*Your uncle is Italian.*
Il nostro è americano.	*Ours is American.*

Oral Practice

Practice saying the following sentences out loud.

Chi sono quei due ragazzi?	*Who are those two boys?*
Questo è mio fratello e quello è mio cugino.	*This one is my brother and that one is my cousin.*
Chi sono quegli uomini?	*Who are those men?*
Questi sono i miei zii e quelli sono i miei cugini.	*These ones are my uncles and those ones are my cousins.*
Chi sono quelle due ragazze?	*Who are those two girls?*
Questa è mia sorella e quella è mia cugina.	*This one is my sister and that one is my cousin.*
Chi sono quelle donne?	*Who are those women?*

Queste sono le mie zie e quelle sono le mie cugine.	*These ones are my aunts and those ones are my cousins.*
Mia sorella è alta, e la tua?	*My sister is tall, and yours?*
Anche la mia è alta.	*Mine is also tall.*
La sua macchina è nuova, e la vostra?	*His car is new, and yours?*
Anche la nostra è nuova.	*Ours is also new.*
La mia amica è americana, e la loro?	*My friend is American, and theirs?*
La loro è italiana.	*Theirs is Italian.*

Written Practice 4

Fill in the blanks with the appropriate pronoun forms of either the demonstrative or the possessive, as necessary.

1. Chi sono quelle due persone? *Who are those two people?*

   _____ è mio fratello e _____ è mio cugino. *This one is my brother and that one is my cousin.*

2. Chi sono queste persone? *Who are these people?*

   _____ sono i miei zii e _____ sono i miei cugini. *These ones are my uncles and those ones are my cousins.*

3. Chi sono quelle due persone? *Who are those two people?*

   _____ è mia sorella e _____ è mia cugina. *This one is my sister and that one is my cousin.*

4. Chi sono quelle persone? *Who are those people?*

   _____ sono le mie zie e _____ sono le mie cugine. *These ones are my aunts and those ones are my cousins.*

5. Mia sorella è simpatica, e _____? *My sister is nice, and yours?*

   Anche _____ è simpatica. *Mine is also nice.*

6. La sua giacca è nuova, e _____? *His jacket is new, and yours (plural)?*

   Anche _____ è nuova. *Ours is also new.*

7. La mia amica è italiana, e _____? *My friend is Italian, and theirs?*

   _____ è francese. *Theirs is French.*

QUIZ

Fill in the blanks with the indicated forms of the imperfect tense. For example:

   (io) cantare *io cantavo* _____

1. (io) leggere _____

   (io) capire _____

   (tu) mangiare _____

   (tu) vedere _____

   (lui) cominciare _____

   (lei) avere _____

   (noi) pagare _____

   (noi) sapere _____

   (voi) mangiare _____

   (voi) potere _____

   (loro) arrivare _____

   (loro) avere _____

Circle the letter of the appropriate present perfect, imperfect, or progressive imperfect verb form that best completes each sentence.

2. Quando mia sorella era giovane, _____ il pianoforte.

   (a) ha suonato

   (b) suonava

   (c) stava suonando

3. Da giovane, lei _____ i capelli lunghi.

   (a) ha avuto

   (b) aveva

   (c) stava avendo

4. Ieri, mentre mio fratello dormiva, io _____ la televisione.

   (a) ho guardato

   (b) guardavo

   (c) stavo guardando

5. Ieri _____ tutta la giornata (*all day long*).

   (a) ho dormito

   (b) dormivo

   (c) stavo dormendo

Fill in the blanks with the missing demonstratives or possessives, as necessary.

6. Chi sono quelle due persone?

   _____ qui vicino è mio fratello e _____ è mio padre. *This one right here is my brother and that one is my father.*

7. Chi sono quelle altre persone?

   _____ qui vicini sono amici e _____ sono le nostre zie. *These ones right here are friends and those ones are our aunts.*

8. Mia sorella si chiama Paola, e _____? *My sister's name is Paula, and yours?*

   _____ si chiama Sara. *Mine is called Sara.*

9. I nostri zii vivono in America e _____? *Our uncles live in America and yours (plural)?*

   Anche _____ vivono in America. *Ours too live in America.*

Personal Matters! Answer the question appropriately.

10. Che cosa dovevi fare di solito da bambino/a?

    _____.

CHAPTER 14

Using the Pluperfect and Past Absolute Tenses

Here's what you will learn in this chapter:

Pluperfect Tense
Past Absolute Tense
Irregular Verbs in the Past Absolute Tense
Transportation

Pluperfect Tense

Lui mi ha detto che aveva già parlato al professore. *He told me that he had already talked to the professor.* The tense used in the verb form **aveva parlato** is called the pluperfect. It corresponds exactly to the English pluperfect: *I had spoken, you had gone,* and so on.

The pluperfect is a compound tense. As such, it is conjugated with an auxiliary verb, which is either **avere** or **essere**, plus the past participle of the action verb.

The pluperfect is formed with the imperfect form of the auxiliary verb plus the past participle of the verb showing the action, in that order.

The following are the complete conjugations of one verb conjugated with **avere**, another with **essere**, and one reflexive verb.

parlare	*to speak*
(io) avevo parlato	*I had spoken*
(tu) avevi parlato	*you (familiar) had spoken*
(Lei) aveva parlato	*you (polite) had spoken*
(lui/lei) aveva parlato	*he/she had spoken*
(noi) avevamo parlato	*we had spoken*
(voi) avevate parlato	*you (familiar plural) had spoken*
(Loro) avevano parlato	*you (polite plural) had spoken*
(loro) avevano parlato	*they had spoken*

partire	*to leave*
(io) ero partito/a	*I had left*
(tu) eri partito/a	*you (familiar) had left*
(Lei) era partito/a	*you (polite) had left*
(lui) era partito	*he had left*
(lei) era partita	*she had left*
(noi) eravamo partiti/e	*we had left*
(voi) eravate partiti/e	*you (familiar plural) had left*
(Loro) erano partiti/e	*you (polite plural) had left*
(loro) erano partiti/e	*they had left*

mettersi	*to put on*
(io) mi ero messo/a	*I had put on*
(tu) ti eri messo/a	*you (familiar) had put on*
(Lei) si era messo/a	*you (polite) had put on*
(lui) si era messo	*he had put on*
(lei) si era messa	*she had put on*
(noi) ci eravamo messi/e	*we had put on*

(voi) vi eravate messi/e	*you (familiar plural) had put on*
(Loro) si erano messi/e	*you (polite plural) had put on*
(loro) si erano messi/e	*they had put on*

The pluperfect tense (literally, "more than perfect" or "more than past") allows you to express an action that occurred before a simple past action.

Dopo che era arrivata, ha telefonato. *After she had arrived, she phoned.*

Oral Practice

Practice saying the following sentences out loud.

Che cosa avevi mangiato ieri, Maria, prima di uscire?	*What had you eaten yesterday, Mary, before going out?*
Non avevo mangiato niente.	*I had not eaten anything.*
A che ora hanno chiuso?	*At what time did they close?*
Avevano già chiuso quando sono arrivato.	*They had already closed up when I arrived.*
A che ora avete finito di studiare?	*At what time did you finish studying?*
Avevamo già finito di studiare quando siete venuti.	*We had already finished studying when you came.*
Ha fatto delle spese ieri tuo fratello?	*Did your brother do some shopping yesterday?*
No, aveva già fatto delle speso il giorno prima.	*No, he had already done some shopping the day before.*
Dove eri andato Marco ieri, quando ho chiamato?	*Where had you gone yesterday, Mark, when I called?*
Ero già andato in centro.	*I had already gone downtown.*
Dove era tuo fratello quando ho chiamato?	*Where was your brother when I called?*
Lui era già uscito.	*He had already gone out.*
Siete venuti anche voi alla festa?	*Did you also come to the party?*
Sì, infatti, eravamo venuti prima di te.	*Yes, in fact, we had come before you.*

Lei si è messa un costume per la festa, vero? — *She wore a costume for the party, right?*

Sì, e si era messa lo stesso costume l'anno scorso. — *Yes, and she had put on the same costume last year.*

Written Practice 1

Fill in the blanks with the appropriate pluperfect forms of the indicated verbs.

1. Che cosa _____ ieri, Maria, prima di uscire? *What had you done yesterday, Mary, before going out?*

   _____ già _____ tutto il libro. *I had already studied the whole book.*

2. A che ora hanno aperto? *At what time did they open up?*

   _____ già _____, quando sei arrivato. *They had already opened up when you arrived.*

3. A che ora avete cominciato a studiare? *At what time did you start studying?*

   _____ già _____ a studiare, quando hai chiamato. *We had already started studying when you called.*

4. Ha comprato la macchina ieri tuo fratello? *Did your brother buy the car yesterday?*

   No, _____ già _____ la macchina il giorno prima. *No, he had already bought the car the day before.*

5. Dove _____, Maria, ieri, quando ho chiamato? *Where had you gone yesterday Mary, when I called?*

   _____ già _____ al cinema. *I had already gone to the movies.*

6. Dove era tuo sorella quando ho chiamato? *Where was your sister when I called?*

   Lei _____ già _____. *She had already gone out.*

7. Siete tornati anche voi alla festa? *Did you also go back to the party?*

   Sì, infatti, _____ prima di te. *Yes, in fact, we had come back before you.*

8. Lei si è alzato presto, vero? *She got up early, right?*

Sì, infatti, _____ prima di voi. *Yes, in fact, she had gotten up before you.*

Past Absolute Tense

Loro andarono in Italia molti anni fa. *They went to Italy many years ago.* In what tense is the verb in this sentence? It is yet another past tense—the last one you will need to learn. It is called the past absolute.

The past absolute is used primarily to refer to actions that occurred in the distant past. The past absolute is translated similarly to the present perfect. For example, the present perfect phrase **Ho parlato** can mean both *I have spoken* and *I spoke*. The past absolute translation is the second option: *I spoke* (**parlai**).

Ieri loro sono andati in Italia.	*Yesterday they went to Italy.*
Molti anni fa andarono in Italia.	*Many years ago they went to Italy.*

The past absolute is formed by dropping the infinitive ending and adding the following endings according to the person (first, second, third) and the verb type. Here is how to form the past absolute of first-conjugation verbs:

cantare	*to sing*
(io) cant**ai**	*I sang*
(tu) cant**asti**	*you* (familiar) *sang*
(Lei) cant**ò**	*you* (polite) *sang*
(lui/lei) cant**ò**	*he/she sang*
(noi) cant**ammo**	*we sang*
(voi) cant**aste**	*you* (familiar plural) *sang*
(Loro) cant**arono**	*you* (polite plural) *sang*
(loro) cant**arono**	*they sang*

PAST ABSOLUTE OF SECOND-CONJUGATION VERBS

The same pattern applies to second-conjugation verbs. Only the endings are different. The following example shows the conjugation of an **-ere** verb. Notice that there are alternative endings for some of the persons in the conjugation.

vendere	to sell
(io) vend**ei** (vend**etti**)	I sold
(tu) vend**esti**	you (familiar) sold
(Lei) vend**è** (vend**ette**)	you (polite) sold
(lui/lei) vend**è** (vend**ette**)	he/she sold
(noi) vend**emmo**	we sold
(voi) vend**este**	you (familiar plural) sold
(Loro) vend**erono** (vend**ettero**)	you (polite plural) sold
(loro) vend**erono** (vend**ettero**)	they sold

PAST ABSOLUTE OF THIRD-CONJUGATION VERBS

Again, the same pattern applies to third-conjugation verbs. Only the endings, as you might expect, are different. Here's an example:

finire	to finish
(io) fin**ii**	I finished
(tu) fin**isti**	you (familiar) finished
(Lei) fin**ì**	you (polite) finished
(lui/lei) fin**ì**	he/she finished
(noi) fin**immo**	we finished
(voi) fin**iste**	you (familiar plural) finished
(Loro) fin**irono**	you (polite plural) finished
(loro) fin**irono**	they finished

The past absolute can be used in place of the present perfect: *I finished, I sang,* and so on. It is used primarily in reference to historical events and events that occurred in the distant past.

I miei genitori tornarono in Italia nel 1986.	*My parents returned to Italy in 1986.*
Finirono quel lavoro tanto tempo fa.	*They finished that job a long time ago.*

The past absolute cannot be used with temporal adverbs such as the following:

ancora	*yet, still*	già	*already*
appena	*just*	poco fa	*a little while ago*

These adverbs limit the action to the immediate past. Only the present perfect can be used in such cases. The exception is **fa**, because it can be used with immediate past and remote past actions.

Alessandro è arrivato poco tempo fa.	*Alexander arrived a little while ago.*
Alessandro arrivò tanti anni fa.	*Alexander arrived many years ago.*
Ho appena telefonato a lei.	*I have just phoned her.*

Oral Practice

Practice saying the following sentences out loud.

Quanto tempo fa studiasti l'italiano, Pina?	*Pina, how long ago did you study Italian?*
Studiai l'italiano in Italia molti anni fa.	*I studied Italian in Italy many years ago.*
Quando comprò la macchina tuo fratello?	*When did your brother buy the car?*
Mio fratello comprò la macchina nel 1997.	*My brother bought the car in 1997.*
Quando imparaste a guidare voi due?	*When did the two of you learn to drive?*
Imparammo venti anni fa.	*We learned twenty years ago.*
Quando tornarono in Italia i tuoi cugini?	*When did your cousins go back to Italy?*
Loro tornarono in Italia dieci anni fa.	*They went back to Italy ten years ago.*
Marco, quando dovesti partire?	*Mark, when did you have to leave?*
Dovei (Dovetti) partire quando ero bambino.	*I had to leave when I was a child.*
Quando potè (potette) venire in America tua zia?	*When could your aunt come to America?*
Mia zia potè (potette) venire nel 1995.	*She was able to come in 1995.*
Quando vendeste la casa voi?	*When did you sell the house?*
Vendemmo la casa molti anni fa.	*We sold the house many years ago.*
Quando doverono (dovettero) tornare loro?	*When did they have to return?*

Loro doverono (dovettero) tornare nel 1999.	*They had to return in 1999.*
Quando partisti per l'Italia, Pina?	*When did you leave for Italy, Pina?*
Partii alcuni anni fa.	*I left several years ago.*
Quando finiste di lavorare voi?	*When did you finish working?*
Finimmo quattro anni fa.	*We finished four years ago.*
Loro si divertirono l'anno scorso, vero?	*They had fun last year, didn't they?*
Quando partì tuo zio per l'Italia?	*When did your uncle leave for Italy?*
Partì molto tempo fa.	*He left a long time ago.*

Written Practice 2

Fill in the blanks with the appropriate past absolute forms of the indicated verbs.

1. Quanto tempo fa _____ l'italiano tua madre? *How long ago did your mom study Italian?*

   _____ l'italiano molti anni fa. *She studied Italian many years ago.*

2. Quando _____ il tuo cellulare, Marco? *When did you buy your cell phone, Mark?*

   _____ questo cellulare tempo fa. *I bought this cell phone a while back.*

3. Quando _____ a guidare loro? *When did they learn to drive?*

   _____ alcuni anni fa. *They learned several years ago.*

4. Quando _____ in Italia voi due? *When did the two of you go back to Italy?*

   Noi _____ in Italia dieci anni fa. *We went back to Italy ten years ago.*

5. Quando _____ partire? *When did they have to leave?*

   _____ partire due anni fa. *They had to leave two years ago.*

6. Quando _____ venire in America tua zia? *When could your aunt come to America?*

Mia zia _____ venire due anni fa. *She was able to come two years ago.*

7. Quando _____ la casa voi? *When did you sell the house?*

_____ la casa molti anni fa. *We sold the house many years ago.*

8. Quando _____ tornare, Giuliana? *When did you have to return, Giuliana?*

Io _____ tornare nel 1999. *I had to return in 1999.*

9. Quando _____ per l'Italia, lei? *When did she leave for Italy?*

_____ alcuni anni fa. *She left several years ago.*

10. Quando _____ di lavorare loro? *When did they finish working?*

_____ quattro anni fa. *They finished four years ago.*

11. Voi due _____ l'anno scorso, vero? *You two had fun last year, didn't you?*

Sì, _____ molto. *Yes, we had a lot of fun.*

12. Tu _____ di lavorare tempo fa, Marco, vero? *Mark, you finished working a while ago, didn't you?*

Sì, io _____ molto tempo fa. *Yes, I finished a long time ago.*

Irregular Verbs in the Past Absolute Tense

Of course, there are irregular verb forms as well. Of the ones you have encountered so far, the following have irregular past absolute forms:

avere   *to have*
(io) ebbi, (tu) avesti, (lui/lei/Lei) ebbe, (noi) avemmo, (voi) aveste, (loro/Loro) ebbero

bere   *to drink*
(io) bevvi (bevetti), (tu) bevesti, (lui/lei/Lei) bevve (bevette), (noi) bevemmo, (voi) beveste, (loro/Loro) bevvero (bevettero)

cadere   *to fall*
(io) caddi, (tu) cadesti, (lui/lei/Lei) cadde, (noi) cademmo, (voi) cadeste, (loro/Loro) caddero

chiedere   *to ask for*
(io) chiesi, (tu) chiedesti, (lui/lei/Lei) chiese, (noi) chiedemmo, (voi) chiedeste, (loro/Loro) chiesero

chiudere   *to close*
(io) chiusi, (tu) chiudesti, (lui/lei/Lei) chiuse, (noi) chiudemmo, (voi) chiudeste, (loro/Loro) chiusero

conoscere   *to know (someone), be familiar with, meet*
(io) conobbi, (tu) conoscesti, (lui/lei/Lei) conobbe, (noi) conoscemmo, (voi) conosceste, (loro/Loro) conobbero

dare   *to give*
(io) diedi, (tu) desti, (lui/lei/Lei) diede, (noi) demmo, (voi) deste, (loro/Loro) diedero

dire   *to say, tell*
(io) dissi, (tu) dicesti, (lui/lei/Lei) disse, (noi) dicemmo, (voi) diceste, (loro/Loro) dissero

essere   *to be*
(io) fui, (tu) fosti, (lui/lei/Lei) fu, (noi) fummo, (voi) foste, (loro/Loro) furono

fare   *to do, make*
(io) feci, (tu) facesti, (lui/lei/Lei) fece, (noi) facemmo, (voi) faceste, (loro/Loro) fecero

leggere   *to read*
(io) lessi, (tu) leggesti, (lui/lei/Lei) lesse, (noi) leggemmo, (voi) leggeste, (loro/Loro) lessero

mettere   *to put*
(io) misi, (tu) mettesti, (lui/lei/Lei) mise, (noi) mettemmo, (voi) metteste, (loro/Loro) misero

prendere   *to take*
(io) presi, (tu) prendesti, (lui/lei/Lei) prese, (noi) prendemmo, (voi) prendeste, (loro/Loro) presero

sapere   *to know*
(io) seppi, (tu) sapesti, (lui/lei/Lei) seppe, (noi) sapemmo, (voi) sapeste, (loro/Loro) seppero

scrivere   *to write*
(io) scrissi, (tu) scrivesti, (lui/lei/Lei) scrisse, (noi) scrivemmo, (voi) scriveste, (loro/Loro) scrissero

stare   *to stay*
(io) stetti, (tu) stesti, (lui/lei/Lei) stette, (noi) stemmo, (voi) steste, (loro/Loro) stettero

vedere   *to see*
(io) vidi, (tu) vedesti, (lui/lei/Lei) vide, (noi) vedemmo, (voi) vedeste, (loro/Loro) videro

venire   *to come*
(io) venni, (tu) venisti, (lui/lei/Lei) venne, (noi) venimmo, (voi) veniste, (loro/Loro) vennero

volere   *to want*
(io) volli, (tu) volesti, (lui/lei/Lei) volle, (noi) volemmo, (voi) voleste, (loro/Loro) vollero

Oral Practice

Practice saying the following sentences out loud.

Giovanni, anche tu avesti una Ford anni fa?	*John, you also had a Ford years ago?*
Sì, ebbi una Ford tanti anni fa.	*Yes, I had a Ford many years ago.*
Lui bevve quel caffè l'anno scorso.	*He drank that coffee last year.*
Dove cadeste voi l'anno scorso?	*Where did you fall last year?*
Che cosa chiesero loro?	*What did they ask for?*
Chiusi il negozio nel 1999.	*I closed the store in 1999.*
Conobbe sua moglie due anni fa.	*He met his wife two years ago.*
A chi deste la vostra macchina due anni fa?	*To whom did you give your car two years ago?*
Demmo la nostra macchina a Bruno.	*We gave our car to Bruno.*
Che cosa dissero loro l'estate scorsa?	*What did they say last summer?*
Quando fosti in Italia l'ultima volta?	*When were you in Italy the last time?*
Fui in Italia l'estate scorsa.	*I was in Italy last summer.*
Che tempo fece quando eravate in Italia?	*How was the weather when you were in Italy?*

Io lessi quel romanzo l'anno scorso.	*I read that novel last year.*
Dove misero la loro macchina?	*Where did they put their car?*
Presi solo il caffè.	*I only had coffee.*
Anche lui seppe la verità, vero?	*He also knew the truth, didn't he?*
Scrissi al professore tempo fa.	*I wrote to the professor a while back.*
Dove stettero loro in Italia?	*Where did they stay in Italy?*
Sì, vidi quel film due anni fa.	*Yes, I saw that movie two years ago.*
Quando venne in America tuo zio?	*When did your uncle come to America?*
Dove vollero andare loro l'anno scorso?	*Where did they want to go last year?*

Written Practice 3

Fill in the blanks with the appropriate past absolute forms of the given verbs.

1. Anche lui _____ una Ford anni fa, vero? *He also had a Ford years ago, right?*

   Sì, _____ una Ford tanti anni fa. *Yes, he had a Ford many years ago.*

2. Quando _____ quel caffè, Maria? *When did you drink that coffee, Mary?*

   Io _____ quel caffè l'anno scorso. *I drank that coffee last year.*

3. Dove _____ lei l'anno scorso? *Where did she fall last year?*

   _____ in Italia. *She fell in Italy.*

4. Che cosa _____, signor Verdi? *What did you ask for, Mr. Verdi?*

   _____ tante cose. *I asked for a lot of things.*

5. Quando _____ il negozio? *When did they close down the store?*

   _____ il negozio nel 2000. *They closed the store in 2000.*

6. Quando _____ tua moglie, Paolo? *When did your meet your wife, Paul?*

   _____ mia moglie due anni fa. *I met my wife two years ago.*

7. A chi _____ la tua macchina, Marco, due anni fa? *To whom did you give your car two years ago, Mark?*

_____ la mia macchina a Bruno. *I gave my car to Bruno.*

8. Che cosa _____ tua sorella tempo fa? *What did your sister say a while ago?*

_____ la verità. *She told the truth.*

9. Quando _____ in Italia l'ultima volta? *When were they in Italy the last time?*

_____ in Italia l'estate scorsa. *They were in Italy last summer.*

10. Che tempo _____ quando eravate in Italia? *How was the weather when you were in Italy?*

_____ sempre bel tempo. *The weather was always nice.*

11. Maria, _____ quel romanzo l'anno scorso, vero? *Mary, did you read that novel last year?*

Sì, io _____ quel romanzo l'anno scorso. *Yes, I read that novel last year.*

12. Dove _____ la loro macchina? *Where did they put their car?*

_____ la macchina in piazza. *They put the car in the square.*

13. Che cosa _____ loro, la settimana scorsa? *What did they have last week?*

_____ solo il caffè. *They only had coffee.*

14. Anche lui _____ la verità, vero? *He also knew the truth, didn't he?*

Sì, anche lui _____ la verità. *Yes, he also knew the truth.*

15. Quando _____ al professore, Marco? *When did you write to the professor, Mark?*

_____ al professore tempo fa. *I wrote to the professor a while back.*

16. Dove _____ lei in Italia? *Where did she stay in Italy?*

_____ in un albergo. *She stayed in a hotel.*

17. Anche lui _____ quel film, vero? *He also saw that movie, right?*

Sì, _____ quel film due anni fa. *Yes, he saw that movie two years ago.*

18. Quando _____ in America i tuoi cugini? *When did your cousins come to America?*

_____ nel 2000. *They came in 2000.*

19. Dove _____ andare i tuoi amici l'anno scorso? *Where did your friends want to go last year?*

_____ andare in vacanza. *They wanted to go on vacation.*

Transportation

As elsewhere, cars (**le automobili** or **le macchine**) are the principle means of transportation in Italy. Buses and subway systems in large cities are also commonly used within the cities and to get from town to town. Trains and airplanes are used to travel longer distances. Train travel is still very popular. Here are some common travel vocabulary words:

l'aereo	*airplane*	il treno	*train*
l'autobus (m.)	*bus*	viaggiare	*to travel*
la metropolitana	*subway*	il viaggio	*trip*

ALITALIA

Alitalia is Italy's main airline (**la linea aerea**). It was founded in 1946. In 1957 it became Italy's national airline, with its head office in Rome; it has branch offices (**le sedi**) throughout the world.

In 1996 Alitalia was reformed as *Alitalia Team* for low-cost medium and long-range connections (**le coincidenze a medio e lungo raggio**). In 1998 it formed partnerships with KLM and Continental, Northwest, and Air France.

Va' in Italia, con Alitalia! You know what this means, don't you?

QUIZ

For each present perfect form give the corresponding pluperfect form. For example:

ho mangiato <u>*avevo mangiato*</u>

1. ho venduto _____

   sono partita _____

ho avuto _____

sei andato _____

hai venduto _____

sei uscito _____

hai fatto _____

è arrivato _____

ha potuto _____

For the following sentences, circle the present perfect, imperfect, or pluperfect form of each verb as required by meaning.

2. Loro _____ quando mi hai chiamato.

   (a) sono già tornati

   (b) tornavano

   (c) erano già tornati

3. Loro _____ per l'Italia ieri.

   (a) sono partiti

   (b) partivano

   (c) erano partiti

4. Loro _____ spesso quando erano giovani.

   (a) sono usciti

   (b) uscivano

   (c) erano usciti

5. Lui mi ha detto che tu _____ quel libro.

   (a) hai già andato

   (b) leggevi

   (c) avevi già letto

6. Lui _____ poco tempo fa.

   (a) è uscito

   (b) usciva

   (c) era uscito

7. Ieri non avevo fame perché _____ .

    (a) ho già mangiato

    (b) mangiavo

    (c) avevo già mangiato

8. Dopo che lui _____ a Roma, vide molte cose.

    (a) è andato

    (b) andava

    (c) era andato

For each present perfect form, give the corresponding past absolute form. For example:

    ho mangiato *mangiai* _____

9. ho venduto _____

   sono partita _____

   ho avuto _____

   sei andato _____

   hai venduto _____

   sei uscito _____

   hai fatto _____

   è arrivato _____

   ha potuto _____

Personal Matters! Answer the question appropriately.

10. Vuoi fare un viaggio in Italia? Dove?

_____ .

CHAPTER 15

More About Nouns and Adjectives

Here's what you will learn in this chapter:

More About Masculine and Feminine Nouns
Nouns of Greek Origin
Position of Adjectives
Form-Changing Adjectives
Human Body

More About Masculine and Feminine Nouns

Amico e amica. *Friend, male or female.* In Chapter 2 you learned that a noun referring to a male ends in **-o** and a noun referring to a female ends in **-a**. This is gener-

ally true, but there are exceptions and there are still a few more rules to Italian nouns, some of which we have already covered. They are repeated here for reinforcement.

Masculine nouns ending in **-tore** often correspond to feminine nouns ending in **-trice**.

Masculine		Feminine	
il pittore	*the (male) painter*	la pittrice	*the (female) painter*
l'autore	*the (male) author*	l'autrice	*the (female) author*
l'attore	*the (male) actor*	l'attrice	*the (female) actor*
lo scultore	*the (male) sculptor*	la scultrice	*the (female) sculptor*
lo scrittore	*the (male) writer*	la scrittrice	*the (female) writer*

Sometimes to form a feminine noun from a masculine noun, the ending **-essa** is added. This means that you must be careful with the ending you use when referring to people!

Masculine		Feminine	
il dottore	*the (male) doctor*	la dottoressa	*the (female) doctor*
il professore	*the (male) professor*	la professoressa	*the (female) professor*
l'elefante	*the (male) elephant*	l'elefantessa	*the (female) elephant*
il leone	*the lion*	la leonessa	*the lioness*

Some of the feminine forms of nouns, however, have been eliminated in Italy, especially with nouns indicating professions.

l'avvocato	*male* or *female lawyer*
il medico	*male* or *female doctor*
lo scultore	*male* or *female sculptor*

Oral Practice

Practice saying the following sentences out loud.

Chi era Raffaello?	*Who was Raphael?*
Era un famoso pittore.	*He was a famous painter.*
Chi è Marialuisa Tadei?	*Who is Marialuisa Tadei?*
Lei è una scultrice contemporanea.	*She is a contemporary sculptress.*

Chi era Marcello Mastroianni?	*Who was Marcello Mastroianni?*
Marcello Mastroianni era un attore.	*Marcello Mastroianni was an actor.*
Chi era Anna Magnani?	*Who was Anna Magnani?*
Anna Magnani era un'attrice.	*Anna Magnani was an actress.*
Chi era Rosalba Carriera?	*Who was Rosalba Carriera?*
Era una pittrice.	*She was a painter.*
Chi era Italo Calvino?	*Who was Italo Calvino?*
Italo Calvino era un autore.	*Italo Calvino was an author.*
Chi era Natalia Ginzburg?	*Who was Natalia Ginzburg?*
Natalia Ginzburg era una scrittrice.	*Natalia Ginzburg was a writer.*
Hai conosciuto la dottoressa Dini?	*Did you meet Dr. Dini?*
Sì, conobbi la dottoressa tempo fa.	*Yes, I met the doctor a while ago.*
Com'è il tuo cane?	*How is your dog?*
È grande come un elefante.	*It is as big as an elephant.*
E la tua gatta?	*And your (female) cat?*
Anche lei è un'elefantessa.	*She is also an elephant.*
Com'è tuo fratello?	*How is your brother?*
Lui è un leone.	*He is a lion.*
Com'è tua sorella?	*How is your sister?*
Anche lei è una leonessa.	*She is also a lioness.*
Che professione fa tuo fratello?	*What profession does your brother do?*
Fa l'avvocato.	*He is a lawyer.*
E tua sorella?	*And your sister?*
Anche lei fa l'avvocato.	*She is also a lawyer.*

Written Practice 1

Fill in the blanks with the appropriate noun forms.

1. Chi era Michelangelo? *Who was Michelangelo?*

   Era un famoso _____. *He was a famous painter.*

2. Chi è Sofia Loren? *Who is Sofia Loren?*

   Lei è un' _____ contemporanea. *She is a contemporary actress.*

3. Chi era Rosalba Carriera? *Who was Rosalba Carriera?*

   Era una _____. *She was a painter.*

4. Chi era Harriet Frishmuth? *Who was Harriet Frishmuth?*

   Lei era una _____ americana. *She was an American sculptor.*

5. Chi era Humphrey Bogart? *Who was Humphrey Bogart?*

   Era un _____ americano. *He was an American actor.*

6. Chi era Dino Buzzati? *Who was Dino Buzzati?*

   Dino Buzzati era un _____. *Dino Buzzati was an author.*

7. Chi era Natalia Ginzburg? *Who was Natalia Ginzburg?*

   Natalia Ginzburg era un' _____. *Natalia Ginzburg was an author.*

8. Hai conosciuto _____ Dini? *Did you meet Dr. Dini?*

   Sì, conobbi _____ tempo fa. *Yes, I met the doctor a while ago.*

9. Com'è la tua gatta? *How is your cat?*

   Lei è grande come un' _____. *She is as big as an elephant.*

10. E il tuo cane? *And your dog?*

    Anche lui è un _____. *He is also an elephant.*

11. Com'è tuo padre? *How is your father?*

    Lui è un _____. *He is a lion.*

12. Com'è tua madre? *How is your mother?*

    Anche lei è una _____. *She is also a lioness.*

13. Che professione fai? *What profession do you do?*

    Faccio l' _____. *I am a lawyer.*

Nouns of Greek Origin

So far you've learned that generally if a noun ends in **-o** it is masculine and if it ends in **-a** it is feminine. However, sometimes a noun ends in **-a** but it is masculine, because it is of Greek origin. Nouns of Greek origin ending in **-amma** and **-ema** correspond to English nouns ending in -*am* and -*em*. They are all masculine.

il problema	*the problem*	il programma	*the program*
il teorema	*the theorem*	il dramma	*the drama*
il sistema	*the system*	il diagramma	*the diagram*

To make these nouns plural, just change the ending to **-i**.

Singular		**Plural**	
il problema	*the problem*	i problemi	*the problems*
il programma	*the program*	i programmi	*the programs*
il diagramma	*the diagram*	i diagrammi	*the diagrams*

Nouns ending in **-si** are also of Greek origin. They correspond to English nouns ending in -*sis*. In this case, however, they are all feminine. And, they are invariable—that is, they do not change in the plural.

Singular		**Plural**	
la crisi	*the crisis*	le crisi	*the crises*
la tesi	*the thesis*	le tesi	*the theses*
l'ipotesi	*the hypothesis*	le ipotesi	*the hypotheses*
l'analisi	*the analysis*	le analisi	*the analyses*

OTHER KINDS OF NOUNS

Remember nouns ending in an accented vowel? You have seen them throughout this book. As you may recall, some are masculine and some feminine. But they are all invariable in the plural.

Singular		**Plural**	
il tè	*the tea*	i tè	*the teas*
la città	*the city*	le città	*the cities*
il caffè	*the coffee*	i caffè	*the coffees*
l'università	*the university*	le università	*the universities*
il tassì	*the taxi*	i tassì	*the taxis*

Sometimes nouns ending in **-o** are feminine, and some ending in **-a** are masculine. These are exceptions! You will simply have to learn them by memory.

la mano	*the hand*	il pianeta	*the planet*
la radio	*the radio*	l'alfabeta	*the alphabet*

Here are the plural forms of these nouns. Take special note of these, because they follow no rules.

le mani	*the hands*	i pianeti	*the planets*
le radio	*the radios*	gli alfabeti	*the alphabets*

Some nouns ending in **-o** are actually an abbreviation of a full word that ends in **-a**. These nouns remain feminine in their abbreviated forms.

Feminine Noun		**Abbreviation**	
la fotografia	*the photograph*	la foto	*the photo*
la motocicletta	*the motorcycle*	la moto	*the motorcycle*

And some nouns ending in **-a** are actually abbreviated masculine nouns ending in **-o**. They remain masculine in their abbreviated forms.

il cinematografo	*the movie theater*	il cinema	*the movies*

Oral Practice

Practice saying the following sentences out loud.

Che tipo di programma preferisci?	*What type of program do you prefer?*
Preferisco i programmi di fantascienza.	*I prefer science fiction programs.*
Che problema hai?	*What problem do you have?*
Non ho problemi.	*I have no problems.*
Conosci qualche teorema matematico?	*Do you know any mathematical theorems?*
Sì, conosco tanti teoremi.	*Yes, I know a lot of theorems.*
Ti piacciono i drammi?	*Do you like dramas?*
Sì, mi piacciono molto.	*Yes, I like them a lot.*

Che diagramma è questo?	*What diagram is this?*
Sono due diagrammi scientifici.	*They are two scientific diagrams.*
Qual è la tua analisi della crisi?	*What is your analysis of the crisis?*
Non c'è crisi!	*There is no crisis!*
Hai una tesi o un'ipotesi?	*Do you have a thesis or hypothesis?*
No, non ho né tesi né ipotesi.	*No, I have neither theses nor hypotheses.*
Preferisci il tè o il caffè?	*Do you prefer tea or coffee?*
Non mi piace né il tè né il caffè.	*I like neither tea nor coffee.*
C'è un'unversità nella tua città?	*Is there a university in your city?*
Ci sono due università.	*There are two universities.*
Usi la mano destra o sinistra per scrivere?	*Do you use the right or left hand to write?*
Uso tutte e due le mani.	*I use both hands.*
Quante radio hai?	*How many radios do you have?*
Non ho la radio.	*I do not have a radio.*
Quanti pianeti conosci?	*How many planets do you know?*
Conosco tutti i pianeti.	*I know all the planets.*
Di chi sono queste foto?	*Whose photos are these?*
Sono le mie.	*They are mine.*

Written Practice 2

Fill in the blanks with the correct forms of the appropriate words.

1. Che tipi di _____ guardi? *What types of programs do you watch?*

   Non guardo la televisione. *I do not watch television.*

2. Quanti _____ hai? *How many problems do you have?*

   Ho solo un _____ grande. *I have only one big problem.*

3. Quanti _____ matematici conosci? *How many mathematical theorems do you know?*

   Conosco solo un _____ . *I know only one theorem.*

4. Ti piacciono i _____? *Do you like dramas?*

   Mi piace solo un _____. *I like only one drama.*

5. Che tipi di _____ sono questi? *What types of diagrams are these?*

   Sono due _____ scientifici. *They are two scientific diagrams.*

6. Qual è la tua _____ della _____? *What is your analysis of the crisis?*

   Non c'è _____! *There is no crisis!*

7. Hai una _____ o un'_____? *Do you have a thesis or hypothesis?*

   No, non ho né _____ né _____. *No, I have neither theses nor hypotheses.*

8. Vuoi il _____ o il _____? *Do you want coffee or tea?*

   Non mi piace né il _____ né il _____. *I like neither coffee nor tea.*

9. C'è un' _____ nella tua città? *Is there a university in your city?*

   No, non ci sono _____. *No, there are no universities.*

10. Usi la _____ destra o sinistra? *Do you use the right or left hand?*

    Uso tutte e due le _____. *I use both hands.*

11. Quante _____ hai? *How many radios do you have?*

    Non ho la _____. *I do not have a radio.*

12. Quanti _____ conosci? *How many planets do you know?*

    Conosco tutti i _____. *I know all the planets.*

13. Conosci l' _____ italiano? *Do you know the Italian alphabet?*

    Sì, conosco gli _____ di molte lingue. *Yes, I know the alphabets of many languages.*

14. Di chi sono queste _____? *Whose photos are these?*

    Sono le sue. *They are hers.*

15. Quante _____ ci sono? *How many motorcycles are there?*

C'è solo una _____. *There is only one motorcycle.*

Position of Adjectives

Sei ricco/a o povero/a? *Are you rich or poor?* **Sei giovane o vecchio/a?** *Are you young or old?* The adjectives used in these sentences are descriptive. Some descriptive adjectives can come either before or after a noun. Here are some common adjectives you may have already encountered:

bello	*beautiful*	grande	*big, large, great*
brutto	*ugly*	piccolo	*little, small*
buono	*good*	povero	*poor*
caro	*dear*	ricco	*rich*
cattivo	*bad*	vecchio	*old*
giovane	*young*		

A few of these adjectives change in meaning depending on their position in a sentence.

È un ragazzo povero.	*He is a poor boy.* (meaning: *not wealthy*)
È un povero ragazzo.	*He is a poor boy.* (meaning: *deserving of pity*)
È un amico vecchio.	*He is an old friend.* (meaning: *in age*)
È un vecchio amico.	*He is an old friend.* (meaning: *for many years*)

Descriptive adjectives can also be separated from the noun they modify by what is called a linking verb. The most common linking verbs are the following three:

essere	*to be*
sembrare	*to seem*
diventare	*to become*

Quella donna è ricca.	*That woman is rich.*
Quell'uomo sembra giovane.	*That man seems young.*
Questa macchina sta diventando vecchia.	*This car is becoming old.*

Adjectives used in this way are known as predicate adjectives because they occur in the predicate slot—after the verb that links them to the noun they modify.

And finally, when these adjectives are accompanied by an adverb, another adjective, or some other part of speech, they must follow the noun.

| È un simpatico ragazzo. | *He is a pleasant boy.* |

But:

| È un ragazzo molto simpatico. | *He is a very pleasant boy.* |
| È un ragazzo simpatico e bravo. | *He is a pleasant and good boy.* |

Oral Practice

Practice saying the following sentences out loud.

Il tuo amico è bello o brutto?	*Is your friend nice looking or ugly?*
Il mio amico sembra bello.	*My friend seems nice looking.*
Hai buoni o cattivi amici?	*Do you have good or bad friends?*
Ho solo buoni amici.	*I have only good friends.*
Chi è quella persona nella foto?	*Who is that person in the photo?*
È una cara amica.	*She is a dear friend.*
Che tipo di casa avete comprato?	*What type of house did you buy?*
Abbiamo comprato una casa grande.	*We bought a big house.*
Chi è quella persona?	*Who is that person?*
Lui è un grande scrittore.	*He is a great writer.*
Tuo zio è ricco o povero?	*Is your uncle rich or poor?*
Lui è molto ricco.	*He is very rich.*
Com'è tua zia?	*How is your aunt?*
È una povera donna.	*She is a poor (wretched) woman.*
Chi è quella persona?	*Who is that person?*
È un vecchio amico.	*He is an old (long-time) friend.*
Com'è tuo padre?	*How is your father?*
Sta diventando vecchio.	*He is becoming old.*

Written Practice 3

Fill in the blanks with the correct forms of the appropriate adjectives.

1. Tuo fratello è _____ o _____? *Is your brother nice looking or ugly?*

   Lui sembra _____. *He seems nice looking.*

2. Hai _____ o _____ genitori? *Do you have good or bad parents?*

   Loro sono molto _____. *They are very good.*

3. Chi è quell'uomo nella foto? *Who is that man in the photo?*

   È un _____ amico. *He is a dear friend.*

4. Che macchina avete comprato? *What car did you buy?*

   Abbiamo comprato una macchina _____. *We bought a big car.*

5. E Marco? *And Mark?*

   Lui ha comprato una macchina _____. *He bought a small car.*

6. Chi è quella persona? *Who is that person?*

   Lei è una _____ scrittrice. *She is a great writer.*

7. Tua zia è _____ o _____? *Is your aunt rich or poor?*

   Lei è molto _____. *She is very rich.*

8. Com'è tuo cugino? *How is your cousin?*

   È un _____ uomo. *He is a poor (wretched) man.*

9. Chi è quella persona? *Who is that person?*

   È un _____ amica. *She is an old (long-time) friend.*

10. Com'è tua madre? *How is your mother?*

    Sta diventando _____. *She is becoming old.*

Form-Changing Adjectives

Of the adjectives you've encountered so far, **buono**, **bello**, and **grande** change in form when they are placed before a noun.

BUONO

- When **buono** is placed before masculine nouns beginning with **z**, **s** + consonant, **gn**, and **ps**, its forms are as follows:

Singular		Plural	
un buono zio	*a good uncle*	dei buoni zii	*some good uncles*
un buono studente	*a good student*	dei buoni studenti	*some good students*

- Before masculine nouns beginning with any other consonant or any vowel, **buono** takes on the following forms:

Singular		Plural	
un buon medico	*a good doctor*	dei buoni medici	*some good doctors*
un buon amico	*a good friend*	dei buoni amici	*some good friends*

- Before feminine nouns beginning with any consonant, the forms are as follows:

Singular		Plural	
una buona pasta	*a good pastry*	delle buone paste	*some good pastries*
una buona donna	*a good woman*	delle buone donne	*some good women*

- Before feminine nouns beginning with any vowel, the forms are as follows:

Singular		Plural	
una buon'amica	*a good friend*	delle buone amiche	*some good friends*
una buon'ora	*a good time (hour)*	delle buone ore	*some good times (hours)*

Don't forget that when **buono** is placed *after* the noun, it is treated as a normal descriptive adjective ending in **-o**.

BELLO

- When **bello** is placed before masculine nouns beginning with **z**, **s** + consonant, **gn**, and **ps**, its forms are as follows:

Singular		Plural	
un bello zaino	*a nice backpack*	dei begli zaini	*some nice backpacks*
un bello sport	*a nice sport*	dei begli sport	*some nice sports*

- Before masculine nouns beginning with any other consonant, its forms are as follows:

Singular		Plural	
un bel cane	*a nice dog*	dei bei cani	*some nice dogs*
un bel gatto	*a nice cat*	dei bei gatti	*some nice cats*

- Before masculine nouns beginning with any vowel, the forms for **bello** are as follows:

Singular		**Plural**	
un bell'amico	*a nice friend*	dei begli amici	*some nice friends*
un bell'orologio	*a nice watch*	dei begli orologi	*some nice watches*

- Before feminine nouns beginning with any consonant, its forms are as follows:

Singular		**Plural**	
una bella borsa	*a nice purse*	delle belle borse	*some nice purses*
una bella camicia	*a nice shirt*	delle belle camicie	*some nice shirts*

- Before feminine nouns beginning with any vowel, the forms for **bello** are as follows:

Singular		**Plural**	
una bell'amica	*a nice friend*	delle belle amiche	*some nice friends*
una bell'estate	*a nice summer*	delle belle estati	*some nice summers*

And don't forget! If placed after the noun, **bello** is treated like a normal descriptive adjective ending in **-o**.

GRANDE

Grande has the optional forms of **gran** (before a masculine singular noun beginning with any consonant except **z**, **s** + consonant, **gn**, and **ps**), and **grand'** (before any singular noun beginning with a vowel). Otherwise, it is treated as a normal adjective ending in **-e**. There is only one plural form: **grandi**.

un gran film	*a great film*	or	un grande film
un grand'amico	*a great friend*	or	un grande amico

Oral Practice

Practice saying the following sentences out loud.

Stai mangiando un panino buono?	*Are you eating a good sandwich?*
Sì, è un buon panino.	*Yes, it is a good sandwich.*
Anche voi state mangiando panini buoni?	*Are you also eating good sandwiches?*

Sì, sono buoni panini.	*Yes, they are good sandwiches.*
Lui è uno studente buono, vero?	*He is a good-hearted student, isn't he?*
Sì, è un buono studente.	*Yes, he is a good-hearted student.*
Questo è un orologio buono, vero?	*This is a good watch, isn't it?*
Sì, è un buon orologio.	*Yes, it is a good watch.*
Questa è una pasta buona, vero?	*This is a good pastry, isn't it?*
Sì, è una buona pasta.	*Yes, it is a good pastry.*
Lei è un'amica buona, vero?	*She is a good friend, isn't she?*
Sì, lei è una buon'amica.	*Yes, she is a good friend.*
Loro sono amiche buone, vero?	*They are good friends, aren't they?*
Sì, sono buone amiche.	*Yes, they are good friends.*
Questo è un vestito bello, vero?	*This is a nice dress, isn't it?*
Sì, è un bel vestito.	*Yes, it is a beautiful dress.*
Questi sono calzini belli, vero?	*These are nice socks, aren't they?*
Sì, sono dei bei calzini.	*Yes, they are some nice socks.*
Questo è uno zaino bello, vero?	*This is a nice backpack, isn't it?*
Sì, è un bello zaino.	*Yes, it is a nice backpack.*
Questi sono stivali belli, vero?	*These are beautiful boots, aren't they?*
Sì, sono begli stivali.	*Yes, they are nice boots.*
Questo è un impermeabile bello, vero?	*This is a nice raincoat, isn't it?*
Sì, è un bell'impermeabile.	*Yes, it is a nice raincoat.*
Questa è una giacca bella, vero?	*This is a nice jacket, isn't it?*
Sì, è una bella giacca.	*Yes, it is a nice jacket.*
Lei è un'attrice bella, vero?	*She is a beautiful actress, isn't she?*
Sì, è una bell'attrice.	*Yes, she is a beautiful actress.*
Loro sono attrici belle, vero?	*They are beautiful actresses, aren't they?*
Sì, sono belle attrici.	*Yes, they are beautiful actresses.*
Questo è un gran libro, no?	*This is a great book, isn't it?*
Sì, è veramente un grande libro.	*Yes, it is truly a great book.*

Written Practice 4

Fill in the blanks with the correct forms of the appropriate adjectives.

1. Stai bevendo un cappuccino _____? *Are you drinking a good cappuccino?*

   Sì, è un _____ cappuccino. *Yes, it is a good cappuccino.*

2. E voi state bevendo cappuccini _____? *And are you drinking good cappuccinos?*

   Sì, sono _____ cappuccini. *Yes, they are good cappuccinos.*

3. Lui è uno zio _____, vero? *He is a good-hearted uncle, isn't he?*

   Sì, è un _____ zio. *Yes, he is a good-hearted uncle.*

4. Lui è un amico _____, vero? *He is a good friend, isn't he?*

   Sì, è un _____ amico. *Yes, he is a good friend.*

5. E anche loro sono amici _____? *And are they also good friends?*

   Sì, anche loro sono _____ amici. *Yes, these are also good friends.*

6. Questa è una minestra _____, vero? *This is a good soup, isn't it?*

   Sì, è una _____ minestra. *Yes, it is a good soup.*

7. Lei è un'amica _____, vero? *She is a good friend, isn't she?*

   Sì, lei è una _____ amica. *Yes, she is a good friend.*

8. Loro sono amiche _____, vero? *They are good friends, aren't they?*

   Sì, sono _____ amiche. *Yes, they are good friends.*

9. Questo è un computer _____, vero? *This is a nice computer, isn't it?*

   Sì, è un _____ computer. *Yes, it is a nice computer.*

10. Questi sono libri _____, vero? *These are nice books, aren't they?*

    Sì, sono dei _____ libri. *Yes, they are some nice books.*

11. Questo è uno zaino _____, vero? *This is a nice backpack, isn't it?*

    Sì, è un _____ zaino. *Yes, it is a nice backpack.*

12. Questi sono stivali _____, vero? *These are beautiful boots, aren't they?*

    Sì, sono _____ stivali. *Yes, they are nice boots.*

13. Questo è un impermeabile _____, vero? *This is a nice raincoat, isn't it?*

    Sì, è un _____ impermeabile. *Yes, it is a nice raincoat.*

14. Questi sono impermeabili _____, vero? *These are nice raincoats, aren't they?*

    Sì, sono _____ impermeabili. *Yes, they are nice raincoats.*

15. Questa è una cravatta _____, vero? *This is a nice tie, isn't it?*

    Sì, è una _____ cravatta. *Yes, it is a nice tie.*

16. Lei è un'attrice _____, vero? *She is a beautiful actress, isn't she?*

    Sì, è una _____ attrice. *Yes, she is a beautiful actress.*

17. Loro sono attrici _____, vero? *They are beautiful actresses, aren't they?*

    Sì, sono _____ attrici. *Yes, they are beautiful actresses.*

Human Body

It is important to be able to name the parts of the human body (**il corpo umano**), or at least some of them. The following is a list of some common body vocabulary words:

la bocca	*mouth*	il labbro	*lip*
il braccio	*arm*	la lingua	*tongue*
i capelli	*hair (on the head)*	la mano	*hand*
il collo	*neck*	il naso	*nose*
il dito	*finger*	l'occhio	*eye*
la faccia	*face*	l'orecchio	*ear*
la fronte	*forehead*	il petto	*chest*
la gamba	*leg*	il piede	*foot*
il ginocchio	*knee*	la spalla	*shoulder*
il gomito	*elbow*	la testa	*head*
la guancia	*cheek*		

Like the English nouns *memorandum* and *compendium*, which have the plural forms *memoranda* and *compendia* (derived from Latin words), Italian also has a few nouns whose plural forms end in **-a**. In Italian these nouns are masculine in the singular but feminine in the plural.

Singular		**Plural**	
il braccio	*the arm*	le braccia	*the arms*
il dito	*the finger*	le dita	*the fingers*
il ginocchio	*the knee*	le ginocchia	*the knees*
il labbro	*the lip*	le labbra	*the lips*

There are not too many of these nouns, and most refer to parts of the human body.

QUIZ

Give the masculine or feminine form for each noun, as necessary. Some of the nouns given here come from previous chapters.

Masculine	**Feminine**
1. l'amico	_____
_____	la dentista
il pianista	_____
_____	la scultrice
il pittore	_____
_____	l'autrice
l'elefante	_____
_____	la leonessa
l'avvocato	_____

Now, give the singular or plural form of the noun (with its definite article), as required.

Singular	**Plural**
2. il problema	_____
_____	i teoremi
il sistema	_____

_____   i programmi

il dramma   _____

_____   i diagrammi

la crisi   _____

_____   le tesi

l'ipotesi   _____

_____   le analisi

For each phrase provided, give the phrase with the opposite meaning. For example:

quel bambino grande _quel bambino piccolo_____

Phrase	**Opposite**
3. quelle belle macchine	_____
quei buoni ravioli	_____
la mia nuova amica	_____
le grandi macchine	_____
quegli uomini ricchi	_____
una professoressa giovane	_____

Reposition each adjective to before the noun, making any changes (if necessary).

4. Questa è una pasta buona.

_____.

5. Lei è un'amica buona.

_____.

6. Questo è un orologio bello.

_____.

7. Questa è un'automobile bella.

_____.

8. Questi sono zaini belli.

_____.

9. Marco ha delle amiche buone.

_____.

Personal Matters! Answer the question appropriately.

10. Che tipo di persona sei? Grande o piccolo/a? Ricco/a o povero/a? Ecc.

_____.

PART THREE TEST

Circle the letter of the word or phrase that best answers each question or completes each sentence.

1. Maria, a che ora _____ di solito?

    (a) si alza

    (b) ti alzi

2. Loro _____ ogni sera.

    (a) ci telefoniamo

    (b) si telefonano

3. Marco, _____! È tardi!

    (a) non ti svegliare

    (b) svegliati

4. Signora, come _____?

    (a) ti chiami

    (b) si chiama

5. Dottoressa Bruni, _____ in Italia!

    (a) divertiti

    (b) si diverta

6. Marco e Maria, _____! Sono già le nove!

    (a) alzatevi

    (b) si alzino

7. Quanto costano quei pantaloni?

    (a) Un terzo di questi.

    (b) In saldo.

8. Signora, _____?

    (a) desidera

    (b) vorrei

9. Marco, non ti _____ quel costume!

    (a) mettere

    (b) metti

10. Signori, _____ alla festa!

    (a) si divertano

    (b) divertitevi

11. Marco, a che ora _____ ieri?

    (a) ti sei alzato

    (b) ti sei alzata

12. Signori, che cosa avete comprato ieri?

    (a) Non abbiamo comprato niente.

    (b) Non avete comprato niente.

13. Dov'è Maria?

    (a) È andata in centro.

    (b) È andato in centro.

14. Chi è venuto alla festa?

    (a) Sono venuti i miei amici.

    (b) Sono usciti i miei amici.

15. Quanti _____ hai guardato ieri sera?

    (a) programmi

    (b) programma

16. Ti piacciono i _____ in televisione?

    (a) dramma

    (b) drammi

17. Anche voi vi siete divertiti alla festa?

    (a) Sì, si sono divertiti.

    (b) Sì, ci siamo divertiti.

18. I tuoi amici sono stati _____ Francia meridionale, non è vero?

    (a) in

    (b) nella

19. Noi viviamo _____ Stati Uniti.

    (a) in

    (b) negli

20. Non ho mai mangiato _____ .

   (a) gnocchi

   (b) gli gnocchi

21. Che cosa facevi, Marco, mentre io dormivo?

   (a) Ho mangiato la pizza.

   (b) Mangiavo la pizza.

22. Che cosa facevano loro spesso da bambini?

   (a) Sono andati spesso in Italia.

   (b) Andavano spesso in Italia.

23. Mentre io pulivo la macchina, tu che cosa facevi?

   (a) Ho guardato un programma alla televisione.

   (b) Stavo guardando un programma alla televisione.

24. Che colore di capelli aveva tua sorella da bambina?

   (a) Ha avuto i capelli biondi.

   (b) Aveva i capelli biondi.

25. Che cosa facevate spesso in Italia da giovani?

   (a) Siamo andati a vedere le città principali.

   (b) Andavamo a vedere le città principali.

26. Come si chiamava il tuo professore d'italiano?

   (a) Si chiamava Giovanni Ritornello.

   (b) Si stava chiamando Giovanni Ritornello.

27. Chi sono quegli uomini?

   (a) Quelli sono i miei amici.

   (b) Quegli sono i miei amici.

28. La mia macchina è nuova, e la loro?

   (a) Anche la loro è nuova.

   (b) Anche loro è nuova.

29. Quale vuoi, questa o _____?

   (a) quella

   (b) quello

30. Desidera?

    (a) Il menù, per favore.

    (b) Niente.

31. I miei genitori _____ in Italia molti anni fa.

    (a) tornano

    (b) tornavano

    (c) tornarono

32. I miei genitori _____ per l'Italia due ore fa.

    (a) sono partiti

    (b) partivano

    (c) partirono

33. I miei genitori _____ spesso in Italia alcuni anni fa.

    (a) sono andati

    (b) andavano

    (c) andarono

34. Lui _____ in Italia per la prima volta quando era molto giovane.

    (a) va

    (b) andava

    (c) andò

35. Michele _____ poco tempo fa.

    (a) è uscito

    (b) usciva

    (c) uscì

36. Non ho fame perché _____ .

    (a) ho già mangiato

    (b) mangiavo

    (c) mangiai

37. Marco _____ a Roma questa mattina.

    (a) è andato

    (b) andava

    (c) andò

38. Dopo che noi _____, loro sono arrivati.

   (a) eravamo usciti

   (b) uscivamo

   (c) uscimmo

39. Loro _____, quando tu hai chiamato.

   (a) avevano già studiato

   (b) studiarono

   (c) hanno studiato

40. Di solito, quando siamo in Italia, stiamo _____.

   (a) in un albergo

   (b) in un bagno

41. Quali _____ guardi di solito?

   (a) programmi

   (b) programma

42. In questo momento ci sono _____, non è vero?

   (a) tante crisi

   (b) tanta crisi

43. Quale _____ usi per scrivere?

   (a) mano

   (b) mani

44. Tua sorella è una _____, vero?

   (a) pittrice

   (b) pittore

45. È stato un _____ mese, non è vero?

   (a) bel

   (b) bello

46. Conosco Marco da molti anni. Lui è _____.

   (a) un vecchio amico

   (b) un amico vecchio

47. Marco è un _____ amico.

    (a) buon

    (b) buono

48. Oggi è una _____ giornata.

    (a) bella

    (b) bel

49. Mio fratello è _____ . Lui è molto famoso.

    (a) un grande matematico

    (b) un matematico grande

50. Loro sono due _____ attrici.

    (a) bei

    (b) belle

PART FOUR

EXTENDING COMPETENCE

CHAPTER 16

Talking About the Future

Here's what you will learn in this chapter:

Using the Future Tense

Irregular Forms in the Future Tense

Future Perfect Tense

Talking About Sports

Using the Future Tense

Dove andrete domani? Andremo in centro. *Where are you going tomorrow? We are going downtown.* The verb used in this sentence is **andare**. It is conjugated in the future tense.

The simple future, as its name implies, allows you to talk about an action that will occur in the future. It is formed by dropping the final **-e** of the infinitives of all three verb types, and then adding on the future tense endings. Also, the **-ar** in the infinitive of first-conjugation verbs must be changed to **-er** before adding the endings.

FUTURE TENSE OF FIRST-CONJUGATION VERBS

Let's start with a first-conjugation verb, such as **parlare**. Note in the following table that the Italian future tense can be translated in three different ways in English. And, remember that the **-ar** of first-conjugation verbs must be changed to **-er** before adding on the future tense endings.

parlare   parler-

(io) parler**ò**	*I will speak, will be speaking, am going to speak*
(tu) parler**ai**	*you (familiar) will speak, will be speaking, are going to speak*
(Lei) parler**à**	*you (polite) will speak, will be speaking, are going to speak*
(lui/lei) parler**à**	*he/she will speak, will be speaking, is going to speak*
(noi) parler**emo**	*we will speak, will be speaking, are going to speak*
(voi) parler**ete**	*you (familiar plural) will speak, will be speaking, are going to speak*
(Loro) parler**anno**	*you (polite plural) will speak, will be speaking, are going to speak*
(loro) parler**anno**	*they will speak, will be speaking, are going to speak*

To indicate that the hard **c** and **g** sounds of verbs ending **-care** and **-gare** are to be maintained, an **h** is added to the spelling. Note the following spelling adjustments, then, for the verbs **cercare** and **pagare**.

cercare   cercher-

(io) cercher**ò**	*I will search, will be searching, am going to search*
(tu) cercher**ai**	*you (familiar) will search, will be searching, are going to search*
(Lei) cercher**à**	*you (polite) will search, will be searching, are going to search*
(lui/lei) cercher**à**	*he/she will search, will be searching, is going to search*
(noi) cercher**emo**	*we will search, will be searching, are going to search*
(voi) cercher**ete**	*you (familiar plural) will search, will be searching, are going to search*
(Loro) cercher**anno**	*you (polite plural) will search, will be searching, are going to search*
(loro) cercher**anno**	*they will search, will be searching, are going to search*

pagare pagher-

(io) pag**herò**	*I will pay, will be paying, am going to pay*
(tu) pag**herai**	*you* (familiar) *will pay, will be paying, are going to pay*
(Lei) pag**herà**	*you* (polite) *will pay, will be paying, are going to pay*
(lui/lei) pag**herà**	*he/she will pay, will be paying, is going to pay*
(noi) pag**heremo**	*we will pay, will be paying, are going to pay*
(voi) pag**herete**	*you* (familiar plural) *will pay, will be paying, are going to pay*
(Loro) pag**heranno**	*you* (polite plural) *will pay, will be paying, are going to pay*
(loro) pag**heranno**	*they will pay, will be paying, are going to pay*

The **-i** of verbs ending in **-ciare** or **-giare** is not maintained in the conjugation of the future tense.

cominciare comincer-

(io) comin**cerò**	*I will start, will be starting, am going to start*
(tu) comin**cerai**	*you* (familiar) *will start, will be starting, are going to start*
(Lei) comin**cerà**	*you* (polite) *will start, will be starting, are going to start*
(lui/lei) comin**cerà**	*he/she will start, will be starting, is going to start*
(noi) comin**ceremo**	*we will start, will be starting, are going to start*
(voi) comin**cerete**	*you* (familiar plural) *will start, will be starting, are going to start*
(Loro) comin**ceranno**	*you* (polite plural) *will start, will be starting, are going to start*
(Loro) comin**ceranno**	*they will start, will be starting, are going to start*

mangiare manger-

(io) man**gerò**	*I will eat, will be eating, am going to eat*
(tu) man**gerai**	*you* (familiar) *will eat, will be eating, are going to eat*
(Lei) man**gerà**	*you* (polite) *will eat, will be eating, are going to eat*
(lui/lei) man**gerà**	*he/she will eat, will be eating, is going to eat*
(noi) man**geremo**	*we will eat, will be eating, are going to eat*
(voi) man**gerete**	*you* (familiar plural) *will eat, will be eating, are going to eat*
(Loro) man**geranno**	*you* (polite plural) *will eat, will be eating, are going to eat*
(loro) man**geranno**	*they will eat, will be eating, are going to eat*

Oral Practice

Practice saying the following sentences out loud. Note that **tra** (or **fra**) can mean *within* or *in* + *a period of time* (in addition to *between* and *among*, as you might recall).

Quando comprerai una nuova macchina, Marco?	*Mark, when will you buy a new car?*
Comprerò una nuova macchina l'anno prossimo.	*I will be buying a new car next year.*
Quando arriverà tuo fratello?	*When will your brother be arriving?*
Arriverà domani.	*He will be arriving tomorrow.*
Marco e Maria, dove aspetterete domani?	*Mark and Mary, where will you be waiting tomorrow?*
Aspetteremo in centro.	*We will be waiting downtown.*
Quando torneranno in Italia, i tuoi cugini?	*When will your cousins be returning to Italy?*
Torneranno tra un anno.	*They will be going back in a year.*
Bruna, comincerai a lavorare tra poco, vero?	*Bruna, you are going to start working soon, right?*
Sì, comincerò fra una settimana.	*Yes, I will be starting in a week.*
Anche tuo fratello mangerà i ravioli, vero?	*Your brother will also eat ravioli, won't he?*
No, lui mangerà solo l'antipasto.	*No, he will only be eating an appetizer.*
Bruna e Paolo, dove cercherete lavoro?	*Bruna and Paul, where will you look for work?*
Cercheremo lavoro negli Stati Uniti.	*We will be looking for work in the United States.*
Pagheranno loro il conto, vero?	*They will be paying the check, won't they?*
Sì, pagheranno loro.	*Yes, they will be paying.*
Quando si alzeranno domani?	*When will they be getting up tomorrow?*
Loro si alzeranno presto.	*They will be getting up early.*

Written Practice 1

Fill in the blanks with the appropriate future tense forms of the indicated verbs.

1. Quando _____ al professore, Marco? *Mark, when are you going to phone the professor?*

   _____ domani. *I will be phoning tomorrow.*

2. Quanto _____ una macchina nuova? *How much will a new car cost?*

   _____ molto. *It will cost a lot.*

3. Marco e Maria, _____ quel programma? *Mark and Mary, will you be watching that program?*

   No, _____ un altro programma. *No, we will be watching another program.*

4. Quando _____, i tuoi cugini? *When will your cousins be arriving?*

   _____ tra una settimana. *They will be arriving in a week.*

5. Tua sorella _____ a lavorare, vero? *Your sister is going to start working, right?*

   Sì, lei _____ fra una settimana. *Yes, she will be starting in a week.*

6. Che cosa _____, tu? *What will you be eating?*

   Io _____ solo l'antipasto. *I will be eating only an appetizer.*

7. Loro _____ lavoro in questa città, vero? *They will be looking for work in this city, right?*

   No, _____ lavoro in un'altra città. *No, they will be looking for work in another city.*

8. _____ voi il conto, vero? *You will be paying the check, won't you?*

   Sì, _____ noi. *Yes, we will be paying.*

9. A che ora _____ domani, Bruna? *At what time will you be getting up tomorrow, Bruna?*

   _____ verso le sei. *I will be getting up around six.*

FUTURE TENSE OF SECOND- AND THIRD-CONJUGATION VERBS

Now, let's look at a second-conjugation and third-conjugation verb, such as **scrivere** and **finire**. Again, we start by dropping the final **-e** of the infinitives, and then adding on the same set of future tense endings as for the **-are** verbs.

scrivere scriver-

(io) scriver**ò**	*I will write, will be writing, am going to write*
(tu) scriver**ai**	*you (familiar) will write, will be writing, are going to write*
(Lei) scriver**à**	*you (polite) will write, will be writing, are going to write*
(lui/lei) scriver**à**	*he/she will write, will be writing, is going to write*
(noi) scriver**emo**	*we will write, will be writing, are going to write*
(voi) scriver**ete**	*you (familiar plural) will write, will be writing, are going to write*
(Loro) scriver**anno**	*you (polite plural) will write, will be writing, are going to write*
(loro) scriver**anno**	*they will write, will be writing, are going to write*

finire finir-

(io) finir**ò**	*I will finish, will be finishing, am going to finish*
(tu) finir**ai**	*you (familiar) will finish, will be finishing, are going to finish*
(Lei) finir**à**	*you (polite) will finish, will be finishing, are going to finish*
(lui/lei) finir**à**	*he/she will finish, will be finishing, is going to finish*
(noi) finir**emo**	*we will finish, will be finishing, are going to finish*
(voi) finir**ete**	*you (familiar plural) will finish, will be finishing, are going to finish*
(Loro) finir**anno**	*you (polite plural) will finish, will be finishing, are going to finish*
(loro) finir**anno**	*they will finish, will be finishing, are going to finish*

As you can see, the Italian future tense corresponds to the English future tense—*I will go, you will write*, and so on. It can also express the idea in English of *going to write* and *will be writing*. In addition, the Italian future tense is used to convey probability.

Sai quanto costa quell'orologio?	*Do you know how much that watch costs?*
Costerà mille euro.	*It probably costs 1000 euros.*

Oral Practice

Practice saying the following sentences out loud.

Che cosa prenderete voi due?	*What will the two of you be having?*
Noi prenderemo solo il caffè.	*We will be having only coffee.*
Quando venderai la tua macchina, Dino?	*Dino, when will you be selling your car?*
Non venderò mai la mia macchina.	*I will never sell my car.*
Che cosa chiederà al professore lo studente?	*What will the student ask the professor?*
Chiederà molte cose.	*He will be asking many things.*
Che cosa leggeranno gli studenti?	*What will the students be reading?*
Gli studenti leggeranno un romanzo.	*The students will be reading a novel.*
Dove dormiranno i tuoi amici?	*Where will your friends be sleeping?*
Dormiranno in un albergo.	*They will be sleeping in a hotel.*
Quando partirete voi due?	*When will the two of you be leaving?*
Partiremo tra una settimana.	*We will be leaving in a week.*
Che cosa preferirà il tuo amico?	*What will your friend (probably) prefer?*
Preferirà solo un bicchiere di vino.	*He will prefer only a glass of wine.*
A che ora uscirai, Paola?	*At what time will you be going out, Paula?*
Uscirò verso le sei.	*I will be going out around six.*
Si divertiranno loro in Italia, vero?	*They are going to have fun in Italy, right?*
Sì, si divertiranno molto.	*Yes, they are going to have a lot of fun.*

Written Practice 2

Fill in the blanks with the appropriate plural forms of the indicated verbs.

1. Che cosa _____ Marco? *What will Mark be having?*

   Lui _____ solo il caffè. *He will be having only coffee.*

2. Quando _____ la macchina, ragazzi? *Guys, when will you be selling your car?*

   Non _____ mai la macchina. *We will never sell the car.*

3. Che cosa _____ al professore gli studenti? *What will the students ask the professor?*

   _____ molte cose. *They will be asking many things.*

4. Che cosa _____, Laura? *What will you be reading, Laura?*

   Io _____ un romanzo. *I will be reading a novel.*

5. Dove _____, Dino e Dina? *Where will you be sleeping, Dino and Dina?*

   _____ in un albergo. *We will be sleeping in a hotel.*

6. Quando _____, Marco? *When will you be leaving, Mark?*

   _____ tra una settimana. *I will be leaving in a week.*

7. Che cosa _____ loro? *What will they (probably) prefer?*

   _____ solo un bicchiere di vino. *They will prefer only a glass of wine.*

8. A che ora _____ lei? *At what time will she be going out?*

   _____ verso le sei. *She will be going out around six.*

9. Che cosa _____ per la festa, Dina? *Dina, what will you be wearing for the party?*

   _____ un vestito nuovo. *I will be putting on a new dress.*

Irregular Forms in the Future Tense

As with the other tenses, there are also irregular forms for the future tense of some verbs. Of those you have encountered so far, the following verbs have irregular future tense forms. Note that many of these irregular forms involve simply dropping both vowels of the infinitive.

andare   *to go*
(io) andrò, (tu) andrai, (lui/lei/Lei) andrà, (noi) andremo, (voi) andrete, (loro/Loro) andranno

avere   *to have*
(io) avrò, (tu) avrai, (lui/lei/Lei) avrà, (noi) avremo, (voi) avrete, (loro/Loro) avranno

bere   *to drink*
(io) berrò, (tu) berrai, (lui/lei/Lei) berrà, (noi) berremo, (voi) berrete, (loro/Loro) berranno

cadere   *to fall*
(io) cadrò, (tu) cadrai, (lui/lei/Lei) cadrà, (noi) cadremo, (voi) cadrete, (loro/Loro) cadranno

dare   *to give*
(io) darò, (tu) darai, (lui/lei/Lei) darà, (noi) daremo, (voi) darete, (loro/Loro) daranno

dire   *to say, tell*
(io) dirò, (tu) dirai, (lui/lei/Lei) dirà, (noi) diremo, (voi) direte, (loro/Loro) diranno

dovere   *to have to*
(io) dovrò, (tu) dovrai, (lui/lei/Lei) dovrà, (noi) dovremo, (voi) dovrete, (loro/Loro) dovranno

essere   *to be*
(io) sarò, (tu) sarai, (lui/lei/Lei) sarà, (noi) saremo, (voi) sarete, (loro/Loro) saranno

fare   *to do, make*
(io) farò, (tu) farai, (lui/lei/Lei) farà, (noi) faremo, (voi) farete, (loro/Loro) faranno

potere   *to be able to*
(io) potrò, (tu) potrai, (lui/lei/Lei) potrà, (noi) potremo, (voi) potrete, (loro/Loro) potranno

sapere   *to know*
(io) saprò, (tu) saprai, (lui/lei/Lei) saprà, (noi) sapremo, (voi) saprete, (loro/Loro) sapranno

stare   *to stay*
(io) starò, (tu) starai, (lui/lei/Lei) starà, (noi) staremo, (voi) starete, (loro/Loro) staranno

vedere   *to see*
(io) vedrò, (tu) vedrai, (lui/lei/Lei) vedrà, (noi) vedremo, (voi) vedrete, (loro/Loro) vedranno

venire   *to come*
(io) verrò, (tu) verrai, (lui/lei/Lei) verrà, (noi) verremo, (voi) verrete, (loro/Loro) verranno

volere   *to want*
(io) vorrò, (tu) vorrai, (lui/lei/Lei) vorrà, (noi) vorremo, (voi) vorrete, (loro/Loro) vorranno

Oral Practice

Practice saying the following sentences out loud.

Marco, andrai anche tu in centro?	*Mark, will you also be going downtown?*
Sì, andrò, anch'io.	*Yes, I will also be going.*
Quanti anni avrà la professoressa?	*How old must the professor be?*
Avrà solo trenta anni.	*She must be only thirty.*
Che cosa berrete voi alla festa?	*What will you be drinking at the party?*
Noi berremo solo il caffè.	*We will be drinking only coffee.*
Che cosa daranno loro agli amici?	*What will they be giving their friends?*
Non daranno niente.	*They will be giving nothing.*
Dove dovrai andare domani, Giovanni?	*Where do you have to go tomorrow, John?*
Dovrò andare a fare delle spese.	*I will have to go shopping.*
Che tempo farà domani?	*How will the weather be tomorrow?*
Farà bel tempo.	*It will be beautiful.*
Franco, potrai venire alla festa?	*Frank, will you be able to come to the party?*
Sì, potrò venire.	*Yes, I will be able to come.*
Gli studenti sapranno parlare bene, vero?	*The students will know how to speak well, won't they?*
Sì, sapranno parlare molto bene.	*Yes, they will know how to speak very well.*
Andrea e Laura, dove starete in Italia?	*Andrew and Laura, where will you be staying in Italy?*

Staremo in un albergo.	*We will be staying in a hotel.*
Quando vedrai i tuoi nonni, Maria?	*When will you be seeing your grand-parents, Mary?*
Vedrò i nonni a Natale.	*I will see my grandparents at Christmas.*
Chi verrà alla festa?	*Who will be coming to the party?*
Tutti verranno.	*Everybody will be coming.*
Che cosa vorrà fare tuo fratello domani?	*What will your brother want to do tomorrow?*
Vorrà andare al cinema.	*He will want to go to the movies.*

Written Practice 3

Fill in the blanks with the appropriate future tense forms of the indicated verbs.

1. _____ anche loro in centro? *Will they also be going downtown?*

   Sì, _____, anche loro. *Yes, they will also be going.*

2. Quanti anni _____ sua madre? *How old must his mother be?*

   _____ circa trent'anni. *She must be around thirty.*

3. Che cosa _____ loro alla festa? *What will they be drinking at the party?*

   Loro _____ solo il caffè. *They will be drinking only coffee.*

4. Che cosa _____ lei agli amici? *What will she be giving the friends?*

   Non _____ niente. *She will be giving nothing.*

5. Dove _____ andare domani, signor Dini? *Where do you have to go tomorrow, Mr. Dini?*

   _____ andare a fare delle spese. *I will have to go shopping.*

6. Chi _____ quelle persone? *Who are those people?*

   _____ i loro cugini. *They must be their cousins.*

7. Che tempo _____ domani? *How will the weather be tomorrow?*

   _____ bel tempo. *It will be beautiful.*

8. Lui _____ venire alla festa? *Will he be able to come to the party?*

   Sì, _____ venire. *Yes, he will be able to come.*

9. Voi _____ parlare bene, vero? *You will know how to speak well, won't you?*

   Sì, _____ parlare molto bene. *Yes, we will know how to speak very well.*

10. Dove _____ loro in Italia? *Where will they be staying in Italy?*

    _____ in un albergo. *They will be staying in a hotel.*

11. Quando _____ i tuoi nonni, Maria? *When will you be seeing your grandparents, Mary?*

    _____ i nonni a Natale. *I will see them at Christmas.*

12. Anche tu _____ alla festa? *Will you also be coming to the party?*

    Sì, _____ anch'io. *Yes, I will be coming, too.*

13. Che cosa _____ fare i tuoi amici domani? *What will your friends want to do tomorrow?*

    _____ andare al cinema. *They will want to go to the movies.*

Future Perfect Tense

The future perfect tense refers to something that occurred *before* a simple future action. Like the present perfect and the pluperfect tenses, the future perfect is a compound tense. It is formed using the future tense conjugation of the auxiliary verb plus the past participle of the verb showing the action, in that order.

Here are two examples of complete future perfect conjugations: one verb is conjugated with **avere** and the other with **essere**.

mangiare	*to eat*
(io) avrò mangiato	*I will have eaten*
(tu) avrai mangiato	*you* (familiar) *will have eaten*
(Lei) avrà mangiato	*you* (polite) *will have eaten*
(lui/lei) avrà mangiato	*he/she will have eaten*
(noi) avremo mangiato	*we will have eaten*
(voi) avrete mangiato	*you* (familiar plural) *will have eaten*
(Loro) avranno mangiato	*you* (polite plural) *will have eaten*
(loro) avranno mangiato	*they will have eaten*

partire	*to leave*
(io) sarò partito/a	*I will have left*
(tu) sarai partito/a	*you* (familiar) *will have left*
(Lei) sarà partito/a	*you* (polite) *will have left*
(lui/lei) sarà partito/a	*he/she will have left*
(noi) saremo partiti/e	*we will have left*
(voi) sarete partiti/e	*you* (familiar plural) *will have left*
(Loro) saranno partiti/e	*you* (polite plural) *will have left*
(loro) saranno partiti/e	*they will have left*

Oral Practice

Practice saying the following sentences out loud.

Che cosa faremo, quando tu avrai pagato il conto?	*What will we be doing, when you will have paid the bill?*
Dopo che io avrò pagato il conto, potremo andare in centro.	*After I will have paid the bill, we can go downtown.*
Chi pagherà il conto, tu o tuo fratello?	*Who will be paying the bill, you or your brother?*
Lui avrà già pagato il conto prima.	*He will have already paid the bill before.*
Che cosa farete, appena sarà arrivato lui?	*What will you be doing, as soon as he will have arrived?*
Appena sarà arrivato, andremo al cinema.	*As soon as he will have arrived, we will be going to the movies.*
Appena sarai arrivata, Maria, che cosa faranno i tuoi amici?	*As soon as you will have arrived, what will your friends be doing, Mary?*

Appena sarò arrivata, non faremo niente.	*As soon as I will have arrived, we will be doing nothing.*
Che cosa farà tua sorella, dopo che sarete usciti?	*What will your sister be doing, after you will have gone out?*
Appena saremo usciti, lei comincerà a studiare.	*As soon as we will have gone out, she will start studying.*
Che cosa farai, quando saranno usciti i tuoi amici?	*What will you be doing, when your friends will have gone out?*
Quando saranno usciti, voglio guardare la televisione.	*When they will have gone out, I want to watch television.*
Che cosa farete, quando i vostri genitori avranno venduto la casa?	*What will you do when your parents will have sold the house?*
Quando avranno venduto la casa, noi andremo in Italia.	*When they will have sold the house, we will be going to Italy.*

Written Practice 4

Fill in the blanks with the appropriate future perfect tense forms of the indicated verbs.

1. Che cosa faremo, quando lui _____ il conto? *What will we be doing, when he will have paid the bill?*

   Dopo che lui _____ il conto, potremo andare in centro. *After he will have paid the bill, we can go downtown.*

2. Chi pagherà il conto, tu o io? *Who will be paying the bill, you or I?*

   Io _____ il conto prima. *I will have already paid the bill before.*

3. Che cosa farete, appena _____ loro? *What will you be doing, as soon as they will have arrived?*

   Appena _____, andremo al cinema. *As soon as they will have arrived, we will be going to the movies.*

4. Appena _____, Dino, che cosa faranno i tuoi amici? *As soon as you will have arrived, what will your friends be doing, Dino?*

   Appena _____, non faremo niente. *As soon as I will have arrived, we will be doing nothing.*

5. Che cosa farà tua madre, dopo che voi _____? *What will your mother be doing, after you will have gone out?*

    Appena _____, lei comincerà a leggere un nuovo romanzo. *As soon as we will have gone out, she will start reading a new novel.*

6. Che cosa farai, quando _____ la tua amica? *What will you be doing, when your friend will have gone out?*

    Quando _____, voglio guardare la televisione. *When she will have gone out, I want to watch television.*

7. Che cosa farete, quando voi _____ la casa? *What will you be doing, when you will have sold the house?*

    Quando noi _____ la casa, compreremo un'altra casa. *When we will have sold the house, we will buy another house.*

8. E che cosa farete, quando loro _____ la macchina? *And what will you be doing, after they will have sold the car?*

    Quando _____ la macchina, compreremo un'altra macchina. *When they will have sold the car, we will buy another car.*

9. Che cosa vorrai fare, dopo che tuo fratello _____? *What will you want to do, after your brother will have woken up?*

    Non voglio fare niente, dopo che _____. *I do not want to do anything, after he will have woken up.*

Talking About Sports

Just as in America and many other parts of the world, sports are an intrinsic part of Italian culture, too. Here are some common sports vocabulary words:

la bicicletta	*bicycle*
il calcio	*soccer*
la ginnastica	*gymnastics*
l'incontro	*match, encounter, meet*
la pallacanestro	*basketball*
la partita	*match, game*
il pattinaggio	*skating*
praticare	*to practice, play (a sport)*

il pugilato	*boxing*
lo sport	*sport*
il tennis	*tennis*
giocare	*to play* (a sport)
si gioca	*one plays*
il giocatore/la giocatrice	*player* (m./f.)
vincere	*to win* (irregular past participle: vinto)
la maglia/la maglietta	*jersey, sweater*
la squadra	*team*

Written Practice 5

Fill in the blanks with the missing words.

1. Di chi è quella _____? *Whose bicycle is that?*

   È la _____ di mia madre. *It is my mother's bike.*

2. Ci sarà un incontro di _____ domani, vero? *There is a soccer match tomorrow, right?*

   Sì, e sarà una bella _____. *Yes, and it will be a great game.*

3. Che tipi di _____ praticano i tuo amici? *What types of sport do your friends play?*

   Loro praticano _____, _____ e _____. *They play basketball, boxing, and tennis.*

4. Anche tu pratichi il _____? *Are you into skating?*

   No, io pratico _____. *No, I am into gymnastics.*

SOCCER IN ITALY

Il calcio was once called **il football** in Italy. It got the name from England where the game of soccer was played over 100 years ago in the English colleges. The first set of rules were established in 1848, and in 1863 the first Football Association was formed in England.

Italians love their **calcio**. Every Sunday the stadiums (**gli stadi**) are packed and the whole day on television revolves around soccer. The winners of the **campionato** (*championship*) wear a **scudetto** (a distinctive emblem) on their jerseys (**le magliette**) the year following their win.

The Italian national team of soccer goes by the name of **gli Azzurri** (*the blue ones*) and each player wears a blue jersey. Blue is the national color of all Italian sports teams. The teams are named after the city for which they play. For example, the team from Milano is called **il Milan** (without the **-o**), the team from Rome is called **il Roma**, and so on. The gender of the name is generally masculine, with a few exceptions: for example, **la Fiorentina**, which plays for **Firenze**. The most famous team is **la Juventus**. It plays for the city of Turin.

QUIZ

For each present indicative verb form provided, give the corresponding future and future perfect forms. For example:

io arrivo *io arriverò* _____ *io sarò arrivato/a* _____

	Simple Future	**Future Perfect**
1. io vendo		
tu mangi		
tu metti		
lui comincia		
lei chiede		
noi paghiamo		
noi chiudiamo		
noi finiamo		
voi cercate		
voi mettete		
loro mangiano		
loro chiedono		

Fill in the blanks with the appropriate future or future perfect forms of the given verbs.

2. Domani mio fratello (andare) _____ in centro per fare delle spese.

3. Dopo che lui (fare) _____ le spese, tornerà subito a casa.

4. Chi (essere) _____ quell'uomo?

5. Appena (venire) _____ i tuoi amici, usciremo.

6. Che tempo (fare) _____ domani?

7. _____ (venire) anche loro alla festa domani?

Personal Matters! Answer each question appropriately.

8. Quali sport pratichi?

_____.

9. Quali sport praticherai forse in futuro?

_____.

10. Che tempo farà domani nella tua città?

_____.

CHAPTER 17

Using the Conditional Tense

Here's what you will learn in this chapter:

Conditional Tense
Irregular Forms in the Conditional Tense
Past Conditional Tense
Using Negatives
Italian People

Conditional Tense

Uscirei oggi, ma devo studiare. *I would go out today, but I have to study.* The first verb in this sentence is in the conditional tense or mood. The conditional mood

allows you to express a condition, as its name implies: *I would go if . . .* or *We would do it, but . . .* , and so on. In addition, the conditional tense is used when making a polite request.

Potrei parlare?	*May I speak?*
Mi darebbe la sua penna?	*Could you give me your pen?*

The present conditional (also known as the simple conditional) is formed like the simple future: the final **-e** of the infinitives of all three verb conjugations is dropped (changing the **-ar** of first-conjugation verbs to **-er**) and then the conditional endings **-ei**, **-esti**, **-ebbe**, **-emmo**, **-este**, and **-ebbero** are added on.

parlare   parler-

(io) parler**ei**	*I would speak*
(tu) parler**esti**	*you (familiar) would speak*
(Lei) parler**ebbe**	*you (polite) would speak*
(lui/lei) parler**ebbe**	*he/she would speak*
(noi) parler**emmo**	*we would speak*
(voi) parler**este**	*you (familiar plural) would speak*
(Loro) parler**ebbero**	*you (polite plural) would speak*
(loro) parler**ebbero**	*they would speak*

scrivere   scriver-

(io) scriver**ei**	*I would write*
(tu) scriver**esti**	*you (familiar) would write*
(Lei) scriver**ebbe**	*you (polite) would write*
(lui/lei) scriver**ebbe**	*he/she would write*
(noi) scriver**emmo**	*we would write*
(voi) scriver**este**	*you (familiar plural) would write*
(Loro) scriver**ebbero**	*you (polite plural) would write*
(loro) scriver**ebbero**	*they would write*

finire   finir-

(io) finir**ei**	*I would finish*
(tu) finir**esti**	*you (familiar) would finish*
(Lei) finir**ebbe**	*you (polite) would finish*
(lui/lei) finir**ebbe**	*he/she would finish*
(noi) finir**emmo**	*we would finish*
(voi) finir**este**	*you (familiar plural) would finish*

| (Loro) finir**ebbero** | *you* (polite plural) *would finish* |
| (loro) finir**ebbero** | *they would finish* |

As with the simple future tense, to indicate that the hard **c** and **g** sounds of verbs ending **-care** and **-gare** are to be maintained, an **h** is added to the spelling. Note, then, the following spelling adjustments for the verbs **cercare** and **pagare**.

cercare   cercher-

(io) cerc**herei**	*I would search*
(tu) cerc**heresti**	*you* (familiar) *would search*
(Lei) cerc**herebbe**	*you* (polite) *would search*
(lui/lei) cerc**herebbe**	*he/she would search*
(noi) cerc**heremmo**	*we would search*
(voi) cerc**hereste**	*you* (familiar plural) *would search*
(Loro) cerc**herebbero**	*you* (polite plural) *would search*
(loro) cerc**herebbero**	*they would search*

pagare   pagher-

(io) pag**herei**	*I would pay*
(tu) pag**heresti**	*you* (familiar) *would pay*
(Lei) pag**herebbe**	*you* (polite) *would pay*
(lui/lei) pag**herebbe**	*he/she would pay*
(noi) pag**heremmo**	*we would pay*
(voi) pag**hereste**	*you* (familiar plural) *would pay*
(Loro) pag**herebbero**	*you* (polite plural) *would pay*
(loro) pag**herebbero**	*they would pay*

And, also as with the future tense, the **-i** of verbs ending in **-ciare** or **-giare** is not maintained in the conditional tense.

cominciare   comincer-

(io) comin**cerei**	*I would start*
(tu) comin**ceresti**	*you* (familiar) *would start*
(Lei) comin**cerebbe**	*you* (polite) *would start*
(lui/lei) comin**cerebbe**	*he/she would start*
(noi) comin**ceremmo**	*we would start*
(voi) comin**cereste**	*you* (familiar plural) *would start*
(Loro) comin**cerebbero**	*you* (polite plural) *would start*
(loro) comin**cerebbero**	*they would start*

mangiare   manger-

(io) man**gerei**	*I would eat*
(tu) man**geresti**	*you* (familiar) *would eat*
(Lei) man**gerebbe**	*you* (polite) *would eat*
(lui/lei) man**gerebbe**	*he/she would eat*
(noi) man**geremmo**	*we would eat*
(voi) man**gereste**	*you* (familiar plural) *would eat*
(Loro) man**gerebbero**	*you* (polite plural) *would eat*
(loro) man**gerebbero**	*they would eat*

Oral Practice

Practice saying the following sentences out loud.

Compreresti questa macchina, Marco?	*Would you buy this car, Mark?*
Sì, comprerei quella macchina.	*Yes, I would buy that car.*
Mangerebbe questi ravioli tuo fratello?	*Would your brother eat these ravioli?*
Sì, mangerebbe i ravioli subito.	*Yes, he would eat the ravioli right away.*
Quando comincereste a lavorare voi?	*When would you start working?*
Noi cominceremmo subito.	*We would begin right away.*
Loro pagherebbero il conto, vero?	*They would pay the bill, wouldn't they?*
Pagherebbero, ma non hanno soldi.	*They would pay, but they do not have money.*
Anche tu cercheresti lavoro, vero?	*You would also be looking for work, right?*
Sì, anch'io cercherei lavoro.	*Yes, I would be looking for work, too.*
Maria, anche tu venderesti la macchina?	*Mary, would you also be selling your car?*
Venderei la macchina, ma non posso.	*I would be selling the car, but I cannot.*
Anche lui prenderebbe il cappuccino, no?	*He would be having cappuccino as well, right?*

Sì, prenderebbe il cappuccino, ma non può.	*Yes, he would be having cappuccino, but he cannot.*
Che cosa chiedereste voi al professore?	*What would you ask the professor?*
Chiederemmo tante cose.	*We would ask a lot of things.*
È vero che loro leggerebbero quel romanzo?	*Is it true that they would read that novel?*
Sì, leggerebbero quel romanzo, ma non hanno tempo.	*Yes, they would read that novel, but they do not have time.*
È vero che partiresti per l'Italia, Gino?	*Is it true that you would be leaving for Italy, Gino?*
Sì, partirei subito, ma ancora non posso.	*Yes, I would be leaving right away, but I cannot yet.*
Che cosa preferirebbe tua sorella?	*What would your sister prefer?*
Lei preferirebbe la minestra.	*She would prefer soup.*
Quando uscireste oggi?	*When would you be going out today?*
Noi usciremmo dopo cena.	*We would go out after dinner.*
Quando aprirebbero i negozi?	*When would stores be opening up?*
Di solito, non aprirebbero prima delle sette.	*Usually, they would not be opening up before seven.*
Marco, a che ora ti alzeresti?	*Mark, at what time would you be getting up?*
Io mi alzerei molto presto.	*I would be getting up very early.*

Written Practice 1

Fill in the blanks with the appropriate conditional forms of the indicated verbs.

1. Loro _____ questa macchina? *Would they buy this car?*

   Sì, _____ quella macchina. *Yes, they would buy that car.*

2. _____ questi ravioli, Marco? *Would you eat these ravioli, Mark?*

Sì, _____ quei ravioli subito. *Yes, I would eat those ravioli right away.*

3. Quando _____ a lavorare lui? *When would he start working?*

Lui _____ subito. *He would begin right away.*

4. È vero che _____ il conto voi? *Is it true that you would pay the bill?*

Sì, _____, ma non abbiamo soldi. *Yes, we would pay, but we do not have money.*

5. Lei _____ lavoro, signor Verdi, vero? *You would be looking for work, Mr. Verdi, right?*

Sì, io _____ lavoro, ma non ho tempo. *Yes, I would be looking for work, but I do not have time.*

6. È vero che anche lei _____ la macchina? *Is it true that she also would be selling her car?*

Sì, _____ la macchina, ma non può. *Yes, she would be selling the car, but she cannot.*

7. Anche tu _____ il cappuccino, no? *You would be having cappuccino as well, right?*

Sì, _____ il cappuccino, ma non posso. *Yes, I would be having cappuccino, but I cannot.*

8. Che cosa _____ voi alla dottoressa? *What would you ask the doctor?*

_____ tante cose. *We would ask a lot of things.*

9. È vero che loro _____ quel romanzo? *Is it true that they would read that novel?*

Sì, _____ quel romanzo, ma non possono. *Yes, they would read that novel, but they cannot.*

10. È vero che lei _____ subito per l'Italia? *Is it true that she would leaving for Italy right away?*

Sì, _____ subito, ma ancora non può. *Yes, she would leave right away, but she cannot yet.*

11. Che cosa _____ voi? *What would you prefer?*

    Noi _____ la minestra. *We would prefer soup.*

12. Quando _____ oggi, Maria? *When would you be going out today, Mary?*

    Io _____ dopo cena. *I would go out after dinner.*

13. Quando _____ i negozi? *When would stores be opening up?*

    Di solito, non _____ prima delle sette. *Usually, they would not be opening up before seven.*

14. Signora, a che ora _____? *Madam, at what time would you be getting up?*

    Io _____ molto presto. *I would be getting up very early.*

Irregular Forms in the Conditional Tense

As you may have guessed, the verbs that are irregular in the future tense are also irregular in the conditional tense in the same way. The same verb stem is used for the conditional as for the future, but this time the conditional endings are added on instead of the future endings. For example, the irregular future and conditional form of **andare** involves dropping both vowels from the infinitive ending (**andr-**) and then adding on the appropriate endings.

Here are some comparisons:

Future		**Conditional**	
io andrò	*I will go*	io andrei	*I would go*
noi saremo	*we will be*	noi saremmo	*we would be*
lui potrà	*he will be able to*	lui potrebbe	*he would be able to*
loro verranno	*they will come*	loro verrebbero	*they would come*

Here are the complete conjugations of the irregular conditional verb forms of the verbs you have encountered so far.

andare *to go*
(io) andrei, (tu) andresti, (lui/lei/Lei) andrebbe, (noi) andremmo, (voi) andreste, (loro/Loro) andrebbero

avere *to have*
(io) avrò, (tu) avresti, (lui/lei/Lei) avrebbe, (noi) avremmo, (voi) avreste, (loro/Loro) avrebbero

bere *to drink*
(io) berrei, (tu) berresti, (lui/lei/Lei) berrebbe, (noi) berremmo, (voi) berreste, (loro/Loro) berrebbero

cadere *to fall*
(io) cadrei, (tu) cadresti, (lui/lei/Lei) cadrebbe, (noi) cadremmo, (voi) cadreste, (loro/Loro) cadrebbero

dare *to give*
(io) darei, (tu) daresti, (lui/lei/Lei) darebbe, (noi) daremmo, (voi) dareste, (loro/Loro) darebbero

dire *to say, tell*
(io) direi, (tu) diresti, (lui/lei/Lei) direbbe, (noi) diremmo, (voi) direste, (loro/Loro) direbbero

dovere *to have to*
(io) dovrei, (tu) dovresti, (lui/lei/Lei) dovrebbe, (noi) dovremmo, (voi) dovreste, (loro/Loro) dovrebbero

essere *to be*
(io) sarei, (tu) saresti, (lui/lei/Lei) sarebbe, (noi) saremmo, (voi) sareste, (loro/Loro) sarebbero

fare *to do, make*
(io) farei, (tu) faresti, (lui/lei/Lei) farebbe, (noi) faremmo, (voi) fareste, (loro/Loro) farebbero

potere *to be able to*
(io) potrei, (tu) potresti, (lui/lei/Lei) potrebbe, (noi) potremmo, (voi) potreste, (loro/Loro) potrebbero

sapere   *to know*
(io) saprei, (tu) sapresti, (lui/lei/Lei) saprebbe, (noi) sapremmo, (voi) sapreste, (loro/Loro) saprebbero

stare   *to stay*
(io) starei, (tu) staresti, (lui/lei/Lei) starebbe, (noi) staremmo, (voi) stareste, (loro/Loro) starebbero

vedere   *to see*
(io) vedrei, (tu) vedresti, (lui/lei/Lei) vedrebbe, (noi) vedremmo, (voi) vedreste, (loro/ Loro) vedrebbero

venire   *to come*
(io) verrei, (tu) verresti, (lui/lei/Lei) verrebbe, (noi) verremmo, (voi) verreste, (loro/Loro) verrebbero

volere   *to want*
(io) vorrei, (tu) vorresti, (lui/lei/Lei) vorrebbe, (noi) vorremmo, (voi) vorreste, (loro/Loro) vorrebbero

Oral Practice

Practice saying the following sentences out loud.

Marco, è vero che andresti in Italia?	*Mark, is it true that you would go to Italy?*
Sì, andrei in Italia volentieri, ma no posso.	*Yes, I would go to Italy gladly, but I cannot.*
È vero che lui non avrebbe pazienza?	*Is it true that he would not have patience?*
Sì, non avrebbe pazienza, anche se ha torto.	*Yes, he would not have patience, even if he is wrong.*
Che cosa berreste voi alla festa?	*What would you be drinking at the party?*
Noi berremmo solo il caffè.	*We would drink only coffee.*
Che cosa darebbero loro agli amici?	*What would they give to their friends?*
Non darebbero niente.	*They would give nothing.*
Dove dovresti andare domani, Giovanni?	*Where should you be going tomorrow, John?*

Dovrei andare a fare delle spese.	*I should be going shopping.*
Chi sarebbe quella persona?	*Who would (must) that person be?*
Non so chi sarebbe.	*I do not know who she must be.*
Che cosa farebbero loro invece di studiare?	*What would they (like to) do instead of studying?*
Farebbero tante cose.	*They would do a lot of things.*
Maria, potresti venire alla festa?	*Mary, would you be able to come to the party?*
No, non potrei venire, perché devo studiare.	*No, I would not be able to come, because I have to study.*
È vero che lui saprebbe tutto?	*Is it true that he would know everything?*
Sì, lui saprebbe tutto.	*Yes, he would know everything.*
Andrea e Laura, dove stareste in Italia?	*Andrew and Laura, where would you be staying in Italy?*
Staremmo in un albergo.	*We would be staying in a hotel.*
Chi verrebbe alla festa?	*Who would come to the party?*
Tutti verrebbero.	*Everybody would come.*
Che cosa vorrebbe fare tuo fratello domani?	*What would your brother want to do tomorrow?*
Vorrebbe andare al cinema.	*He would want to go to the movies.*

Written Practice 2

Fill in the blanks with the appropriate conditional forms of the indicated verbs.

1. È vero che tuo fratello _____ in Italia? *Is it true that your brother would go to Italy?*

   Sì, _____ in Italia volentieri, ma non può. *Yes, he would go to Italy gladly, but he cannot.*

2. È vero che tu non _____ pazienza con noi, Marco? *Is it true that you would not have patience with us, Mark?*

   Sì, non _____ pazienza. *Yes, I would not have patience.*

3. Che cosa _____ loro alla festa? *What would they be drinking at the party?*

   Loro _____ solo il caffè. *They would be drinking only coffee.*

4. Che cosa _____ voi agli amici? *What would you give to your friends?*

   Non _____ niente. *We would give nothing.*

5. Dove _____ andare domani, il tuo amico? *Where should your friend be going tomorrow?*

   _____ andare a fare delle spese. *He should be going shopping.*

6. Chi _____ quella donna? *Who must that woman be?*

   Non so chi _____. *I do not know who she must be.*

7. Che cosa _____, Dino, invece di studiare? *What would you (like to) do, Dino, instead of studying?*

   _____ tante cose. *I would be doing a lot of things.*

8. Franco, _____ venire alla festa? *Frank, would you be able to come to the party?*

   No, non _____ venire, perché devo studiare. *No, I would not be able to come, because I have to study.*

9. È vero che loro _____ tutto? *Is it true that they would know everything?*

   Sì, _____ tutto. *Yes, they would know everything.*

10. Ragazzi, dove _____ in Italia? *Guys, where would you be staying in Italy?*

    _____ in un albergo. *We would be staying in a hotel.*

11. _____ anche tu, Pino, alla festa? *Would you come to the party, too, Pino?*

    Sì, _____, anch'io. *Yes, I would come, too.*

12. Che cosa _____ fare lei domani? *What would she want to do tomorrow?*

    _____ andare al cinema. *She would want to go to the movies.*

Past Conditional Tense

The past conditional (also known as the conditional perfect) is a compound tense. It is formed with the conditional of the auxiliary verb plus the past participle of the verb showing the action, in that order. Here are two examples of complete verb conjugations for you: one is conjugated with **avere** and the other with **essere**.

mangiare	*to eat*
(io) avrei mangiato	*I would have eaten*
(tu) avresti mangiato	*you* (familiar) *would have eaten*
(Lei) avrebbe mangiato	*you* (polite) *would have eaten*
(lui/lei) avrebbe mangiato	*he/she would have eaten*
(noi) avremmo mangiato	*we would have eaten*
(voi) avreste mangiato	*you* (familiar plural) *would have eaten*
(Loro) avrebbero mangiato	*you* (polite plural) *would have eaten*
(loro) avrebbero mangiato	*they would have eaten*

partire	*to leave*
(io) sarei partito/a	*I would have left*
(tu) saresti partito/a	*you* (familiar) *would have left*
(Lei) sarebbe partito/a	*you* (polite) *would have left*
(lui/lei) sarebbe partito/a	*he/she would have left*
(noi) saremmo partiti/e	*we would have left*
(voi) sareste partiti/e	*you* (familiar plural) *would have left*
(Loro) sarebbero partiti/e	*you* (polite plural) *would have left*
(loro) sarebbero partiti/e	*they would have left*

The Italian conditional perfect tense corresponds to the English past conditional—*I would have . . .* , *you would have . . .* , and so on. It is used to refer to conditional or hypothetical actions that can only logically be expressed in a perfect tense.

Ha detto che sarebbe venuto.	*He said that he would have come.*
Sapeva che io avrei capito.	*He knew that I would have understood.*
Avrei voluto comprare quella macchina, ma non avevo soldi.	*I would have wanted to buy that car, but I did not have the money.*

Oral Practice

Practice saying the following sentences out loud.

Marco, avresti pagato il conto?	*Mark, would you have paid the bill?*
Sì, avrei pagato il conto, ma non avevo soldi.	*Yes, I would have paid the bill, but I did not have any money.*
È vero che i tuoi cugini sarebbero già arrivati?	*Is it true that your cousins would have already arrived?*
Sì, sarebbero arrivati ieri sera.	*Yes, they would have arrived last night.*
Quando saresti uscita ieri, Pina?	*When would you have gone out yesterday, Pina?*
Sarei uscita presto, ma invece non sono uscita affatto.	*I would have gone out early, but instead I did not go out at all.*
Marco e Maria, è vero che avreste venduto la macchina?	*Mark and Maria, is it true that you would have sold the car?*
Sì, avremmo venduto la macchina, ma nessuno la voleva.	*Yes, we would have sold the car, but no one wanted it.*
Anche i nostri genitori avrebbero venduto la macchina.	*Our parents would also have sold the car.*

Written Practice 3

Fill in the blanks with the appropriate past conditional forms of the indicated verbs.

1. Voi _____ il conto? *Would you have paid the bill?*

   Sì, _____ il conto, ma non avevamo soldi. *Yes, we would have paid the bill, but we did not have any money.*

   Anche loro _____ il conto, ma anche loro non avevano soldi. *They would also have paid the bill, but they also did not have money.*

2. È vero che tuo fratello _____? *Is it true that your brother would have arrived?*

Sì, _____ ieri sera. *Yes, he would have arrived last night.*

3. Anche i tuoi amici, _____ iera sera, vero? *Even your friends would have arrived last night, right?*

Sì, anche loro _____. *Yes, they would also have arrived.*

4. Quando _____ ieri, Maria? *When would you have gone out yesterday, Mary?*

_____ presto, ma invece non sono uscita affatto. *I would have gone out early, but instead I did not go out at all.*

5. Anche voi _____, vero? *You also would have gone out, right?*

Sì, anche noi _____. *Yes, we would also have gone out.*

6. Maria, è vero che _____ la macchina? *Mary, is it true that you would have sold the car?*

Sì, _____ la macchina, ma nessuno la voleva. *Yes, I would have sold the car, but no one wanted it.*

Anche mio fratello _____ la macchina. *My brother would also have sold the car.*

Using Negatives

Negatives are words that allow you to deny, refuse, or oppose something. Any sentence can be made negative in Italian by simply putting **non** before the verb.

Non conosco nessuno qui.	*I do not know anyone here.*
Non pratico più lo sport.	*I do not do sports anymore.*

The following are some common negative constructions. You have seen virtually all of them in previous chapters. Notice that **non** is a part of each construction.

non... affatto	*not at all*
non... mai	*never, not ever*
non... nessuno	*no one*
non... niente, nulla	*nothing*
non... più	*no more, no longer*
non... neanche, non... nemmeno	*not even*
non... né... né	*neither . . . nor*
non... mica	*not really, not quite, not at all*

Oral Practice

Practice saying the following sentences out loud.

Marco sa cantare bene, vero?	*Mark knows how to sing well, doesn't he?*
No, non sa cantare affatto.	*No, he does not know how to sing at all.*
È vero che tu bevi sempre l'espresso?	*Is it true that you always drink espresso?*
No, non bevo mai l'espresso.	*No, I never drink espresso.*
È vero che lui va spesso in centro?	*Is it true that he goes downtown often?*
No, lui non va mai in centro.	*No, he never goes downtown.*
Conosci qualcuno in questa città?	*Do you know someone in this city?*
No, non conosco nessuno.	*No, I do not know anyone.*
Marco, che cosa vuoi fare oggi?	*Mark, what do you want to do today?*
Non voglio fare niente.	*I do not want to do anything.*
C'è qualcosa da fare?	*Is there something to do?*
No, non c'è nulla da fare.	*No, there is nothing to do.*
Voi andate sempre in Italia, no?	*You always go to Italy, don't you?*
No, non andiamo più in Italia.	*No, we do not go to Italy anymore.*
Ti piace l'espresso?	*Do you like espresso?*
No, e non mi piace nemmeno il cappuccino.	*No, and I do not like cappuccino either.*
Vuoi la pasta o la minestra?	*Do you want pasta or soup?*
Non voglio né pasta né minestra.	*I want neither pasta nor soup.*
È vero che viene anche lui alla festa?	*Is it true that he is also coming to the party?*
No, non è mica vero.	*No, it is not true at all.*

Written Practice 4

Complete each negative sentence by filling in the blank with the appropriate negative construction.

1. Tuo fratello sa suonare bene il pianoforte, vero? *Your brother knows how to play the piano well, doesn't he?*

   No, non sa suonare _____. *No, he does not know how to play at all.*

2. È vero che tu guardi sempre la televisione? *Is it true that you always watch television?*

   No, non guardo _____ la televisione. *No, I never watch television.*

3. È vero che lui va spesso al cinema? *Is it true that he goes to the movies often?*

   No, lui non va _____ al cinema. *No, he never goes to the movies.*

4. Conosci qualcuno in Italia? *Do you know someone in Italy?*

   No, non conosco _____. *No, I do not know anyone.*

5. Pino, che cosa vuoi fare oggi? *Pino, what do you want to do today?*

   Non voglio fare _____. *I do not want to do anything.*

6. Hai qualcosa da dire? *Do you have something to say?*

   No, non ho _____ da dire. *No, I have nothing to say.*

7. Voi andate sempre in vacanza, no? *You always go on vacation, don't you?*

   No, non andiamo _____. *No, we do not go anymore.*

8. Ti piace la carne? *Do you like meat?*

   No, e non mi piace _____ la pasta. *No, and I do not like pasta either.*

9. Vuoi l'espresso o il cappuccino? *Do you want espresso or cappuccino?*

   Non voglio _____ l'espresso _____ il cappuccino. *I want neither espresso nor cappuccino.*

10. È vero che vieni anche tu alla festa? *Is it true that you are also coming to the party?*

    No, non è _____ vero. *No, it is not true at all.*

Italian People

Most of Italy's people live in urban areas (**i centri urbani**). Italy's largest cities, in order of population, are Rome (**Roma**), Milan (**Milano**), and Naples (**Napoli**). Each has more than a million people. Many of the country's cities are surrounded by large metropolitan areas.

The most densely populated areas of the country are the industrialized regions (**le regioni**) of Lombardy (**la Lombardia**) and Liguria (**la Liguria**) in the northwest and the region of Campania (**la Campania**) in the south. The areas with the lowest population density are the mountainous regions of both the north and south.

Most of Italy's people are ethnic Italians. The only sizable ethnic minorities (**le minoranze**) are Germans who live in **il Trentino Alto Adige** region, which borders Austria; and Slovenes who inhabit the Trieste area, along the border of Italy and Slovenia. In addition, a number of ethnic French people live in the Valle D'Aosta (**la Valle d'Aosta**) region, near Italy's border with France and Switzerland.

Italians have also emigrated throughout the world. There are many Italians in the United States today who can trace their origins to Italy.

QUIZ

For each future tense verb provided, give the corresponding conditional and conditional perfect forms. For example:

io arriverò	*io arriverei*	*io sarei arrivato/a*
	Simple Conditional	**Conditional Perfect**
1. io venderò		
io preferirò		
tu mangerai		
tu metterai		
lui comincerà		
lei chiederà		
noi pagheremo		
noi chiuderemo		
voi cercherete		

voi metterete   _____   _____

loro mangeranno   _____   _____

loro chiederanno   _____   _____

Choose the appropriate future, future perfect, conditional, or conditional perfect tense for the following sentences, as necessary.

2. Lui _____ il conto, ma non ha soldi.

  (a) pagherà   (c) pagherebbe

  (b) avrà pagato   (d) avrebbe pagato

3. Mia sorella _____ la macchina, ma è ancora troppo giovane.

  (a) comprerà   (c) comprerebbe

  (b) avrà comprato   (d) avrebbe comprato

4. Domani lui _____ il conto di sicuro.

  (a) pagherà   (c) pagherebbe

  (b) avrà pagato   (d) avrebbe pagato

5. _____ dire qualcosa, per favore?

  (a) Potrò   (c) Potrei

  (b) Avrò potuto   (d) Avrei potuto

6. Mi _____ la sua matita, professore?

  (a) darà   (c) darebbe

  (b) avrà dato   (d) avrebbe dato

7. Quella ragazza _____ l'italiano l'anno prossimo.

  (a) studierà   (c) studierebbe

  (b) avrà studiato   (d) avrebbe studiato

8. Mi ha detto che sua sorella _____ alla festa, ma deve studiare.

  (a) verrà   (c) verrebbe

  (b) sarà venuta   (d) sarebbe venuta

Rewrite each sentence, using a negative construction.

9. Lui mangia sempre gli spaghetti.

    _____.

    Ieri ho mangiato la carne e le patate.

    _____.

    Marco conosce tutti in quella scuola.

    _____.

    Lui vuole qualcosa.

    _____.

    Quello è proprio vero.

    _____.

Personal Matters! Answer the question appropriately.

10. Quali grandi città italiane vorresti vedere?

    _____.

CHAPTER 18

Using Object Pronouns

Here's what you will learn in this chapter:

Object Pronouns

Object Pronouns with Past Participles

A Bit More About Adjectives

Adverbs

Computers and the Internet

Object Pronouns

Mi hai telefonato ieri sera? Sì, ti ho telefonato verso le sei. *Did you call me last night? Yes, I called you around six.* In these two sentences you see the object pro-

nouns **mi** and **ti**. Object pronouns occur often in conversation. Their main use is to replace direct or indirect objects. Take a look.

Direct Object

Marco sta leggendo **quel libro** adesso.

*Marco is reading **that book** now.*

Direct Object Pronoun

Marco **lo** sta leggendo adesso.

*Marco is reading **it** now.*

Indirect Object

Marco darà quel libro **a sua sorella** domani.

*Marco will give that book **to his sister** tomorrow.*

Indirect Object Pronoun

Marco **le** darà quel libro domani.

*Marco will give that book **to her** tomorrow.*

Note from the previous example sentences that, though the Italian direct and indirect objects *follow* the verb in a sentence, the object pronouns generally *precede* the verb.

Think of direct object pronouns as corresponding to the English pronouns *me, her, us,* and so on; and of indirect object pronouns as corresponding to the English use of *to me, to her, to us,* and so on.

Here are the object pronouns in Italian:

Direct		Indirect	
mi	*me*	mi	*to me*
ti	*you* (familiar)	ti	*to you* (familiar)
La	*you* (polite)	Le	*to you* (polite)
lo	*him*	gli	*to him*
la	*her*	le	*to her*
ci	*us*	ci	*to us*
vi	*you* (familiar plural)	vi	*to you* (familiar plural)
li	*them* (masculine)	gli	*to them* (masculine)
le	*them* (feminine)	gli	*to them* (feminine)

Notice that the plural of the indirect object pronouns **gli** (*to him*) and **le** (*to her*) is **gli** (*to them*). This is the case in current Italian. It can be confusing, so pay very close attention to these forms in the Oral Practice.

Also, avoid confusion by remembering that the verb in a sentence agrees with the subject, not the object pronoun. For example, in the sentence (**Io**) **la chiamo spesso**, translate each part: *I-her-call-often*. Note how the verb *call* agrees with *I*, just as in the Italian sentence, the verb **chiamo** agrees with **io**.

Lastly, don't forget to keep familiar and polite forms distinct.

Oral Practice

Practice saying the following sentences out loud.

È vero che Maria ti chiama spesso, Pina?	*Is it true, Pina, that Mary calls you often?*
Sì, Maria mi chiama spesso.	*Yes, Mary calls me often.*
Angela, è vero che tu chiami Marco spesso?	*Angela, is it true that you call Mark often?*
Sì, lo chiamo spesso.	*Yes, I call him often.*
È vero che tu ci inviterai alla tua festa?	*Is it true that you are going to invite us to your party?*
Sì, vi inviterò volentieri.	*Yes, I am going to invite you gladly.*
Pino, quando mi darai il tuo indirizzo?	*Pino, when are you going to give your address to me?*
Ti ho già dato il mio indirizzo.	*I have already given my address to you.*
Signor Dini, quando mi darà il Suo indirizzo?	*Mr. Dini, when are you going to give your address to me?*
Le ho già dato il mio indirizzo.	*I have already given my address to you.*
Marco, quando parlerai al professore?	*Mark, when are you going to speak to the (male) professor?*
Gli ho già parlato.	*I have already spoken to him.*
E quando parlerai alla professoressa?	*And when will you speak to the (female) professor?*
Le ho già parlato.	*I have already spoken to her.*
Maria, quando ci scriverai?	*Mary, when will you write to us?*
Vi scriverò tra poco.	*I will write to you in a little while.*

Written Practice 1

Fill in the blanks with the appropriate object pronouns.

1. Maria, perché _____ chiami spesso? *Mary, why do you call me often?*

   Io _____ chiamo spesso, perché non ho niente da fare. *I call you often, because I have nothing to do.*

2. Signora Dini, perché _____ chiama spesso? *Mrs. Dini, why do you call me often?*

   Io _____ chiamo spesso, perché non ho niente da fare. *I call you often, because I have nothing to do.*

3. Maria, quante volte chiami Marco ogni giorno? *Mary, how many times do you call Mark every day?*

   _____ chiamo spesso. *I call him often.*

4. Marco, quante volte chiami Maria ogni giorno? *Mark, how many times do you call Mary every day?*

   _____ chiamo spesso. *I call her often.*

5. Pina, _____ inviterai alla tua festa? *Pina, are going to invite us to your party?*

   Sì, _____ inviterò. *Yes, I am going to invite you.*

6. Inviterai anche i nostri amici? *Are you also going to invite our friends?*

   Sì, _____ inviterò. *Yes, I am going to invite them.*

7. Inviterai anche le mie amiche? *Will you also be inviting my (female) friends?*

   Sì, _____ inviterò di sicuro. *Yes, I will invite them for sure.*

8. Pino, perché non _____ dai il tuo indirizzo? *Pino, why don't you give your address to me?*

   _____ ho già dato il mio indirizzo. *I have already given my address to you.*

9. Signor Dini, perché non _____ dà il Suo indirizzo? *Mr. Dini, why don't you give your address to me?*

   _____ ho già dato il mio indirizzo. *I have already given my address to you.*

10. Quando parlerai a mio fratello? *When are you going to speak to my brother?*

     _____ ho già parlato. *I have already spoken to him.*

11. E quando parlerai a mia sorella? *And when will you speak to my sister?*

     _____ ho già parlato. *I have already spoken to her.*

12. Signora Verdi, quando _____ scriverà? *Mrs. Verdi, when will you write to us?*

     _____ scriverò tra poco. *I will write to you in a little while.*

13. E quando scriverà ai Suoi amici? *And, when will you write to your friends?*

     _____ scriverò subito. *I will write to them right away.*

14. E quando scriverà alle Sue amiche? *And when will you write to your (female) friends?*

     _____ scriverò subito. *I will write to them right away.*

FORMS AND USES OF THE DIRECT OBJECT PRONOUN *LO*

The English direct object pronoun *it* (plural: *them*) is expressed by using a form of the third person direct object pronoun in Italian. Be careful! Choose the pronoun according to the gender and number of the noun it replaces.

Masculine Singular

Marco comprerà il gelato domani.	*Marco will buy the ice cream tomorrow.*
Marco lo comprerà domani.	*Marco will buy it tomorrow.*

Masculine Plural

Maria comprerà i biglietti domani.	*Mary will buy the tickets tomorrow.*
Maria li comprerà domani.	*Mary will buy them tomorrow.*

Feminine Singular

Il signor Verdi comprerà la rivista domani.	*Mr. Verdi will buy the magazine tomorrow.*
Il signor Verdi la comprerà domani.	*Mr. Verdi will buy it tomorrow.*

Feminine Plural

La signora Dini comprerà le riviste domani.	*Mrs. Dini will buy the magazines tomorrow.*
La signora Dini le comprerà domani.	*Mrs. Dini will buy them tomorrow.*

Oral Practice

Practice saying the following sentences out loud.

Franco, vuoi lo zucchero?	*Frank, do you want sugar?*
No, non lo voglio.	*No, I do not want it.*
Maria, hai gli stivali?	*Mary, do you have boots?*
No, non li ho.	*No, I do not have them.*
Giovanni quando pulirai la casa?	*John, when are you going to clean the house?*
La pulirò domani.	*I am going to clean it tomorrow.*
Pina, quando comprerai le scarpe nuove?	*Pina, when are you going to buy new shoes?*
Le comprerò tra poco.	*I am going to buy them in a little while.*
Anche tu mangerai la carne?	*Are you also going to eat the meat?*
Sì, anch'io la mangerò.	*Yes, I am also going to eat it.*
Mangerai anche le patate?	*Are you also going to eat the potatoes?*
No, non le mangerò.	*No, I will not eat them.*
Signora, vuole questi stivali?	*Madam, would you like these boots?*
Sì, li compro volentieri.	*Yes, I will buy them gladly.*

Written Practice 2

Fill in the blanks with the appropriate object pronouns.

1. Dina, vuoi il cappuccino? *Dina, do you want cappuccino?*

   No, non _____ voglio. *No, I do not want it.*

2. Giovanni, hai i biglietti? *John, do you have the tickets?*

   No, non _____ ho. *No, I do not have them.*

3. Signor Marchi, quando comprerà quella macchina? *Mr. Marchi, when are you going to buy that car?*

   _____ comprerò domani. *I am going to buy it tomorrow.*

4. Signora, quando comprerà quelle scarpe? *Madam, when are you going to buy those shoes?*

   _____ comprerò tra poco. *I am going to buy them in a little while.*

5. Volete la minestra? *Do you want soup?*

   No, non _____ vogliamo. *No, we do not want it.*

6. Mangerete le patate? *Are you going to eat the potatoes?*

   Sì _____ mangeremo. *Yes, we will eat them.*

7. Signora, vuole il tè? *Madam, would you like tea?*

   No, non _____ voglio. *No, I do not want it.*

8. Signora, vuole i ravioli? *Madam, would you like ravioli?*

   Sì, _____ mangio volentieri. *Yes, I will eat them gladly.*

Object Pronouns with Past Participles

When the verb is in a compound tense, the past participle agrees in gender and number with these four direct object pronouns: **lo**, **la**, **li**, and **le**.

Masculine Singular

Marco ha comprato il gelato ieri.	*Mark bought the ice cream yesterday.*
Marco **lo** ha comprat**o** ieri.	*Mark bought it yesterday.*

Masculine Plural

Marco ha comprato i biglietti ieri.	*Mark bought the tickets yesterday.*
Marco **li** ha comprat**i** ieri.	*Mark bought them yesterday.*

Feminine Singular

Marco ha comprato la rivista ieri.	*Mark bought the magazine yesterday.*
Marco **la** ha comprat**a** ieri.	*Mark bought it yesterday.*

Feminine Plural

Marco ha comprato le riviste ieri.	*Mark bought the magazines yesterday.*
Marco **le** ha comprat**e** ieri.	*Mark bought them yesterday.*

NOTE: *Only the singular forms **lo** and **la** can be elided and only with these auxiliary forms of **avere**: **ho**, **hai**, **ha**, **hanno**.*

Marco lo ha comprato ieri.	=	Marco l'ha comprato ieri.
Marco la ha comprata ieri.	=	Marco l'ha comprata ieri.

Agreement with the other direct object pronouns is optional.

Giovanni ci ha chiamato.	*John called us.*

Or:

Giovanni ci ha chiamati.	*John called us.*

There is no agreement with indirect object pronouns.

Giovanni gli ha scritto.	*John wrote to him/them.*
Giovanni le ha scritto.	*John wrote to her.*

Be very careful! Remember that the pronoun form **le** has two meanings.

As a Direct Object Pronoun: Agreement

Lui ha già mangiato le patate.	*He already ate the potatoes.*
Lui **le** ha già mangiat**e**.	*He already ate them.*

As an Indirect Object Pronoun: No Agreement

Lui ha scritto a sua sorella.	*He wrote to his sister.*
Lui le ha scritto.	*He wrote to her.*

Oral Practice

Practice saying the following sentences out loud.

Marco, hai letto quel romanzo?	*Mark, did you read that novel?*
Sì, l'ho già letto.	*Yes, I have already read it.*
Maria, hai mangiato i ravioli?	*Mary, did you eat the ravioli?*
Sì, li ho mangiati.	*Yes, I ate them.*
Signor Verdi, ha venduto la casa?	*Mr. Verdi, did you sell the house?*
Sì, l'ho venduta due settimane fa.	*Yes, I sold it two weeks ago.*
Signora Marchi, ha comprato le scarpe?	*Mrs. Marchi, did you buy the shoes?*
Sì, le ho comprate una settimana fa.	*Yes, I bought them a week ago.*
Marco e Maria, avete visto quel film?	*Mark and Mary, did you see that movie?*
No, non lo abbiamo visto.	*No, we did not see it.*
Gino, i tuoi amici hanno visto la partita?	*Gino, did your friends see the game?*
No, non l'hanno vista.	*No, they did not see it.*
Signora Dini, ha comprato i biglietti?	*Mrs. Dini, did you buy the tickets?*
Sì, li ho già comprati.	*Yes, I have already bought them.*
Signor Verdi, ha scritto le e-mail?	*Mr. Verdi, did you write the e-mails?*
Sì, le ho scritte tutte.	*Yes, I wrote them all.*

Written Practice 3

Fill in the blanks with the appropriate object pronouns, making the necessary changes to the past participles.

1. Marco, hai letto il giornale? *Mark, did you read the newspaper?*

   Sì, _____ ho già lett_____. *Yes, I have already read it.*

2. Maria, hai mangiato gli spaghetti? *Mary, did you eat the spaghetti?*

Sì, _____ ho mangiat_____. *Yes, I ate it.* (Be careful! In Italian, this is plural.)

3. Signor Verdi, ha venduto la macchina? *Mr. Verdi, did you sell the car?*

   Sì, _____ ho vendut_____ due settimane fa. *Yes, I sold it two weeks ago.*

4. Signora Marchi, ha comprato le riviste? *Mrs. Marchi, did you buy the magazines?*

   Sì, _____ ho comprat_____ ieri. *Yes, I bought them yesterday.*

5. Marco e Maria, avete visto quel programma? *Mark and Mary, did you see that program?*

   No, non _____ abbiamo vist_____. *No, we did not see it.*

6. Gino, i tuoi amici hanno letto la rivista? *Gino, did your friends read the magazine?*

   No, non _____ hanno lett_____. *No, they did not read it.*

7. Signora Dini, ha comprato gli stivali? *Mrs. Dini, did you buy the boots?*

   Sì, _____ ho già comprat_____. *Yes, I have already bought them.*

8. Signor Verdi, ha comprato le scarpe? *Mr. Verdi, did you buy the shoes?*

   Sì, _____ ho comprat_____. *Yes, I bought them.*

A Bit More About Adjectives

In addition to all of the adjectives you have been using, there are certain words that sometimes function like adjectives, though they may not always be classified as such. Here are the most common. Note that you have already come across many of them.

abbastanza	*enough*	poco	*little, few*
altro	*other*	qualsiasi	*whichever, any*
assai	*quite, enough*	stesso	*same*
certo	*certain*	tanto	*much, many, a lot*
molto	*much, many, a lot*	troppo	*too much*
ogni	*each, every*	tutto	*all*
parecchio	*several, quite a few*	ultimo	*last*

Oral Practice

Practice saying the following sentences out loud.

Vuoi ancora zucchero nel caffè?	*Would you like more sugar in your coffee?*
No, c'è abbastanza zucchero.	*No, there is enough sugar in it.*
Vuoi un'altra pasta?	*Would you like another pastry?*
Sì, vorrei lo stesso tipo di pasta.	*Yes, I would like the same type of pastry.*
Vuoi ancora patate?	*Do you want more potatoes?*
No, ho assai patate.	*No, I have enough potatoes.*
Conosci un certo uomo che si chiama Dino?	*Do you know a certain man named Dino?*
Conosco tanti uomini che si chiamano Dino.	*I know many men named Dino.*
Vuoi molta o poca pasta?	*Would you like a lot or a little pasta?*
Voglio tutta la pasta che hai.	*I want all the pasta that you have.*
Quante volte vai in centro ogni settimana?	*How many times do you go downtown each week?*
Vado parecchie volte.	*I go several times.*
Quale frutta vuoi?	*Which fruit do you want?*
Qualsiasi frutta va bene per me.	*Any fruit is fine with me.*
Vuoi anche quest'ultima patata?	*Would you also like this last potato?*
No, ho mangiato troppe patate.	*No, I have eaten too many potatoes.*

Written Practice 4

Fill in the blanks with the correct forms of the appropriate adjectives, as they have been classified here.

1. Vuoi ancora spaghetti? *Would you like more spaghetti?*

   No, ho mangiato _____. *No, I have eaten enough.*

2. Vuoi un _____ panino? *Would you like another sandwich?*

   Sì, vorrei _____ panino al formaggio. *Yes, I would like the same cheese sandwich.*

3. Vuoi ancora carne? *Would you like more meat?*

   No, ho mangiato _____ carne. *No, I have eaten enough meat.*

4. Conosci una _____ donna che si chiama Pina? *Do you know a certain woman named Pina?*

   Conosco _____ donne che si chiamano Pina. *I know many women named Pina.*

5. Vuoi _____ o _____ zucchero? *Would you like a lot or a little sugar?*

   Voglio _____ lo zucchero che hai. *I want all the sugar that you have.*

6. Quante volte vai al cinema _____ mese? *How many times do you go to the movies each month?*

   Vado _____ volte. *I go several times.*

7. Quale panino vuoi? *Which sandwich do you want?*

   _____ panino va bene per me. *Any sandwich is fine with me.*

8. Vuoi anche quest'_____ bicchiere? *Would you also like this last glass?*

   No, ho bevuto _____ bicchieri. *No, I have drunk too many glasses.*

Adverbs

Adverbs modify verbs, adjectives, or other adverbs. They convey relations of time, place, degree of intensity, and manner.

Maria guida lentamente.	*Maria drives slowly.*
Questa casa è molto bella.	*This house is very beautiful.*
Giovanni guida troppo velocemente.	*John drives too quickly.*

The following guidelines describe how to form adverbs of manner. Notice that the adverb ending **-mente** corresponds to the English adverb ending *-ly*.

- Change the **-o** ending of a descriptive adjective to **-a**.

  certo   *certain*   certa-
  lento   *slow*   lenta-

- Add the adverb ending **-mente**.

  certa-   certamente   *certainly*
  lenta-   lentamente   *slowly*

- If the adjective ends in **-e**, instead of **-o**, then simply add on **-mente**.

  elegante   *elegant*   elegantemente   *elegantly*
  semplice   *simple*   semplicemente   *simply*

- However, if the adjective ends in **-le** or **-re** and is preceded by a vowel, then the **-e** is dropped.

  facile   *easy*   facilmente   *easily*
  popolare   *popular*   popolarmente   *popularly*

- A few exceptions to these rules are the following:

  benevolo   *benevolent*   benevolmente   *benevolently*
  leggero   *light*   leggermente   *lightly*
  violento   *violent*   violentemente   *violently*

Here are some common Italian adverbs of manner:

Adjective		Adverb of Manner	
enorme	*enormous*	enormemente	*enormously*
felice	*happy*	felicemente	*happily*
preciso	*precise*	precisamente	*precisely*
raro	*rare*	raramente	*rarely*
regolare	*regular*	regolarmente	*regularly*
speciale	*special*	specialmente	*especially*
triste	*sad*	tristemente	*sadly*
utile	*useful*	utilmente	*usefully*
vero	*true*	veramente	*truly*

Oral Practice

Practice saying the following sentences out loud.

Sta dicendo la verità?   *Is he telling the truth?*
Certamente.   *Certainly.*

Come guida lei?	*How does she drive?*
Lentamente.	*Slowly.*
Come insegna l'italiano il professore?	*How does the professor teach Italian?*
Facilmente.	*Easily.*
Come è percepito quel film?	*How is that movie perceived?*
Popolarmente.	*Popularly.*
Come dobbiamo trattare la gente?	*How must we treat people?*
Benevolmente.	*Benevolently.*
Come devo condire l'insalata?	*How should I dress the salad?*
Leggermente.	*Lightly.*
Ti piace l'italiano?	*Do you like Italian?*
Enormemente.	*Enormously.*

Written Practice 5

Answer each question with the correct adverb, as indicated.

1. Come hanno reagito? *How did they react?*

   _____. *Happily.*

2. Come hanno fatto quella cosa? *How did they do that thing?*

   _____. *Precisely.*

3. Quante volte viene lui con voi? *How many times does he come with you?*

   _____. *Rarely.*

4. Quante volte guardi la televisione? *How many times do you watch television?*

   _____. *Regularly.*

5. Anche lui deve studiare, vero? *He also has to study, doesn't he?*

   _____ lui! *Especially him!*

6. Come suona lui di solito? *How does he usually play?*

   _____. *Sadly.*

OTHER TYPES OF ADVERBS

Adverbs cover a wide range of meanings, from time relations to quantity. Here are some very common adverbs and adverbial phrases, many of which have been introduced in previous chapters.

allora	*then, thus*	poi	*after, then*
anche	*also, too*	presto	*early*
ancora	*again, still, yet*	prima	*first, before*
anzi	*as a matter of fact*	purtroppo	*unfortunately*
appena	*just, barely*	quasi	*almost*
di nuovo	*again, anew*	qui	*here*
domani	*tomorrow*	solo	*only*
fra (tra) poco	*in a little while*	spesso	*often*
già	*already*	stamani	*this morning*
ieri	*yesterday*	stasera	*this evening*
lì, là	*there*	subito	*right away*
lontano	*far*	tardi	*late*
male	*bad(ly)*	vicino	*near(by)*
oggi	*today*		

The adjectives **molto**, **tanto**, **poco**, **troppo**, and **parecchio** can also be used as adverbs. But be careful! When used as adverbs, there is no agreement as there is when used as adjectives.

Adjective		**Adverb**	
Lei ha molti soldi.	*She has a lot of money.*	Lei è molto intelligente.	*She is very intelligent.*
Ci sono pochi studenti.	*There are few students.*	Loro studiano poco.	*They study little.*

To determine if a word such as **molto** is an adjective or adverb, check the word that follows it in the sentence. If it is a noun, then **molto** is an adjective, agreeing with the noun. Otherwise, it is an adverb. In this case, no agreement pattern is required.

Oral Practice

Practice saying the following sentences out loud.

Loro vanno spesso al cinema?	*Do they often go to the movies?*
Purtroppo.	*Unfortunately.*
Marco l'ha fatto ancora una volta?	*Did Mark do it again (one more time)?*
Sì, ieri.	*Yes, yesterday.*
Dove abitano?	*Where do they live?*
Lei abita lontano, e lui vicino.	*She lives far, and he nearby.*
È tardi?	*Is it late?*
Sì, sono quasi le tre.	*Yes, it is almost three o'clock.*
Lui ha appena finito di lavorare?	*Has he just finished working?*
Sì, e anzi ha lavorato tanto oggi.	*Yes, and, as a matter of fact, he worked a lot today.*
Che cosa farai domani?	*What are you going to do tomorrow?*
Prima voglio studiare e poi uscire.	*First I want to study, and then go out.*

Written Practice 6

Fill in the blanks with the appropriate adverbs or adjectives, as necessary.

1. Quando verrai, stamani o stasera? *When are you coming, this morning or tonight?*

   Vengo _____. *I am coming right away.*

2. Chi va con Gino in centro? *Who is going with Gino downtown?*

   _____ io. *Only I.*

3. Dov'è il computer, lì? *Where is the computer, there?*

   No, è _____. *No, it is here.*

4. Quando andrai in centro? *When are you going downtown?*

   _____. *In a little while.*

5. Allora, perché non vieni anche tu? *Then, why don't you also come?*

   Perché sto _____. *Because I feel bad (unwell).*

6. Hai fame, Maria? *Are you hungry, Mary?*

   Sì, ho _____ fame. *Yes, I am very hungry.*

7. Quanto tempo hai lavorato ieri, Maria? *How much time did you work yesterday, Mary?*

   _____. *A little.*

Computers and the Internet

The topic of computers and the Internet is very important in today's world. So, here are some useful Italian vocabulary words to learn:

il computer	*computer*
il software	*software*
l'hardware	*hardware*
lo schermo	*monitor, screen*
la stampante	*printer*
la tastiera	*keyboard*
il mouse	*mouse*
Internet (no article is used in Italian)	*Internet*
il sito web	*website*
l'indirizzo e-mail	*e-mail address*
navigare	*to navigate*
chiocciola	*@*
punto	*dot*

QUIZ

Answer each question affirmatively with an appropriate direct object pronoun. For example:

Mi hai chiamato ieri?   *Did you call me yesterday?*

Sì, ti ho chiamato ieri.   *Yes, I called you yesterday.*

1. Mi chiamerai stasera?

   _____.

Ti ho invitato alla festa, vero?

_____.

Chiamerai Giovanni domani?

_____.

Vedrai Maria domani?

_____.

Ci inviterai alla festa?

_____.

Vi ho invitato alla festa, vero?

_____.

Vedrai le tue amiche domani?

_____.

Vedrai i tuoi genitori domani?

_____.

Answer each question affirmatively with an appropriate indirect object pronoun.

2. Mi dirai il tuo nome?

_____.

Ti ho dato il mio indirizzo, vero?

_____.

Parlerai alla professoressa domani?

_____.

Parlerai al signor Mirri domani?

_____.

Ci scriverai per Natale?

_____.

Vi ho scritto per Natale, vero?

_____.

Parlerai alle tue amiche domani?

_____.

Parlerai ai tuoi genitori domani?

_____.

Answer each question affirmatively, replacing the italicized direct object with an appropriate direct object pronoun and making any necessary changes to the past participle.

3. Hai letto *il giornale*?

_____.

Hai letto *la rivista*?

_____.

Hai chiamato *gli zii*?

_____.

Hai chiamato *le zie*?

_____.

Hai mangiato *la carne*?

_____.

Hai mangiato *le patate*?

_____.

Hai guardato *quel programma*?

_____.

Hai guardato *quei programmi*?

_____.

Change each adjective into an adverb of manner or vice versa, as necessary.

4. certamente _____

   semplice _____

   facilmente _____

   popolare _____

benevolmente _____

leggero _____

enorme _____

felicemente _____

preciso _____

specialmente _____

utile _____

veramente _____

Choose the appropriate adverb for each sentence.

5. Noi andiamo _____ al cinema.

   (a) spesso

   (b) già

6. Lui l'ha fatto _____ una volta.

   (a) ancora

   (b) sempre

7. Mio fratello vive _____, e mia sorella vicino.

   (a) lontano

   (b) sempre

8. È _____ l'una.

   (a) quasi

   (b) poi

Personal Matters! Answer each question appropriately.

9. Che tipo di computer hai?

   _____.

10. Qual è il tuo indirizzo e-mail?

   _____.

CHAPTER 19

Using Double and Attached Object Pronouns

Here's what you will learn in this chapter:

Double Object Pronouns

Dove sono le riviste? Te le ho già date. *Where are the magazines? I have already given them to you.* You may have noticed that the second sentence contains two pronouns in sequence: **te le**. The first pronoun is really the indirect object pronoun **ti**, with a slight modification, and the second one is the direct object pronoun **le**, which replaces **le riviste**.

When both direct and indirect object pronouns are required in a sentence, the following rules apply:

- The indirect object pronoun always precedes the direct object pronoun, and the only possible direct object forms in this case are: **lo**, **la**, **li**, and **le**.

Marco **mi** darà **il libro** domani.	*Mark will give **the book to me** tomorrow.*
Marco **me lo** darà domani.	*Mark will give **it to me** tomorrow.*

- The indirect pronouns **mi**, **ti**, **ci**, and **vi** are changed to **me**, **te**, **ce**, and **ve**, respectively.

Maria **ti** darà **i libri** domani.	*Mary will give **you the books** tomorrow.*
Maria **te li** darà domani.	*Mary will give **them to you** tomorrow.*
Maria **vi** comprerà **le scarpe** per Natale.	*Mary will buy **you shoes** for Christmas.*
Maria **ve le** comprerà per Natale.	*Mary will buy **you them** for Christmas.*
Maria **ci** ha dato **i suoi libri**.	*Mary has given **her books to us**.*
Maria **ce li** ha dati.	*Mary has given **them to us**.*

> **NOTE:** *In the previous example there is still agreement between the direct object pronoun and the past participle.*

- The indirect pronouns **gli** and **le** are both changed to **glie**, and attached to **lo**, **la**, **li**, and **le** to form one word: **glielo**, **glieli**, **gliela**, **gliele**.

Marco darà **il libro a Paolo** domani.	*Mark will give **the book to Paul** tomorrow.*
Marco **glielo** darà domani.	*Mark will give **it to him** tomorrow.*

Maria darà **quella borsa a sua sorella**.	*Mary will give **her sister that purse**.*
Maria **gliela** darà.	*Mary will give **it to her**.*
Ho dato **i libri a mio fratello** ieri.	*I gave **the books to my brother** yesterday.*
Glieli ho dati ieri.	*I gave **them to him** yesterday.*
Ho dato **le mie chiavi a Maria** stamani.	*I gave **my keys to Mary** this morning.*
Io **gliele** ho date stamani.	*I gave **them to her** this morning.*

Reflexive pronouns also make a change to **me**, **te**, **se**, **ce**, **ve**, and **se** before direct object pronouns.

Marco **si mette** sempre **la giacca**.	*Marco always **puts on a jacket**.*
Marco **se la mette** sempre.	*Marco always **puts it on**.*

In compound tenses, agreement is between the past participle and the object pronoun, not the subject.

Agreement with the Subject

Marco **si è messo la giacca** ieri.	*Marco **put on his jacket** yesterday.*

Agreement with the Object Pronoun

Marco **se la è messa** ieri.	*Marco **put it on** yesterday.*

Oral Practice

Practice saying the following sentences out loud.

Gina, mi compreresti il giornale?	*Gina, could you buy me the newspaper?*
Sì, te lo comprerò volentieri.	*Yes, I will gladly buy it for you.*
Paolo, ci hai dato i tuoi libri?	*Paul, did you give your books to us?*
Sì, ve li ho dati.	*Yes, I gave them to you.*
Signora, ha dato la chiave a suo marito?	*Madam, did you give the key to your husband?*
Sì, gliel'ho data ieri.	*Yes, I gave it to him yesterday.*

Signor Dini, ha comprato le scarpe a sua figlia?	*Mr. Dini, did you buy the shoes for your daughter?*
No, non gliele ho ancora comprate.	*No, I have not bought them for her yet.*
Maria, hai ancora comprato il portatile a tua sorella?	*Mary, have you bought the laptop for your sister yet?*
Sì, gliel'ho comprato ieri.	*Yes, I bought it for her yesterday.*
Marco, hai dato i tuoi libri agli altri studenti?	*Mark, did you give your books to the other students?*
Si, glieli ho già dati.	*Yes, I already gave them to them.*
Maria, ti sei messa quelle scarpe, vero?	*Mary, you put on those shoes, didn't you?*
Sì, me le sono messe.	*Yes, I put them on.*

Written Practice 1

Replace the words in bold print with the appropriate double pronouns.

1. Giovanni, **mi** hai detto **la verità**? *John, did you tell me the truth?*

   Sì, _____ ho detta. *Yes, I told it to you.*

2. Maria, hai dato **il tuo indirizzo a Paolo?** *Mary, did you give your address to Paul?*

   Sì, _____ ho dato ieri. *Yes, I gave it to him yesterday.*

3. Marco, hai comprato **il computer a Maria?** *Mark, did you buy the computer for Mary?*

   Sì, _____ ho comprato ieri. *Yes, I bought it for her yesterday.*

4. Signora, ha dato **i libri a suo figlio?** *Madam, did you give the books to your son?*

   Sì, _____ ho dati ieri. *Yes, I gave them to him yesterday.*

5. Gina, hai comprato **la rivista a Maria**? *Gina, did you buy Mary the magazine?*

   Sì, _____ ho comprata stamani. *Yes, I bought it for her this morning.*

6. Dino, hai comprato **le riviste ai tuoi amici**? *Dino, did you buy the magazines for your friends?*

   Sì, _____ ho comprate poco fa. *Yes, I bought them for them a little while ago.*

7. Giovanni, **ti** ho dato **la penna**? *John, did I give you the pen?*

   Sì, _____ hai data ieri. *Yes, you gave it to me yesterday.*

8. Ragazzi, **vi** ho dato **i biglietti**? *Guys, did I give you the tickets?*

   Sì, _____ hai dati. *Yes, you gave them to us.*

9. Signora, **ci** ha dato **le chiavi**? *Madam, did you give us the keys?*

   Sì, _____ ho già date. *Yes, I already gave them to you.*

10. Maria, **ti** sei messa **gli stivali**? *Mary, did you wear boots?*

    Sì, _____ sono messi. *Yes, I wore them.*

Attached Object Pronouns

Object pronouns are sometimes attached to verb forms. In this case, the double pronouns are always written as one word. The following shows how this is done, using the word **ecco** (this is an important and commonly used construction):

Ecco la matita.	*Here is the pencil.*
Eccola.	*Here it is.*
Ecco Marco e Maria.	*Here are Mark and Mary.*
Eccoli.	*Here they are.*
Ecco i libri per te.	*Here are the books for you.*
Eccoteli.	*Here they are for you.*

With the modal verbs (**potere**, **dovere**, and **volere**) you can either attach the object pronouns to the infinitive of the verb showing the action, or put them before the modal verb. Note that when you attach pronouns to the infinitive, you must drop the final **-e** of the infinitive.

Non posso mangiare la carne.	*I cannot eat meat.*
Non la posso mangiare.	*I cannot eat it.*

Or:

Non posso mangiarla.	*I cannot eat it.*
Tu devi dare il libro per Natale a Maria.	*You must give Mary the book for Christmas.*
Tu glielo devi dare per Natale.	*You must give it to her for Christmas.*

Or:

Tu devi darglielo per Natale.	*You must give it to her for Christmas.*
Lui mi vuole dare la macchina.	*He wants to give me his car.*
Lui me la vuole dare.	*He wants to give it to me.*

Or:

Lui vuole darmela.	*He wants to give it to me.*

The object pronouns are also attached to the familiar forms of the imperative. They are not attached to the polite **Lei** and **Loro** forms.

Familiar

Marco, mangia la mela!	*Mark, eat the apple.*
Marco, mangiala!	*Mark, eat it!*
Maria, scrivi l'e-mail a tuo fratello!	*Mary, write your brother the e-mail.*
Maria, scrivigliela!	*Mary, write it to him!*
Marco e Maria, date la vostra penna a me!	*Mark and Mary, give your pen to me.*
Marco e Maria, datemela!	*Mark and Maria, give it to me!*

Polite

Signor Verdi, mangi la mela!	*Mr. Verdi, eat the apple.*
Signor Verdi, la mangi!	*Mr. Verdi, eat it!*
Signora Rossi, scriva l'e-mail a Suo fratello!	*Mrs. Rossi, write your brother the e-mail.*
Signora Rossi, gliela scriva!	*Mrs. Rossi, write it to him!*

Signor Verdi e signora Rossi, diano la Loro penna a me!	*Mr. Verdi and Mrs. Rossi, give your pen to me.*
Signor Verdi e signor Rossi, me la diano!	*Mr. Verdi and Mrs. Rossi, give it to me!*

When attaching pronouns to familiar forms of the imperative that end with an apostrophe (**da'**, **di'**, **fa'**, **sta'** and **va'**), you must double the first letter (sound) of the pronoun.

Dammi la penna!	*Give me the pen!*
Dilla!	*Tell it!*
Fallo!	*Do it!*

There is, of course, no double **gl**.

Digli la verità!	*Tell him the truth!*
Faglielo!	*Do it for him!*

Oral Practice

Practice saying the following sentences out loud.

Dov'è la rivista?	*Where is the magazine?*
Eccola.	*Here it is.*
Dove sono i tuoi amici?	*Where are your friends?*
Eccoli.	*Here they are.*
Dove sono i libri per me?	*Where are the books for me?*
Eccoteli.	*Here they are for you.*
Puoi bere il caffè?	*Can you drink coffee?*
Sì, lo posso bere./Sì, posso berlo.	*Yes, I can drink it.*
Devi fare la spesa oggi?	*Do you have to do food shopping today?*
Sì, la devo fare./Sì, devo farla.	*Yes, I have to do it.*
Vuoi mangiare le patate?	*Do you want to eat potatoes?*
Sì, le voglio mangiare./Sì, voglio mangiarle.	*Yes, I want to eat them.*

Marco, mangia la carne!	*Mark, eat the meat!*
Marco, mangiala!	*Mark, eat it!*
Maria, scrivi l'e-mail a tua sorella!	*Mary, write your sister the e-mail!*
Maria, scrivigliela!	*Mary, write it to him!*
Signor Verdi, mangi la carne!	*Mr. Verdi, eat the meat!*
Signor Verdi, la mangi!	*Mr. Verdi, eat it!*
Maria, dammi la penna!	*Mary, give me the pen!*
Maria, dammela!	*Mary, give it to me!*
Maria, digli la verità!	*Mary, tell him the truth!*
Maria, digliela!	*Mary, tell it to him!*

Written Practice 2

Using the English translations as a guide, translate the following responses with the appropriate pronouns.

1. Dov'è il mio portatile? *Where is my laptop?*

   _____. *Here it is.*

2. Dove sono le mie scarpe? *Where are my shoes?*

   _____. *Here they are.*

3. Dove sono le riviste per me? *Where are the magazines for me?*

   _____. *Here they are for you.*

4. Puoi mangiare i ravioli? *Can you eat the ravioli?*

   _____. *Yes, I can eat them.*

5. Devi studiare la nuova lezione? *Do you have to study the new lesson?*

   _____. *Yes, I have to study it.*

6. Vuoi comprare gli stivali nuovi? *Do you want to buy new boots?*

   _____. *Yes, I want to buy them.*

7. Maria, comprami quella rivista! *Mary, buy me that magazine.*

   _____! *Mary, buy it for me!*

8. Mario, dammi il tuo indirizzo! *Mario, give me your address.*

   _____! *Mario, give it to me!*

Stressed Pronouns

There is another type of object pronoun that goes after the verb. It is known as a stressed or tonic pronoun.

Before		**After**	
Direct			
mi	*me*	me	*me*
ti	*you* (familiar)	te	*you* (familiar)
La	*you* (polite)	Lei	*you* (polite)
lo	*him*	lui	*him*
la	*her*	lei	*her*
ci	*us*	noi	*us*
vi	*you* (familiar plural)	voi	*you* (familiar plural)
li	*them* (masculine)	loro	*them*
le	*them* (feminine)	loro	*them*

Indirect			
mi	*to me*	a me	*to me*
ti	*to you* (familiar)	a te	*to you* (familiar)
Le	*to you* (polite)	a Lei	*to you* (polite)
gli	*to him*	a lui	*to him*
le	*to her*	a lei	*to her*
ci	*to us*	a noi	*to us*
vi	*to you* (familiar plural)	a voi	*to you* (familiar plural)
gli	*to them* (masculine)	a loro	*to them*
gli	*to them* (feminine)	a loro	*to them*

For most purposes, the two types can be used interchangeably. However, the stressed forms are more appropriate when emphasis is required or in order to avoid ambiguity.

Marco lo darà a me, non a te!	*Mark will give it to me, not to you!*
Ieri ho scritto a te, e solo a te!	*Yesterday I wrote to you, and only you!*

Also, these are the only object pronouns that can be used after a preposition.

Maria viene con noi.	*Mary is coming with us.*
Il professore parla di te.	*The professor is speaking of you.*
L'ha fatto per me.	*He did it for me.*

Oral Practice

Practice saying the following sentences out loud.

È vero che Marco ti inviterà?	*Is it true that Mark will invite you?*
Sì, inviterà anche me!	*Yes, he will invite me as well!*
Verrai con noi alla festa?	*Will you come with us to the party?*
No, non verrò con voi; andrò con loro.	*No, I will not come with you; I will go with them.*
A chi darai il tuo portatile?	*To whom will you give your laptop?*
Lo darò a lui o forse a lei, ma non a te.	*I will give it to him or maybe to her, but not to you.*
Ci hai dato il tuo indirizzo?	*Did you give us your address?*
No, non l'ho dato a voi; l'ho dato a loro.	*No, I did not give it to you; I gave it to them.*
Vi ho dato il mio indirizzo?	*Did I give you my address?*
No, non lo hai dato a noi; lo hai dato a loro.	*No, you did not give it to us; you gave it to them.*

Written Practice 3

Fill in the blanks with stressed pronouns as indicated.

1. Mi hai chiamato ieri? *Did you call me yesterday?*

   No, non ho chiamato _____; ho chiamato _____. *No, I did not call you; I called him.*

2. Ti ho invitato alla festa? *Did I invite you to the party?*

   No, non hai invitato _____; hai invitato _____. *No, you did not invite me; you invited her.*

3. Ci hai chiamato ieri? *Did you call us yesterday?*

   No, non ho chiamato _____; ho chiamato _____. *No, I did not call you; I called them.*

4. A chi hai dato il tuo indirizzo? *To whom did you give your address?*

   L'ho dato a _____ due e a _____. *I gave it to you two and to them.*

Still More About the Verb *Piacere*

The verb **piacere**, as you know, is used for expressing likes and dislikes. But it is a tricky verb because it really means *to be pleasing to.*

Mi piace la pizza.	*I like pizza. = To me is pleasing the pizza.*
Non gli è piaciuta la pizza.	*He did not like the pizza. = To him was not pleasing the pizza.*

Because this verb can be difficult, let's look a little more closely at its conjugations. The verb **piacere** is regular in all the tenses, except the following two.

Present Indicative
(io) piaccio, (tu) piaci, (lui/lei/Lei) piace, (noi) piacciamo, (voi) piacete, (loro/Loro) piacciono

Past Absolute
(io) piacqui, (tu) piacesti, (lui/lei/Lei) piacque, (noi) piacemmo, (voi) piaceste, (loro/Loro) piacquero

Piacere is conjugated with the auxiliary **essere** in compound tenses.

Non mi è piaciuta la pasta.	*I did not like the pasta.*
Non gli sono piaciuti gli spaghetti.	*He did not like the spaghetti.*

When saying that you or someone else likes something, translate the English expression in your mind as *to be pleasing to* and then follow the word order in the formula below:

Expression	**Translate to**	**Italian Expression**
I like that book.	*To me is pleasing that book.*	Mi piace quel libro.
We like those books.	*To us are pleasing those books.*	Ci piacciono quei libri.
She likes her brothers.	*To her are pleasing her brothers.*	Le piacciono i suoi fratelli.
The brothers like her.	*She is pleasing to her brothers.*	Lei piace ai suoi fratelli.

If you think this way, you will have an easier time using **piacere**. Notice that the subject is sometimes put at the end of the sentence (although this is not necessary).

> *Mary likes John.*   *To Mary is pleasing John.*   A Maria piace Giovanni.

Or:

> *John is pleasing to Mary.*   Giovanni piace a Maria.

As mentioned, in compound tenses, **piacere** is conjugated with **essere**. This means, of course, that the past participle agrees with the subject.

> *I did not like her.*   *Not to me was pleasing she.*   (Lei) non mi è piaciuta.
>
> *She did not like us.*   *Not to her were pleasing we.*   (Noi) non le siamo piaciuti.

In some sentences with **piacere**, you can use the object pronouns that come after the verb for reasons of emphasis or clarity.

> La musica piace a me, non a te!   *I like the music, not you! (= The music is pleasing to me, not to you!)*

Oral Practice

Practice saying the following sentences out loud.

> Marco, ti piace la minestra?   *Mark, do you like the soup?*
> *(Mark, is the soup pleasing to you?)*
>
> Sì, mi piace.   *Yes, I like it.*
> *(Yes, it is pleasing to me.)*
>
> Signora, quale Le piacerà?   *Madam, which one will you like (want)?*
> *(Madam, which one will be pleasing to you?)*
>
> Mi piacerà questa.   *I will like this one.*
> *(This one will be pleasing to me.)*
>
> Maria, ti piaccio?   *Mary, do you like me?*
> *(Mary, am I pleasing to you?)*

Sì, mi piaci molto.	*Yes, I like you a lot.*
	(Yes, you please me very much.)
Sono piaciuti i ravioli a Mario?	*Did Mario like the ravioli?*
	(Were the ravioli pleasing to Mario?)
Sì, gli sono piaciuti molto.	*Yes, he liked them a lot.*
	(Yes, they pleased him very much.)
Piacque l'Italia a tua sorella?	*Did your sister like Italy?*
	(Was Italy pleasing to your sister?)
Sì, le piacque molto.	*Yes, she liked it a lot.*
	(Yes, it pleased her very much.)

Written Practice 4

Fill in the blanks with the appropriate forms of piacere, as indicated.

1. Marco, ti _____ le mie scarpe? *Mark, do you like my shoes?*

   Sì, mi _____ molto. *Yes, I like them a lot.*

2. Maria, ti _____ mia sorella? *Mary, did you like my sister?*

   Sì, mi _____ molto. *Yes, I liked her a lot.*

3. E i miei amici _____? *And did you like my friends?*

   Sì, anche loro _____ molto. *Yes, I liked them a lot, too.*

4. Marco, ti _____? *Mark, do you like me?*

   Sì, mi _____ molto. *Yes, I like you a lot.*

5. Signora, Le _____ andare in centro? *Madam, would you like to go downtown?*

   Sì, mi _____ molto. *Yes, I would like it a lot.*

6. Marco e Mario, vi _____? *Mark and Mary, do you like us?*

   Sì, ci _____ molto. *Yes, we like you a lot.*

QUIZ

Give the double pronoun form by replacing each noun phrase with a direct object pronoun (**lo**, **li**, **la**, **le**) and making the appropriate modification to each indirect object pronoun. For example:

    mi/il libro *me lo* _____ *to me/the book*

1. mi/i libri _____

   mi/la penna _____

   mi/le scarpe _____

   ti/il cappello _____

   ti/i ravioli _____

   ti/la macchina _____

   ti/le scarpe _____

   gli/il computer _____

   gli/i biglietti _____

   gli/la matita _____

   gli/le matite _____

   ci/il portatile _____

   ci/i televisori _____

   ci/le patate _____

   le/l'indirizzo _____

   le/gli indirizzi _____

   le/la matita _____

   le/le borse _____

   vi/il cappotto _____

   vi/gli stivali _____

   vi/la camicia _____

   vi/le camicie _____

Choose the correct answer for each question. One of the two given answers is actually wrong, reflecting a typical blunder with learners of Italian.

2. Marco, hai comprato quelle riviste a tuo fratello, vero?
    (a) Sì, gliele ho comprate ieri.
    (b) Sì, gliele ho comprato ieri.
3. Maria, dove sono le tue amiche?
    (a) Eccole.
    (b) Le ecco.
4. Sono tue queste scarpe?
    (a) Sì, dammele subito!
    (b) Sì, me le da' subito!
5. Vuoi mangiare la carne?
    (a) Sì, voglio mangiarla.
    (b) Sì, voglio la mangiare.

Give the corresponding stressed or unstressed form of the pronoun, as required.

Unstressed	Stressed
6. _____	me
le (*to her*)	_____
_____	a te
gli (*to him*)	_____
_____	noi
gli (*to them*)	_____
_____	a me
Le (*to you*, polite)	_____
_____	a voi

For each of the following sentences, choose the correct form of the verb **piacere**.

7. Maria, ti _____ quel film?

   (a) piace

   (b) piaccio

8. Maria, io ti _____?

   (a) piace

   (b) piaccio

9. A lui non _____ quei libri.

   (a) piacerà

   (b) piaceranno

Personal Matters! Answer the question appropriately.

10. Che cosa ti piace fare regolarmente?

_____ .

CHAPTER 20

Making Comparisons

Here's what you will learn in this chapter:

More About Pronouns

Adjectives of Comparison

Adverbs of Comparison

Relative Pronouns

Italian Coffee

More About Pronouns

Mi piace molto! *I like it a lot!* Words such as **molto**, **tanto**, and so on, which you have been using since the beginning of this book as adjectives and adverbs, can also function as pronouns.

Lui mangia molto.	*He eats a lot.*
Tuo fratello dorme molto, no?	*Your brother sleeps a lot, doesn't he?*
Ieri ho mangiato troppo.	*Yesterday I ate too much.*

When referring to people in general, use the plural forms **molti**, **alcuni**, **tanti**, **pochi**, **parecchi**, **tutti**, and so on.

Molti vanno in Italia quest'anno.	*Many are going to Italy this year.*
Alcuni dormono, ma parecchi lavorano.	*Some are sleeping, but quite a few are working.*
Tutti sanno quello.	*Everyone knows that.*

Use the corresponding feminine forms (**molte**, **alcune**, etc.) when referring to females.

Di quelle ragazze, molte sono italiane.	*Of those girls, many are Italian.*
Di quelle donne, alcune sono americane.	*Of those women, some are American.*

Notice the following useful expression:

alcuni... altri *some . . . others*

Alcuni andranno in Italia; **altri**, invece, andranno in Francia.	***Some*** *will go to Italy;* ***others****, instead, will go to France.*

Oral Practice

Practice saying the following sentences out loud.

Tua sorella mangia molto, vero?	*Your sister eats a lot, doesn't she?*
No, lei mangia poco.	*No, she eats little.*
Tuo fratello dorme poco, no?	*Your brother sleeps little, doesn't he?*
No, lui dorme tanto.	*No, he sleeps a lot.*
Quanti vogliono andare in Italia?	*How many want to go to Italy?*
Molti vogliono andare.	*Many want to go.*
E quanti vogliono vedere Napoli?	*And how many want to see Naples?*
Alcuni, ma parecchi vogliono vedere Roma.	*Some, but quite a few want to see Rome.*
Chi sa quello?	*Who knows that?*
Tutti sanno quello.	*Everyone knows that.*
Quante ragazze ci sono in classe?	*How many girls are there in class?*
Molte, ma ieri poche sono venute.	*Many, but yesterday few came.*
Quante ragazze andranno in Italia?	*How many girls are going to Italy?*
Alcune andranno; altre, invece, no.	*Some are going; others, instead, are not.*

Written Practice 1

Fill in the blanks with the appropriate pronouns.

1. La tua amica mangia _____, vero? *Your sister eats little, doesn't she?*

   No, lei mangia _____. *No, she eats a lot.*

2. Tua mamma dorme _____, no? *Your mother sleeps a lot, doesn't she?*

   No, lei dorme molto _____. *No, she sleeps very little.*

3. Chi vuole andare in Italia quest'anno? *Who wants to go to Italy this year?*

_____ vogliono andare. *Many want to go.*

4. E quanti vogliono vedere Firenze? *And how many want to see Florence?*

_____ , ma _____ vogliono vedere Pisa. *Some, but quite a few want to see Pisa.*

5. Chi dice quello? *Who is saying that?*

_____ dicono quello. *Everyone is saying that.*

6. Quante ragazze ci sono in classe? *How many girls are there in class?*

_____ , ma ieri _____ sono venute. *A few, but yesterday many came.*

ITALIAN PRONOUNS *NE* AND *CI*

The pronoun **ne** is usually placed before the verb in a sentence and it is used to replace the following structures:

- Partitives

  Comprerai anche **delle patate**?   *Will you also buy **some potatoes**?*

  Sì, **ne** comprerò.   *Yes, I will buy **some**.*

- Numbers and quantitative expressions

  Quanti **libri** hai letto?   *How many **books** did you read?*

  Ne ho letti **due**.   *I read **two of them**.*

  NOTE: *Notice the agreement between **ne** and the past participle.*

- Indefinite expressions

  Hai letto molti **libri**, non è vero?   *You read a lot of **books**, isn't that true?*

  Sì, **ne** ho letti **molti**.   *Yes, I read **a lot of them**.*

- Topic phrases introduced by **di**

  Ha parlato **di matematica**, vero?   *He spoke **of mathematics**, didn't he?*

  Sì, **ne** ha parlato.   *Yes, he spoke **about it**.*

  NOTE: *Notice that in this particular case there is no agreement. **Ne** does not refer to any quantity.*

The locative (place) pronoun **ci** means *there*. It, too, goes before the verb.

Andate **in Italia**, non è vero?	*You are going **to Italy**, aren't you?*
Sì, **ci** andiamo domani.	*Yes, we are going **there** tomorrow.*
Marco vive **a Perugia**, non è vero?	*Marco lives **in Perugia**, doesn't he?*
Sì, **ci** vive da molti anni.	*Yes, he has been living **there** for many years.*

Oral Practice

Practice saying the following sentences out loud.

Hai mangiato dei panini?	*Did you eat some sandwiches?*
Sì, ne ho mangiati tre.	*Yes, I ate three of them.*
Vuoi delle patate?	*Do you want some potatoes?*
No, non ne voglio.	*No, I do not want any of them.*
Quanti libri hai comprato?	*How many books did you buy?*
Ne ho comprati alcuni.	*I bought a few of them.*
Quanti amici hai invitato alla festa?	*How many friends did you invite to the party?*
Ne ho invitati molti.	*I invited many of them.*
Ha parlato di Dante, il professore?	*Did the professor speak about Dante?*
Sì, ne ha parlato.	*Yes, he spoke about him.*
Quando andrete in Italia?	*When are you going to Italy?*
Ci vogliamo andare l'anno prossimo.	*We want to go there next year.*
Maria vive a Milano, non è vero?	*Mary lives in Milan, doesn't she?*
Sì, ci vive da molti anni.	*Yes, she has been living there for many years.*

Written Practice 2

Fill in the blanks with *ne* or *ci*, as necessary.

1. Tu vivi negli Stati Uniti, non è vero? *You live in the United States, don't you?*

   Sì, _____ vivo da molto. *Yes, I have been living there for a while.*

2. Hanno parlato di televisione, vero? *They spoke about television, didn't they?*

   Sì, _____ hanno parlato. *Yes, they spoke about it.*

3. Quando andranno in Italia? *When are they going to Italy?*

   _____ andranno l'anno prossimo. *They are going there next year.*

4. Hai preso del caffè? *Did you have some coffee?*

   Sì, _____ ha bevuti tre. *Yes, I drank three of them.*

5. Vuoi delle paste? *Would you like some pastries?*

   No, non _____ voglio. *No, I do not want any of them.*

6. Quanti cappuccini hai bevuto? *How many cappuccinos did you drink?*

   _____ ho bevuti alcuni. *I drank a few of them.*

7. Quanti amici hai chiamato ieri? *How many friends did you call yesterday?*

   _____ ho chiamati molti. *I called many of them.*

Adjectives of Comparison

Marco è più alto di Maria. *Mark is taller than Mary.* The adjective in this sentence is a comparison between two people. Adjectives can be used to indicate that someone or something has a relatively equal, greater, or lesser degree of some quality. The three degrees of comparison are called: positive, comparative, and superlative.

For the positive degree in Italian, use the construction **così... come** or **tanto... quanto**.

Alessandro è così felice come sua sorella.	*Alexander is as happy as his sister.*
Loro sono tanto buoni quanto gli altri.	*They are as nice as the others.*

The first words in these contructions (**così** and **tanto**) are optional.

Alessandro è felice come sua sorella.	*Alexander is as happy as his sister.*
Loro sono buoni quanto gli altri.	*They are as nice as the others.*

For the comparative degree simply use **più** (*more*) or **meno** (*less*), as the case may be.

Marco è intelligente.	*Marco is intelligent.*	Maria è più intelligente.	*Maria is more intelligent.*
Lui è simpatico.	*He is nice.*	Lei è meno simpatica.	*She is less nice.*
Sara è alta.	*Sarah is tall.*	Alessandro è più alto.	*Alexander is taller.*

For the superlative degree use the definite article (in its proper form) followed by **più** or **meno**, as the case may be.

Maria è la più intelligente della sua classe.	*Mary is the most intelligent in her class.*
Quel ragazzo è il più simpatico della famiglia.	*That boy is the nicest in the family.*
Quelle patate sono le meno buone.	*Those potatoes are the least good.*

In superlative constructions the definite article is not repeated if it already appears before a noun.

Maria è la ragazza più intelligente della classe.	*Mary is the most intelligent girl in the class.*
Lui è il ragazzo meno intelligente della classe.	*He is the least intelligent boy in the class.*

In comparative constructions the word *than* is rendered in two ways:

- If two structures (nouns, substantives, or noun phrases) are compared by one adjective, the preposition **di** is used.

Giovanni è più alto **di** Pietro.	*John is taller **than** Peter.*
Maria è meno elegante **di** sua sorella.	*Mary is less elegant **than** her sister.*

- If two adjectives are used to compare the same structure (a noun, a substantive, or a noun phrase), the word **che** is used instead.

Giovanni è più simpatico **che** intelligente.	*John is nicer **than** he is intelligent.*
Maria è meno elegante **che** simpatica.	*Mary is less elegant **than** she is nice.*

Some adjectives have both regular and irregular comparative and superlative forms.

buono	*good*	più buono *or* migliore	*better*
cattivo	*bad*	più cattivo *or* peggiore	*worse*
grande	*big*	più grande *or* maggiore	*bigger (older)*
piccolo	*small*	più piccolo *or* minore	*smaller (younger)*

Questo vino è buono, ma quello è migliore.	*This wine is good, but that one is better.*
Questo caffè è cattivo, ma quello è peggiore.	*This coffee is bad, but that one is worse.*
Lui è il fratello maggiore.	*He is the oldest brother.*
Lei è la sorella minore.	*She is the youngest sister.*

To express *very* emphatically (*very, very* or *the very most of something*) as part of the adjective, just drop the final vowel and add **-issimo**.

buono	*change to*	buon-	+	-issimo	=	buonissimo	*very, very good*
alto	*change to*	alt-	+	-issimo	=	altissimo	*very, very tall*
grande	*change to*	grand-	+	-issimo	=	grandissimo	*very, very big*
facile	*change to*	facil-	+	-issimo	=	facilissimo	*very, very easy*

Giovanni è intelligentissimo.	*John is very very, very intelligent.*
Anche Maria è intelligentissima.	*Mary is also very, very intelligent.*

Oral Practice

Practice saying the following sentences out loud.

Com'è Alessandro?	*How is Alexander?*
Alessandro è così bravo come sua sorella.	*Alexander is as nice as his sister.*
Com'è Marco?	*How is Mark?*
Lui è più intelligente di Pino.	*He is more intelligent than Pino.*
Ma è meno intelligente di Maria.	*But he is less intelligent than Mary.*
Com'è Maria?	*How is Mary?*
Lei è più intelligente che simpatica.	*She is more intelligent than she is nice.*
Ma lei è più simpatica di te.	*But she is nicer than you.*
Chi è la persona piu alta della famiglia?	*Who is the tallest person in your family?*
Mio fratello è la persona più alta.	*My brother is the tallest person.*
Io sono la meno alta.	*I am the least tall.*
Com'è quel panino?	*How is that sandwich?*
È buono, ma questo è migliore.	*It is good, but this one is better.*
Com'è quel cappuccino?	*How is that cappuccino?*
È cattivo, ma quello è peggiore.	*It is bad, but that one is worse.*
Chi è lui?	*Who is he?*
Lui è il fratello maggiore.	*He is the oldest brother.*
Chi è lei?	*Who is she?*
Lei è la sorella minore.	*She is the youngest sister.*

Written Practice 3

Fill in the blanks with the appropriate comparison structures.

1. Com'è tuo fratello? *How is your brother?*

   Lui è _____ felice _____ sua sorella. *He is as happy as his sister.*

2. Come sono i tuoi genitori? *How are your parents?*

   Loro sono _____ simpatici _____ i tuoi. *They are as nice as yours.*

3. Com'è il tuo amico? *How is your friend?*

   Lui è _____ bravo _____ tuo amico. *He is nicer than your friend.*

   Ma è _____ bravo _____ tua sorella. *But he is less nice than your sister.*

4. Com'è la tua amica? *How is your friend?*

   Lei è _____ elegante _____ simpatica. *She is more elegant than she is nice.*

   E lei è _____ simpatica _____ te. *And she is nicer than you.*

5. Chi è _____ intelligente della classe? *Who is the most intelligent in the class?*

   Mio fratello è _____ intelligente. *My brother is the most intelligent.*

   Io sono _____ intelligente. *I am the least intelligent.*

6. Com'è quel vino? *How is that wine?*

   È buono, ma questo è _____. *It is good, but this one is better.*

7. Com'è quella pasta? *How is that pastry?*

   È cattiva, ma quella è _____. *It is bad, but that one is worse.*

8. Chi è lui? *Who is he?*

   Lui è il fratello _____. *He is the oldest brother.*

9. Chi è lei? *Who is she?*

   Lei è la sorella _____. *She is the youngest sister.*

Oral Practice

Practice saying the following sentences out loud.

È vero che Marco è molto intelligente?	*Is it true that Mark is very intelligent?*
Sì, è intelligentissimo.	*Yes, he is very, very intelligent.*

È vero che Alessandro è molto alto?   *Is it true that Alexander is very tall?*

Sì, è altissimo.   *Yes, he is very, very tall.*

È vero che Sara è molto simpatica?   *Is it true that Sarah is very nice?*

Sì, è simpaticissima.   *Yes, she is very, very nice.*

È vero che la loro casa è molto   *Is it true that their house is very big?*
  grande?

Sì, è grandissima.   *Yes, it is very, very big.*

È vero che loro sono molto bravi?   *Is it true that they are very nice?*

Sì, sono bravissimi.   *Yes, they are very, very nice.*

È vero che le ragazze sono molto   *Is it true that the girls are very happy?*
  felici?

Sì, sono felicissime.   *Yes, they are very, very happy.*

Written Practice 4

Fill in the blanks with the appropriate forms of the indicated adjectives.

1. È vero che lui è molto ricco? *Is it true that he is very rich?*

   Sì, è _____. *Yes, he is very, very rich.*

2. È vero che lei è molto alta? *Is it true that she is very tall?*

   Sì, è _____. *Yes, she is very, very tall.*

3. È vero che la loro casa è molto bella? *Is it true that their house is very beautiful?*

   Sì, è _____. *Yes, it is very, very beautiful.*

4. È vero che loro sono molto felici? *Is it true that they are very happy?*

   Sì, sono _____. *Yes, they are very, very happy.*

5. È vero che le ragazze sono molto eleganti? *Is it true that the girls are very elegant?*

   Sì, sono _____. *Yes, they are very, very elegant.*

Adverbs of Comparison

Adverbs are compared in the same manner as adjectives. Note that the comparative degree is the most frequently used form for adverbs.

lentamente	*slowly*	più lentamente	*more slowly*
facilmente	*easily*	meno facilmente	*less easily*
lontano	*far*	più lontano	*farther*
velocemente	*quickly*	più velocemente	*more quickly*

Note the following irregular comparative forms for adverbs:

Adverb		Comparative		Superlative	
bene	*well*	più bene = meglio	*better*	il meglio	*the best*
male	*bad(ly)*	più male = peggio	*worse*	il peggio	*the worst*

Oral Practice

Practice saying the following sentences out loud.

Come guida Marco?	*How does Mark drive?*
Lui guida più lentamente di me.	*He drives more slowly than I do.*
Ma guida meno lentamente di mia sorella.	*But he drives less slowly than my sister.*
Lui studia volentieri, vero?	*He studies gladly, doesn't he?*
Sì, ma studia meno volentieri di me.	*Yes, but he studies less gladly than I do.*
Come stai, Maria?	*How are you Mary?*
Oggi sto meglio.	*Today, I am better.*
E come sta tuo fratello?	*And how is our brother?*
Lui sta peggio.	*He is worse.*

Written Practice 5

Fill in the blanks with the missing words, as indicated.

1. Come guida tuo fratello? *How does your brother drive?*

    Lui guida _____ velocemente _____ te. *He drives more quickly than you do.*

    Ma guida _____ velocemente _____ me. *But he drives less quickly than I do.*

2. Lui capisce tutto facilmente, vero? *He understands everything easily, doesn't he?*

    Sì, ma capisce _____ facilmente _____ me. *Yes, but he understands less easily than I do.*

3. Come sta tuo fratello? *How is your brother?*

    Oggi sta _____. *Today, he is better.*

4. E come sta tuo cugino? *And how is your cousin?*

    Lui sta _____. *He is worse.*

Relative Pronouns

Throughout this book you have been using **che** to express *that*, *which*, or *who*. This is called a relative pronoun. Relative pronouns connect two clauses, which are essentially two mini-sentences. Note that in Italian **che** must be used, whereas in English, the corresponding English form may be omitted.

La ragazza **che** legge il giornale è italiana.	*The girl **who** is reading the newspaper is Italian.*

After a preposition, however, the form **cui** is used instead of **che**.

La ragazza **con cui** hai parlato è mia sorella.	*The girl **with whom** you spoke is my sister.*

The pronoun **chi** is used to mean *he*, *she*, *they*, and *who* or more simply *whoever*.

Chi va in Italia si divertirà.	***Whoever*** *goes to Italy will enjoy himself/* *herself.*

And, finally, **quello che** means *what* in the sense of *that which*. It also has two idiomatic forms: **quel che** or **ciò che**.

Quello che dici è vero.	*What (**That which**) you are saying is true.*
Non sai **quel che** dici.	*You do not know **what** you are saying.*
Ciò che dici non mi piace.	*I do not like **what** you are saying.*

Oral Practice

Practice saying the following sentences out loud.

Chi è la donna che legge il giornale?	*Who is the woman reading the newspaper?*
La donna che legge il giornale è mia madre.	*The woman who is reading the newspaper is my mother.*
Com'è il vestito che hai comprato ieri?	*How is the dress you bought yesterday?*
Il vestito che ho comprato ieri è molto bello.	*The dress I bought yesterday is very beautiful.*
Ti piace il libro che stai leggendo?	*Do you like the book you are reading?*
Sì, mi piace il libro che sto leggendo.	*Yes, I like the book I am reading.*
Chi è il ragazzo a cui hai dato il libro?	*Who is the boy to whom you gave the book?*
Il ragazzo a cui ho dato il libro è mio cugino.	*The boy to whom I gave the book is my cousin.*
Dov'è il mio libro?	*Where is my book?*
Non trovo lo zaino in cui ho messo il tuo libro.	*I cannot find the backpack in which I put your book.*
Che cosa hai detto?	*What did you say?*
Chi va a Roma si divertirà molto.	*Whoever goes to Rome will enjoy himself/herself.*
Chi ha detto quello?	*Who said that?*

Chi ha detto quello non sa niente.	*Whoever said that knows nothing.*
Che cosa devo fare?	*What should I do?*
Devi fare quello che ti dico io.	*You must do what I tell you.*
Che cosa ha fatto lui?	*What did he do?*
Ha fatto quel che doveva fare.	*He did what he had to do.*

Written Practice 6

Fill in the blanks with the missing pronouns—relative or otherwise.

1. _____ è l'uomo _____ mangia il panino? *Who is the man eating the sandwich?*

   L'uomo _____ mangia il panino è mio padre. *The man who is eating the sandwich is my father.*

2. Com'è il caffè _____ hai bevuto ieri? *How is the coffee that you drank yesterday?*

   Il caffè _____ ho bevuto ieri era molto buono. *The coffee I drank yesterday was very good.*

3. Chi è la persona a _____ hai dato il libro? *Who is the person to whom you gave the book?*

   La persona a _____ ho dato il libro è mio cugino. *The person to whom I gave the book is my cousin.*

4. Dov'è il libro _____ ti ho dato ieri? *Where is the book that I gave you yesterday?*

   Non trovo la scatola in _____ l'ho messo. *I cannot find the box in which I put it.*

5. _____ ha detto tuo fratello? *What did your brother say?*

   _____ va in centro oggi si divertirà. *Whoever goes downtown today will enjoy himself/herself.*

6. _____ ha detto quello? *Who said that?*

   _____ ha detto quello non sa niente. *Whoever said that knows nothing.*

7. _____ devo fare? *What should I do?*

   Devi fare _____ ti dico io. *You must do what I tell you.*

Italian Coffee

Italians love their coffee! Coffee bars are everywhere. So, here are some of the ways to order and enjoy Italian coffee:

un caffellatte	*coffee and steamed milk in equal portions; a "latte"*
un cappuccino	*cappuccino (espresso coffee with steamed milk)*
corretto	*with a dash of liqueur*
decaffeinato	*decaffeinated*
doppio	*double*
un espresso	*espresso coffee*
lungo	*less concentrated; long*
macchiato	*with a drop of milk*
ristretto	*strong; short*

QUIZ

Choose the appropriate answer to each question.

1. Quanti andranno in Italia quest'anno?

    (a) Molti ci andranno.

    (b) Andremo in Italia.

2. È vero che hai comprato delle paste ieri?

    (a) Sì, ne ho comprate molte.

    (b) Sì, ho comprato molte.

3. Quante ne avete comprate, precisamente?

    (a) Ne abbiamo comprate sette.

    (b) Abbiamo comprato sette.

4. Andrete anche voi in Italia?

    (a) Sì, ci andremo di sicuro.

    (b) Sì, vado di sicuro.

Provide the missing forms of the given adjectives. For example:

bravo   <u>*più bravo*</u>   il più bravo   <u>*bravissimo*</u>

Positive	Comparative	Superlative	Emphatic Superlative
5. _____	più alta	la più alta	_____
bravi	_____	i più bravi	_____
eleganti	_____	le più eleganti	_____
_____	più belli	_____	bellissimi
buono	_____	il migliore	_____
piccolo	_____	_____	piccolissimo
grande	maggiore	_____	_____

Match the questions in the left column with the answers in the right column.

_____ 6. Come sta tuo fratello?

_____ 7. Chi è la persona che parla con lui?

_____ 8. Dove ha messo la mia penna?

_____ 9. Che devo fare?

a. È mio fratello.

b. Non trovo la scatola in cui l'ho messa.

c. Devi fare quello che ti dico io.

d. Oggi sta meglio.

Personal Matters! Answer the question appropriately.

10. Che tipo di caffè ti piace?

_____ .

Circle the letter of the word or phrase that best completes the sentence or answers the question.

1. Dove _____ domani, Marco?

    (a) andrai

    (b) sarai andato

2. Che cosa _____ in Italia, Pina e Giovanni?

    (a) farete

    (b) farai

3. Signora Verdi, che cosa _____ in quel negozio?

    (a) comprerà

    (b) comprerai

4. Quando _____ i tuoi amici per l'Italia?

    (a) partiranno

    (b) saranno partiti

5. A che ora _____ voi stasera?

    (a) saranno usciti

    (b) uscirete

6. Appena _____, andrò in centro.

    (a) mi alzerò

    (b) mi sarò alzato

7. Quanto _____ quella macchina?

    (a) costeranno

    (b) costerà

8. Quanti anni _____ il professore?

    (a) avrà avuto

    (b) avrà

9. Il calcio si gioca _____.

    (a) negli stadi

    (b) a casa

10. Lo sport più popolare in Italia è _____ .

   (a) il calcio

   (b) il tennis

11. Loro _____ in Italia, ma non hanno tempo.

   (a) andrebbero

   (b) andranno

12. Signor Verdi, quando _____ andare in vacanza, fra una settimana o due?

   (a) vorrebbe

   (b) sarebbe voluto

13. Mia sorella _____ solo quel programma ogni sera, anche se è lo stesso programma.

   (a) guarderebbe

   (b) guarderà

14. Loro _____ quella macchina, ma non hanno soldi.

   (a) comprerebbero

   (b) compreranno

15. A che ora _____ arrivare i tuoi amici?

   (a) dovrebbero

   (b) saranno dovuti

16. Loro _____ la loro macchina, ma nessuno l'ha voluta.

   (a) venderebbero

   (b) avrebbero già venduto

17. Io non conosco _____ in questa città.

   (a) nessuno

   (b) qualcuno

18. Anche lui non vuole _____ , vero?

   (a) niente

   (b) qualcosa

19. Loro non vanno _____ in Italia ogni anno.

   (a) più

   (b) mai

20. Quella pizza non mi piace _____.

    (a) affatto

    (b) qualcosa

21. Marco, quando _____ hai chiamato ieri sera?

    (a) mi

    (b) ti

22. Hai parlato al professore? Sì, _____ ho già parlato.

    (a) gli

    (b) lo

23. Hai parlato alla professoressa? Sì, _____ ho già parlato.

    (a) le

    (b) la

24. Avete comprato le scarpe ieri? Sì _____ abbiamo comprate.

    (a) le

    (b) gli

25. Hai guardato quei programmi? Sì, _____ ho guardati.

    (a) li

    (b) gli

26. Vado in centro _____ sabato.

    (a) altro

    (b) ogni

27. Ho mangiato _____ carne.

    (a) troppo

    (b) troppa

28. Ho veramente _____ fame.

    (a) molto

    (b) molta

29. Lui è _____ una brava persona.

    (a) vera

    (b) veramente

30. Guardiamo _____ quel tipo di programma.

    (a) abbastanza

    (b) spesso

31. Giovanni, mi hai comprato la giacca?

    (a) Sì, te l'ho comprata.

    (b) Sì, gliel'ho comprata.

32. Signora, ha comprato quella giacca a suo figlio?

    (a) Sì, te l'ho comprata.

    (b) Sì, gliel'ho comprata.

33. Dove sono i tuoi amici?

    (a) Eccoli.

    (b) Eccogli.

34. Marco, vuoi mangiare la pizza?

    (a) Sì, voglio mangiarla.

    (b) Sì, mangiala.

35. Maria, dove sono le mie scarpe?

    (a) Dammele!

    (b) Dagliele!

36. Hai dato il tuo portatile a mio fratello?

    (a) No, non l'ho dato a lui; l'ho dato a loro.

    (b) No, non glielo ho dato; glielo ho dato.

37. Marco, ti _____ io?

    (a) piace

    (b) piaccio

38. Signora, Le _____ i ravioli?

    (a) sono piaciuti

    (b) è piaciuto

39. Maria, ti _____ andare in Francia?

    (a) piacerebbe

    (b) piaccio

40. Signora Verdi e signor Rossi, Le _____ gli spaghetti?

    (a) sono piaciuti

    (b) piacque

41. Quante patate vuoi?

    (a) Ne voglio alcune.

    (b) Ci vogliono alcune.

42. Anche voi verrete in centro con noi?

    (a) Sì, ci verremo anche noi.

    (b) Sì, ne verremo anche noi.

43. Quanti vogliono andare in Italia quest'anno?

    (a) Molti.

    (b) Molte.

44. Marco è più alto _____ Maria.

    (a) di

    (b) che

45. Maria è _____ intelligente della sua classe.

    (a) la più

    (b) più

46. Quel panino è buono, ma questo è _____.

    (a) migliore

    (b) meglio

47. Chi è quella persona _____ sta leggendo il giornale?

    (a) cui

    (b) che

48. Chi è la persona a _____ hai parlato ieri?

    (a) cui

    (b) che

49. _____ va in Italia si divertirà.

    (a) Che

    (b) Chi

50. Devi fare _____ ti ho detto.

    (a) chi

    (b) quello che

FINAL EXAM

Practice what you've learned by choosing the correct answer for each of the following.

1. Come si chiama tuo fratello?

    (a) Mi chiamo Paolo.

    (b) Si chiama Paolo.

2. Signore, come si chiama?

    (a) Mi chiamo Marco Signorelli.

    (b) Si chiama Marco Signorelli.

3. Ti presento _____ .

    (a) la dottoressa Maria Rinaldi

    (b) Maria Rinaldi

4. Le presento _____ .

    (a) la dottoressa Maria Rinaldi

    (b) Maria Rinaldi

5. Pina è la _____ di Marco.

    (a) sorella

    (b) fratello

6. Che cosa è?

    (a) È l'orologio di Marco.

    (b) È lo zio di Marco.

7. Chi sono quelle due persone?

    (a) Sono le scarpe di Maria.

    (b) Sono le amiche di Maria.

8. Che cos'è?

    (a) È mia cugina.

    (b) È la mia giacca.

9. Buongiorno, dottoressa. _____

    (a) Come sta?

    (b) Come stai?

10. Ciao, Stefano.

   (a) Come sta?

   (b) Come stai?

11. Grazie per il caffè.

   (a) Prego.

   (b) Per favore.

12. Ciao, Maria.

   (a) Arrivederci.

   (b) ArrivederLa.

13. Quelle due ragazze sono _____.

   (a) greci

   (b) greche

14. Quei due bambini sono _____.

   (a) tedeschi

   (b) tedesche

15. Che giorno è?

   (a) È lunedì.

   (b) È febbraio.

16. Di quale nazionalità sei, Maria?

   (a) Sono italiana.

   (b) Sono americano.

17. Di dove sei?

   (a) Sono di Firenze.

   (b) Sono italiana.

18. Le amiche di Maria sono _____.

   (a) americane

   (b) americani

19. Com'è quella donna?

   (a) È simpaticissimo.

   (b) È simpaticissima.

20. Sono _____ zii di Pina.

    (a) gli

    (b) i

21. Lui è _____ psicologo americano.

    (a) uno

    (b) un

22. Dove hai messi i miei libri?

    (a) Eccoli.

    (b) Ci sono i libri.

23. Vuoi qualcosa, Maria?

    (a) No, non ho fame.

    (b) No, non hai fame.

24. Quanti anni _____, signora Verdi?

    (a) hai

    (b) ha

25. Non _____ la carne.

    (a) mi piace

    (b) mi piacciono

26. Che cosa bevono i tuoi amici di solito?

    (a) Beviamo il caffè.

    (b) Bevono il caffè.

27. Chi è il tuo _____?

    (a) dentista

    (b) dentisti

28. Chi sono quelle ragazze _____?

    (a) simpatici

    (b) simpatiche

29. Dove abiti, Maria?

    (a) In via Dante, numero 34.

    (b) Domani.

30. Che cosa legge, signora, di solito?

    (a) Leggo il giornale.

    (b) Legge il giornale.

31. Che cosa farai domani?

    (a) Farò delle spese in centro.

    (b) Farà delle spese in centro.

32. Dov'è tua sorella?

    (a) Il medico.

    (b) Dal medico.

33. A che ora arriveranno i tuoi amici?

    (a) Sono le cinque.

    (b) Alle cinque.

34. Che ora è?

    (a) Sono le due e mezzo.

    (b) Domani.

35. Dov'è la mia penna?

    (a) Con la scatola.

    (b) Nella scatola.

36. Quando partite voi?

    (a) Partono domani.

    (b) Partiamo domani.

37. Mi capisci?

    (a) Sì, ti capisci.

    (b) Sì, ti capisco.

38. Quando uscirete?

    (a) Quando avremo finito di studiare.

    (b) Quando studieremo.

39. Oggi è _____ marzo.

    (a) il primo

    (b) primo

40. Di chi sono _____ pantaloni?

    (a) quei

    (b) quegli

41. Chi sono _____ uomini?

    (a) quei

    (b) quegli

42. Che cosa sta dicendo tuo fratello?

    (a) Non sta dicendo niente.

    (b) Non stai dicendo niente.

43. Cosa sta facendo Lei, signora?

    (a) Sto leggendo.

    (b) Sta leggendo.

44. Come si chiama _____ amica, Maria?

    (a) la tua

    (b) la Sua

45. Quando arriva _____ zia, signora Verdi?

    (a) tua

    (b) Sua

46. Di solito fa _____ tempo in primavera.

    (a) bel

    (b) bello

47. Maria, _____ alla festa anche tu!

    (a) vieni

    (b) venga

48. Signor Verdi, _____ la verità!

    (a) dica

    (b) di'

49. Maria, anche tu vuoi _____ minestra?

    (a) qualche

    (b) un po' di

50. Preferiamo mangiare _____.

    (a) di spaghetti

    (b) degli spaghetti

51. Signora, a che ora _____ di solito?

    (a) si alza

    (b) ti alzi

52. Maria, _____! È tardi!

    (a) si alzi

    (b) alzati

53. Marco e Maria, _____! Sono già le otto e mezzo!

    (a) svegliatevi

    (b) si sveglino

54. Pino, non ti _____ quella giacca!

    (a) mettere

    (b) metti

55. Signor Verdi, non si _____ quella giacca!

    (a) metta

    (b) metti

56. Dottoressa, a che ora _____ ieri?

    (a) si è alzato

    (b) si è alzata

57. Chi è venuto con te in centro?

    (a) Sono venuti loro.

    (b) Sono venuto loro.

58. Quei _____ sono veramente belli?

    (a) programmi

    (b) programma

59. Anche loro si sono divertiti alla festa?

    (a) Sì, si sono divertiti.

    (b) Sì, ci siamo divertiti.

60. Loro sono stati _____ Italia, non è vero?

    (a) in

    (b) nell'

61. Sì, sono stati _____ Italia centrale.

    (a) in

    (b) nell'

62. Che cosa facevi, Maria, mentre io studiavo?

    (a) Ho guardato la televisione.

    (b) Guardavo la televisione.

63. Che colore di capelli avevi da bambina, Maria?

    (a) Ha avuto i capelli biondi.

    (b) Avevo i capelli biondi.

64. Chi sono quei bambini?

    (a) Quelli sono i miei cugini.

    (b) Quegli sono i miei cugini.

65. Io _____ in Italia spesso da bambino.

    (a) andavo

    (b) sono andato

66. Loro _____ per l'Italia alcuni minuti fa.

    (a) partivano

    (b) sono partiti

67. Loro _____ in America molti anni fa.

    (a) venivano

    (b) vennero

68. Lei _____ poco tempo fa.

    (a) è uscita

    (b) usciva

69. Mia sorella _____ a Roma stamani.

    (a) è andata

    (b) andava

70. Loro _____ quando tu hai chiamato.

    (a) erano già usciti

    (b) uscivano

71. Lui è un _____ uomo, non è vero?

    (a) bell'

    (b) bel

72. E lei è una _____ donna, non è vero?

    (a) bella

    (b) bel

73. Lui è un _____ amico.

    (a) buono

    (b) buon

74. _____ pomeriggio!

    (a) Buono

    (b) Buon

75. _____ sera!

    (a) Buon

    (b) Buona

76. Dove _____ domani, signora Verdi e signor Marchi?

    (a) andranno

    (b) sarete andati

77. Maria, che cosa _____ in quel negozio?

    (a) comprerà

    (b) comprerai

78. A che ora _____ loro stasera?

    (a) saranno usciti

    (b) usciranno

79. Quanto _____ quelle scarpe?

    (a) costeranno

    (b) costerà

80. Quanti anni _____ la dottoressa Mirri?

    (a) avrà avuto

    (b) avrà

81. Noi _____ in Italia, ma non abbiamo i soldi.

    (a) andrebbero

    (b) andremmo

82. Signor Verdi, che cosa _____ fare domani?

    (a) vorrebbe

    (b) volle

83. Io _____ quella macchina, ma non ho abbastanza soldi.

    (a) comprerebbero

    (b) comprerei

84. Quando _____ arrivare i tuoi genitori?

    (a) dovrebbero

    (b) dovettero

85. Lui non conosce _____ in questa città.

    (a) nessuno

    (b) qualcuno

86. Io non voglio _____, grazie.

    (a) niente

    (b) qualcosa

87. Non voglio _____.

    (a) spaghetti

    (b) degli spaghetti

88. Noi non andiamo _____ in Italia, perché non abbiamo soldi.

    (a) più

    (b) affatto

89. Quella minestra non mi piace _____.

    (a) affatto

    (b) nulla

90. Marco, mi hai dato il tuo indirizzo?

    (a) Sì, te l'ho dato.

    (b) Sì, gliel'ho dato.

91. Hai parlato al signor Marchi? Sì, _____ ho già parlato.

    (a) gli

    (b) lo

92. Hai parlato alla signora Marchi? Sì, _____ ho già parlato.

    (a) le

    (b) la

93. Avete comprato gli stivali ieri? Sì _____ abbiamo comprati.

    (a) li

    (b) gli

94. Maria, mi hai comprato quella camicia?

    (a) Sì, te l'ho comprata.

    (b) Sì, gliel'ho comprata.

95. Signora, gli ha comprato quella macchina?

    (a) Sì, te l'ho comprata.

    (b) Sì, gliel'ho comprata.

96. Dove sono le tue amiche?

    (a) Eccoli.

    (b) Eccole.

97. Maria, vuoi mangiare questa pasta?

    (a) Sì, voglio mangiarla.

    (b) Sì, mangiala.

98. Maria, dove hai messo le mie scarpe? _____

    (a) Dammele!

    (b) Dagliele!

99. Maria, ti _____ io?

    (a) piace

    (b) piaccio

100. Alessandro è più alto _____ Maria.
    (a) di
    (b) che

ITALIAN-ENGLISH GLOSSARY

Adjectives are given only in their masculine singular form.

To differentiate between masculine or feminine nouns for nouns ending in **-e**, the abbreviations (*m.*) and (*f.*) are used.

a at, to, in
A presto! See you soon!
abbastanza enough
abitare to live, dwell
acqua water
adesso now
aereo airplane
affatto at all
agosto August
albergo hotel
albero tree
alfabeto (*m.*) alphabet
allora then
alto tall
altrettanto and also, as much/many
altro other
alzarsi to get up
americano American
amico/amica friend (*m./f.*)

analisi (*f.*) analysis
anche also, too
ancora still, yet
andare to go
andare in onda to be broadcast
anno year
antipasto starter, hors d'oeuvres, appetizer
anzi as a matter of fact, in fact
appena as soon as, just, barely
aprile April
aprire to open
arancione orange (adj.)
arrivare to arrive
arrivederci/arrivederLa good-bye (familiar/polite)
aspettare to wait (for)
assai rather, quite
attore/attrice actor/actress
Australia Australia
australiano Australian
autobus (*m.*) bus
automobile (*f.*) automobile
autore/autrice author (*m./f.*)
autunno autumn
avere to have

avere... anni to be . . . years old
avere bisogno di to need
avere fame to be hungry
avere ragione to be right
avere sete to be thirsty
avere sonno to be sleepy
avere torto to be wrong
avvocato lawyer
azzurro blue
bacio kiss
bagno washroom
bambino/bambina child (*m./f.*)
banca bank
bello beautiful, handsome, nice
bene well
bere to drink
bianco white
bibita soft drink
bicchiere (*m.*) drinking glass
bicicletta bicycle
biglietto ticket
biologo biologist
biondo blond
bistecca steak
blu dark blue
bocca mouth
borsa purse
bottiglia bottle
braccio arm
bravo good (person)
brutto ugly, bad
buco hole
bugia lie
Buon appetito! Eat up! (Literally: Have a good appetite!)
buon pomeriggio good afternoon
buonanotte good night
buonasera good evening
buongiorno good morning, good day
buono good
cadere to fall

caffè (*m.*) coffee
caffellatte (*m.*) coffee and steamed milk, a latte
calcio soccer
caldo hot
calza stocking
calzino sock
camera bedroom, room
cameriere/cameriera waiter/waitress
camicetta blouse
camicia shirt
campagna countryside
Canada Canada
canadese Canadian
cane (*m.*) dog
cantare to sing
capelli (*m. pl.*) hair (on the head)
capire to understand
cappello hat
cappotto coat
cappuccino cappuccino coffee
carne (*f.*) meat
caro dear
carta di credito credit card
casa house
cattivo bad
cellulare (*m.*) cell phone
cena dinner
centrale central
centro downtown
cercare to look for, search for
certo certain
chat chatroom
che what, that, which, who
che cosa what
chi who
chiamare to call
chiamarsi to be called, named
chiave (*f.*) key
chiedere to ask for
chiudere to close

Ci vediamo! See you later!
ciao hi, bye
Cina China
cinema (*m.*) movies, cinema
cinese Chinese
città (*f.*) city
classe (*f.*) class (of students), classroom
cliente (*m.* or *f.*) customer
cognome (*m.*) surname
colazione (*f.*) breakfast
collo neck
colore (*m.*) color
coltello knife
come how, like, as
Come si chiama? What is your name? (polite)
Come sta? How are you? (polite)
Come stai? How are you? (familiar)
Come ti chiami? What is your name? (familiar)
Come va? How is it going?
cominciare to begin, start
commedia comedy
commesso/commessa salesclerk (*m./f.*)
comprare to buy
computer computer
con with
condire to put on dressing/condiments
conoscere to know
contemporaneo contemporary
conto bill, check
corretto coffee with a dash of liqueur
cosa thing
così so, thus
costare to cost
costume (*m.*) costume
cravatta tie
crisi (*f.*) crisis
cucina kitchen
cugino/cugina cousin (*m./f.*)
da from, as a

da capo from the start
dare to give
data date
davanti (a) in front of
decaffeinato decaffeinated
dentista (*m.* or *f.*) dentist
destro right
di of
di nuovo again
di solito usually
diagramma (*m.*) diagram
dicembre December
dire to say
discoteca discothèque, disco
dito finger
divano couch, sofa
diventare to become
divertirsi to enjoy oneself, have fun
documentario documentary
dolce (*m.*) dessert, sweet
dollaro dollar
domani tomorrow
domenica Sunday
donna woman
dopo after
doppio double
dormire to sleep
dottore/dottoressa Dr., doctor (*m./f.*)
dove where
dovere to have to
dozzina dozen
dramma (*m.*) drama
durare to last
e and
ecco here is/here are, there is/there are
elefante/elefantessa elephant (*m./f.*)
elegante elegant
enorme enormous
entrare to enter
espresso espresso coffee
esserci to be here/there

essere to be
estate (*f.*) summer
euro euro
fa ago
faccia face
facile easy
fame (*f.*) hunger
famoso famous
fantascienza science fiction
fare to do
fare delle spese to do some shopping
fare la spesa to do food shopping
fare male to hurt
farmacia pharmacy
farmacista (*m.* or *f.*) pharmacist
febbraio February
felice happy
festa party, feast
figlia daughter
figlio son
film movie
finestra window
finire to finish
forchetta fork
formaggio cheese
forse maybe
foto (*f.*) photo
francese French
Francia France
fratello brother
freddo cold
fronte (*f.*) forehead
frutta fruit
gamba leg
gatto cat
gelato ice cream
genitori (*m. pl.*) parents
gennaio January
gente (*f.*) people
Germania Germany
già already

giacca jacket
giallo yellow
Giappone (*m.*) Japan
giapponese Japanese
giardino garden
ginnastica gymnastics
giocare to play (a sport/game)
giocatore/giocatrice (*m./f.*) player
gioco game
giornale (*m.*) newspaper
giornata day (in its entirety)
giorno day
giovane young
giovedì Thursday
gioventù (*f.*) youth
giugno June
gnocco dumpling
gomito elbow
gonna skirt
grande big, large
grazie thank you, thanks
greco Greek
grigio gray
guancia cheek
guardare to watch, look at
ieri yesterday
imparare to learn
impermeabile (*m.*) overcoat, raincoat
in in, to
incontro encounter, match
indirizzo address
infatti in fact
infermiere/infermiera nurse (*m./f.*)
infine finally
ingegnere (*m.* or *f.*) engineer
Inghilterra England
inglese English
insalata salad
insegnare to teach
insieme together
intelligente intelligent

invece instead
inverno winter
invitare to invite
io I
ipotesi (*f.*) hypothesis
isola island
Italia Italy
italiano Italian
jazz jazz
karatè (*m.*) karate
là there
labbro lip
lago lake
lasagne (*f./pl.*) lasagna
lasciare to leave (behind)
lavarsi to wash oneself
Le presento... (polite) Let me introduce you to . . .
leggere to read
leggero light
lei she
Lei you (polite)
lente (*f.*) magnifying glass, lens
lento slow
leone/leonessa lion/lioness
letto bed
lezione (*f.*) lesson, class
lì/là there
libro book
lingua language
lontano far
loro/Loro they/you (polite plural)
loro/Loro their, theirs/your, yours (polite plural)
luglio July
lui he
lunedì Monday
lungo long
luogo place
ma but
macchiato coffee with a drop of milk

macchina car
madre (*f.*) mother
maggio May
maglia sweater, jersey
mai ever, never
mail (e-mail) (*f.*) e-mail
male bad, badly
mamma mom
mancia tip
mangiare to eat
mano (*f.*) hand
marito husband
marrone brown
martedì Tuesday
marzo March
matematica mathematics
matita pencil
mattina morning
medico (*m.* or *f.*) doctor
mela apple
melone (*m.*) cantaloupe
meno minus, less
mentre while
menù (*m.*) menu
mercoledì Wednesday
meridionale southern
mese (*m.*) month
metà (*f.*) half (noun)
metropolitana subway
mettere to put
mettersi to put on, wear, set about, begin to
mezzanotte (*f.*) midnight
mezzo half (adj.)
mezzogiorno noon
mica quite, at all
minerale mineral
minestra soup
mio my, mine
mobile (*m.*) piece of furniture
moda fashion
moglie (*f.*) wife

molto much, many, a lot, very
momento moment
moto (*f.*) motorcycle
muro wall
naso nose
navigare to navigate
nazionalità nationality
né... né neither . . . nor
neanche neither, not even, not . . . either
negozio store
nero black
nessuno no one, none
nevicare to snow
niente nothing, anything
no no
noi we
nome (*m.*) name
non not
non c'è male not bad
nonno/nonna grandfather/grandmother
nostro our, ours
notte (*f.*) night
novembre November
nulla nothing
numero number
nuovo new
o or
occhio eye
oggi today
ogni each, every
ora hour
orecchio ear
orologio watch
orzo barley
ottobre October
padre (*m.*) father
pagare to pay
paio pair
panino sandwich, bun
pantaloni (*m. pl.*) pants
papà (*m.*) dad

parecchio several, quite a few
parete (*f.*) partition
parlare to speak
partire to leave
partita game, match
pasta pasta, pastry
patata potato
pattinaggio skating
pavimento floor
pazienza patience
penna pen
per for
per favore/per piacere please
percepito perceived
perché why, because
perfetto perfect
periferia suburbs
persona person
pesca peach
petto chest
piacere to like, to be pleasing to
pianeta (*m.*) planet
pianista (*m. or f.*) pianist
piano floor (story of a building)
piatto dish
piazza square, plaza
piccolo little
piede (*m.*) foot
piovere to rain
pittore/pittrice painter (*m./f.*)
più plus, more, anymore
pizza pizza
poco little, few
poi after, then
pomeriggio afternoon
pomodoro tomato
popolare popular
popolazione (*f.*) population
porta door
portare to wear, carry
portatile (*m.*) laptop

portoghese Portuguese
potere to be able to
povero poor
pranzo lunch
praticare to practice (sports)
preciso precise
preferire to prefer
prego you're welcome, may I help you
prendere to
    take, have something to eat/drink
presto early, fast
prima before
primavera spring
primo piatto first dish/serving/course
problema (*m.*) problem
professione (*f.*) profession
professore/professoressa professor (*m./f.*)
programma (*m.*) program
programma (*m.*) **a puntate** series
proprio really
prosciutto ham (cured)
prossimo next
provarsi to try on
psicologo/psicologa psychologist (*m./f.*)
pulire to clean
pure as well
purtroppo unfortunately
qualcosa something
qualcuno someone
quale which
qualsiasi whichever, any
quando when
quanto how much
quarto quarter
quasi almost
qui here
radio (*f.*) radio
ragazzo/ragazza boy/girl
ragione (*f.*) reason
raro rare
ravioli (*m. pl.*) ravioli

reagire to react
regolare regular
ricco rich
riga ruler
ripetere to repeat
ristorante (*m.*) restaurant
ristretto strong/short coffee
rivista magazine
romanzo novel
rosa pink
rosso red
Russia Russia
russo Russian
sabato Saturday
saldo sale
salotto living room
Salute! To your health!
sapere to know (how to)
sbaglio mistake
scarpa shoe
scatola box
schermo monitor (computer)
sciarpa scarf
scientifico scientific
scorso last (week, month, etc.)
scrittore/scrittrice writer (*m./f.*)
scrivere to write
scultore/scultrice sculptor
scuola school
se if
secondo piatto second dish/serving/course
sedia chair
sembrare to seem
semplice simple
sempre always
sentire to feel
sentirsi to feel
sera evening
sete (*f.*) thirst
settembre September
settimana week

sì yes
sicuro sure
signora lady, madam, Mrs.
signore gentleman, sir, Mr.
signorina miss, Ms.
simpatico nice
sinistro left
sistema (*m.*) system
sito web website
solo only
sonno sleep
sopra over, on top
sorella sister
sotto under
spaghetti (*m. pl.*) spaghetti
Spagna Spain
spagnolo Spanish
spalla shoulder
speciale special
specialista (*m.* or *f.*) specialist
spesso often
spettacolo variety show
spia spy
sport sport
squadra team
stagione (*f.*) season
stamani this morning
stampante (*f.*) printer
stanco tired
stare to stay, to be
stare bene to be (feel) well
stare male to be (feel) bad
stasera tonight
Stati Uniti United States
stesso same
stivale (*m.*) boot
strano strange
studente/studentessa student (*m./f.*)
studiare to study
su on
subito right away

succo juice
suo his, her, hers
Suo your, yours (polite)
suonare to play an instrument
svegliarsi to wake up
Svizzera Switzerland
taglia measurement, size
tanto much, many, a lot
tardi late
tassì (*m.*) taxi
tastiera keyboard
tavola dining table
tavolo table
tazza cup
tè (*m.*) tea
tedesco German
telecomando TV remote control
telefonare to phone
telegiornale (*m.*) TV newscast
telequiz TV quiz show
televisione (*f.*) television
televisore (*m.*) TV set
tempo time, weather
tennis (*m.*) tennis
teorema (*m.*) theorem
tesi (*f.*) thesis
testa head
tetto roof
Ti presento... Let me introduce you . . .
  (familiar)
tipo type
tornare to return, come back
torto crooked(ness), fault
tra, fra between, among, within
trattare to treat
trattoria (family) restaurant
treno train
triste sad
troppo too much
tu you (familiar)
tuo your, yours (familiar)

tutto all, every
ultimo last
università (*f.*) university
uomo man
usare to use
uscire to go out
utile useful
vacanza vacation
valigia suitcase
vecchio old
vedere to see
vendere to sell
venerdì Friday
venire to come
verde green
verità (*f.*) truth
vero true
verso around, toward
vestirsi to get dressed
vestito dress, suit
via street

viaggiare to travel
viaggio trip
vicino near
vincere to win
vino wine
viola violet, purple
violento violent
virtù (*f.*) virtue
voce (*f.*) voice
voi you (familiar plural)
volentieri gladly
volere to want
volta time (in a sequence)
vostro your, yours
weekend weekend
yacht yacht
zaino backpack
zio/zia uncle/aunt
zitto quiet
zucchero sugar

ENGLISH-ITALIAN GLOSSARY

actor/actress attore/attrice
address indirizzo
after dopo
after, then poi
afternoon pomeriggio
again di nuovo
ago fa
airplane aereo
all, every tutto
almost quasi
alphabet alfabeto (*m.*)
already già
also, too anche
always sempre
American americano
analysis analisi (*f.*)
and e
and also, as much/many altrettanto
apple mela
April aprile
arm braccio
around, toward verso
arrive (to) arrivare
as a matter of fact, in fact anzi
ask for (to) chiedere

as soon as, just, barely appena
as well pure
at all affatto
at, to, in a
August agosto
Australia Australia
Australian australiano
author autore/autrice (*m./f.*)
automobile automobile (*f.*)
autumn autunno
backpack zaino
bad cattivo
bad, badly male
bank banca
barley orzo
be (to) essere
be able to (to) potere
be broadcast (to) andare in onda
be called (to) chiamarsi
be here/there (to) esserci
be hungry (to) avere fame
be right (to) avere ragione
be sleepy (to) avere sonno
be thirsty (to) avere sete
be wrong (to) avere torto

be . . . years old (to) avere... anni
beautiful, handsome, nice bello
become (to) diventare
bed letto
bedroom, room camera
before prima
begin (to) cominciare
between, among, within tra, fra
bicycle bicicletta
big, large grande
bill, check conto
biologist biologo
black nero
blond biondo
blouse camicetta
blue azzurro
book libro
boot stivale (*m.*)
bottle bottiglia
box scatola
boy ragazzo
breakfast colazione (*f.*)
brother fratello
brown marrone
bus autobus (*m.*)
but ma
buy (to) comprare
call (to) chiamare
Canada Canada
Canadian canadese
cantaloupe melone (*m.*)
cappuccino coffee cappuccino
car macchina
carry (to) portare
cat gatto
cell phone cellulare (*m.*)
central centrale
certain certo
chair sedia
chatroom chat
cheek guancia

cheese formaggio
chest petto
child bambino/bambina (*m./f.*)
China Cina
Chinese cinese
city città (*f.*)
class (of students), classroom classe (*f.*)
clean (to) pulire
close (to) chiudere
coat cappotto
coffee caffè (*m.*)
coffee and steamed milk, a latte caffellatte (*m.*)
coffee with a dash of liqueur corretto
coffee with a drop of milk macchiato
cold freddo
color colore (*m.*)
come (to) venire
comedy commedia
computer computer
contemporary contemporaneo
cost (to) costare
costume costume (*m.*)
couch, sofa divano
countryside campagna
cousin cugino/cugina (*m./f.*)
credit card carta di credito
crisis crisi (*f.*)
crooked(ness), fault torto
cup tazza
customer cliente (*m.* or *f.*)
dad papà (*m.*)
dark blue blu
date data
daughter figlia
day giorno
day (in its entirety) giornata
dear caro
decaffeinated decaffeinato
December dicembre
dentist dentista (*m.* or *f.*)

dessert, sweet dolce (*m.*)
diagram diagramma (*m.*)
dining table tavola
dinner cena
discothèque, disco discoteca
dish piatto
do (to) fare
doctor medico (*m.* or *f.*)
documentary documentario
do food shopping (to) fare la spesa
dog cane (*m.*)
dollar dollaro
door porta
do some shopping (to) fare delle spese
double doppio
downtown centro
dozen dozzina
Dr., doctor dottore/dottoressa (*m.*/*f.*)
drama dramma (*m.*)
dress, suit vestito
drink (to) bere
drinking glass bicchiere (*m.*)
dumpling gnocco
each, every ogni
ear orecchio
early, fast presto
easy facile
eat (to) mangiare
Eat up! (Literally: **Have a good
  appetite!**) Buon appetito!
elbow gomito
elegant elegante
elephant elefante/elefantessa (*m.*/*f.*)
e-mail mail (e-mail) (*f.*)
encounter, match incontro
engineer ingegnere (*m.* or *f.*)
England Inghilterra
English inglese
enjoy oneself, have fun (to) divertirsi
enormous enorme
enough abbastanza

enter (to) entrare
espresso coffee espresso
euro euro
evening sera
ever, never mai
eye occhio
face faccia
fall (to) cadere
famous famoso
far lontano
fashion moda
father padre (*m.*)
February febbraio
feel (to) sentirsi
feel (to) sentire
feel bad (to) stare male
feel well (to) stare bene
finally infine
finger dito
finish (to) finire
first dish/serving/course primo piatto
floor pavimento
floor (story of a building) piano
foot piede (*m.*)
for per
forehead fronte (*f.*)
fork forchetta
France Francia
French francese
Friday venerdì
friend amico/amica (*m.*/*f.*)
from the start da capo
from, as a da
fruit frutta
game gioco
game, match partita
garden giardino
gentleman, sir, Mr. signore
German tedesco
Germany Germania
get dressed (to) vestirsi

get up (to) alzarsi
girl ragazza
give (to) dare
gladly volentieri
go (to) andare
go out (to) uscire
good buono
good (person) bravo
good afternoon buon pomeriggio
good evening buonasera
good morning, good day buongiorno
good night buonanotte
good-bye
     (familiar/polite) arrivederci/arrivederLa
grandfather/grandmother nonno/nonna
gray grigio
Greek greco
green verde
gymnastics ginnastica
hair (head) capelli (*m. pl.*)
half (noun) metà (*f.*)
half (adj.) mezzo
ham (cured) prosciutto
hand mano (*f.*)
handsome bello
happy felice
hat cappello
have (to) avere
have to (to) dovere
he lui
head testa
hear (to) sentire
here qui
here is/here are, there is/there are ecco
hi, bye ciao
his, her, hers suo
hole buco
hot caldo
hotel albergo
hour ora
house casa

How are you? (familiar) Come stai?
How are you? (polite) Come sta?
how much quanto
how, like, as come
How is it going? Come va?
hunger fame (*f.*)
hurt (to) fare male
husband marito
hypothesis ipotesi (*f.*)
I io
ice cream gelato
if se
in, to in
in fact infatti
in front of davanti (a)
instead invece
intelligent intelligente
invite (to) invitare
island isola
Italian italiano
Italy Italia
jacket giacca
January gennaio
Japan Giappone
Japanese giapponese
jazz jazz
juice succo
July luglio
June giugno
karate karatè (*m.*)
key chiave (*f.*)
keyboard tastiera
kiss bacio
kitchen cucina
knife coltello
know (to) conoscere
know (how to) (to) sapere
lady, madam, Mrs. signora
lake lago
language lingua
laptop portatile (*m.*)

lasagna lasagne (*f. pl.*)
last (to) durare
last ultimo
last (week, month, etc.) scorso
late tardi
lawyer avvocato
learn (to) imparare
leave (to) partire
leave (behind) (to) lasciare
left sinistro
leg gamba
lesson, class lezione (*f.*)
Let me introduce you . . . (familiar) Ti presento...
Let me introduce you to . . . (polite) Le presento...
lie bugia
light leggero
like, be pleasing to (to) piacere
lion/lioness leone/leonessa
lip labbro
little piccolo
little, few poco
live, dwell (to) abitare
living room salotto
long lungo
look for, search for (to) cercare
lunch pranzo
magazine rivista
magnifying glass, lens lente (*f.*)
man uomo
March marzo
mathematics matematica
May maggio
maybe forse
measurement, size taglia
meat carne (*f.*)
menu menù (*m.*)
midnight mezzanotte (*f.*)
mineral minerale
minus, less meno

miss, Ms. signorina
mistake sbaglio
mom mamma
moment momento
Monday lunedì
monitor (computer) schermo
month mese (*m.*)
morning mattina
mother madre (*f.*)
motorcycle moto (*f.*)
mouth bocca
movie film
movies, cinema cinema (*m.*)
much, many, a lot tanto
much, many, a lot, very molto
my, mine mio
name nome (*m.*)
nationality nazionalità
navigate (to) navigare
near vicino
neck collo
need (to) avere bisogno di
neither, not even, not . . . either neanche
neither . . . nor né... né
new nuovo
newspaper giornale (*m.*)
next prossimo
nice bello, simpatico
night notte (*f.*)
no no
no one, none nessuno
noon mezzogiorno
nose naso
not non
not bad non c'è male
nothing nulla
nothing, anything niente
novel romanzo
November novembre
now adesso
number numero

nurse infermiere/infermiera (*m./f.*)
October ottobre
of di
often spesso
old vecchio
on su
only solo
open (**to**) aprire
or o
orange arancione (*adj.*)
other altro
our, ours nostro
over, on top sopra
overcoat, raincoat impermeabile (*m.*)
painter pittore/pittrice (*m./f.*)
pair paio
pants pantaloni (*m., pl.*)
parents genitori (*m., pl.*)
partition parete (*f.*)
party, feast festa
pasta, pastry pasta
patience pazienza
pay (**to**) pagare
peach pesca
pen penna
pencil matita
people gente (*f.*)
perceived percepito
perfect perfetto
person persona
pharmacist farmacista (*m.* or *f.*)
pharmacy farmacia
phone (**to**) telefonare
photo foto (*f.*)
pianist pianista (*m.* or *f.*)
piece of furniture mobile (*m.*)
pink rosa
pizza pizza
place luogo
planet pianeta (*m.*)
play (**a sport/game**) (**to**) giocare

play an instrument (**to**) suonare
player giocatore/giocatrice (*m./f.*)
please per favore/per piacere
plus, more, anymore più
poor povero
popular popolare
population popolazione (*f.*)
Portuguese portoghese
potato patata
practice (**sports**) (**to**) praticare
precise preciso
prefer (**to**) preferire
printer stampante (*f.*)
problem problema (*m.*)
profession professione
professor professore/professoressa (*m./f.*)
program programma (*m.*)
psychologist psicologo/psicologa (*m./f.*)
purse borsa
put (**to**) mettere
put on (**to**) mettersi
to put on dressing/condiments
 (**to**) condire
quarter quarto
quiet zitto
quite, at all mica
radio radio (*f.*)
rain (**to**) piovere
rare raro
rather, quite assai
ravioli ravioli (*m. pl.*)
react (**to**) reagire
read (**to**) leggere
really proprio
reason ragione (*f.*)
red rosso
regular regolare
repeat (**to**) ripetere
restaurant (**family**) trattoria
restaurant ristorante (*m.*)
return, come back (**to**) tornare

rich ricco
right destro
right away subito
roof tetto
ruler riga
Russia Russia
Russian russo
sad triste
salad insalata
sale saldo
salesclerk commesso/commessa (*m./f.*)
same stesso
sandwich, bun panino
Saturday sabato
say (to) dire
scarf sciarpa
school scuola
science fiction fantascienza
scientific scientifico
sculptor scultore/scultrice (*m./f.*)
season stagione (*f.*)
second dish/serving/course secondo piatto
see (to) vedere
seem (to) sembrare
sell (to) vendere
See you later! Ci vediamo!
See you soon! A presto!
September settembre
series programma (*m.*) a puntate
several, quite a few parecchio
she lei
shirt camicia
shoe scarpa
shoulder spalla
simple semplice
sing (to) cantare
sister sorella
skating pattinaggio
skirt gonna
sleep sonno
slow lento

sleep (to) dormire
snow (to) nevicare
so, thus così
soccer calcio
sock calzino
soft drink bibita
someone qualcuno
something qualcosa
son figlio
soup minestra
southern meridionale
spaghetti spaghetti (*m. pl.*)
Spain Spagna
Spanish spagnolo
speak (to) parlare
special speciale
specialist specialista (*m. or f.*)
sport sport
spring primavera
spy spia
square, plaza piazza
starter, hors d'oeuvres, appetizer antipasto
stay, be (to) stare
steak bistecca
still, yet ancora
stocking calza
store negozio
strange strano
street via
strong/short coffee ristretto
student studente/studentessa (*m./f.*)
study (to) studiare
suburbs periferia
subway metropolitana
sugar zucchero
suitcase valigia
summer estate (*f.*)
Sunday domenica
sure sicuro
surname cognome (*m.*)

sweater, jersey maglia
Switzerland Svizzera
system sistema (*m.*)
table tavolo
take (to) prendere
tall alto
taxi tassì (*m.*)
tea tè (*m.*)
teach (to) insegnare
team squadra
television televisione (*f.*)
tennis tennis (*m.*)
thank you, thanks grazie
their, theirs/your, yours (polite plural)
   loro/Loro
then allora
theorem teorema (*m.*)
there lì/là
thesis tesi (*f.*)
they/you (polite, plural) loro/Loro
thing cosa
thirst sete (*f.*)
this morning stamani
Thursday giovedì
ticket biglietto
tie cravatta
time (in a sequence) volta
time, weather tempo
tip mancia
tired stanco
To your health! Salute!
today oggi
together insieme
tomato pomodoro
tomorrow domani
tonight stasera
too much troppo
train treno
travel (to) viaggiare
treat (to) trattare
tree albero

trip viaggio
true vero
truth verità (*f.*)
try on (to) provarsi
Tuesday martedì
TV newscast telegiornale (*m.*)
TV quiz show telequiz
TV remote control telecomando
TV set televisore (*m.*)
type tipo
ugly, bad brutto
uncle/aunt zio/zia
under sotto
understand (to) capire
unfortunately purtroppo
United States Stati Uniti
university università (*f.*)
use (to) usare
useful utile
usually di solito
vacation vacanza
variety show spettacolo
violent violento
violet, purple viola
virtue virtù (*f.*)
voice voce (*f.*)
wait (for) (to) aspettare
waiter/waitress cameriere/cameriera
wake up (to) svegliarsi
wall muro
want (to) volere
wash oneself (to) lavarsi
washroom bagno
watch orologio
watch, look at (to) guardare
water acqua
we noi
wear (to) portare
website sito web
Wednesday mercoledì
week settimana

weekend weekend
well bene
what che cosa
what, that, which, who che
What is your name? (familiar) Come ti chiami?
What is your name? (polite) Come si chiama?
when quando
where dove
which quale
whichever, any qualsiasi
while mentre
white bianco
who chi
why, because perché
wife moglie (*f.*)
win (to) vincere
window finestra
wine vino

winter inverno
with con
woman donna
write (to) scrivere
writer scrittore/scrittrice (*m./f.*)
yacht yacht
year anno
yellow giallo
yes sì
yesterday ieri
you (familiar) tu
you (familiar plural) voi
you (polite) Lei
young giovane
your, yours (familiar) tuo
your, yours (plural) vostro
your, yours (polite) Suo
you're welcome prego
you're welcome, may I help you prego
youth gioventù (*f.*)

ANSWER KEY

PART ONE: CHAPTER 1

Written Practice 1

1. Ti presento Giuseppe. Ciao, Giuseppe.   2. Ti presento Alessandro. Ciao, Alessandro.   3. Le presento il signor Vecchiarelli. Piacere, signor Vecchiarelli.

Written Practice 2

1. Come va, professoressa Dini?   2. Come va, dottor Franceschi?
3. Come va, dottoressa Martini?

QUIZ

1. Mi chiamo Arnaldo. / Mi chiamo Edoardo. / Mi chiamo Eleonora. / Mi chiamo Ilaria. / Mi chiamo Isabella.   2. Lui si chiama Umberto. / Lui si chiama Pietro. / Lui si chiama Tommaso. / Lui si chiama Giovanni.   3. Lei si chiama Maria. / Lei si chiama Pina. / Lei si chiama Claudia. / Lei si chiama Bianca.   4. Il mio amico si chiama Guglielmo. / Il mio amico si chiama Cesare. / Il mio amico si chiama Osvaldo. / Il mio amico si chiama Cristofero. / Il mio amico si chiama Giuseppe.   5. La mia amica si chiama Pasqualina. / La mia amica si chiama Sara. / La mia amica si chiama Rachele. / La mia amica si chiama Maria. / La mia amica si chiama Chiara.   6. Ti presento Alessandro. / Ti presento Annabella.   7. Le presento il professor Giovanni Rossini. / Le presento la professoressa Gina Marchi. / Le presento la signorina Maria Franceschi. / Le presento la signora Vittoria Dini. / Le presento il signor Marco Rossi. / Le presento il dottor Piero Roccia. / Le presento la dottoressa Sara Loggia.
8. Mi piace il jazz. / Mi piace il weekend. / Mi piace la città. / Mi piace il caffè. / Mi piace l'università.   9. Mi chiamo (*insert your name*).   10. Sì, mi piace. / No, non mi piace.

CHAPTER 2

Written Practice 1
1. l'americana   2. l'italiana   3. la francese   4. l'inglese   5. la
canadese   6. Carla   7. Paola

Written Practice 2
1. È un pavimento.   2. È un cognome.   3. È una parete.   4. È un nome.
5. È un'automobile.   6. È un divano.   7. È una chiave.   8. È un mobile.
9. È una sedia.

Written Practice 3
1. Sono due giardini.   2. Sono due sedie.   3. Sono due giornali.
4. Sono due pareti.   5. Sono due tassì.   6. Sono due chat.

Written Practice 4
1. Come stai, Maria?   2. Come sta, signora Bianchi?   3. Come va,
Claudia?   4. Come va, signor Marchi?   5. Ciao, Marco!
6. ArrivederLa, signora Dini.

QUIZ
1. la ragazza / il padre / l'americana / l'amico / la figlia / l'italiano / la zia / il
francese / l'inglese / il canadese   2. muri / casa / giardini / sedia / tavole /
pavimento / caffè / città / sport / tassì /chat / computer   3. È il figlio di
Alessandro. / È la figlia di Sara. / È la casa di Alessandro. / È la chiave di Sara.
4. Buongiorno / Ciao, Maria. / Buongiorno, signorina Giusti. / Buongiorno / Ciao,
Marco. / Buongiorno, professor Marchi.   5. Buonasera/Ciao, Claudia. Come
stai? Bene, grazie. / Buonasera, professoressa Giusti. Come sta? Non c'è male. /
Buonasera/Ciao, Giovanni. Come stai? Così, così. / Buonasera, dottor Bruni.
Come sta? Bene, grazie.   6. b   7. b   8. a   9. Mi chiamo (*insert your
first name*).   10. Sono il signor/la signora/la signorina (*insert your last name*).

CHAPTER 3

Written Practice 1
1. Sono amiche.   2. Sono giochi.   3. Sono buchi.   4. Sono banche.
5. Sono laghi.   6. Sono orologi.   7. Sono farmacie.   8. Sono valige.

Written Practice 2
1. È mercoledì.   2. È giovedì.   3. È venerdì.   4. È agosto.   5. È
settembre.   6. È ottobre.   7. È novembre.   8. È dicembre.

Written Practice 3
1. Parlo russo.   2. Parlo spagnolo.   3. Sono americano/a.   4. Sono
inglese.   5. Sono australiano/a.

Written Practice 4
1. Sì, Sara è americana.   2. No, non mi piace il caffè.   3. Sì, mi piace il tè.

Written Practice 5
1. Sono di Napoli.   2. Sono di Palermo.   3. Sono di Venezia.   4. Sono di Firenze.   5. Sono di Genova.   6. Sono di Perugia.   7. Sono di Bari.

QUIZ
1. tedeschi / buchi / giochi / greci / amici / luoghi / laghi / biologi / amiche
2. riga / banca / orologio / bacio / faccia / farmacia / camicia   3. Oggi è lunedì. / Oggi è martedì. / Oggi è mercoledì. / Oggi è sabato. / Oggi è giovedì.   4. È il mese di gennaio. / È il mese di giugno. / È il mese di ottobre. / È il mese di maggio. / È il mese di febbraio. / È il mese di marzo. / È il mese di aprile.
5. Parlo portoghese, ma non sono portoghese. / Parlo italiano, ma non sono italiano/a. / Parlo russo, ma non sono russo/a. / Parlo inglese, ma non sono inglese. / Parlo tedesco, ma non sono tedesco/a.   6. Il mio giorno della settimana preferito è (*insert day of the week*).   7. Sono americano/a (*or other nationality*).   8. Parlo inglese e italiano (*or insert any other languages*).
9. Mi chiamo (*insert your name*).   10. Sono di (*insert city name*).

CHAPTER 4

Written Practice 1
1. sono   2. è   3. è   4. è   5. siamo   6. sono

Written Practice 2
1. nuova   2. bianco   3. nere   4. azzurri   5. verde   6. gialla
7. intelligenti   8. intelligenti

Written Practice 3
1. simpatica   2. simpatiche   3. simpatico   4. simpatici   5. lungo
6. lunghi   7. lunga   8. lunghe

Written Practice 4
1. Forse costa tredici o quattordici dollari.   2. Forse costa quindici o sedici dollari.   3. Forse costa diciassette o diciotto euro.   4. Forse costa diciannove o venti euro.

Written Practice 5
1. Forse costa settantatré o novantotto euro.   2. Forse costa quarantanove o cinquantasette dollari.   3. Forse costa zero o cento dollari.

QUIZ
1. Anche tu sei americano/a. / Anche lei è australiana. / Anche noi siamo inglesi. / Anche voi siete francesi. / Anche loro sono canadesi. / Anche io (Anch'io) sono russo/a. / Anche lui è cinese. / Anche Paolo è italiano. / Anche il signor Giusti è

italiano. / Anche la signorina Dini è americana.   2. a   3. a   4. b
5. ragazza intelligente / amico alto / zia alta / uomo intelligente / madre simpatica
/ amico italiano / ragazza francese / uomo simpatico   6. vestiti rosa / sciarpa
rossa / uomini alti / zaino marrone / uomini simpatici / sciarpa grigia   7. Forse
costa settantotto o settantanove euro. / Forse costa ottantasette o ottantotto dollari.
/ Forse costa sedici o diciassette dollari. / Forse costa ventitré o ventiquattro euro.
/ Forse costa sessantuno o sessantadue euro.   8. Il mio colore perferito è
(*insert color word*).   9. Sono americano/a (*or other nationality*).   10. Il mio
amico/La mia amica si chiama (*insert name in Italian* [*if possible*]).

CHAPTER 5

Written Practice 1
1. uno   2. un   3. una   4. un'   5. un   6. uno, una   7. un
8. un'   9. una   10. un, un

Written Practice 2
1. lo   2. il   3. l'   4. l'   5. la   6. il   7. l'

Written Practice 3
1. i   2. gli   3. gli   4. le   5. le

Written Practice 4
1. l'   2. le   3. la; no article

Written Practice 5
1. È   2. Sono   3. c'è   4. ci sono   5. Ecco

Written Practice 6
1. ho   2. hai   3. ha   4. abbiamo   5. avete   6. hanno

Written Practice 7
1. Sto   2. stai   3. Stiamo   4. sta   5. stanno   6. state

Written Practice 8
1. ti piace   2. Le piace   3. ti piacciono   4. Le piacciono

QUIZ
1. il ragazzo / la ragazza / l'americano / l'italiana / lo studente / l'amico
2. i ragazzi / le madri / gli americani / le studentesse / gli studenti / gli italiani /
i cani / gli orologi / gli gnocchi / le ore   3. a. m   b. h   c. n   d. i   e. j   f. k
g. l   4. Anch'io ho sete. / Anche il fratello di Maria ha sonno. / Anche tu hai
ragione. / Anch'io sto bene. / Anche noi stiamo assai bene.   5. b   6. a
7. Ho (*insert age number word*) anni.   8. Sto bene. / Sto assai bene. / Sto molto
bene. / Sto così, così.   9. Sì, mi piace. / No, non mi piace.   10. Sì, mi
piacciono./No, non mi piacciono.

PART ONE TEST

1. a	2. b	3. a	4. a	5. b	6. b	7. a	8. a	9. a	
10. b	11. a	12. b	13. b	14. b	15. a	16. a	17. b		
18. a	19. a	20. a	21. a	22. a	23. b	24. a	25. b		
26. b	27. a	28. a	29. b	30. a	31. a	32. b	33. b		
34. a	35. a	36. a	37. a	38. a	39. b	40. a	41. a		
42. b	43. a	44. a	45. b	46. a	47. b	48. a	49. b		
50. a									

PART TWO: CHAPTER 6

Written Practice 1

1. parla; parlo   2. arrivano; arrivano   3. entra; entra   4. guardate; guardiamo   5. impari; imparo   6. tornano; torniamo

Written Practice 2

1. comincio   2. cominci   3. comincia   4. cominciamo
5. cerchiamo   6. cercano   7. cercate   8. cerchi   9. paghi
10. pago   11. pagate   12. paghiamo   13. mangi   14. mangio
15. mangia   16. mangiano

Written Practice 3

1. dai   2. do   3. bevi   4. bevo   5. dà   6. do   7. beve
8. bevo   9. dà   10. dà   11. beve   12. beve   13. date
14. diamo   15. bevete   16. beviamo   17. danno   18. danno
19. bevono   20. bevono

Written Practice 4

1. mangi   2. Mangio   3. mangiate   4. mangiamo   5. bevi
6. bevo   7. mangiate   8. Mangiamo

Written Practice 5

1. infermiere   2. infermiere   3. spie   4. persona   5. dentisti
6. pianiste   7. farmacista   8. specialista

Written Practice 6

1. Quattrocento novantasei.   2. Novecento.   3. Novecento quindici.
4. Quattrocento due.   5. Ottocentotré.   6. Trecento sessantuno.
7. Seicento trenta.   8. Duecentodue.

QUIZ

1. arriv**ano** / guard**i** / impar**a** / chiam**ate** / torn**iamo** / parl**ano** / chiam**a**   2. a
3. b   4. a   5. b   6. l'infermiera / le cameriere / la dentista / le pianiste / la farmacista / le specialiste   7. a   8. b   9. Per colazione, di solito mangio (*insert food name*) e bevo (*insert drink name*).   10. Per pranzo, di solito mangio (*insert food name*) e bevo (*insert drink name*).

CHAPTER 7

Written Practice 1

1. vede; Vedo   2. ripetono; ripetono   3. vende; vende   4. leggete;
leggiamo   5. prendi; prendo   6. mettono; mettiamo   7. vivi; Vivo

Written Practice 2

1. dici   2. dico   3. fai   4. faccio   5. fate   6. facciamo   7. dice
8. dico   9. fanno   10. fanno   11. fate   12. facciamo   13. dicono
14. dicono

Written Practice 3

1. ai   2. dello   3. sul   4. delle   5. negli   6. con la/colla
7. sotto la

Written Practice 4

1. a   2. nell'   3. del   4. dai   5. da

Written Practice 5

1. nove milioni   2. trecento milioni   3. cinquantun   4. trentun
5. ventidue mila   6. diciotto mila   7. nessun   8. nessuna

Written Practice 6

1. Sono le due e mezzo/mezza. *or* Sono le due e trenta.   2. È l'una e
trentacinque di pomeriggio/del pomeriggio. *or* Sono le tredici e trentacinque.
3. Arriva alle sette e quarantacinque di sera/della sera. *or* Arriva alle venti meno
un quarto.   4. Arrivano a mezzanotte.   5. Il film c'è alle cinque in punto di
pomeriggio/del pomeriggio. *or* Il film c'è alle diciassette in punto.   6. Arrivano
alle quattro e un quarto. *or* Arrivano alle quattro e quindici.   7. Sono le sei e
uno.   8. Sono le quattro meno venti.

QUIZ

1. ved**i** / viv**ono** / ripet**o** / vend**ete** / legg**iamo** / prende / mette   2. allo zio /
degli amici / dal medico / nei ristoranti / sulla sedia / coll'amico / all'amica / delle
amiche   3. nella / degli / sulla/sotto la / dal / alle / a / nella   4. a   5. a
6. b   7. b   8. Ho (*insert age number word*) anni.   9. Adesso è/sono
(*insert time of day*).   10. Di solito studio alle (*insert time of day*).

CHAPTER 8

Written Practice 1

1. parte; Parto   2. dormi; dormo   3. apre; aprono   4. sentite; Sentiamo

Written Practice 2

1. capisce; capisco   2. preferiscono; Preferiscono   3. pulisci; pulisco
4. finite; Finiamo   5. finiscono; Finiscono   6. pulite; puliamo
7. capisce; capisce

Written Practice 3

1. vai; Vado   2. va; va   3. andate; Andiamo   4. vanno; Vanno
5. esci; Esco   6. esce; esce   7. uscite; usciamo   8. escono; Escono
9. vieni; vengo   10. viene; Viene   11. Venite; veniamo   12. Vengono; vengono

Written Practice 4

1. il ventiseiesimo piano   2. la dodicesima volta   3. il quarantatreesimo giorno   4. la cinquantottesima volta   5. la sesta settimana   6. l'ottavo mese

Written Practice 5

1. questo/quest'   2. questi   3. questo   4. questo/quest'   5. questi
6. questo   7. questi   8. questa   9. queste   10. questa/quest'
11. queste

Written Practice 6

1. quell'   2. quegli   3. quel   4. quell'   5. quei   6. quello
7. quegli   8. quella   9. quelle   10. quell'   11. quelle

Written Practice 7

1. il sedici agosto   2. il nove luglio, 2009 (duemila nove)   3. sono nato il venticinque marzo   4. sono nata il primo aprile

QUIZ

1. sen**ti** / apr**ono** / par**to** / cap**isce** / prefer**iamo** / pul**ite** / fin**iscono**   2. a
3. a   4. b   5. a   6. a   7. b   8. questi bambini / quella ragazza / questi amici / quell'amica / quelle ragazze / queste bambine / quello studente / quegli zii / quell'uomo   9. vero / vero / vero / vero   10. Capisco l'italiano (*insert any other languages*).

CHAPTER 9

Written Practice 1

1. facendo; mangiando   2. sta; sta   3. facendo; pulendo   4. stanno; Stanno   5. facendo; Sto   6. dicendo; dicendo   7. sta; Sta

Written Practice 2

1. puoi; posso   2. può; può   3. potete; possiamo   4. possono; possono
5. vuoi; Voglio   6. vuole; vuole   7. volete; vogliamo   8. vogliono; vogliono   9. devi; devo   10. deve; deve   11. dovete; Dobbiamo
12. devono; Devono

Written Practice 3

1. il tuo; il mio   2. la tua; la mia   3. i tuoi; i miei   4. le tue; le mie
5. la Sua; la mia   6. i Suoi; I miei   7. il suo; il suo   8. la sua; la sua

9. i suoi; i suoi   10. le sue; le sue   11. il vostro; il nostro   12. la vostra; la nostra   13. i vostri; i nostri   14. le vostre; le nostre   15. il loro; la loro   16. i loro; i loro   17. le loro; le loro

Written Practice 4

1. mia/la mia   2. mia/la mia   3. nostro/il nostro   4. i nostri   5. sua   6. la nostra   7. il loro

Written Practice 5

1. il suo   2. il suo   3. i suoi   4. i suoi   5. le sue   6. le sue

Written Practice 6

1. Fa brutto tempo!   2. Domani fa bel tempo!   3. Nevica molto!   4. Fa caldo!   5. Tira vento e piove!   6. Fa freddo e spesso nevica.

QUIZ

1. io comincio / tu stai mettendo / lui dorme / noi stiamo facendo / lei dà / voi state bevendo / loro dicono   2. io posso / tu puoi / lui può / lei può / noi possiamo / voi potete / loro possono   3. io voglio / tu vuoi / lui vuole / lei vuole / noi vogliamo / voi volete / loro vogliono   4. io devo / tu devi / lui deve / lei deve / noi dobbiamo / voi dovete / loro devono   5. la nostra amica / il nostro libro / la vostra amica / il vostro amico / la sua amica / la loro casa   6. i miei orologii / le mie camicie / i tuoi cani / le tue automobili / i suoi gatti / i loro amici   7. no article / no article / il / no article / no article / il / il / la   8. il suo / il suo / le sue / le sue / Sua / Sua / la Loro   9. Voglio andare a (*insert city name*).   10. Oggi fa (*insert weather word*).

CHAPTER 10

Written Practice 1

1. parla; parli; Parliamo   2. chiamate; chiamino   3. mangia; mangi; Mangiamo   4. pagate; paghino

Written Practice 2

1. leggi; legga; Leggiamo   2. mettete; mettano   3. apri; apra; Apriamo   4. dormite; dormano   5. finisci; finisca; Finiamo   6. pulite; puliscano

Written Practice 3

1. vada; vadano   2. abbi; abbiate   3. beva; bevete   4. da'; dia   5. dite; dicano   6. sii; siate   7. faccia; fa'   8. sta'; state   9. esci; esca   10. vieni; venga

Written Practice 4

1. mangiare; mangi   2. uscire; esca   3. fare; faccia   4. pulite; puliscano

Written Practice 5

1. sapete; sappiamo   2. conosce; conosco   3. sa; sa   4. sai; so
5. sapete; sappiamo   6. conosce; conosce   7. conosce; conoscono
8. conosci; conosco

Written Practice 6

1. un po' di; dello   2. degli   3. degli   4. della; un po' di   5. dei,
delle, dei   6. del; un po' di   7. della   8. dell'; un po' d'

Written Practice 7

1. alcuni; qualche   2. alcune; qualche   3. alcuni; qualche   4. alcune;
qualche   5. dello/un po' di

QUIZ

1. Mangi la mela! / Aspetti qui! / Finisca la mela! / Paghi il conto! / Chiuda la
porta! / Aprano le porte! / Finiscano di studiare! / Vada a dormire!   2.
Comincio a mangiare! / Apri la porta! / Non cercare la chiave! / Non scrivere
l'e-mail! / Dormi! / Non chiudete le porte! / Abbia pazienza!   3. Maria,
mangia la mela! / Maria, non bere l'acqua! / Maria, chiudi la porta! / Maria, apri
la finestra!   4. Maria e Marco, mangiate la mela! / Maria e Marco, non bevete
l'acqua! / Maria e Marco, chiudete la porta! / Maria e Marco, aprite la finestra!
5. Signora Verdi, mangi la mela! / Signora Verdi, non beva l'acqua! / Signora
Verdi, chiuda la porta! / Signora Verdi, apra la finestra!   6. Signora Verdi e
signor Rossi, mangino la mela! / Signora Verdi e signor Rossi, non bevano l'acqua! /
Signora Verdi e signor Rossi, chiudano la porta! / Signora Verdi e signor Rossi,
aprano la finestra!   7. alcune penne, qualche penna / degli zii, alcuni zii /
delle mele, qualche mela / alcuni amici, qualche amico / delle ragazze, alcune
ragazze   8. Il mio indirizzo è (*insert your address*).   9. Vivo in (*insert your
country name*).   10. In futuro voglio vivere in (*insert country name*).

PART TWO TEST

1. a   2. a   3. a   4. a   5. a   6. b   7. b   8. b   9. b
10. b   11. a   12. a   13. a   14. a   15. a   16. b   17. b
18. b   19. b   20. b   21. a   22. b   23. a   24. a   25. b
26. a   27. a   28. b   29. b   30. a   31. b   32. a   33. a
34. a   35. a   36. b   37. b   38. a   39. a   40. b   41. a
42. b   43. a   44. b   45. a   46. a   47. b   48. b   49. b
50. a

PART THREE: CHAPTER 11

Written Practice 1

1. vi alzate; ci alziamo   2. si svegliano; si svegliano   3. ti vesti; Mi vesto
4. si sente; mi sento   5. si mettono; Si mettono   6. ti chiami; Mi chiamo
7. si diverte; si diverte   8. si vestono; Ci vestiamo

Written Practice 2

1. svegliati   2. si svegli   3. metterti/ti mettere   4. si metta
5. divertitevi   6. si divertano   7. alzati   8. si alzi   9. Svegliamoci
10. svegliamoci   11. lavati   12. si vesta   13. alzarti/ti alzare   14. si
alzi

Written Practice 3

1. si telefonano; si telefonano   2. vi parlate; ci parliamo   3. si vedono; si
vedono   4. vi capite; ci capiamo

Written Practice 4

1. costa; la metà   2. Quanta; Tre quinti   3. Un quarto, sette ottavi; nove
ottavi   4. vuoi; Il doppio   5. costano; un terzo   6. hai bisogno;
sessantina   7. Quante; centinaia   8. Quanti; Due dozzine
9. Quante; migliaia

Written Practice 5

1. Desidera   2. comprare   3. taglia   4. porto   5. si provi
6. costa   7. saldo   8. commesso   9. commessa   10. i clienti
11. Desidera   12. una cravatta   13. i pantaloni   14. Si provi   15. Ho
bisogno di   16. un paio   17. dei calzini, delle calze   18. un impermeabile

QUIZ

1. Maria, divertiti alla festa! / Maria, non metterti (ti mettere) i pantaloni rossi!
2. Marco, provati quel cappotto! / Marco, alzati presto domani!   3. Maria e
Marco, divertitevi alla festa! / Maria e Marco, non mettetevi un costume!
4. Maria e Claudia, provatevi dei nuovi vestiti! / Maria e Claudia, telefonatevi più
spesso!   5. Signora Dini, si diverta alla festa! / Signora Dini, non si metta i
pantaloni rossi!   6. si provi quel cappotto! / si alzi presto domani!   7. a
8. a   9. Di solito mi alzo alle (*insert time of day*).   10. Porto il (*insert your
size*).

CHAPTER 12

Written Practice 1

1. avete cominciato; Abbiamo cominciato   2. hai cominciato; ho cominciato
3. hanno cominciato; hanno cominciato   4. hai ripetuto; ho ripetuto
5. avete ripetuto; abbiamo ripetuto   6. hanno ripetuto; hanno ripetuto

7. hai, pulito; ho, pulito   8. avete pulito; abbiamo pulito   9. hanno pulito; hanno pulito

Written Practice 2

1. sei caduta; sono caduta   2. sono durati; sono durati   3. è entrato; è entrato   4. è sembrato; è sembrato   5. sono diventati; sono diventati
6. è costata; È costata   7. vi siete svegliati; Ci siamo svegliati   8. si è sentita; Mi sono sentita

Written Practice 3

1. hai chiuso; Ho chiuso   2. ha preso; Ho preso   3. avete aperto; abbiamo aperto   4. hanno dato; Hanno dato   5. Ha detto; ha detto   6. è stata; è stata   7. ha fatto; Ha fatto   8. hai mai letto; ho già letto   9. hai messo; Ho messo   10. hai bevuto; ho bevuto   11. hanno scritto; abbiamo già scritto
12. è stata; È stata   13. ha visto; ha visto   14. Sono venuti; sono venuti

Written Practice 4

1. la; La   2. la; La   3. gli; Gli   4. la; La, nell'   5. nell'   6. gli
7. il; Il   8. la; no article   9. l'   10. il; in   11. la; La

QUIZ

1. ho comprato / ha venduto / hai dormito / ci siamo divertiti/e / siete venuti/e / sono arrivati si sono alzate   2. **ha** visto   3. **si sono** divertiti   4. è costa**ta**
5. è dura**to**   6. **siete** anda**ti**   7. a   8. a   9. Di solito il sabato o la domenica (*insert what you usually do*).   10. Nella mia città ieri (*insert yesterday's weather*).

CHAPTER 13

Written Practice 1

1. andava; Andava, studiava   2. guardavate, studiavamo; guardavamo, studiavate   3. mangiavate, studiavo; Mangiavamo, studiavi   4. ti alzavi; mi alzavo   5. aveva; aveva   6. conoscevate; conoscevamo   7. dovevano; dovevano   8. ti mettevi; mi mettevo   9. finiva; Finiva   10. dormivate; dormivamo, puliva   11. usciva; usciva, veniva   12. ti divertivi; mi divertivo

Written Practice 2

1. beveva; beveva   2. davi; davo   3. dicevano, leggevo; dicevano
4. era, parlava; era   5. facevate, ero; facevamo, eri   6. stavi; stavo

Written Practice 3

1. stava bevendo; Stavo bevendo   2. stavate leggendo; stavamo leggendo
3. stavano dicendo; stavano dicendo   4. stavano facendo; stava pulendo, stava leggendo   5. stavi facendo; stavo facendo   6. stavi facendo, si stava vestendo; mi stavo vestendo

Written Practice 4

1. Questo, quello 2. Questi, quelli 3. Questa, quella 4. Queste, quelle
5. la tua; la mia 6. la vostra; la nostra 7. la loro; La loro

QUIZ

1. io leggevo / io capivo / tu mangiavi / tu vedevi / lui cominciava / lei aveva / noi pagavamo / noi sapevamo / voi mangiavate / voi potevate / loro arrivavano / loro avevano 2. b 3. b 4. b *or* c 5. a 6. Questo, quello
7. Questi, quelle 8. la tua; La mia 9. i vostri; i nostri 10. Da bambino/a, di solito dovevo (*insert what you had to do as a child*).

CHAPTER 14

Written Practice 1

1. avevi fatto; Avevo, studiato 2. Avevano, aperto 3. Avevamo, cominciato 4. aveva, comprato 5. eri andata; Ero, andata 6. era, uscita
7. eravamo tornati 8. si era alzata

Written Practice 2

1. studiò; Studiò 2. comprasti; Comprai 3. impararono; Impararono
4. tornaste; tornammo 5. doverono (dovettero); Doverono (Dovettero)
6. potè (potette); potè (potette) 7. vendeste; Vendemmo 8. dovesti; dovei (dovetti) 9. partì; Partì 10. finirono; Finirono 11. vi divertiste; ci divertimmo 12. finisti; finii

Written Practice 3

1. ebbe; ebbe 2. bevesti; bevvi (bevetti) 3. cadde; Cadde 4. chiese; Chiesi 5. chiusero; Chiusero 6. conoscesti; Conobbi 7. desti; Diedi
8. disse; Disse 9. furono; Furono 10. fece; Fece 11. leggesti; lessi
12. misero; Misero 13. presero; Presero 14. seppe; seppe
15. scrivesti; Scrissi 16. stette; Stette 17. vide; vide 18. vennero; Vennero 19. vollero; Vollero

QUIZ

1. avevo venduto / ero partita / avevo avuto / eri andato / avevi venduto / eri uscito / avevi fatto / era arrivato / aveva potuto 2. c 3. a 4. b 5. c 6. a
7. c 8. c 9. vendei (vendetti) / partii / ebbi / andasti / vendesti / uscisti / facesti / arrivò / potè (potette) 10. Answers will vary.

CHAPTER 15

Written Practice 1
1. pittore   2. attrice   3. pittrice   4. scultrice   5. attore   6. autore
7. autrice   8. il dottor/la dottoressa; il dottore/la dottoressa   9. elefantessa
10. elefante   11. leone   12. leonessa   13. avvocato

Written Practice 2
1. programmi   2. problemi; problema   3. teoremi; teorema   4. drammi;
dramma   5. diagrammi; diagrammi   6. analisi, crisi; crisi   7. tesi,
ipotesi; tesi, ipotesi   8. caffè, tè; caffè, tè   9. università; università
10. mano; mani   11. radio; radio   12. pianeti; pianeti   13. alfabeta;
alfabeti   14. foto   15. moto; moto

Written Practice 3
1. bello, brutto; bello   2. buoni, cattivi; buoni   3. caro   4. grande
5. piccola   6. grande   7. ricca, povera; ricca   8. povero   9. vecchia
10. vecchia

Written Practice 4
1. buono; buon   2. buoni; buoni   3. buono; buono   4. buono; buon
5. buoni; buoni   6. buona; buona   7. buona; buon'   8. buone; buone
9. bello; bel   10. belli; bei   11. bello; bello   12. belli; begli
13. bello; bell'   14. belli; begli   15. bella; bella   16. bella; bell'
17. belle; belle

QUIZ
1. l'amica / il dentista / la pianista / lo scultore / la pittrice / l'autore / l'elefantessa /
il leone / l'avvocato   2. i problemi / il teorema / i sistemi / il programma / i
drammi / il diagramma / le crisi / la tesi / le ipotesi / l'analisi   3. quelle brutte
macchine / quei cattivi ravioli / la mia vecchia amica / le piccole macchine /
quegli uomini poveri / una professoressa vecchia   4. Questa è una buona pasta.
5. Lei è una buon'amica.   6. Questo è un bell'orologio.   7. Questa è una
bell'automobile.   8. Questi sono begli zaini.   9. Marco ha delle buone
amiche.   10. Sono una persona (*insert the type of person you are*).

PART THREE TEST
1. b   2. b   3. b   4. b   5. b   6. a   7. a   8. a   9. a
10. a   11. a   12. a   13. a   14. a   15. a   16. b   17. b
18. b   19. b   20. b   21. b   22. b   23. b   24. b   25. b
26. a   27. a   28. a   29. a   30. a   31. c   32. a   33. b
34. c   35. a   36. a   37. a   38. a   39. a   40. a   41. a
42. a   43. a   44. a   45. a   46. a   47. a   48. a   49. a
50. b

PART FOUR: CHAPTER 16

Written Practice 1

1. telefonerai; Telefonerò   2. costerà; Costerà   3. guarderete; guarderemo
4. arriveranno; Arriveranno   5. comincerà; comincerà   6. mangerai;
mangerò   7. cercheranno; cercheranno   8. Pagherete; pagheremo   9. ti
alzerai; Mi alzerò

Written Practice 2

1. prenderà; prenderà   2. venderete; venderemo   3. chiederanno;
Chiederanno   4. leggerai; leggerò   5. dormirete; Dormiremo   6. partirai;
Partirò   7. preferiranno; Preferiranno   8. uscirà; Uscirà   9. ti metterai;
Mi metterò

Written Practice 3

1. Andranno; andranno   2. avrà; Avrà   3. berranno; berranno   4. darà;
darà   5. dovrà; Dovrò   6. saranno; Saranno   7. farà; Farà   8. potrà;
potrà   9. saprete; sapremo   10. staranno; Staranno   11. vedrai; Vedrò
12. verrai; verrò   13. vorranno; Vorranno

Written Practice 4

1. avrà pagato; avrà pagato   2. avrò già pagato   3. saranno arrivati/e;
saranno arrivati/e   4. sarai arrivato; sarò arrivato   5. sarete usciti/e; saremo
usciti/e   6. sarà uscita; sarà uscita   7. avrete venduto; avremo venduto
8. avranno venduto; avranno venduto   9. si sarà svegliato; si sarà svegliato

Written Practice 5

1. bicicletta; bicicletta   2. calcio; partita   3. sport; la pallacanestro, il
pugilato, il tennis   4. pattinaggio; la ginnastica

QUIZ

1. io venderò, io avrò venduto / tu mangerai, tu avrai mangiato / tu metterai, tu
avrai messo / lui comincerà, lui avrà cominciato / lei chiederà, lei avrà chiesto /
noi pagheremo, noi avremo pagato / noi chiuderemo, noi avremo chiuso / noi
finiremo, noi avremo finito / voi cercherete, voi avrete cercato / voi metterete, voi
avrete messo / loro mangeranno, loro avranno mangiato / loro chiederanno, loro
avranno chiesto   2. andrà   3. avrà fatto   4. sarà   5. saranno venuti
6. farà   7. Verranno   8. Pratico (*insert the sports you play*).   9. Forse
praticherò (*insert sports you may do in the future*).   10. Domani (*insert
weather for tomorrow*).

CHAPTER 17

Written Practice 1

1. comprerebbero; comprerebbero 2. Mangeresti; mangerei
3. comincerebbe; comincerebbe 4. paghereste; pagheremmo
5. cercherebbe; cercherei 6. venderebbe; venderebbe 7. prenderesti;
prenderei 8. chiedereste; Chiederemmo 9. leggerebbero; leggerebbero
10. partirebbe; partirebbe 11. preferireste; preferiremmo 12. usciresti;
uscirei 13. aprirebbero; aprirebbero 14. si alzerebbe; mi alzerei

Written Practice 2

1. andrebbe; andrebbe 2. avresti; avrei 3. berrebbero; berrebbero
4. dareste; daremmo 5. dovrebbe; Dovrebbe 6. sarebbe; sarebbe
7. faresti; Farei 8. potresti; potrei 9. saprebbero; saprebbero
10. stareste; Staremmo 11. Verresti; verrei 12. vorrebbe; Vorrebbe

Written Practice 3

1. avreste pagato; avremmo pagato; avrebbero pagato 2. sarebbe arrivato;
sarebbe arrivato 3. sarebbero arrivati; sarebbero arrivati 4. saresti uscita;
Sarei uscita 5. sareste usciti/e; saremmo usciti/e 6. avresti venduto; avrei
venduto; avrebbe venduto

Written Practice 4

1. affatto 2. mai 3. mai 4. nessuno 5. niente/nulla 6. niente/
nulla 7. più 8. neanche / nemmeno 9. né, né 10. mica

QUIZ

1. io venderei, avrei venduto / io preferirei, avrei preferito / tu mangeresti, avresti
mangiato / tu metteresti, avresti messo / lui comincerebbe, avrebbe cominciato /
lei chiederebbe, avrebbe chiesto / noi pagheremmo, avremmo pagato / noi
chiuderemmo, avremmo chiuso / voi cerchereste, avreste cercato / voi mettereste,
avreste messo / loro mangerebbero, avrebbero mangiato / loro chiederebbero,
avrebbero chiesto 2. c 3. c 4. a 5. c 6. c 7. a 8. d
9. Lui non mangia mai gli spaghetti. / Ieri non ho mangiato né la carne né le
patate. / Marco non conosce nessuno in quella scuola. / Lui non vuole niente/nulla. /
Quello non è mica vero. 10. Vorrei vedere (*insert city name*).

CHAPTER 18

Written Practice 1

1. mi; ti 2. mi; La 3. Lo 4. La 5. ci; vi 6. li 7. le
8. mi; Ti 9. mi; Le 10. Gli 11. Le 12. ci; Vi 13. Gli
14. Gli

Written Practice 2

1. lo   2. li   3. La   4. Le   5. la   6. le   7. lo   8. li

Written Practice 3

1. **l'**ho già lett**o**   2. **li** ho mangiat**i**   3. **l'**ho vendut**a**   4. **le** ho comprat**e**
5. **lo** abbiamo vist**o**   6. **l'**hanno lett**a**   7. **li** ho già comprat**i**   8. **le** ho comprat**e**

Written Practice 4

1. abbastanza/assai   2. altro; lo stesso   3. abbastanza/assai   4. certa; molte/tante   5. molto/tanto, poco; tutto   6. ogni; parecchie   7. Qualsiasi
8. ultimo; troppi

Written Practice 5

1. Felicemente   2. Precisamente   3. Raramente   4. Regolarmente
5. Specialmente   6. Tristemente

Written Practice 6

1. subito   2. Solo   3. qui   4. Tra/Fra poco   5. male   6. molta
7. Poco

QUIZ

1. Sì, ti chiamerò stasera. / Sì, mi hai invitato alla festa. / Sì, lo chiamerò domani. / Sì, la vedrò domani. / Sì, vi inviterò. / Sì, ci hai invitato. / Sì, le vedrò. / Sì, li vedrò.   2. Sì, ti dirò il mio nome. / Sì, mi hai dato il tuo indirizzo. / Sì, le parlerò domani. / Sì, gli parlerò domani. / Sì, vi scriverò. / Sì, ci hai scritto. / Sì, gli parlerò. / Sì, gli parlerò.   3. Sì, l'ho letto. / Sì, l'ho letta. / Sì, li ho chiamati. / Sì, le ho chiamate. / Sì, l'ho mangiata. / Sì, le ho mangiate. / Sì, l'ho guardato. / Sì, li ho guardati.   4. certo / semplicemente / facile / popolarmente / benevolo / leggermente / enormemente / felice / precisamente / speciale / utilmente / vero
5. a   6. a   7. a   8. a   9. Io ho (*insert your type of computer*: un Mac/ un IBM, etc.).   10. Il mio indirizzo e-mail è (*insert your e-mail address*).

CHAPTER 19

Written Practice 1

1. te la/te l'   2. glielo/gliel'   3. glielo/gliel'   4. glieli   5. gliela/gliel'
6. gliele   7. me la / me l'   8. ce li   9. ve le   10. me li

Written Practice 2

1. Eccolo   2. Eccole   3. Eccotele   4. Sì, li posso mangiare/Sì, posso mangiarli   5. Sì, la devo studiare/Sì, devo studiarla   6. Sì, li voglio comprare/Sì, voglio comprarli   7. Maria, compramela   8. Mario, dammelo

Written Practice 3

1. te, lui   2. me, lei   3. voi, loro   4. voi, loro

Written Practice 4
1. piacciono; piacciono   2. è piaciuta; è piaciuta   3. ti sono piaciuti; sono piaciuti   4. piaccio; piaci   5. piacerebbe; piacerebbe   6. piacciamo; piacete

QUIZ
1. me li / me la / me le / te lo / te li / te la / te le / glielo / glieli / gliela / gliele / ce lo / ce li / ce le / glielo / glieli / gliela / gliele / ve lo / ve li / ve la / ve le   2. a
3. a   4. a   5. a   6. mi / a lei / ti / a lui / ci / a loro / mi / a Lei / vi
7. a   8. b   9. b   10. Regolarmente mi piace (*insert what you like to do*: studiare/fare delle spese, etc.).

CHAPTER 20

Written Practice 1
1. poco; molto/tanto   2. molto/tanto; poco   3. Molti   4. Alcuni, parecchi   5. Tutti   6. Poche/Alcune, molte/tante

Written Practice 2
1. ci   2. ne   3. Ci   4. ne   5. ne   6. Ne   7. Ne

Written Practice 3
1. così, come   2. tanto, quanto   3. più, del; meno, di   4. più, che; più, di   5. il più; il più; il/la meno   6. migliore   7. peggiore   8. maggiore
9. minore

Written Practice 4
1. ricchissimo   2. altissima   3. bellissima   4. felicissimi
5. elegantissime

Written Practice 5
1. più, di; meno, di   2. meno, di   3. meglio   4. peggio

Written Practice 6
1. Chi, che; che   2. che; che   3. cui; cui   4. che; cui   5. Che/Che cosa/Cosa; Chi   6. Chi; Chi   7. Che/Che cosa/Cosa; quello che/quel che/ciò che

QUIZ
1. a   2. a   3. a   4. a   5. alta, altissima / più bravi, bravissimi / più eleganti, elegantissimi / belli, i più belli / migliore, buonissimo / minore, il minore / il/la maggiore, grandissimo/a   6. d   7. a   8. b   9. c   10. Mi piace (*insert type of coffee you like*).

PART FOUR TEST
1. a   2. a   3. a   4. a   5. b   6. b   7. b   8. b   9. a
10. a   11. a   12. a   13. a   14. a   15. a   16. b   17. a

18. a   19. a   20. a   21. a   22. a   23. a   24. a   25. a
26. b   27. b   28. b   29. b   30. b   31. a   32. b   33. a
34. a   35. a   36. a   37. b   38. a   39. a   40. a   41. a
42. a   43. a   44. a   45. a   46. a   47. b   48. a   49. b
50. b

FINAL EXAM

1. b   2. a   3. b   4. a   5. a   6. a   7. b   8. b   9. a
10. b   11. a   12. a   13. b   14. a   15. a   16. a   17. a
18. a   19. b   20. a   21. a   22. a   23. a   24. b   25. a
26. b   27. a   28. b   29. a   30. a   31. a   32. b   33. b
34. a   35. b   36. b   37. b   38. a   39. a   40. a   41. b
42. a   43. a   44. a   45. b   46. a   47. a   48. a   49. b
50. b   51. a   52. b   53. a   54. a   55. a   56. b   57. a
58. a   59. a   60. a   61. b   62. b   63. b   64. a   65. a
66. b   67. b   68. a   69. a   70. a   71. a   72. a   73. b
74. b   75. b   76. a   77. b   78. b   79. a   80. b   81. b
82. a   83. b   84. a   85. a   86. a   87. a   88. a   89. a
90. a   91. a   92. a   93. a   94. a   95. b   96. b   97. a
98. a   99. b   100. a

INDEX

ABOUT THE AUTHOR

Marcel Danesi, a native of Italy, is Professor of Semiotics and Anthropology at the University of Toronto. He has been a visiting professor at Rutgers University, the University of Rome "La Sapienza," the Catholic University of Milan, the University of Lugano, and has given lectures throughout the academic world. Danesi has also authored and coauthored many books on learning Italian and Spanish.

uno
due
tre
quattro
cinque